Health as Communication Nexus

A Service-Learning Approach

Kendall Hunt
publishing company

Marifran Mattson

Jennifer Gibb Hall

Book Team

Chairman and Chief Executive Officer   Mark C. Falb
President and Chief Operating Officer   Chad M. Chandlee
Vice President, Higher Education   David L. Tart
Director of Publishing Partnerships   Paul B. Carty
Editorial Manager   Georgia Botsford
Senior Editor   Angela Willenbring
Vice President, Operations   Timothy J. Beitzel
Assistant Vice President, Production Services   Christine E. O'Brien
Senior Production Editor   Mary Melloy
Permissions Editor   Carla Kipper
Cover Designer   Jenifer Chapman
Senior Web Project Editor   Sheena Reed

Cover image © 2011 Shutterstock, Inc.

www.kendallhunt.com
Send all inquiries to:
4050 Westmark Drive
Dubuque, IA 52004-1840

Printed in the United States of America
10 9 8 7 6 5 4 3 2 1

*for James—always unconditionally
and unflinchingly supportive*

*for the students who contribute
to the Motorcycle Safety at Purdue (MS@P) campaign—
without your input and energy,
the campaign wouldn't be possible!*

MM

*for my girls—you remind me every day
what life is really about*

JGH

Brief Contents

Contents

Preface

Passion, Vision, and Learning Methods

Passion

My passion for the study and practice of health communication was spurred decades ago by a telephone call from a boyfriend I had while in primary school. One day when I was getting close to graduating from college I was surprised by Craig's voice on the other end of the telephone line. He just returned to our home-town after living in another state for several years. After talking for a few minutes he told me that he had AIDS and he came home to die in the care of his family. Toward the end of our conversation he pointedly asked me, "What can you do with your degree in Communication that will help people like me or help people avoid contracting HIV?" I was caught off guard by the question and became silent because I did not have an answer. However, Craig's question certainly got me thinking and sparked my interest in health communication.

Neither St. Norbert College, where I achieved a bachelor's degree, nor Marquette University, where I achieved a Master's degree, had a program, concentration, or even a class in health communication; not many departments of Communication did at the time. However, I began to research the topic of health communication on my own and when possible integrated that research into my class papers and projects, always with my friend Craig's question from that fateful phone call in the back of my mind. It wasn't until I began the PhD program at Arizona State University that I could focus on health communication and begin to understand how I might answer Craig's question. Under the guidance of my advisors Kathy Miller and Jim Stiff, I crafted a dissertation project that considered the persuasive strategies utilized by HIV test counselors to influence clients to practice safer sex (Mattson, 1999). The counselors' strategies and clients' reactions to those strategies were fascinating and sometimes effective. The most unique and controversial strategy occurred when a counselor suggested to clients that perhaps they should lie to their relational partners because the clients did not want to tell their relational partners that they had unsafe sex with someone else (Mattson & Roberts, 2001). This project at least provided a partial answer to Craig's question—I could tell him, unfortunately posthumously, that a few persuasive strategies seemed to be effective in persuading people to practice safer sex. I wonder what Craig would think about that deception strategy!

I've been teaching health communication courses at both the undergraduate and graduate levels since joining the Department of Communication at Purdue University in 1995. Then in 2006, I was involved in a devastating motorcycle accident that claimed most of my left leg and dramatically changed my life both personally and professionally. After returning to university duties almost a year after the accident and my subsequent recovery and rehabilitation, I often joked that I finally felt like a legitimate professor of health communication because I had been a patient for so long. With the urging of a class of graduate students, I shifted my professional health communication efforts toward designing, implementing, and evaluating the Motorcycle Safety at Purdue campaign (MS@P; www.ItInvolvesYou.com). Also at about this juncture in my career, I decided to write a health communication textbook aimed toward undergraduates, beginning graduate students, and anyone else who may want to learn about the growing field of health communication. Although there were a few excellent textbooks of health communication already available, I wanted to approach the topic with a unique combination of learning methods that I suspected would effectively engage students, stir their passion for this field of study and practice, answer some challenging health questions they may be grappling with, and perhaps in the process change their lives too.

One of the students I met through teaching health communication became my co-author of this book. Jennifer Gibb Hall achieved both her Master of Arts and PhD degrees at Purdue University. And she too experienced a major, unexpected health situation; a high-risk pregnancy that resulted in the birth of triplets. Like me, Jen did not major in health communication as an undergraduate but as she excelled in the discipline of Communication and struggled with health issues as a graduate student, she realized the importance of and great opportunities within the emerging field of health communication. Also, because of her tireless work on the MS@P campaign through classes she took with me, I knew she valued service to the community. I invited Jen to work on this book project with me because I was confident her insights would add depth to our treatment of health communication. I'm exceedingly grateful that she agreed to participate in this project and that she injected her creativity and can-do attitude.

Vision

Our vision for this book is to present a comprehensive survey of the health communication topics, concepts, and issues we teach, research, and otherwise engage within academia, health care-related environments and occupations, and/or as part of our daily lives. Our mission is to appeal to undergraduate students, beginning graduate students, or anyone who aspires to learn about the field of health communication from the perspective of those who teach, conduct research, and have applied experiences within the discipline of Communication.

Learning Methods

The unique combination of learning methods we utilize includes a *critical incident case study method* with a *service-learning approach.* A critical incident case study method is integrated across the chapters of the book because it provides a rich, in-depth example to illustrate the wide variety of topics and issues considered within the realm of health communication. This critical incident case study method also provides a common point of entry and reentry because some students may not have experience with challenging health issues. In addition, a service-learning approach is forwarded to offer pragmatic ideas for how instructors and students of health communication can incorporate health communication knowledge and skills to benefit themselves, their families, their friends, and their communities. The remainder of this Preface discusses these two learning methods in more detail.

Critical Incident Case Study Method

In essence, we are combining two research methods, the critical incident technique and the case study method, to create the critical incident case study method.

Critical Incident Technique

The *critical incident technique* was developed by John Flanagan (1954), a World War II military psychologist, to determine why so many training planes were crashing. He defined the technique as "a set of procedures for collecting direct observations of human behavior in such a way as to facilitate their potential usefulness in solving practical problems . . . collecting observed incidents having special significance" (p. 237). Later, this technique was used in other types of organizations to learn about "war stories" and then try to determine root causes and solutions to avoid these war stories reoccurring in the future (Kain, 2004; Zemke & Kramlinger, 1989).

Critical incidents also are used in the counseling and teaching professions. In the counseling context, critical incidents are considered a therapy tool to debrief about the stress experienced by trauma victims. Cohen and Smith (1976) put it this way, "The critical incident concept evolved with the observation that certain [types of] critical situations emerge and repeat themselves time and again" (p. 115). The commonalities of these incidents can promote understanding and enhance ways of learning to respond to these situations.

In the education context, Tripp (1993) proposed that teachers document critical incidents to learn more about how they react to students and to determine strategies for improving their teaching. And Cooper (1998) specifically suggested integrating the critical incident technique into service-learning courses to help students reflect upon and better understand their service-learning experiences. Strategies for promoting reflection include class and small group discussions, journaling, and debriefing sessions. We encourage these strategies throughout the book.

Based on its connection to real-world examples and its usefulness in the early stages of understanding a phenomenon (Kain, 2004), the critical incident technique is particularly well suited to a book designed to introduce readers to theory, research, and practice in health communication. Although we are using the critical incident technique in a slightly different way than it was originally intended because we are primarily focusing on one critical incident to analyze health communication topics and issues rather than gathering, pooling, and analyzing many critical incidents, we remain true to the central idea of the critical incident technique that individuals learn from extensive examples. We combined the critical incident technique with the case study method because the case study method tends to emphasize one illustrative case.

Case Study Method

The *case study method* is defined as a specific instance of a phenomenon selected for study with the goal of seeking to discern and pursue understanding of issues intrinsic to knowledge of the particular case. The illustrative case should be chosen and used to stimulate learning and understanding of particular concepts, issues, or problems (Burawoy, 1991; Mier, 1982; Schwandt, 2001; Stake, 1995; Yin, 2003). Our choice of the case involving my motorcycle accident and its aftermath is based on the authors' close familiarity with the case, the comprehensive nature of the case, and the rich data to draw upon from the case. Highlighting aspects of this complex case throughout the book assists us in displaying a wide-range of health communication phenomena within a real-life situation. More specifically, our close familiarity with the case affords us the unique opportunity to apply the principles, theories, and issues relevant to health communication to the case in an effort to make the material more accessible, comprehendible, interesting, and practical to students.

Although the motorcycle accident and its aftermath serves as the primary critical incident case study throughout the book, we include other supplementary health and illness examples. Also, throughout the book students are asked to think about and write down their unique, personal examples which serve as their critical incidents or mini case studies for reflection and analysis about health communication.

Service-Learning Approach

The second learning method we employ to enhance learning and application of health communication concepts and issues is *service learning*. According to the Corporation for National & Community Service (2010),

> Service learning combines service objectives with learning objectives with the intent that the activity changes both the recipient and the provider of the service. This is accomplished by combining service tasks with structured opportunities that link the task to self-reflection, self-discovery, and the acquisition and comprehension of values, skills, and knowledge content.

In other words, service learning is a teaching and learning strategy that integrates meaningful community service with instruction and reflection to enrich the learning experience, teach civic responsibility, and strengthen communities. Service learning is associated with a variety of benefits and learning outcomes (National Survey of Student Engagement, 2007; Oster-Aaland, Sellnow, Nelson, & Pearson, 2004; Panici & Lasky, 2002; Rice & Brown, 1998), including:

◆ Integration of theory with practice
◆ Career/vocational clarification
◆ Possible career connections

- ◆ Sense of purpose
- ◆ Sense of social responsibility
- ◆ Enjoyable experience
- ◆ Regard for cultural differences
- ◆ Cognitive skills
- ◆ Problem solving
- ◆ Increased knowledge of course content
- ◆ Interpersonal skills

The history of service learning dates back to the early 1900s and experienced resurgent interest and activity into the present. In the beginning of the 20th century, John Dewey and William James developed the philosophical foundations for service learning when they independently wrote about the importance of engaging students in educational experiences outside the classroom while integrating the values of citizenship. On university, college, and community college campuses throughout the United States faith-based and Greek organizations historically are noted for their community service initiatives. In the 1960s, the civil rights movement spurred activists and lead to the formation of the Peace Corps and the Volunteers in Service to America (VISTA) which engaged students in community service work. The first conference dedicated to merging ideas about service and learning also was held during this decade. The following recommendations from that conference set the agenda for past and present service-learning initiatives:

- ◆ Colleges and universities should encourage students to participate in community service, help to make sure that academic learning is a part of this service, and give academic recognition for that learning.
- ◆ Colleges and universities, private organizations, and federal, regional, and state governments should provide the opportunities and funds for students wanting to participate in service learning.
- ◆ Students, public and private agency officials, and college and university faculty should participate in planning and implementing service-learning programs.

These recommendations are engaged in a variety of ways. For example, Purdue University's definition of service learning, created by its Community of Service-Learning Faculty Fellows, addresses the recommendations (www.purdue.edu/servicelearning/Service-Learning/about.html). In campus-wide communications service learning is defined as a course-based, credit-bearing, educational experience in which students:

- ◆ Participate in an organized service activity that meets identified community needs;
- ◆ Use knowledge and skills directly related to a course or discipline; and
- ◆ Reflect on the service activity in such a way as to gain
    - ❖ further understanding of course content,
    - ❖ a broader appreciation of the discipline, and
    - ❖ an enhanced sense of personal values and civic responsibility.

To further differentiate service learning from other types of coursework, Furco (1996) distinguished between service learning, community service, field education, volunteerism and internships. As the Service-Learning Continuum (Figure P.1) illustrates, service-learning projects aspire to equally serve the needs of service recipients and the student learners who are providing the service—considered an uppercase S, uppercase L project, which is positioned toward the right end of the continuum.

For example, the Motorcycle Safety at Purdue (MS@P; www.ItInvolvesYou. com) campaign that students are exposed to throughout this book is an ongoing service-learning program because students work on real-time traffic safety projects that benefit the community while they learn about relevant concepts and issues in health communication such as health campaign design, implementation, and evaluation.

If a class project focuses more on the service being provided it likely is a community service or volunteerism project. Or service learning with an emphasis on Service rather than learning—an uppercase S, lowercase l project, which is positioned toward the left side of the continuum. For example, having students spend a weekend volunteering for Habitat for Humanity to build a house for a family in the community without or with minimal linking of that experience to course content is considered a volunteer or community service project.

If the project focuses more on student learning than on service to the community it likely is a field education or internship experience. Or service learning with an emphasis on learning rather than service—a lowercase s, uppercase L project, which is positioned more toward the right side of the continuum. For example, placing students in commercial pharmacies to observe and assist practicing pharmacists in order to gain hands-on learning experience and write a term paper about the communication of pharmacists is considered field education or if done for an extended period of time may be an internship. The Service-Learning Continuum is a helpful tool not only to define service learning but also to consider when planning course activities and projects.

RMC Research Corporation, through National Service-Learning Clearinghouse (www.servicelearning.org), offers standards for effective service-learning practice. These standards are:

◆ Meaningful service—project actively engages participants in meaningful and personally relevant service activities
◆ Link to curriculum—service learning intentionally used as an instructional strategy to meet learning and content goals

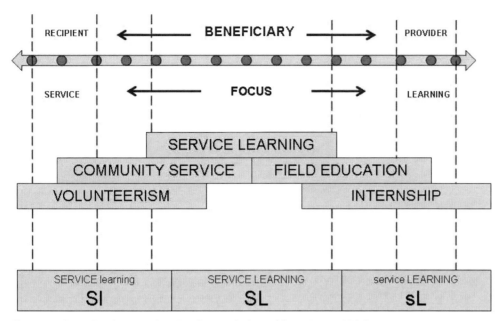

Figure P.1 ◆ *Service-Learning Continuum (adapted from Furco, 1996)*

◆ Reflection—project incorporates multiple challenging reflection activities that prompt deep thinking and analysis about oneself and one's relationship to society

◆ Diversity—project promotes understanding of diversity and mutual respect among all participants

◆ Student voice—project provides students with active voice in planning, implementing, and evaluating service-learning experiences with guidance from instructor

◆ Partnerships—partnerships are collaborative, mutually beneficial, and address community needs

◆ Progress monitoring—project engages participants in an ongoing process to assess the quality of implementation and progress toward meeting specified goals, and uses results for improvement and sustainability

◆ Duration and intensity—project is of sufficient duration and intensity to address community needs and meet specified outcomes

In the Service-Learning Application section of each chapter, we highlight one of these service-learning standards and use examples from the many facets of the MS@P campaign to illustrate various aspects of community engagement while promoting student learning about health communication theory, research, and practice. The photos on these pages are from MS@P service-learning projects.

Photo courtesy of MS@P

Motorcycle Safety at Purdue at Community Event

Engaging in a service-learning project is an effective learning method to better understand the intricacies of health communication. It provides a practical way to directly apply concepts being learned to actual health-related situations. Further, by integrating a service-learning approach with the critical incident case

Table P.1 ◆ *Example Service-Learning Projects*

◆ Study oral history, social support, and volunteerism while collecting stories at a local nursing home

◆ Study public policy and civic responsibility while writing letters to state legislators to support legislation to mandate health insurance coverage for prosthetics

◆ Study communication with and among the disabled by volunteering with Special Olympics

◆ Study the role of technology in health communication while designing a Web site for a nonprofit hospital

◆ Study the role of media in health by pitching related stories to local media outlets

This list of projects is provided to give you a sense of the wide variety of service-learning activities within the realm of health communication and to spur your own ideas for projects.

Motorcycle Safety at Purdue at College Mentors for Kids Event

study method already discussed, instructors can tangibly illustrate the concepts and issues that shape health communication. Consequently, it is likely that students can better apply course material to past, present, and future health-oriented experiences and projects. To learn more about MS@P go to www.ItInvolvesYou.com. For additional service-learning examples and project ideas, refer to Table P.1 and this book's companion Web site.

It is exciting and incredibly fulfilling to bring this book project to fruition. We sincerely hope that our passion for health communication, our vision for this book, and the learning methods we incorporate enhance students' understandings and experiences of health.

Take Special Care,

Marifran Mattson

Marifran Mattson, PhD
mmattson@purdue.edu

Organization of the Text

To assist instructors in guiding students on their journey into the study of health communication, this book is organized into twelve chapters.

Chapter 1—Introducing Health as Communication Nexus

The opening chapter focuses on the pervasiveness of health communication in our lives and explains the model of Health as Communication Nexus. The health status of Americans is discussed, along with reasons for health disparities. The field of health communication and its history is outlined and career paths in the field are identified.

Chapter 2—Linking Health Communication with Ethics

What constitutes an ethical dilemma? Why is unethical behavior considered common? Chapter 2 considers these questions in the context of health by explaining the criteria for an ethical dilemma, including the interconnections between values, morals, and ethics. The Hippocratic Oath is discussed, along with other ethical orientations and several strategies for ethical health communication. The service-learning application illustrates how a MORT analysis can be used to interact with community partners about the ethical practices of a health campaign.

Chapter 3—Linking Health Communication with Theories Informed by Health Communication

Theory is defined and its purposes listed, as well as the importance of incorporating theory into health communication practices and programs. Four theories that are uniquely situated within health communication are highlighted. Suggestions for integrating theories into service-learning projects are offered with examples.

Chapter 4—Linking Health Communication with Patient Interaction

This chapter reviews the history of patient/health care provider interaction and discusses the micro-level and macro-level influences on their interaction. Patient-centered communication is defined and compared to traditional communication approaches to health care. In addition, skills patients need to fully participate in patient-centered communication are identified. Conversation starters are one tool patients can use to better interact with health care providers and the service-learning application specifically explains how health campaign practitioners can work with target audience members to design and implement this helpful tool while providing a meaningful experience for students.

Chapter 5—Linking Health Communication with Health Care Provider Interaction

The many influences on health care provider/patient interaction are discussed, as well as the benefits of patient-centered communication for health care providers. The skills health care providers need to practice patient-centered care are reviewed, including techniques to improve patients' health literacy. The service-learning application considers incorporating the diversity of a health campaign team and the campaign target audience when developing communication training materials.

Chapter 6—Linking Health Communication with Social Support

In this chapter the types, components, health benefits, and key aspects of social support are discussed. In-person and online support groups are compared, including the benefits and drawbacks of social support groups. The service-learning application explains how to start a support group and emphasizes establishing and maintaining community partnerships.

Chapter 7—Linking Health Communication with Health Campaign Theories

The definition of theory is revisited with an emphasis on its importance in health campaigns. An ecological framework is used to organize health campaign theories. In addition the contexts of influence relevant to health campaign design, implementation, and evaluation are explained. The service-learning application reconsiders how to link course curriculum with a community project by providing a specific example of integrating theory into a real-time health campaign.

Chapter 8—Linking Health Communication with Health Campaign Practice

This chapter begins by defining public health, health education and health promotion and compares these concepts with health communication. The ten essential public services that public health provides are outlined. The Messaging Model for Health Communication Campaigns (MMHCC) is introduced and the four phases within this process are explained, including the 4 Ps of social marketing. Needs assessment is highlighted, including a definition, uses, and an example of a SWOT analysis. Progress monitoring in health campaigns is the focus of the service-learning application, which works through an example of how to use the MMHCC to design and correct a campaign.

Chapter 9—Linking Health Communication with Risk Communication and Crisis Communication

Risk communication and crisis communication are compared and contrasted in this chapter. Each topic is then further explored separately, suggesting strategies and best practices. A discussion of integrating students' and community members' voices into service-learning projects is presented in the service-learning application along with an example.

Chapter 10—Linking Health Communication with Entertainment Education

This chapter defines entertainment education, reviews its history, and provides examples. In addition, creating entertainment education programming in different formats is discussed. Opportunities for employment in entertainment education also are identified. In the service-learning application the role of critical reflection is explored through a video game project example.

Chapter 11—Linking Health Communication with Media

In this chapter health communication in the context of media is considered. Media is defined and its role in contemporary society is considered. Agenda-Setting Theory and Media Framing Theory are offered as explanations for the influence of media on health communication. The four steps of media advocacy planning are listed and discussed. An in-progress media advocacy project is highlighted in the service-learning application, which also emphasizes incorporating critical reflection.

Chapter 12—Linking Health Communication with e-Health

The final chapter begins with the role of technology in health tourism. This is followed by an outline of the major milestones in the history of health and technology. After reviewing the many terms linking health and technology, a rationale for adopting the term e-Health is provided and the processes, implications, and benefits of e-Health on health communication are explained. The service-learning application accentuates the importance of demonstrating impact and celebrating success by providing an example project that incorporates both these standards into a campaign Web site.

Web Site

The companion Web site to this book was designed to provide a significant collection of resources for instructors and students. This Web site includes additional text material and links to relevant information for further review. Wherever you see the Webcom icon in the margin of the text, it indicates relevant material is available on the companion Web site. The companion Web site also includes:

- ◆ Poll questions
- ◆ Quiz questions
- ◆ Interactive exercises
- ◆ Service-learning application ideas

References

Burawoy, M. (1991). The extended case method. In M. Burawoy, A. Burton, A. A. Ferguson, K. J. Fox, J. Gamson, N. Gartrell, L. Hurst, C. Kurzman, L. Salzinger, J. Schiffman, & S. Ui (Eds.), *Ethnography unbound: Power and resistance in the modern metropolis* (pp. 271–287). Berkeley: University of California Press.

Cohen, A. M., & Smith, R. D. (1976). *The critical incident in growth groups: Theory and technique* (Vol. 1). La Jolla, CA: University Associates.

Cooper, D. D. (1998). Reading, writing, and reflection. In R. A. Rhoads & J. P. F. Howard (Eds.), *New directions for teaching and learning: Academic service learning: A pedagogy of action and reflection* (pp. 47–56). San Francisco: Jossey-Bass.

Corporation for National & Community Service (2010). Learn and Serve America's National Service-Learning Clearinghouse. Retrieved January 15, 2010, from www.servicelearning.org.

Flanagan, J. C. (1954). The critical incident technique. *Psychological Bulletin, 51,* 327–358.

Furco, A. (1996). Service-learning: A balanced approach to experiential education *Expanding Boundaries: Service and Learning* (pp. 2–6). Washington, DC: Corporation for National Service.

Kain, D. L. (2004). Owning significance: The critical incident technique in research. In K. deMarrais & S. D. Lapan (Eds.), *Foundation for research: Methods of inquiry in education and the social sciences* (pp. 69–85). Mahwah, NJ: Lawrence Erlbaum Associates.

Mattson, M. (1999). Reconceptualizing communication cues to action in the health belief model: HIV test counseling. *Communication Monographs, 66,* 240–265.

Mattson, M., & Roberts, F. (2001). Overcoming truth telling as an obstacle to initiating safer sex: Discussing deception in pre-HIV test counseling sessions. *Health Communication, 13,* 343–362.

Mier, D. (1982). From concepts to practices: Student case study work in organizational communication. *Communication Education, 31,* 151–154.

National Survey of Student Engagement. (2007). Experiences that matter: Enhancing student learning and success. Bloomington, IN: Indiana University Center for Postsecondary Research.

Oster-Aaland, L. K., Sellnow, T. L., Nelson, P. E., & Pearson, J. C. (2004). The status of service learning in departments of communication: A follow-up study. *Communication Education, 53,* 348–356.

Panici, D., & Lasky, K. (2002). Service learning's foothold in communication scholarship. *Journalism & Mass Communication Educator, 57,* 113–125.

Rice, K. L., & Brown, J. R. (1998). Transforming educational curriculum and service learning. *Journal of Experiential Education, 21,* 140–146.

Schwandt, T. A. (2001). *Dictionary of qualitative inquiry* (2nd ed.). Thousand Oaks, CA: Sage.

Stake, R. S. (1995). *The art of case study research.* Thousand Oaks, CA: Sage.

Tripp, D. (1993). *Critical incidents in teaching: Developing professional judgment.* London: Routledge.

Yin, R. K. (2003). *Case study research: Design and methods* (3rd ed.). Thousand Oaks, CA: Sage.

Zemke, R., & Kramlinger, T. (1989). *Figuring things out: A trainer's guide to needs and task analysis.* Reading, MA: Addison-Wesley.

Acknowledgments

We gratefully acknowledge the constructive comments of our colleagues who provided reviews for the text. These colleagues include:

David Anderson
George Mason University

Julie Andsager
University of Iowa

Michael Arrington
University of Kentucky

Jaye Atkinson
Georgia State University

Austin Babrow
Purdue University

Jo Ann Beine
Arapahoe Community College

Dina Borzekowski
Johns Hopkins University

Lisa Bradford
University of Wisconsin—Milwaukee

Maria Brann
West Virginia University

Stefne Broz
Wittenberg University

Lori Byers
Ball State University

Brenda Coppard
Creighton University

Joy Cypher
Rowan University

Lynda Dixon
Bowling Green State University

Kelly Dorgan
East Tennessee State University

Nichole Egbert
Kent State University

Vicki Freimuth
University of Georgia

Steven Giles
Wake Forest University

Dairlyn Gower
Lake Superior College

Diane Gronefeld
Northern Kentucky University

Marceline Thompson-Hayes
Arkansas State University—Jonesboro

Amy Hedman
Minnesota State University—Mankato

Madeline Keaveney
California State University—Chico

Carole Kimberlin
University of Florida

Janice Krieger
Ohio State University

Deb LeHew
Anoka Technical College

Elaine Jenks
West Chester University

Douglas Lawrence
Marywood University

Lyn Lepre
University of Tennessee

Cynthia Lundgren
Houston Community College

Claudia McCalman
Southeastern Louisiana University

Lynn McKelvey
Odessa College

Kelly McNeilis
Missouri State University

Gretchen Norling
University of West Florida

Charles Okigbo
North Dakota State University

Cynthia Petri
University of Alabama—Birmingham

Michael P. Pagano
Fairfield University

Claire Sullivan
University of Maine

Kandi Walker
University of Louisville

Claire Wheeler
Portland State University

Holley Wilkin
Georgia State University

Barbara Williams
University of Southern Indiana

Edward Woods
Marshall University

Jeff Ybarguen
Idaho State University

Marco Yzer
University of Minnesota

Xiaoquan Zhao
George Mason University

We also greatly appreciate the valuable working relationships we fostered with Paul, Angela, Mary, and Sheena at Kendall Hunt Publishing Company. Through your patience, expertise, and guidance this idea became a pedagogical tool for health communication.

About the Authors

*Marifran Mattson, PhD
(Arizona State University,
1995)*

Professor Mattson's research and teaching program explores the intersection of organizing health communication initiatives, health advocacy, and health communication pedagogy. She is particularly interested in the role of communication processes in addressing problems related to human health and safety. Theoretically, she seeks to identify critical interactive features to improve communication and reduce harm among people in diverse contexts, including public health campaigns, public policy debates, aviation organizations, HIV testing, interactions about pain medication, and patient/health care provider confidentiality. Her methodological choices are predicated upon her research questions and typically involve mixed methodologies, including observations, interviews, focus groups, and surveys. Her current research and teaching project, the Motorcycle Safety at Purdue campaign (www.ItInvolvesYou.com), integrates her professional interests. This campaign was founded with a team of graduate students after Professor Mattson was involved in a life-altering motorcycle crash. Mattson's health communication research is published in journals, including *Communication Monographs, Communication Studies, Health Communication, Health Marketing Quarterly, Health Promotion Practice, Journal of Applied Communication Research,* and *Journal of Health Communication.*

*Jennifer Gibb Hall, PhD
(Purdue University, 2010)*

Lecturer Hall's research and teaching are centered on a fundamental interest in how individuals, groups, organizations and cultures communicate about their health and use communication to improve health. Specifically she is interested in the integration of narratives as people think about, talk about, and make sense of their health-related situations. Her current research explores how women who experience high-risk pregnancies integrate the many narratives around them into the narratives they create to assist in making sense of their experiences, in making decisions, and in asserting their identities. Hall's health communication research is published in journals, including *Cases in Public Health Communication & Marketing* and *Health Communication.*

CHAPTER 1

Introducing Health as Communication Nexus

© 2011, Morgan Lane Photography, Shutterstock, Inc.

Chapter Learning Objectives

◆ Realize the pervasiveness of health communication in our lives
◆ Understand the idea of and model for Health as Communication Nexus
◆ Highlight the general health status of Americans and young adults
◆ Explain reasons for health disparities and offer examples
◆ Define the concepts of health, communication, and health communication
◆ Outline the history of the field of health communication
◆ Identify career paths in health communication

Chapter Preview

This chapter introduces you to the field of health communication from a communication perspective. After sharing a traumatic health-related challenge experienced by one of the authors of this book, we discuss the pervasiveness of health communication in our daily lives and challenge you to identify examples of health communication in your life. Next we offer a model of Health as Communication Nexus that frames the organization of this book. This model positions health as a crucial linking pin that connects many of the concentration areas that are studied in the discipline of communication. Stemming directly from the Health as Communication Nexus model, we then outline the chapter-by-chapter layout of the book to give you an initial sense of the topics and issues you'll learn more about. An overview of the health status of Americans is provided next to give you a sense of the many health challenges that health communication can address. After this discussion we build a definition of health communication. This is followed by a historical timeline of health communication to situate our current study within its historical roots. The chapter concludes by identifying and describing career paths you might follow in health communication and considers the job market for those career paths.

So let's begin our journey into the exciting subject of health communication by presenting a health-related situation experienced by one of the authors.

By Joanne Hammer

A Crawfordsville woman riding a motorcycle severed her leg during a crash with a semi truck Sunday, Indiana State Police said. Marifran Mattson, 40, was attempting to navigate a curve on Indiana 47 at the 7.5 mile marker in Parke County when she drifted into the northbound lane, according to a crash report by State Trooper Chris Carter, Terre Haute post. Mattson, who was riding a 2003 Harley-Davidson motorcycle, crashed into a 1996 Volvo semi truck driven by Bryan Smith of Waveland, police said. She suffered a severed leg and was transported to West Central Community Hospital in Clinton, police said. Information about her condition was not available by press time Sunday. Parke County and Montgomery County Sheriff departments also responded.

From *Journal Review* by Joanne Hammer. Copyright © *Journal Review.* Reprinted by permission.

The motorcycle accident referred to in the newspaper clipping happened to one of the authors of this book, Professor Marifran Mattson. Although the newspaper article describes the situation from a factual standpoint, Professor Mattson, as the person injured in the crash, describes what happened in the following much more personal way.

"On a richly colorful and warm fall afternoon in 2004 I was riding my motorcycle with a small group of friends. As I negotiated around a curve on the narrow, two-lane state highway we were traveling, I glanced ahead to realize I was about to collide with an oncoming semi truck. I screamed and as that scream faded my personal and academic life was irreversibly changed. The direct impact with the front bumper of the truck caused severe injuries, including an immediately severed left leg to above the knee, a broken femur, and a broken hip in three places. The collision threw me from my motorcycle and I remember rolling over backwards three times. I also remember being thankful that I was wearing a helmet. After a life-saving emergency helicopter transport, a month-long stay in a trauma unit, eight surgeries and several months in rehabilitation and recovery, I returned to my career as a professor. I'm not sure I'll ever completely recover from this life-threatening experience and its aftermath but due to the ongoing encouragement of my husband, Jim, and the many students I have worked with since the accident, I have dedicated myself to motorcycle safety—not only to protect motorcycle riders but for the sake of drivers of cars and trucks, and the loved ones of motorcycle riders too. Since that fateful fall day, experiences spawned from an unfortunate accident have led to the formation of a comprehensive motorcycle safety campaign; have informed health communication pedagogy, health campaign model building, applied research, dissertation projects, funding opportunities, and community outreach. All of these activities have been a very positive way to channel the energy from a devastating experience into creative approaches to teaching and learning and into service to the community."

We start the book with two accounts of this motorcycle accident for two reasons. First, as these two accounts suggest, this motorcycle accident and its aftermath is a rich example of a complex health-oriented situation that will help us explore the many facets of health communication throughout this book. Second, since you may be wondering if it will be difficult to study health communication if you don't have very many health-oriented experiences to draw upon, we utilize the motorcycle crash and its aftermath as a detailed example, or a critical incident case study, throughout the book. As each chapter delves into a different facet of the study of health communication, we will revisit Professor Mattson's health communication experiences since her motorcycle accident to highlight relevant concepts and issues in health communication.

In addition, we will include examples from the other author, Lecturer Jennifer Hall's, unique personal experience of having triplets. Of course, we will include many other examples to illustrate the concepts and issues involved in the study of health communication. Actually, at times throughout the book, you will be asked to think about and write down your own examples pertaining to health communication. And we suspect you'll be surprised by how many health communication experiences you have without even realizing it—refer to the list of critical health incidents in the sidebar to spark your thinking. We are confident this approach will help you learn about the exciting and growing field of health communication!

List of critical health incidents you might relate to:

- Binge drinking by a friend
- Car accident
- Accident while babysitting
- Death of a loved one from an illness or disease
- Sports injury—such as a torn ACL (anterior cruciate ligament)

Use this list to stimulate your thinking about personal examples you can write about and learn from throughout your study of health communication.

Pervasiveness of Health Communication

Like the newspaper clipping that begins this chapter and reports on the motorcycle crash experienced by Professor Mattson, much of the local, state, and national news communicates health issues that affect individuals, communities, organizations, and the government. A quick scan of today's headlines via CNN, the local newspaper, a favorite magazine, or YouTube will likely yield at least another story or video about a health-related incident. Take a few minutes to complete Health Communication Nexus Interlude 1.1. These interludes present an opportunity to link to your own health communication experiences.

Health Communication Nexus Interlude 1.1

Suspend reading this book for a few minutes and pick up either the nearest or your favorite mass media communication tool—the TV remote, a cereal box, your laptop computer, a magazine, a smartphone, or the mail—and identify at least one health topic or issue discussed via this communication tool. Jot down that topic in your notebook to serve as a reminder of how closely health topics and issues surround you. Think about this health topic/issue and answer the following questions in your notebook.

- Is the health topic or issue relevant to you? Why or why not?

- Might the health topic or issue be relevant to someone you care about—now or in the future? Why or why not?

Although you may not have experienced any health issues, either serious or minor, chances are you've been exposed to countless health issues through the media. This activity also helps us illustrate the purpose of this book and our vision for engaging you in learning more about health communication topics and issues.

Health as Communication Nexus Model

Now that we've gotten your attention with some explicit examples that will frame our study of health communication, we'd like to explain the main title of this book. "Health as Communication Nexus" refers to our central belief and core argument that health communication serves as a crucial linking pin that connects many of the concentration areas of interest and research in the discipline of communication. Because health or lack thereof is a fundamental experience of all humans, it serves as the ideal context within which to consider the concentration areas in the discipline of communication. Consequently, health communication becomes the core concept from which the topics and issues relevant to health communication emanate and become linked to the other topics and issues. The model of Health as Communication Nexus is illustrated below. A brief outline of the chapters of this book, which are organized around the topics presented in the model, is provided following the model.

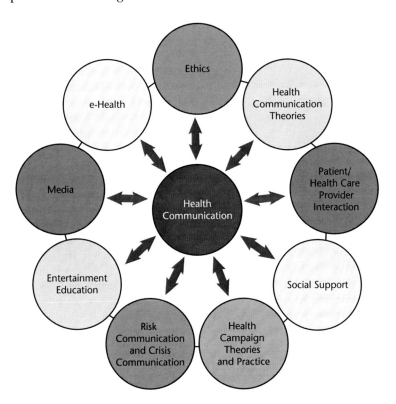

Figure 1.1 ◆ *Health as Communication Nexus model*

The topic of ethics is strategically located at the top center of the Health as Communication Nexus model and is the focus of the chapter following this introductory chapter because ethics must infuse the study of all other topics and issues in health communication. We also position health communication theories toward the top of the model and cover this topic early in the book because a consideration of theory should guide our discussion of the other content areas in health communication. The remaining chapters are organized from more micro topics, such as patient interaction and health care provider interaction, to more macro topics, such as health campaigns, health in the media, and technology. Also, within each chapter we profile experts working in the field whose careers involve aspects of health communication relevant to the chapter.

Vision and Outline of Chapters

Our vision for this book is to present a comprehensive survey of the health communication topics, concepts, and issues found in health-care–related environments and occupations and/or as part of our daily lives. Our hope is that this book appeals to anyone who desires to learn more about the field of health communication from the perspectives of people who teach, conduct research, and have applied experience within the discipline of communication.

To give you a sense of the topics, concepts, and issues within health communication, an outline of the chapters of this book follows.

◆ In the remainder of Chapter 1, "Introducing Health as Communication Nexus," we continue introducing you to the concept of health communication by providing some essential definitions, offering a historical timeline of health communication within the discipline of communication, and discussing career opportunities in the growing field of health communication.

◆ In Chapter 2, "Linking Health Communication with Ethics," we argue that a consideration of values and ethics must infuse the study of health communication. Ethical issues and dilemmas pervade the real-life health situations and challenges that you may encounter both personally and professionally. To understand and/or prepare for these ethical issues and dilemmas, this chapter presents traditional and contemporary perspectives on ethics and offers strategies for dealing with ethical issues and dilemmas. Also, we purposely devote an entire chapter to discussing ethics early in the book to encourage you to further consider ethics throughout our discussion of health communication in subsequent chapters.

◆ In Chapter 3, "Linking Health Communication with Theories Informed by Health Communication," we present four theories that we believe are unique to the field of health communication, although they may originally stem from other disciplines. Learning these theories and applying them to actual situations will help you appreciate the role of theory in understanding and practicing health communication.

◆ In Chapter 4, "Linking Health Communication with Patient Interaction," we emphasize the patient's perspective on interaction with health care providers by summarizing the history of the patient/health care provider relationship and discussing various micro-level and macro-level influences on this relationship. In addition, patient rights including informed decision making and informed consent are considered along with the foundations of patient-centered communication and patient skill development for effectively interacting with health care providers.

◆ In Chapter 5, "Linking Health Communication with Health Care Provider Interaction," the health care provider's perspective on interaction with patients is emphasized by discussing the many macro-level and micro-level influences on health care providers' communication with patients and emphasizing the importance of and skills for developing a patient-centered approach. In addition, techniques for improving patients' health literacy are considered.

◆ In Chapter 6, "Linking Health Communication with Social Support," we outline the types and benefits of social support and discuss communication that is supportive, support seeking, and the role of support networks and support groups in helping people cope with health issues and challenges.

◆ In Chapter 7, "Linking Health Communication with Health Campaign Theories," and Chapter 8, "Linking Health Communication with Health Campaign Practice," we discuss a health communication perspective on the ways in which health campaigns are theoretically framed and designed, implemented, and evaluated. The Messaging Model for Health Communication Campaigns is offered as a tool for establishing a health campaign.

◆ In Chapter 9, "Linking Health Communication with Risk Communication and Crisis Communication," we distinguish between the concepts of risk communication and crisis communication, discuss perceptions of hazard and outrage, suggest emotion management strategies, and offer guidelines and best practices for conducting effective risk and crisis communication.

◆ In Chapter 10, "Linking Health Communication with Entertainment Education," we review the history, provide examples, present the 3-step process of creating programming, and consider career opportunities for using entertainment media to educate mass audiences about health issues.

◆ In Chapter 11, "Linking Health Communication with Media," we consider the role of the media and media consumers in co-constructing health communication. Relevant theories are reviewed along with techniques for media literacy and media advocacy.

◆ Finally, in Chapter 12, "Linking Health Communication with e-Health," we address theories, concepts, and issues at the intersection of health and technology, including the historical roots of technology in health contexts and exciting new e-Health applications such as telemedicine, electronic medical records, and video games.

By reading and studying these chapters, you will gain a better understanding of and perhaps an appreciation for health communication. We also hope you will become a more effective health communicator to meet any health-related challenges and opportunities that may surround you, your family, your friends, your colleagues, and/or your community. To begin your quest for a better understanding and appreciation of health communication, let's consider the health status of Americans in general and young adults in particular.

Health Status of Americans

One of the main reasons that health communication is so important is that although most of us want to be healthy, there are so many competing choices that challenge our abilities to make healthy decisions. So effective health communication may foster health by helping us make healthy choices. However, ineffective health communication also may contribute to lack of health by contributing to our unhealthy choices. Let's review the health status of Americans and then begin considering the role of health communication in helping people make healthy choices. Although the United States remains among the healthiest countries in the world, there is ongoing concern about the health status of Americans in several categories. In 2008, the Centers for Disease Control and Prevention (CDC; 2008) reported the following about the status of Americans' health.

Life and Death Rates

◆ Men and women can expect to live longer than ever before. On average, for all races, men live to be 75.1 years of age and women live to be 80.2 years of age.

- Mortality (death) rates from heart disease, stroke, and cancer, for all races, declined in recent years.
- Infant mortality rates, for all races, declined from 29.2 per 1,000 live births in 1950 to 6.7 in 2006.

Although longer life spans are considered desirable, with longer life spans and an aging population comes increasing prevalence of chronic diseases and other adverse health conditions, including associated disabilities (limitations in usual activities).

Chronic Diseases and Conditions

- 65% of men and 80% of women age 75 years and over reported either having high blood pressure or taking medication to control hypertension. This compares with 36% of adults age 45 to 54.
- 16% of adults have high cholesterol, with women age 55 years and over being much more likely to have high cholesterol than men in the same age range.
- Almost 25% of adults age 60 and over have diabetes.

Risk Factors for Chronic Diseases and Conditions

There is growing concern about the number of people with risk factors, such as obesity and insufficient exercise, because these risk factors are associated with chronic diseases and conditions such as heart disease, diabetes, and hypertension.

- Obesity rates remain at unacceptable levels, with over 1/3 of adults age 20 and over considered obese.
- Nearly 1/5 of women and high school students and 1/4 of men currently smoke cigarettes.
- Almost 11% of pregnant women smoke cigarettes.
- About 1/3 of adults age 18 and over engage in regular physical activity and about 1/5 engage in regular strength training.

Infectious Diseases

- Due to vaccines and other prevention initiatives, new cases of many infectious diseases, including hepatitis types A, B, and C, measles, mumps, rubella, and invasive pneumococcal disease, decreased substantially.
- Incidence rates of other communicable diseases such as pertussis (whooping cough) and chlamydia increased in recent years.
- Newly recognized infectious diseases emerged, including severe acute respiratory syndrome, influenza A (H1N1) virus, and methicillin-resistant staphylococcus aureus.
- Influenza and pneumonia remain major causes of death, especially among those age 65 and over.
- HIV/AIDS continues to spread.

Unintentional Injuries

◆ Accidents are the #1 cause of death for those age 1 to 44.

◆ Due to use of seat belts, helmets, and other public health initiatives, deaths from unintended injuries declined since 1970. This, however, does not include deaths from motorcycle crashes, which continue to increase each year (National Highway Transportation Safety Administration, 2008).

Health Disparities

The above statistics about the health status of Americans also are influenced by major *health disparities* that exist in health and health care access depending on individuals' socioeconomic status, race, ethnicity, and health insurance status. In other words, some income, racial, and ethnic groups are less healthy because they are less likely to have access to health care than other groups; and for some groups, the health disparity gap is becoming wider. Following are just a few example statistics about health disparities.

◆ On average, Blacks have a life expectancy of 73.2 years, while Whites have a life expectancy of 78.2 years.

◆ 53% of Black women over the age of 20 are obese compared with 42% of women of Mexican origin and 32% of White women.

◆ Among persons under age 65, those of Hispanic origin, American Indians, and Alaska Natives are less likely to have health insurance than other racial and ethnic groups.

◆ Percentage of mothers with early prenatal care is lowest among American Indian or Alaska Natives and highest among Whites.

◆ Mammography levels are lower among Hispanic and Asian women compared with Black and White women.

Healthy People 2020 is a comprehensive set of disease prevention and health promotion objectives for the United States to achieve over the next decade. Created by scientists both inside and outside the government, it identifies a wide range of public health priorities and specific, measurable objectives.

Goals of *Healthy People 2020:*

• Attain high-quality, longer lives free of preventable disease, disability, injury, and premature death.
• Achieve health equity, eliminate disparities, and improve the health of all groups.
• Create social and physical environments that promote good health for all.
• Promote quality of life, healthy development, and healthy behaviors across all life stages.

Topics:

• Access to health services
• Adolescent health

continued

- Arthritis, osteoporosis, and chronic back conditions
- Blood disorders and blood safety
- Cancer
- Chronic kidney disease
- Dementias including Alzheimer's Disease
- Diabetes
- Disability
- Early and middle childhood
- Educational and community-based programs
- Environmental health
- Family planning
- Food safety
- Genomics
- Global health
- Healthcare associated infections
- Health communication and health information technology
- Health-related quality of life
- Hearing and other sensory or communication disorders
- Heart disease and stroke
- HIV
- Immunization and infectious diseases
- Injury and violence prevention
- Lesbian, gay, bisexual and transgender health issues
- Maternal, infant, and child health
- Medical product safety
- Mental health and mental disorders
- Nutrition and weight status
- Occupational safety and health
- Older adults
- Oral health
- Physical activity
- Preparedness
- Public health infrastructure
- Respiratory diseases
- Sexually transmitted diseases
- Sleep health
- Social determinants of health
- Substance abuse
- Tobacco use
- Vision

(U.S. Department of Health and Human Services, 2010; www.healthypeople.gov)

Take a break from reading and pick up your notebook. Jot down your first reaction to each of the following questions about the health status of young adults.

- What do you think is the most common chronic disease or illness among young adults?
- What percentage of young adults smoke cigarettes?
- How many drinks does it take for a young adult to be considered a heavy drinker?
- What do you think are the top two illegal drugs most often used by young adults?
- What do you think is the biggest health concern young adults face and why?

As you read on, you will find out whether your reactions to these questions were accurate according to the most current data available.

Within its report on the health status of Americans, CDC (2008) also provided a special feature report on the health status of young adults age 18 to 29. The introduction of the report states that this age range is usually a "transitional period in terms of education, marital status, family structure, and employment; and a critical time when many behaviors and risk factors are established that will affect health status later in life" (p. 72). During this time in their lives, young adults usually assume increased responsibility for their own decisions. Often their decisions directly or indirectly affect their current and future health status. Decisions surrounding alcohol, cigarette, and illegal drug use or nonuse, sexual activity, childbearing, exercise, and eating habits all influence health.

Cigarette smoking, heavy drinking, use of illegal drugs, sexually-transmitted diseases, and forced sexual activity are common risk factors for young adults, which may have long-term effects. Although the prevalence of cigarette smoking and alcohol consumption leveled off over the past decade, both of these behaviors remain public health concerns. About 30% of young men smoke cigarettes compared with about 20% of young women. Young men were 37% more likely to smoke cigarettes than young women.

Six percent to 8% of young men and 3% to 5% of young women reported heavy drinking (more than 14 drinks per week for men and more than 7 drinks per week for women). In addition, about 25% of young men and 3% to 9% of young women reported having 5 or more drinks in a day on at least 12 days in the past year.

Young adults 18–29 years: Cigarette and alcohol use

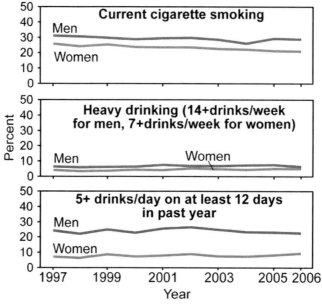

CDC/NCHS, *Health, United States*, 2008.

Between 25% and 40% of young adults reported using an illicit drug in the past year. Illicit drugs include heroin, marijuana, cocaine, and methamphetamine, or non-medical use prescription drugs such as pain relievers, tranquilizers, stimulants, and sedatives. Marijuana was the most commonly used illicit drug reported, with non-medical prescription drugs being the second most common.

Young adults: Illicit drug use, 2006

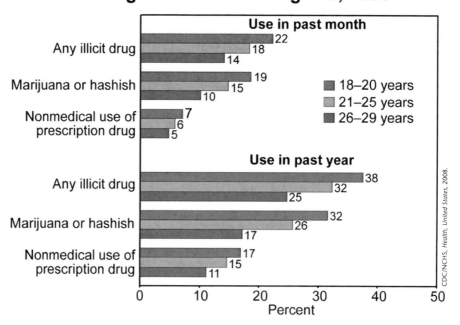

A pressing health issue for young women is sexually-transmitted diseases. Forty-five percent of young women age 20 to 24 were infected with human papillomavirus (HPV), which is transmitted through sexual contact and is associated with cervical, anal, and other genital cancers. The number of sexual partners is the most consistent risk factor for HPV. Sixty-two percent of women age 20 to 29 who had three or more sexual partners in the past year were HPV-positive compared with 32% of women who had one partner in the past year. Approximately 1/5 of women between the ages of 18 and 44 reported forced sexual intercourse before age 30.

Although most young adults reported being in good health, 18% of young women and 12% of young men reported at least one of six serious health conditions, including arthritis, asthma, cancer, diabetes, heart disease, and hypertension. Asthma was the most commonly reported of the six conditions, followed in order by arthritis, hypertension, cancer, diabetes, and heart disease. In addition, 4% to 5% of young adults reported overall fair or poor health or an activity limitation due to a chronic health condition.

So, based on the information about the health status of young adults, how accurate were your responses to the questions in Health Communication Nexus Interlude 1.2? What information was most surprising to you and why? What information was most concerning to you and why?

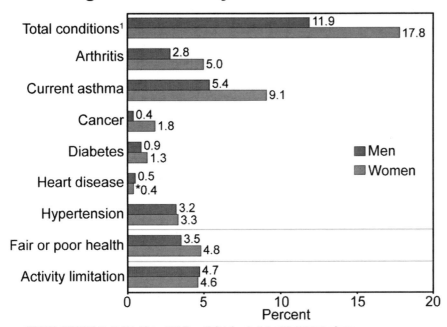

Young adults 18–29 years: Health status

SOURCES: CDC/NCHS, *Health, United States, 2008*, Figure 35. Data from the National Health Interview Survey.
[1]At least one of these physician-diagnosed conditions (arthritis, current asthma, cancer, diabetes, heart disease, or hypertension).
* Relative standard error 20%–30%.

Now that you have a sense of some of the health challenges facing Americans, let's explore how health communication can help us in turning these health challenges into opportunities to improve and maintain health. First, we need to agree on a definition of health communication from the variety of definitions that have been offered. Agreeing on a definition of the concept of health communication allows us to share a common understanding of what the concept means as we branch out into the many areas of health communication in the chapters that follow.

Defining Health Communication

Although the term health communication is not yet included in many dictionaries, those who study and practice health communication have defined it in a variety of ways (see Schiavo, 2007 for review of definitions).

In our effort to understand what is meant by the term health communication, we need to consider the component parts of the concept of health communication. In preparation for this, please complete Health Communication Nexus Interlude 1.3.

Health Communication Nexus Interlude 1.3

Stop reading for a few minutes and jot down your response to this question in your notebook: How do you define "health?"

Consider for another minute or two a related question: Do you think health is a human right? Why or why not? Jot down your response in your notebook.

OK, just a couple more questions and a few more minutes before you get back to the reading: How do you define "communication?"

Now try putting the two concepts together: How do you define "health communication?" Again, jot down your response in your notebook.

Keep your responses, as you'll need them later for comparison purposes.

We followed a similar approach to what we asked you to do in Health Communication Nexus Interlude 1.3 to determine our working definition of health communication. We took each concept within the term health communication —"health" and "communication"—and considered how these concepts have been defined independently and then we put those concepts together to create our definition.

Defining Health

We researched definitions of the concept health and, of course, we found many legitimate and relatively similar definitions. For example, the *Mosby Medical*

Encyclopedia defines health as "a state of physical, mental, and social well-being and the absence of disease or other abnormal condition. It is a condition that involves constant change and adaptation to stress" (Glanze, Anderson, & Anderson, 1992, p. 360).

In the Merriam-Webster (2008) online dictionary, health is defined as "the condition of being sound in body, mind, or spirit; *especially:* freedom from physical disease or pain." These definitions are similar in that they both consider the states of physical and mental soundness or well-being as essential. The definitions are different in that one includes social well-being, while the other incorporates sound spirit as necessary for health. Also, one definition considers health to be a process because it involves adaptation and change; the other definition emphasizes health as being the absence of disease or pain.

Despite the variety of definitions of health to choose from, we kept returning to the often-quoted and well-recognized definition by the World Health Organization (WHO), which states that "health is a state of complete physical, mental and social well-being and not merely the absence of disease or infirmity (2006)." Like so many others, we appreciate this comprehensive definition of health that was developed over 50 years ago.

However, Saracci (1997), while recognizing that the WHO provided a major advance when it broadened the conceptualization of health from a state of physical well-being by including psychological and social dimensions, aptly questioned whether the WHO definition of health is now too broad and impractical. Interestingly, he wondered whether "a state of complete physical, mental, and social well-being corresponds much more closely to happiness than to health" (p. 1). This is an especially important question when we consider whether health is a human right. When you completed Health Communication Nexus Interlude 1.3, did you argue, like many would, that health is a human right and that it is an appropriate use of resources to fulfill people's health needs? However, expanding this argument further, if our definition of health is synonymous with happiness, as Saracci suggested, then is happiness a human right that we should use societal resources to ensure?

Saracci went on to discuss four consequences of failing to distinguish health from happiness:

1. Any disturbance in happiness may be considered a health problem.
2. If the quest for happiness is boundless, so too will the quest for health and health services be boundless.
3. Attempting to guarantee happiness and health for every citizen will deplete resources and seriously jeopardize the possibility of attaining equity in health.
4. Equating happiness and health assumes one way of achieving and maintaining health and happiness, which undermines personal autonomy and smacks of tyranny.

In an effort to resolve this definitional dilemma, Saracci (1997) suggested a way to link the WHO's idealistic definition of health with individual and societal health realities by adding a measurable descriptor of health such as: "Health is a condition of well being free of disease or infirmity and a basic and universal human right" (p. 2). This descriptor of health provides a way to measure health or lack of health using mortality (e.g., death rates), morbidity (e.g., rate of disease), and quality of life (e.g., air quality) indicators. So, given what you already learned in this chapter about the health status of Americans and young adults and about health disparities, does thinking about all this, especially in light of Saracci's perspective, change your response to the question "Is health a human right?" Why or why not? To learn our answer to this important, thought-provoking question, let's get back to our task of defining health.

Adapted from the WHO's (2006) and Saracci's (1997) definitions, we coin the following definition of *health*:

> Ideally, health is a state of complete physical, mental, and social well-being. However, health is more commonly experienced as the absence of physical, mental, social disease, or illness and should be considered a basic, universal human right.

Defining Communication

We also researched definitions of the concept of communication within the discipline of communication, and again we found a variety of definitions, from the very simple to the more descriptive and complex. At the most basic level, communication is the "process of understanding and sharing meaning" (Pearson & Nelson, 2000, p. 3).

Building upon this definition, Hoover (2005) defined communication as a "process of creating shared meanings in order to bring people and ideas together" (p. 23). In addition to referring to communication as a process of gaining and sharing meaning, this definition includes the goal of communication as bringing people and their ideas together. Although we consider this an adequate definition of communication, we're concerned that it does not capture the complexity of the communication process.

One reason many of us have difficulty communicating, especially in health care settings, is because we don't understand and appreciate the complexity of the communication process. We have the wrong model or process of communication in mind—that is, we consider communication to be a simple one-way process between sender and receiver and we assume that the message sent will be the message received. So, before we forward a more comprehensive definition of communication, let's graphically illustrate the complicated nature of communication using a health care example. After we present the health care example, you will be asked to stop reading and participate in a Health Communication Nexus Interlude, which asks you to draw out all the components of the communication process using the example.

The following health care example happened to Lecturer Hall, one of the authors of this book. When Jennifer Hall was a graduate student at Purdue

University, she and her husband, Brian, were considering trying to have another child after their daughter turned two, which was in about six months. Jennifer had been feeling funky, so she decided to take a home pregnancy test. The test was positive, so she called to confirm the result with her OB-GYN. During what should have been a rather routine check-up and pregnancy test, the physician started asking some unusual questions, such as "What if you had more than one baby in there?" However, he did not wait for a response before moving on with the examination. At the end of the visit, the physician confirmed that Jennifer was pregnant and then asked, without explanation, that she return the following week for an ultrasound test. Jennifer and Brian attended the next appointment together, during which the physician told them, "You are not just pregnant with one baby, there are three babies!—yes, triplets!!!" Jennifer and Brian stared at each other in disbelief. Jennifer started to cry and asked her physician how this could have happened, while Brian stood nearby shaking his head in continued disbelief.

Health Communication Nexus Interlude 1.4

Now, based on the health care example just presented take a few minutes to draw out all the components of this interaction into a model of communication in your notebook. Be creative. As a hint to get you started, draw three people to represent Jennifer, Brian, and the physician. People are key components of communication so they need to be included in your graphic model of communication. How would you illustrate the message(s) sent between these communicants? How were those messages sent and how would you illustrate how the messages were sent? Continue drawing all the aspects of communication you can think of within this interaction between Jennifer, Brian, and their physician. Try to draw as complete a communication model as possible. Remember, we're trying to illustrate that communication is a complex process of sharing and understanding meaning.

It is likely that the model of communication you drew in Health Communication Nexus Interlude 1.4 is more complex than you initially anticipated. If not, you may need to revisit the example and your model to make sure the model exemplifies the complexity of the communication process involved in this interaction.

Let's consider a definition of *communication* that more aptly captures the intricate interaction occurring in the Health Communication Nexus Interlude example.

Communication is a complex transactional process that involves the generation, transmission, receipt, and interpretation of symbols that may be verbal or nonverbal.

We prefer this definition because it is more specific about what the process of communication involves and it indicates that communication occurs both in words and through body language or actions. Did you capture all of these aspects of the communication process in your model of communication? Graphic representation of communication should include all the following components:

◆ *People*—the individuals involved in the interaction.
◆ *Message(s)*—the information or request and the symbols that convey the information or request.
◆ *Channel(s)*—mode or method of communication (e.g., cell phone to make and confirm appointment with physician, face-to-face appointment with physician).
◆ *Feedback*—evaluative information returned in response or reaction to a previous message (e.g., bursting into tears upon being told that she is pregnant with triplets; interpretation may be positive or negative).
◆ *Noise*—physical or psychological interference with a message (e.g., a ringing cell phone takes your psychological attention away from what the physician is discussing with you even if you don't answer the cell phone).
◆ *Context*—the setting or situation within which the communication occurs (e.g., emergency room, over the telephone with a representative of the health insurance company). Ideally, you want the context of communication to be conducive to effective interaction; and regardless of the context, you need to adapt your communication to the setting.

Figure 1.2 ◆ *Model of Communication*

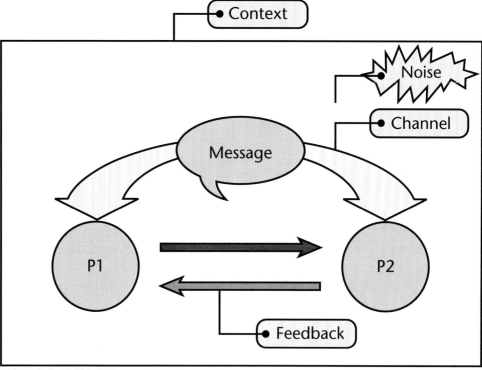

CDC/NCHS, *Health, United States,* 2008.

To illustrate each of these components, we offer a model of communication in Figure 1.2. Compare it with the model of communication that you drew. Are the models comparable? How is your model similar to our model? How is our model different than your model? If our models are different, why are they different? By drawing and thinking about these models, we demonstrated the complexity of the communication process.

Now let's further consider the context of communication or the setting within which the communication occurs, because it may impact the process and effectiveness of communication. Redmond (2000) distinguished among six communication settings with each setting requiring different communication skills to fulfill different communication goals.

1. *Intrapersonal Context*

   Communication with oneself or talk directed toward ourselves often takes the form of cognitive analysis of self, others, problems, and situations. For example, rehearsing in your mind how you will respond to your physician about the timeline and symptoms of an earache. Sometimes our intrapersonal communication can cause noise that interferes with our communication with others. We may get so caught up in our own rehearsal of what we want to say, we don't listen to the physician's questions and treatment steps to reduce or eliminate the earache.

   Whether we actually communicate with ourselves is somewhat controversial within the discipline of communication. Some scholars argue that intrapersonal communication is the same as cognition or thinking and does not constitute communication because we are not converting our thoughts into symbols to create a message to send to another person or persons. In other words, communication needs to be a social activity (Miller, 2002; Vocate, 1994). Either way, internal states such as thinking, planning, and feeling emotions are important to consider when we communicate with others in health-related situations.

2. *Interpersonal Context*

   This communication setting often is referred to as conversation, which usually takes place one-to-one or among very few people. The primary goal is to develop, maintain, and improve relationships. Discussing your earache with a physician is an example of interpersonal communication. Through this interaction you both are involved in creating and maintaining a relationship with the immediate goal of determining the cause and treatment for your earache. If the conversation is successful and your earache subsides, it is likely that both you and your physician also will consider the relationship effective and you may decide to visit the same physician in the future if you are having a health problem.

   Some scholars refer to the interpersonal context of communication within a health care setting as interviewing. *Interviewing* is a specialized form of interpersonal communication, because it is goal-structured, with primarily one person, the health care provider, asking the questions and the other person, the patient, responding (Redmond, 2000). However, because we emphasize that interactants in any health communication context have mutual responsibility for effective communication, we encourage patients to both respond to questions and ask questions. Further, we suggest that patients write down their questions in advance to aid recall and staying on track during appointments with their health care providers.

3. *Small Group or Team Context*
Small aggregates of people can form either a small group or a team. These communication contexts are closely aligned, but there is one key difference. According to Myers and Anderson (2008), a small group is "three or more people working interdependently for the purpose of accomplishing a task" (p. 7). Katzenbach and Smith (1993) defined a team as "a small number of people with complementary skills who are committed to a common purpose, performance goals, and approach for which they hold themselves mutually accountable" (p. 45). So a team is a small group but adds the dimension of members holding each other mutually accountable for their work as a team. This is consistent with our emphasis on health communication being an endeavor for which interactants have mutual responsibility for effectiveness.

A support group for individuals caring for someone with Alzheimer's disease (for more information go to this book's Web site) is an example of small group health communication because individuals who attend these support groups are seeking support through interaction with others in a similar situation.

An example of a health care team is the trauma unit at the regional medical center where Professor Mattson was a patient for a month after her motorcycle accident. The health care team integrated the patient's care by having regular meetings attended by the surgeon, the surgeon's nurse, a psychiatrist, an infectious disease specialist, a physical therapist, and a social worker. Sometimes, these meetings took place at Professor Mattson's bedside to encourage her and her husband to provide input. Together the health care providers discussed, planned, and executed how to best serve the physical and psychological needs of Professor Mattson as she recovered from a traumatic accident.

4. *Organizational Context*
Communication takes place in a social collectivity with common goals, coordinated activity, environmental embeddedness, structure, and communication. The health care team in the trauma unit previously mentioned also operates within the hospital's organizational context. The entire regional hospital staff shares the common goal of diagnosing and treating patients' health problems by working together, through communication, within the rules of the organization and in response to a

constantly changing health care environment which harbors diseases, illnesses, and social, economic, and political pressures and challenges.

5. *Public Context/Mass Communication Context*

In preparing and delivering a message to an audience in a public or media setting, the communication goal is to make a presentation that meets the needs of a particular situation. Often the speaker is working to disseminate information and act as a catalyst for change.

An example is an amputee testifying in front of the public health policy committee of a state legislature about the need for insurance companies to cover prosthetic limbs under private health insurance plans. The goal of this prepared public message is to persuade the legislators that there is a need to pass a law mandating insurance companies to reimburse for prosthetic care because prosthetic limbs are necessary for amputees to remain healthy and productive members of society, and insurance companies have been eliminating or unrealistically capping coverage for these devices and services (for more information about state and federal prosthetic parity legislation, go to this book's Web site).

6. *Intercultural or Multicultural Context*

Communication occurs among people of diverse cultures. Basically, people within a culture share a common denominator such as race, religion, gender, ethnicity, region, lifestyle, or occupation. People of different cultures have different values, attitudes, traditions, customs, and languages, which can challenge effective communication. Similar to the larger society, health care environments are intercultural or multicultural contexts.

For example, CBS News (2008) highlighted the Community DentCare Network's mobile van project, which is designed to provide dental care to underserved preschool children who do not have dental insurance. The most common chronic disease in children is dental decay. The DentCare van is set up to communicate with and treat children. The van even is equipped with stuffed animals whose teeth the children can brush while the health care providers work with them. As the mobile van moves through the neighborhoods of Manhattan, uninsured adults constantly bang on the door to the van seeking treatment for themselves. Even though the project is not designed for adults, the health care providers help adults in extreme need of dental care and adapt their communication accordingly. Similarly, the community clinic in your hometown needs to adapt its communication to the unique needs of the various cultures that seek treatment there.

Each of these contexts provides unique challenges to effective communication. Realizing this and understanding that some or all aspects of the communication process may need to be adjusted depending on the context is an important step toward effective health communication.

Attributes of Communication

There are a few other attributes of the communication process that are worth noting and keeping in mind as we study health communication, including:

◆ Meanings are in people, not in words
◆ Communication is a process
◆ Communication is a transactional process
◆ Communication is the relationship
◆ Most communication is nonverbal
◆ Effective communication skills are learned

Meanings are in people, not in words. Meanings of words are ambiguous or vague and vary among people, with some words and phrases being easier to comprehend than others. For example, "I feel nauseous" versus "I feel funky." Variability in meaning should be taken into consideration when communicating. More ambiguous meanings likely will need more distinct explanation. If you initially say to a physician, "I feel funky," follow up with a more descriptive explanation of what feeling funky means to you so the physician can better understand and work more effectively with you.

Communication is a process. Interaction is a relatively systematic series of continuously changing actions depending on the context and people involved. For example, a visit to the urgent care clinic typically involves several steps from arrival, briefly explaining the problem to the intake staff, paperwork, waiting, greeting the health care provider, explaining the problem and symptoms, diagnosis, treatment, and follow-up. However, the content of each of these steps will vary depending on the situation. For example, a busy versus a not-busy clinic and the complexity and urgency of the health problem, such as a gunshot wound versus an earache due to wax build-up.

Communication is a transactional process. The process of communication is a two-way rather than a one-way process as we simultaneously send and receive messages. For example, when a technician at your local pharmacy is asking if you have any questions for the pharmacist about the medication you are picking up at the drive-thru window, you are, at the same time, nonverbally addressing the question by beginning to shake your head from side to side to nonverbally signal "No." This also indicates that the transaction is almost complete and you are free to leave.

Communication is the relationship. The relationship between the interactants is created through communication, and the effectiveness of and satisfaction with the relationship is based on the people involved and the situation. For example, without communication there would be no way to realize or express that you have a "long-distance" relationship with your parents or your significant other. In the same way, when you decide to switch physicians to someone who is closer to where you are currently living, this decision involves the relationship aspect of your communication with that person.

Most communication is nonverbal. Communication goes beyond the verbal message, that is, the words expressed, to nonverbal aspects of the message, including facial expressions, tone of voice, and other actions. Estimates vary but suggest that between 65% and 93% of information is communicated nonverbally (Andersen, 2008). Although this is a broad range, it basically indicates that more than 50% of our communication is nonverbal. Further, there is a major irony associated with nonverbal communication. Even though nonverbal communication is more ambiguous, or difficult to interpret because each nonverbal action can have several meanings, nonverbal messages are trusted more as a source of accurate information when they contradict the verbal message. This is, in part, because nonverbal communication provides insight into emotions.

For example, when your mom calls you on your cell phone and asks, "How are you doing?" and you say, "Fine," how can she always seem to tell when you're really not feeling fine? Well, it's because there is much more communicated through your tone of voice than what your mom interprets from your verbal "fine." However, with people such as your health care providers, who are not as familiar with you as your mom likely is, you may need to be much more explicit in your verbal messages to avoid misinterpretations that can result from misunderstanding your nonverbal messages.

Effective communication skills are learned. Good communication is not an innate ability or a skill that we are born with or inherit. If this were the case, so many relationships would not fail due to an inability to communicate. Also, it takes more than common sense to be an effective communicator. Instead, communication is a skill that can be taught and learned. This is a key underlying assumption of this book. Learning about health communication and the skills associated with communicating in health settings will make you a more effective and satisfied communicator in these unique situations.

Defining Health Communication

Now that we understand more about how health is defined and about the complexity of the communication process, we need to integrate the concepts of health and communication into a definition of health communication to frame your further study of this concept.

There are many definitions of health communication; ranging from simply seeking and transmitting health information (Freimuth & Quinn, 2004; Kreps & Thornton, 1992) to attempting to influence people's health behaviors through communication strategies (U.S. Department of Health and Human Services, 2001). Of the many available definitions (for more examples, see Schiavo, 2007), we prefer to start with Brashers and Babrow's (1996) description of communication within the context of health:

> Communication in health and illness constitutes the most vital of human experiences. No other human phenomenon is more elemental than health and illness; none connects us more viscerally with our aspirations, or confronts us more palpably with our limitations. Moreover, given the dynamics of these elemental experiences, and especially given that they are constituted in the communicative interweaving of body, mind, and society, health

communication represents among the most complex, challenging, and potentially rewarding areas for inquiry. (p. 243)

We favor this description because it locates communication within human experiences of health and is consistent with our sense that health is a communication nexus—meaning that communication, in all its manifestations, is at the center and creates our experiences of health.

We also believe that it is important for a definition of health communication to emphasize the role of communication in addressing health issues. This belief is based in part on The Joint Commission's (2010) report which determined that one of its seven National Patient Safety Goals was to "improve the effectiveness of communication among caregivers" because it identified communication errors as a root cause for many unexpected occurrences involving death or serious injury or the risk thereof in health care situations. Therefore, students in health care–oriented programs need to be knowledgeable about health communication and learn effective health communication strategies.

What Is The Joint Commission?

The Joint Commission is an independent, not-for-profit organization that accredits and certifies more than 17,000 health care organizations and programs in the United States. Joint Commission accreditation and certification is recognized nationwide as a symbol of quality that reflects an organization's commitment to meeting certain performance standards.

Mission Statement: To continuously improve health care for the public, in collaboration with other stakeholders, by evaluating health care organizations and inspiring them to excel in providing safe and effective care of the highest quality and value.

Vision Statement: All people always experience the safest, highest quality, best-value health care across all settings.

(For more information go to this book's Web site) © The Joint Commission, 2010. Reprinted with permission.

So, if we integrate the notion of health as a communication nexus with the need to be knowledgeable about and learn effective communication strategies for health contexts, the following new definition of *health communication* emerges:

Health communication is the multifaceted study and use of effective, ethical approaches to share information and motivate audiences at the individual, organizational, and community levels about health issues and decisions that enhance health.

Now that we've built a definition of health communication, let's situate our current study of this topic within the historical roots of health communication.

Historical Timeline of Health Communication

Health communication is a relatively new area of the discipline of communication. According to the National Communication Association (NCA; www.natcom. org), "The field of health communication has been attracting increased attention in recent years due to the growing recognition of the role that communication plays in enhancing health promotion and disease prevention." Several significant milestones have distinguished health communication as an important area of study and consideration. The timeline in Table 1.1 illustrates these milestones.

1960s Communication established as an academic discipline.

1970s Health communication established as an emphasis area within the discipline of communication.

1975 Health Communication Division of the International Communication Association (ICA) founded. This division encourages theory development, research, and effective practice of health communication by publication of a newsletter, programming of research panels at ICA's annual meeting, and sponsorship of a midyear and a summer conference.

1977 Costello (1977) and Cassata (1977) reviewed the area of health communication in *Communication Yearbook*. However, these chapters were based on research of authors in other academic disciplines, such as medicine, nursing, and clinical psychology (see for example, Korsch, Freeman, & Negrete, 1971; Korsch, Gozzi, & Francis, 1968).

1980s and 1990s Interest and research in health communication grew exponentially.

1984 Thompson's (1984) review of health communication in the health and social service professions published in a communication journal and was strongly influenced by research published in communication outlets or presented at communication conferences.

1986 Health Communication Division of NCA formed. This division plays a significant role in representing the discipline as it works to advance theory, research, teaching, and practical applications of human and mediated communication to health care and health promotion.

1989 *Health Communication* launched as first academic journal devoted to dissemination of research on communication and health issues.

1996 CDC established Office of Health Communication to integrate health communication into overall prevention programs as a means of influencing individual behavior to reduce risks to health.

ICA was formed in 1950 to bring together academicians and other professionals whose interests are focused on the systematic study of communication theories, processes, and skills. The association maintains an active membership of more than 3,100 individuals residing around the world. Two-thirds of these individuals teach and conduct research in colleges, universities, and schools, while other members are in government, the media, communication technology, business law, medicine, and other professions. To learn more about ICA go to this book's Web site.

NCA is an academic society with a mission to promote effective and ethical communication by supporting the communication research, teaching, public service, and practice of a diverse community of scholars, educators, administrators, students, practitioners, and publics. To learn more about NCA go to this book's Web site.

CDC is a federal government agency that promotes health and quality of life by preventing and controlling disease, injury, and disability. It accomplishes this mission by working with partners throughout the nation and the world. To learn more about CDC go to this book's Web site.

Table 1.1 ◆ *Timeline of Health Communication Milestones*

(continued)

1996	*Journal of Health Communication* becomes the second journal in the field.
1997	American Public Health Association recognized health communication through its Public Health Education and Health Promotion section.

NCI is the principal government's principal agency for cancer research, training, and information dissemination. To learn more about NCI go to this book's Web site.

2000s **Role of health communication in national public health initiatives recognized and emphasized.**

2000	The National Cancer Institute (NCI) formed Health Communication and Informatics Research branch to contribute to the reduction in death and suffering due to cancer by supporting interdisciplinary research and development of a seamless health communication and informatics infrastructure.
2001	Health communication added as a focus area to *Healthy People 2010*. The goal of this focus area was to use communication strategies to improve health.
2002– 2004	Institute of Medicine (IOM) report highlighted the centrality of communication in health through the following conferences:

2002	Speaking of Health: Assessing Health Communication Strategies for Diverse Populations
2002	Who Will Keep the Public Healthy: Educating Public Health Professionals for the 21st Century
2004	Health Literacy: A Prescription to End Confusion

2004	NCI awarded Centers of Excellence in Cancer Communication to four universities.
2004	*American Journal of Public Health* featured a series of editorials on the importance of health communication to the discipline of public health.
	Major professional organizations outside the discipline of communication (e.g., the American Public Health Association, the Society of Behavioral Medicine) offered forums for sharing health communication scholarship.

Healthy People 2010 and 2020 is a comprehensive set of national health objectives designed to identify the most significant preventable threats to health and to establish goals to reduce these threats. It can be used by many different people, states, communities, professional organizations, and others to help develop programs to improve health. *Healthy People 2020* was developed through a broad consultation process, built on scientific knowledge, and designed to measure programs over time. To learn more about *Healthy People 2020,* go to this book's Web site.

IOM is a component of the National Academy of Sciences that provides unbiased, evidence-based, and authoritative information and advice concerning health and science policy to policy-makers, professionals, leaders in every sector of society, and the public at large. To learn more about IOM go to this book's Web site.

Careers and Job Market in Health Communication

Career Prospects

Now that you've learned how health communication is uniquely defined and you have a sense of the history of health communication, you may be wondering how you could play a role in the future of health communication or, more precisely, how health communication could play a role in your professional future.

Overall, the prospects for jobs in health-related fields are very encouraging. The United States government reports that most jobs in health communication-related occupations likely will be plentiful over the next few decades. According to the most recent data from the Bureau of Labor Statistics (2010), of the 16 professional occupation categories listed, 8 are health related and could be filled by a person with health communication knowledge and training.

For example, the outlook for "Public Relations Specialists" within the "Media and Communications-Related Occupations" category is expected to grow faster than most other occupations. However, competition for entry-level positions, with the minimum of a bachelor's degree and some field experience, is expected to be intense. In health organizations, public relations specialists serve as advocates for the organization and its clients and work to build positive relationships with the organization's audiences. Example audiences include the media, the community, and the government.

One common task of these occupations is writing press releases including working with the media to place those press releases within media programming. Other tasks may involve writing speeches for organization officials, giving presentations within the community, and preparing funding proposals and annual reports on behalf of the organization. Individuals who relish busy environments and who are creative, take initiative, practice good judgment, and can communicate ideas clearly and succinctly most often thrive in these occupations. An example job description for a Communications Coordinator at a YWCA—essentially a public relations or communication specialist position—reads:

> Responsible for the planning, implementation, and representation of a comprehensive internal and external communications program. Ongoing responsibilities include: preparation and publication of comprehensive seasonal program schedule, hiring and oversight of internship staff, participation in relevant community events to advertise programs and services, coordinating with local media to pitch story ideas, writing and distributing employee newsletter, organization of staff promotional events.

Public Relations/Marketing Specialist

Franklin Regional Medical Center is currently seeking a **Public Relations/ Marketing Specialist** to join our team!

The Specialist coordinates projects for public/media relations, internal communications, and marketing, specifically contributing support for information-gathering, writing, planning special events, and relating to the media, the community, and patients.

A minimum of a Bachelor's degree in journalism, mass communications or an appropriately related field is required. Two to five years experience in media, public relations, marketing, or related field and health care experience are preferred.

(example job ad from www.monster.com)

In another relevant occupation category, "Community and Social Services Occupations," the outlook for the position of a "Health Educator" is even more promising. Employment opportunities for this occupation are expected to grow much faster than the average for all occupations. There is expected to be high demand for these positions because of the rising cost of health care and the increased understanding that specialization in health education and/or health communication is needed to be effective. However, some employers require advanced degrees, especially to fill positions beyond entry level. Examples of non-entry-level positions include executive director and senior health educator.

Basically, health educators work to encourage healthy lifestyles and prevention of disease through education. Tasks involve assessing health needs and planning, implementing, and evaluating relevant health programs. Most health educators work in medical care settings, schools, public health departments, non-profit organizations and businesses. The goals and tasks of health educators vary slightly depending on the type of organization. Individuals who prefer to work with a variety of people both individually and in groups, serve as a health resource, and split their time within and outside an office adapt well to this occupation. An example job description for an HIV Health Educator position at a public health department reads:

> Provides HIV prevention programs to schools, community organizations, and businesses tailoring programs to fit the needs of the group. Performs workplace training as needed in businesses, social service agencies, shelters, and nursing homes. Assesses community needs and priorities through analysis of previous program results, other community resources, and national, state and local data. Researches, develops, and implements HIV prevention programs focusing on risk reduction education for high-risk groups including: IV drug users, men who have sex with men, and high-risk heterosexuals. Collaborates with area service organizations to promote social support networks for HIV risk reduction, HIV testing and counseling, and other available services for at-risk population. Provides counseling and testing according to department protocol, which includes collecting, storing, and transporting specimens. Ensures anonymity and documentation of results as required by law. Complies with laws for proper handling of biohazardous material. Provides test results, post-test counseling, and treatment referrals to HIV clinics, STD clinics, drug treatment programs, and other community services. Plans and promotes conferences on issues related to HIV. Coordinates and implements conference schedule, including agenda, organizing speakers and rooms, and attending to conference projects. Other duties as assigned.

Research on the Job Market

Scant published research considers the job prospects in the area of health communication. Two academic research studies have been conducted to assess the career options for health communication professionals and the core competencies needed to become a health communication professional. The findings from these studies are consistent. Both report exciting career prospects for those with education in health communication, but to attain these positions, both articles strongly recommend internships and volunteer opportunities to enhance your educational background.

In 1999, Fowler, Celebuski, Edgar, Kroger, and Ratzan conducted a telephone survey of supervisors of health communication practitioners in small, medium, and large organizations and determined that the job outlook was positive, but for most of the core competencies required of health communication practitioners, a graduate degree was preferred by the employer. Given that health communication was a relatively new area of research and practice at the time of the study, the authors suspected that most health communication practitioners would not have majored in a health communication program. Instead, they would have academic degrees in other, related disciplines and professional programs, such as health psychology, medical sociology, behavioral health, nursing, social work, and public health. Therefore, in this study, a health communication practitioner was broadly defined as someone who "focuses specifically on communication issues in health care settings" (p. 327). The core health communication responsibilities that the supervisors were asked about in the study were determined by a working group of health communication academics and practitioners. According to supervisors, in order of most often hired for and supervised, the nine core health communication responsibilities were:

1. Design programs, campaigns, or materials
2. Evaluate programs, campaigns, or materials
3. Teach classes or provide training about health
4. Conduct research to develop programs, campaigns, or materials
5. Market health-related products or services
6. Develop health-related public relations
7. Administer health information consumer services
8. Organize coalitions or act as an advocate
9. Obtain funding for communicating about health

Interestingly, the rank ordering of items changed when supervisors were asked to anticipate the responsibilities that would be in greatest need in the future. From responses to this request, the list of core health communication responsibilities emerged as:

1. Design programs, campaigns, or materials
2. Conduct research to develop programs, campaigns, or materials
3. Administer health information consumer services
4. Organize coalitions or act as an advocate
5. Obtain funding for communicating about health
6. Evaluate programs, campaigns, or materials
7. Teach classes or provide training about health
8. Develop health-related public relations
9. Market health-related products or services

For all of these responsibilities, the supervisors expected their organizations to be hiring over the next few years.

In order to competently perform the core responsibilities identified, supervisors reported that health communication practitioners needed at least a general knowledge of relevant health issues. In addition, good oral and written communication skills were deemed important across all the core responsibilities. With regard to training and experience, accomplishing some responsibilities, such as public relations and health information services, do not require an advanced degree. However, for other responsibilities, such as conducting research and obtaining funding, an advanced degree is preferred. For those seeking entry-level positions as health communication practitioners, gaining experience through an internship or by volunteering is recommended.

PROFILE

Searching for Employment in Health Communication

Timothy Edgar, PhD—Associate Professor and Graduate Program Director, Emerson College

Because health communication is a relatively new field, some may question what sorts of job opportunities are available for those with a degree in health communication. Timothy Edgar frequently answers this question in his position as the Graduate Program Director for the Health Communication Program at Emerson College. He explains that graduates of health communication programs will have the same opportunities as those graduating from public health programs, although health communication students generally gravitate toward positions with a communication focus such as public relations or marketing. Some of the potential jobs for those with health communication degrees include working for non-profits, health insurance agencies on the prevention side, worksite wellness programs, or in pharmaceutical sales. He recommends that health communication students take courses in public health in order to have a better understanding of the field and the language and vocabulary of health promotion. In addition, a broad understanding of health issues will be extremely beneficial to those trying to create and deliver messages about health issues.

Prior to his position at Emerson College, Edgar worked as a consultant with Centers for Disease Control and Prevention (CDC) and was involved in a variety of projects including evaluating the VERB campaign which encouraged children to engage in more physical activity. Although he enjoyed this job very much, he decided to pursue an opportunity to join the faculty and teach at Emerson College. He was excited about the applied nature of the health communication program and looked forward to training the next generation of professionals in the field.

As he teaches students, he considers it important for them to be able to explain what they do and why it has value. He explains that many people think that health communication is easy. You put some information into a brochure, add some colorful pictures and graphics, and you're done. In reality, effective health communication projects, initiatives, and campaigns involve knowledge about behavior change and communication theories, solid research, planning, and evaluation. Those with an academic background in health communication are trained in these areas and can help communication efforts be more effective.

Additionally, Edgar thinks it is important for those in health communication to recognize and appreciate the many barriers individuals face as they try to live healthier lifestyles. He illustrates this with the example of obesity. Many people who are overweight lack the money to buy healthy, low-calorie foods or to join a gym. Many live in areas where it is unsafe to go outside to exercise. Or some people are working two jobs to survive financially and do not have the time and energy to exercise. Health communication campaigns need to take these complex factors into account in order to succeed.

In a more recent study, Edgar and Hyde (2005) surveyed alumni of the master's of health communication program jointly offered by Emerson College and Tufts University, which at the time of the study graduated more students than any other graduate program in health communication. Results from this survey demonstrated that graduates were very marketable in both the private and public sectors working in either nonprofit or for-profit organizations. Respondents attained positions in a variety of types of organizations, with the six that topped the list being the government, hospital or medical practice, advertising/public relations/marketing, educational institution, pharmaceutical or biotech firm, and nonprofit advocacy or voluntary organization. Respondents also reported much flexibility in being able to pursue their career interests. In other words, a degree in health communication seems to support a wide array of career options. Regarding salary expectations, the researchers noted that pursuing a career in health communication "might not be a path to wealth, but respectable salaries exist" (p. 20).

Two of the most compelling results from this survey concerned needed knowledge/skills and trends in health communication. When asked about knowledge and skills, there was much crossover with the earlier study we discussed. More than 10% of the respondents in the more recent study reported that they had acquired the following necessary skills/knowledge in the health communication program:

1. Knowledge of message strategy and campaign planning
2. Knowledge of behavioral and communication theory
3. Presentation skills
4. Medical knowledge/content
5. Research methods
6. Skill in epidemiology and biostatistics

In addition, more than 10% of the respondents suggested that new technologies and health care finance/business skills should have been addressed in the program.

The respondents' ideas about the emerging trends in health communication that academic programs should consider including also were very telling. The categories mentioned included:

1. Risk communication
2. Crisis communication/bioterrorism
3. Internet/e-learning
4. Public health funding and finance
5. Cultural competence
6. Technological advances in medicine
7. Health literacy
8. Obesity
9. Issues in the pharmaceutical/biotechnology industry
10. Social marketing
11. Ethics

We encourage you to consider and heed the challenges posed by these two research articles about the necessary knowledge and skills to pursue a career in health communication. Reading this book is definitely a step in the right direction because we cover all of the topics identified in the research and sample job descriptions and job ads as important to a career path in health communication.

Chapter Summary

In this chapter we introduced you to the topic of health communication. Using a personal example of a traumatic motorcycle accident as a backdrop, we considered and offered a model of how health is a communication nexus linking many of the areas of research and practice in the discipline of communication (refer back to the Health as Communication Nexus Model in Figure 1.1). We also asked you to think of health communication examples from your own experiences to illustrate the pervasiveness of health communication. This was followed by an outline of the health status of Americans which identified several health challenges and opportunities for effective health communication. We then built a definition of health communication to serve as a common jumping-off point to further study the intricacies of health communication. Next we couched our current study of health communication within the historical timeline of the field of health communication. Looking ahead to your further endeavors, we concluded the chapter by presenting an overview of some exciting career choices and the encouraging job market outlook for students of health communication.

References

Andersen, P. A. (2008). *Nonverbal communication: Forms and functions* (2nd ed.). Long Grove, IL: Waveland Press.

Brashers, D. E., & Babrow, A. S. (1996). Theorizing health communication. *Communication Studies, 47,* 243–251.

Bureau of Labor Statistics (2010). *Occupational outlook handbook, 2010–11 edition.* Washington, DC: U.S. Department of Labor.

Cassata, D. M. (1977). Health communication theory and research: An overview of the communication specialist interface. In B. D. Ruben (Ed.), *Communication yearbook 2* (pp. 495–503). New Brunswick, NJ: Transaction Books.

CBS News (2008). Dental insurance crisis [Television]. *The other America.* Retrieved June 30, 2008, from http://www.cbsnews.com/video/watch/?id=4217889n.

Centers for Disease Control and Prevention (2008). Health, United States, 2008. Retrieved January 30, 2010, from http://www.cdc.gov/nchs/data/hus/hus08.pdf#executive-summary.

Costello, D. E. (1977). Health communication theory and research: An overview. In B. D. Ruben (Ed.), *Communication yearbook 1* (pp. 557–568). New Brunswick, NJ: Transaction Books.

Edgar, T., & Hyde, J. N. (2005). An alumni-based evaluation of graduate training in health communication: Results of a survey on careers, salaries, competencies, and emerging trends. *Journal of Health Communication, 10,* 5–25.

Fowler, K., Celebuski, C., Edgar, T., Kroger, F., & Ratzan, S. C. (1999). An assessment of the health communication job market across multiple types of organizations. *Journal of Health Communication, 4,* 327–342.

Freimuth, V. S., & Quinn, S. C. (2004). The contributions of health communication to eliminating health disparities. *American Journal of Public Health, 94*(12), 2053–2055.

Glanze, W. D., Anderson, K. N., & Anderson, L. E. (Eds.). (1992). *The Mosby medical encyclopedia* (2nd ed.). New York: Plume.

Hoover, J. H. (2005). *Effective small group and team communication* (2nd ed.). Belmont, CA: Thomson Wadsworth.

Katzenbach, J., & Smith, D. (1993). *The wisdom of teams.* Cambridge, MA: Harvard Business School Press.

Korsch, B. M., Freeman, B., & Negrete, V. F. (1971). Practical implications of doctor-patient interaction analyses for pediatric practice. *American Journal of Diseases of Children, 121,* 110–114.

Korsch, B. M., Gozzi, E. K., & Francis, V. (1968). Gaps in doctor-patient communication: Doctor-patient interaction and patient satisfaction. *Pediatrics, 42,* 855–871.

Kreps, G. L., & Thornton, B. C. (1992). *Health communication: Theory & practice* (2nd ed.). Prospect Heights, IL: Waveland.

Merriam-Webster's Dictionary. (2008). Retrieved June 16, 2008, from http://www.merriam-webster.com/dictionary/health.

Miller, K. I. (2002). *Communication theories: Perspectives, processes, and contexts.* Boston: McGraw-Hill.

Myers, S. A., & Anderson, C. M. (2008). *The fundamentals of small group communication.* Thousand Oaks, CA: Sage.

National Highway Transportation Safety Administration (2008). Traffic safety facts 2007: Motorcycles. Retrieved April 27, 2009, from http://www.nhtsa.gov.

Pearson, J. C., & Nelson, P. E. (2000). *An introduction to human communication: Understanding and sharing* (8th ed.). Boston: McGraw-Hill.

Redmond, M. V. (2000). *Communication: Theories and applications.* Boston: Houghton Mifflin.

Saracci, R. (1997). The World Health Organisation needs to reconsider its definition of health. *British Medical Journal, 314,* 1409–1410.

Schiavo, R. (2007). *Health communication: From theory to practice.* San Francisco: John Wiley & Sons.

The Joint Commission (2010). National patient safety goals. Retrieved January 10, 2010, from http://www.JointCommission.org/PatientSafety/NationalPatientSafetyGoals.

Thompson, T. L. (1984). The invisible helping hand: The role of communication in the health and social service professions. *Communication Quarterly, 32,* 148–163.

U.S. Department of Health and Human Services (2001). Healthy People 2010. Retrieved July 2, 2008, from http://www.healthypeople.gov/document/html/volume1/11 healthcom.htm.

U.S. Department of Health and Human Services (2010). Healthy People 2020. Retrieved January 17, 2011, from www.healthypeople.gov.

Vocate, D. R. (Ed.). (1994). *Intrapersonal communication: Different voices, different minds.* Hillsdale, NJ: Lawrence Erlbaum Associated.

World Health Organization (2006). Constitution of the World Health Organization Supplement (pp. 1–18).

CHAPTER 2   Linking Health Communication with . . .

Ethics

Chapter Learning Objectives

◆ List and explain the criteria for what constitutes an ethical dilemma
◆ Define and describe the interrelationships between values, morals, and ethics
◆ Identify reasons unethical behavior is considered common
◆ Explicate the four principles espoused in the Hippocratic Oath
◆ Compare and contrast traditional and contemporary orientations to ethics in health care
◆ Apply ethical strategies and tools within health communication

Chapter Preview

In this chapter we emphasize the importance of ethics in health communication. After considering an example of an ethical dilemma, we present the criteria for what constitutes an ethical dilemma so that you can recognize ethical issues throughout your personal and professional life. Next we define key concepts, including values, morals, and ethics, and ask you to think about how these concepts are interrelated. We then discuss why unethical behavior is considered to be so common. To contend with unethical behavior in health care, we present the Hippocratic Oath and discuss how it formed the roots of bioethics and the Four Principles Approach to ethics in health care. This is followed by introducing you to both traditional and contemporary approaches to ethics and the implications of those approaches for a variety of health communication experiences. From these orientations to ethics, several strategies and guidelines for ethical health communication emerge, including professional codes of ethics. The chapter concludes with a service-learning application that offers an ethical analysis tool for health communication campaigns complete with specific examples to illustrate how to use this ethics tool from an existing campaign.

Ethical dilemmas and decisions pervade the real-life health issues and challenges that we may encounter and need to communicate about both personally and professionally. Guttman (2003) argued that by definition, health communication involves ethics because predominantly health communication is a purposeful attempt to influence people to adopt health recommendations. Consider the following ethical dilemma encountered and described by one of the authors of this book. Professor Mattson and her husband, Jim, faced an ethical decision soon after her motorcycle accident.

An Ethical Dilemma and A Decision

"After my motorcycle crash, I was eventually transported via emergency helicopter to a regional hospital with a trauma unit. Soon after arriving at the hospital and briefly talking with emergency room personnel, I was given medication to make me unconscious for the surgery which would begin repairing the area where my leg was severed. After surgery I was placed in the intensive care unit where I remained unconscious for several days. During one of the initial conversations that my husband, Jim, and I had after I became more conscious and able to process information, he mentioned that the man who was driving the truck I collided with had been calling the hospital to inquire about my condition. Jim already had spoken with the truck driver a few times. In addition to wondering how I was doing, the truck driver expressed concern that I might want to sue him for his involvement in the accident. He told my husband that he had a sick family member whose medical bills already were overwhelming and that a lawsuit would be an additional burden.

Although my top priority at the time was recovering from my injuries, the topic of how to handle the cause and responsibility for the accident began to weigh on my mind and became part of an ongoing discussion with my husband. There was much to consider, including peace of mind, finances, and legal representation. After several surgeries and days in intensive care, I was transferred to a regular room in the trauma unit. One evening while lying in bed watching TV, the phone rang and I picked up the receiver and weakly said 'Hello.' The person on the other end of the line hesitated. I said 'hello' again. This time he spoke. I don't remember exactly what he said but he told me he was the truck driver and that he did not see me or realize that he had struck something until he heard the thump and looked in his side-view mirror to see me flying sideways off my motorcycle. We talked for a minute or two and then said good-by and I hung up the phone. I knew from that moment that I would not pursue suing him for his role in the accident. Mainly because suing him would not change the outcome of the crash. It would not reattach my severed leg and it would likely cause additional pain and hardship—for me and the truck driver.

We never spoke with the truck driver again. He did not try to contact me after our phone call and I never tried to contact him. However, whether or not to pursue legal action against the truck driver was something Jim and I spoke about occasionally—Jim wondering if I should reconsider my decision. I later learned from the crash report that the police officer at the scene determined, after considering available evidence, including talking with witnesses, that I had swerved into the truck's path. Although I don't necessarily agree with this assessment, and I was never interviewed for my point of view as the driver of the motorcycle, I decided to accept the outcome. For me it was the only way that I could proceed in a positive direction with my recovery."

So, why is this situation an *ethical dilemma* that involves health communication? The decision of whether or not to sue involves a choice, which will significantly influence the health and well-being of humans, and that choice can be judged by moral standards of right and wrong. Professor Mattson decided not to pursue suing the truck driver because she believed that doing so would only cause more harm to the individuals involved in the situation, including her husband, herself, the truck driver, and his family. She reasoned that because suing would not change the outcome of the accident and likely would inflict unnecessary pain, suing was not morally justified. Without realizing it at the time, Professor Mattson not only was experiencing and illustrating the criteria for an ethical dilemma, but she also was invoking aspects of ethical orientations in her decision making about the situation. As this chapter progresses, try to pinpoint which ethical orientation or combination of orientations Professor Mattson was exhibiting.

To help you understand and prepare for the variety of ethical dilemmas you undoubtedly will face throughout your life, like the entirely unexpected ethical dilemma Professor Mattson describes in the introduction, this chapter presents traditional and contemporary perspectives on ethics and offers practical strategies for dealing with ethical dilemmas in a variety of health communication situations.

Just as ethics pervade health communication, we believe that ethics should pervade our study of health communication. Therefore, we devote an entire chapter to discussing health communication ethics early in the book and revisit this topic in subsequent chapters to encourage you to further consider ethics throughout our discussion of health communication. Our approach to introducing ethics early on and revisiting ethics periodically throughout the book is endorsed by Cheney and his colleagues (2004, 2009), who argued that we all need to allow thinking and discussions about ethics to infuse both our personal and professional activities. Further, instead of simply treating ethics as a way of regulating behavior, we ought to consider ethics an essential aspect of our being human in interaction with other humans.

How do we know when we are facing an ethical issue or dilemma? The next section provides criteria for recognizing ethical situations.

Criteria for an Ethical Dilemma

As illustrated in Professor Mattson's narrative about deciding whether or not to sue the truck driver, without even consciously realizing it she was invoking Jensen's (1997) criteria for what constitutes an ethical issue or dilemma by talking with the truck driver and her husband and then making the decision not to pursue a lawsuit. Jensen's criteria for what constitutes an ethical situation or dilemma include the following:

◆ *Significant impact on others*—decision or action will affect self and others.
◆ *Conscious choice between means and ends*—decision or action involves selecting between process and outcome. Although the desired outcome

may be desirable, what will occur in the process of achieving that outcome must also be considered. For example, although winning a lawsuit may provide vindication and a monetary settlement, reliving the motorcycle crash and its aftermath again and again during testimony may strain family relationships.

◆ *Communication can be judged by standards of right and wrong*—interaction in the situation can be considered honest or deceitful according to commonly agreed upon rules of behavior. For example, it would be inappropriate to threaten another with a lawsuit in the hopes of receiving a monetary settlement if one has no intention of pursuing that threat.

Jensen's Criteria for an Ethical Dilemma

- Significant impact on others
- Conscious choice between means and ends
- Communication can be judged by standards of right and wrong

(from Jensen, 1997)

Now that you know the criteria for an ethical dilemma and you've read about those criteria being applied to one example, complete Health Communication Nexus Interlude 2.1. Doing so gives you practice applying the criteria to situations.

Health Communication Nexus Interlude 2.1

Begin this interlude by reading through the following list of potential ethical issues/situations/dilemmas.

List of Potential Ethical Issues/Situations/Dilemmas

- Whether or not to share your concerns with a friend and/or someone else about that friend's excessive alcohol consumption
- Exaggerating about a symptom to a health care provider to gain medication or treatment
- Using someone else's prescription medication
- Sharing a patient's medical history with another health care provider to get ideas for how to respond to the patient's situation

continued

- Underestimating or overestimating when a health care provider asks about amount of exercise, food intake, alcohol consumption, smoking, medication use
- Not telling a child that he or she has a terminal illness

Now, while going through the list, write down your answers to the following questions in your notebook:

1. Based on Jensen's (1997) criteria for an ethical dilemma, which situations on this list are ethical issues, situations, or dilemmas? Also note why or why not.

2. Did you find the criteria for an ethical dilemma useful? Why or why not?

3. Are there any other criteria for an ethical issue/situation/dilemma that you think should be added to Jensen's list of criteria? Why?

Defining Ethics: Foundational Concepts

For many, the broad term ethics is difficult to define and comprehend. To address this difficulty, we build a definition of ethics by first defining the following three related concepts:

- ◆ Values
- ◆ Morals
- ◆ Ethics

It is helpful to first grasp these concepts and their role in shaping your own and others' perspectives about and reactions to ethical issues and dilemmas.

The first foundational concept associated with ethics is values. *Values* are defined as "conceptions of The Good or The Desirable that motivate human behavior and that function as criteria in our making of choices and judgments" (Johannesen, Valde, & Wedbee, 2008, p. 1). In other words, values are those ideals, either positive or negative (such as freedom, integrity, individualism, physical fitness, obesity) that a culture, society, or community considers important to embrace or repel. Can you think of any health-related values that the community you grew up in, also known as your community of origin, hold dear? Are the health-related values of your community of origin the same or different than the values of your current community? If the values are different, how has this influenced your thinking and behavior regarding health and health-related issues?

Our values form our morals. *Morals* are defined as generally agreed-upon, culturally-transmitted standards or rules of right and wrong conduct (Gert, 2008). When values and morals intersect with or influence what is considered appropriate conduct, ethics are involved.

Ethics is defined as a system of moral principles for right and wrong human behavior (Johannesen et al., 2008, p. 1). Ethics do not necessarily tell us what to do in a given situation but instead what to consider in that situation before we decide how to act. For example, *medical ethics* or *biomedical ethics* refers to moral values and responsibilities in the context of medical practice and research (Wells, 2002).

Perceptions of Ethical Behavior in Health-Related Professions

So why be concerned about ethics and ethical issues and dilemmas in health communication? Because both as health care consumers and/or patients and as health care providers or others in health-related professions (such as public relations specialists, public health campaigners, health care administrators) you likely will encounter situations that require decision making and attention to ethics or what is considered right and wrong behavior. And although many perceive those in health-related professions as inherently honest and ethical, those in business-related professions, including the health industry, do not fare as well in terms of the public's perception of the ethicality of their behaviors. A recent Gallup poll (Saad, 2008) announced that for the seventh straight year, nurses were considered the most honest and ethical professionals of the 21 professions surveyed. Pharmacists and medical doctors also received high integrity ratings. Journalists, some of whom report on health issues, were more neutrally rated in terms of honesty and ethics. And among those professionals on the most negative end of the honesty and ethics continuum were lobbyists, telemarketers, and advertising practitioners, perhaps because they are tasked with persuading legislators and/or the public toward a certain way of thinking or behaving.

Reasons Unethical Behavior Considered Common

Why is dishonest or unethical behavior perceived to be so common in general and in particular professions? Five reasons for unethical behavior pervade the literature and are relevant to health situations (Mitchell & Silver, 1990):

- ◆ Ethic of personal advantage
- ◆ Lying and cheating as cultural traits
- ◆ Pressure to compete
- ◆ Culture of looting
- ◆ Complex structure of society and organizations

The first reason for the pervasiveness of unethical behavior is that many in American society aspire to the ethic of personal advantage. The *ethic of personal advantage* values short-term gain rather than a long-term perspective, is focused on achieving an outcome rather than on how that outcome is achieved, and emphasizes the individual over the community (Mitchell & Silver, 1990). Consequently individuals and organizations within society emphasize personal and organizational success at any cost.

The second reason that unethical behavior is considered common stems from the first reason. In aspiring to the ethic of personal advantage, many in our society consider *lying and cheating as cultural traits,* meaning that not telling each other or the public the truth is so common that many consider it inevitable and even acceptable for members of our culture to lie. According to prominent ethics scholar Sissela Bok (1989a, 1989b), a *lie* is an intentional effort to mislead. The suggestion that lying is a cultural trait implies that generally people believe that almost everyone and every organization is misrepresenting the truth to gain some advantage.

In the early 1990s, the cover of *Time* magazine conveyed this sentiment with the headline "Lying: Everybody's Doin' It (Honest)." Inside, the lead story, "Lies, Lies, Lies," discussed the public's growing disenchantment with politicians because they are believed to be dishonest in order to appease different groups or special interests, including health care interests (such as organizations that represent hospitals and health insurance companies) within their constituencies in order to win elections (Gray, 1992).

More recently, Chopra (2008) argued that a "Cycle of Lies" exists in national politics for the following reasons:

◆ Politics is elitist and attracts rich, white males who stick together.
◆ Ideology links politicians and gives them more reason to protect each other.
◆ Special interests and lobbyists bought their way into politics many years ago and formed a cohesive group which can outlast any political term.
◆ The interests of the poor and ethnic minorities have been suspended indefinitely, so these groups must be fed false promises to conceal political reality.
◆ Core support from religious conservatives demands that politicians show public piety even though the religious convictions of these politicians are mild or nonexistent.
◆ Democracy is a ritual enacted every four years at election time and after which politicians return to business as usual.

Chopra further argued that it is difficult to reverse this cycle because, ironically, each of the reasons actually perpetuates the cycle of lies. However, Chopra also suggested that we've reached a critical point in the cycle of lying because the public seems to be craving honesty and trustworthiness in politics rather than ugly political wrangling and inertia.

Keep in mind, this notion of lying to win does not occur only in politics, within major organizations, and by adults. In order to be considered a cultural trait, lying must be occurring across the culture. A biannual ethics survey of high school students conducted by the Josephson Institute (2008) confirmed that lying and cheating are increasing among youth. In 2008, more than 75% of youth surveyed said they lied to a parent about something significant, and 64% admitted cheating on a test in the past year. Interestingly, the study also found that "despite these high levels of dishonesty, the respondents have a high self-image when it comes to ethics. A whopping 93% said they were satisfied with their personal ethics and character and 77% said that when it comes to doing what is right, I am better than most people I know." In his book *The Cheating Culture: Why More Americans Are Doing Wrong to Get Ahead*, Callahan (2004) confirmed that the culture of lying and cheating is instilled at an early age and is part of childhood socialization through families, friends, and schools.

These disturbing statistics beg the question—why has lying become a cultural trait? The following list covers the most compelling reasons according to those who have researched and written on the subject (Callahan, 2004; Weaver, 1998; Wexler, 2000):

- ◆ The competitive economy has shifted our values from equal opportunity toward a focus on money, selfishness, and material possessions.
- ◆ Focus on money and profits creates pressure to cut corners, lie, and cheat to report more profits and gain more wealth.
- ◆ The assumption exists that everyone else is lying and cheating, so it is okay to lie and cheat too.
- ◆ There is no accountability and punishment for lying and cheating (in part due to lack of resources by government and other regulatory agencies).
- ◆ Youths witness parents getting away with lying and cheating.

As alluded to in the list above, the third reason that unethical behavior is considered to be so common is that people in health-related professions and many of us in everyday situations feel a strong sense of *pressure to compete* with others in order to judge ourselves as successful. For many in our society, success is achieved by surpassing the accomplishments of others. If this need to be competitive is strong enough, some may try to achieve the feeling of accomplishment at any cost, including ill health and compromising relationships and personal integrity. Consider, as an example, the proliferation of illegal substance use in athletics today. Steroids and other performance-enhancing substances were banned in athletic training and competitions because they give athletes an unfair advantage, and overuse of these drugs can be very harmful to athletes' health (KidsHealth, 2009; United States Anti-Doping Agency, 2009). Because athletes have such a strong drive to perform better than their opponents, some athletes ingest or inject banned substances despite the health risks, and then adamantly deny it when asked about their illegal behavior. The fear of both athletic and financial failure may be too great to ignore or turn down the opportunity to cheat to achieve success. Numerous cases of this very type of unethical behavior in sports may come to mind, including the use and denial of illegal substances by famous runners, baseball players, and cyclists.

A fourth reason for the seemingly ordinariness of unethical behavior is referred to by Lerner (1992) as the *culture of looting,* defined as the unfair appropriation or random destruction of the collective goods of others for the sake of personal and private benefit. Originally coined in the context of the Los Angeles riots that followed the acquittal of four police officers charged with beating Rodney King, this phrase applies the concept of looting to describe a fundamental character of American society. In other words, individuals' ultimate pursuit is to look out for themselves and in doing so take what they can get when they can get it.

Looting can take many forms. It can be stealing from a shopkeeper who cannot defend the shop in the face of a riot; corporations exploiting natural resources to create consumer products in order to gain huge profits; or politicians who compromise their campaign promises to keep donors giving. Lerner argued that the culture of looting has become a dominant way of life and that we all are complicit in it by at times compromising to gain our own advantages. Perhaps, for example, you have taken or bought a prescription drug from a friend because you thought it would help you sleep or help you concentrate better. In doing so, you took advantage of others who may need to pay more for prescription medications due to your and your friends' illegal behavior which took advantage of the prescription medication system. Also, you may have compromised your own health and safety and that of your friend by taking a medication that was not prescribed to you.

A fifth reason for the perceived commonness of unethical behavior is the *complex structure of society and organizations*. You may be wondering how the structure of society and organizations can influence unethical behavior. As our society grows—currently the United States grows at an annual rate of 0.9%, meaning that our country's population doubles every 77 years (Rosenberg, 2009)—cities and towns become larger, and interactions between people tend to become more fleeting and impersonal, which may make it easier to act unethically toward people we consider strangers. Similarly, as organizations become larger and larger, there is an increase in their complex structures; there are more and more levels of organizational hierarchy and a corresponding increase in role differentiation and specialization among employees. This complexity creates impersonal organizations where employees often feel lost in the vastness of the organization, which may facilitate unethical, immoral, or irresponsible conduct because behavior or responsibility for behavior can become disassociated from individuals or diffused among many individuals. These complex hierarchical webs make it more difficult to assign individual responsibility or blame for a given action. Often in large, complex organizations, how well the individual meshes with the organization's goals is important even if that meshing compromises personal morals or integrity.

For example, the ethics surrounding communication by members of Merck & Co., Inc. about the prescription drug Vioxx have been widely questioned (Berenson, 2005; Lyon, 2007; Ross, Hill, Egilman, & Krumholz, 2008). Vioxx, an anti-inflammatory medication prescribed to treat arthritis and other acute pain conditions, was withdrawn from the market in 2004 because of safety concerns. Lyon's (2007) case study about the health communication surrounding Vioxx found that pharmaceutical sales representatives employed by Merck were constrained from discussing the risks of Vioxx with health care providers. They were instructed and trained in specific strategies, including scripted responses and visual aids, to avoid the topic of the risks of Vioxx and to redirect questions about risks to the benefits of the drug. Specifically, sales representatives were told to tell physicians that they could not discuss concerns about heart-attack risks because these risks were not on the drug's label, which had been approved by the U.S. Food and Drug Administration. To redirect the conversation, sales representatives were given a "Cardiovascular Card" produced by the company that included graphs and charts emphasizing the drug's safety. Generally, the massive sales staff at Merck followed these sales directives issued by the company in order to comply with the company's economic priorities and achieve personal gains, including sales bonuses. Due to the complex structure of this large organization, it would be difficult to attribute blame for unethical behavior to individuals within the sales force.

The study of ethical and unethical behavior has been around for a long time. Next we consider three historically relevant and interrelated perspectives on health care ethics: the Hippocratic Oath, bioethics, and the Four Principles Approach.

Hippocratic Oath

Generally interest in medical ethics dates back to the ancient Greek physician Hippocrates (460–377 BC) who put forward the first moral standard in the practice of

---

THE HIPPOCRATIC OATH: Classical Version

Today, few medical schools require students to recite the classical version of the oath.

I swear by Apollo Physician and Asclepius and Hygieia and Panaceia and all the gods and goddesses, making them my witnesses, that I will fulfill according to my ability and judgment this oath and this covenant:

To hold him who has taught me this art as equal to my parents and to live my life in partnership with him, and if he is in need of money to give him a share of mine, and to regard his offspring as equal to my brothers in male lineage and to teach them this art—if they desire to learn it—without fee and covenant; to give a share of precepts and oral instruction and all the other learning to my sons and to the sons of him who has instructed me and to pupils who have signed the covenant and have taken an oath according to the medical law, but no one else.

I will apply dietetic measures for the benefit of the sick according to my ability and judgment; I will keep them from harm and injustice.

I will neither give a deadly drug to anybody who asked for it, nor will I make a suggestion to this effect. Similarly I will not give to a woman an abortive remedy. In purity and holiness I will guard my life and my art.

I will not use the knife, not even on sufferers from stone, but will withdraw in favor of such men as are engaged in this work.

Whatever houses I may visit, I will come for the benefit of the sick, remaining free of all intentional injustice, of all mischief and in particular of sexual relations with both female and male persons, be they free or slaves.

What I may see or hear in the course of the treatment or even outside of the treatment in regard to the life of men, which on no account one must spread abroad, I will keep to myself, holding such things shameful to be spoken about.

If I fulfill this oath and do not violate it, may it be granted to me to enjoy life and art, being honored with fame among all men for all time to come; if I transgress it and swear falsely, may the opposite of all this be my lot.

Edelstein, Ludwig. *The Hippocratic Oath: Text, Translation, and Interpretation*, p. 3 © 1996 The Johns Hopkins University Press. Reprinted with permission of The Johns Hopkins University Press.

---

medicine: "Do no harm." This standard formed the basis of the Hippocratic Oath, which many new medical school graduates still recite today. Keep in mind, however, that like ethical perspectives and approaches generally, the Hippocratic Oath has been debated and changed over the years (Graham, 2000; Orr, Pang, Pellegrino, & Siegler, 1997). Read and compare the classical version and a modern version of the Hippocratic oath found in the sidebars. Despite these debates and changes, however, physicians, like those in other professional communities inside and outside the health care industry, often are bound by codes of ethics. Codes of ethics shape and are shaped by the shared community and culture of the individuals who choose to become part of that profession.

THE HIPPOCRATIC OATH: Modern Version

During graduation ceremonies, many medical students take a modern version of the oath written by Louis Lasagna in 1964.

I swear to fulfill, to the best of my ability and judgment, this covenant:

I will respect the hard-won scientific gains of those physicians in whose steps I walk, and gladly share such knowledge as is mine with those who are to follow.

I will apply, for the benefit of the sick, all measures [that] are required, avoiding those twin traps of overtreatment and therapeutic nihilism.

I will remember that there is art to medicine as well as science, and that warmth, sympathy, and understanding may outweigh the surgeon's knife or the chemist's drug.

I will not be ashamed to say "I know not," nor will I fail to call in my colleagues when the skills of another are needed for a patient's recovery.

I will respect the privacy of my patients, for their problems are not disclosed to me that the world may know. Most especially must I tread with care in matters of life and death. If it is given me to save a life, all thanks. But it may also be within my power to take a life; this awesome responsibility must be faced with great humbleness and awareness of my own frailty. Above all, I must not play at God.

I will remember that I do not treat a fever chart, a cancerous growth, but a sick human being, whose illness may affect the person's family and economic stability. My responsibility includes these related problems, if I am to care adequately for the sick.

I will prevent disease whenever I can, for prevention is preferable to cure.

I will remember that I remain a member of society, with special obligations to all my fellow human beings, those sound of mind and body as well as the infirm.

If I do not violate this oath, may I enjoy life and art, respected while I live and remembered with affection thereafter. May I always act so as to preserve the finest traditions of my calling and may I long experience the joy of healing those who seek my help.

The Hippocratic Oath: Modern version written by Louis Lasagna, 1964.

Bioethics

In more recent history, *bioethics*, which is rooted in the discipline of philosophy, became a field of study dedicated to considering the ethical implications of biological and medical procedures, technologies, and treatments. Although revelations about the inhumane treatment of research participants during biomedical experiments conducted by the Nazis during World War II began focusing attention on bioethics, technological advances and corresponding questions about humanity in a variety of situations, including beginning and ending of life, organ transplantation, medical research, and individual rights versus the public good, continue to shape bioethics (Pence, 2008).

Four Principles Approach to Health Care Ethics

Taken together, the Hippocratic Oath and bioethics are based in and espouse four ethical principles or moral obligations:

- ◆ Do good—promote health and protect individuals from potential risks.
- ◆ Do no harm—avoid instilling intended or unintended physical, psychological, social, and cultural damage upon individuals.
- ◆ Respect personal autonomy and privacy—individuals have the right to make decisions and choices on their own, and their confidentiality should be protected.
- ◆ Ensure justice—reduce barriers to equal access to resources that encourage health and avoid health risks.

These four principles may seem obvious to strive for but may be difficult to apply in everyday health situations. Beauchamp and Childress (2009) referred to these foundational principles as the *Four Principles Approach* to ethical decision making. One limitation in applying these four principles is that individuals involved in an ethical decision may disagree about the relative weight to apply to each principle. While completing Health Communication Nexus Interlude 2.2, think about how each of the individual perspectives on the case may weight the importance of each of the four ethical principles differently, thus coming to a different decision.

Health Communication Nexus Interlude 2.2

Four Principles Approach to Analyzing Ethical Issues/Decisions
(adapted from Beauchamp & Childress, 2009)

Carefully read through the program description and program transcript presented here. Then using the table provided, jot down in your notebook how you think each individual role addressed the ethical issues/decisions in the case.

Written by Joan I. Greco. Used with permission of Fred Friendly Seminars, Inc.

continued

Directions: Weight each role on each of the four ethical principles using a scale of 1 to 5 (1 = least important and 5 = most important).

	Do Good	Do No Harm	Autonomy/Privacy	Justice
Patient				
Family				
Physicians				
Nurses				
Spiritual Advisor				

Program Description

In a program from the long-running PBS Series, The Fred Friendly Seminars entitled "Before I Die: Medical Care and Personal Choices" (Schatz, 1996), experts from a variety of perspectives, including bioethics, medicine, nursing, spirituality, family, and the patient, discussed both actual and hypothetical case studies that involved challenging ethical questions and decisions.

For this interlude, we chose the case study of Cathleen, a woman with a young family who has advanced breast cancer. Each expert on the show is asked to role-play or comment from a different perspective in this case. Topics explored in this case study include the inability of many people to talk about and face death, the impreciseness of advance directives, the moral question of physician-assisted suicide, the strain of patient/physician communication in end-of-life situations, the effect of managed care on end-of-life options, the complexity of pain control, the promises of hospice care, the role of spirituality, the final authority on treatment options, and the necessity of end-of-life medical training.

Discussing both hypothetical and actual case studies is an interesting and common practice in the study of ethics and in everyday conversations because it allows discussants to identify, articulate, and further consider how different ethical perspectives and approaches can be applied to a variety of situations (Pence, 2008).

Program Transcript

Introduction by Tim Russert: In hospitals, doctors' offices and medical schools, there is one word that is rarely, if ever, heard—the word "death." Most Americans—even doctors—don't like to hear or think about it, as if not breathing the monster's name will prevent its next visit.

continued

But avoidance has its costs; and today what we fear most is not so much death itself as the modern medical nightmare: a death alone, in pain, tethered to expensive machines that merely prolong dying.

Our experiences with the death of loved ones has made us all wonder: isn't there a better way to die? Is dying in America more impersonal, painful and expensive than it needs to be? Should physician-assisted suicide be an option? Has medical technology made us think of dying as a failure rather than a natural part of life?

Now let us join our distinguished panelists as they wrestle with these profoundly personal questions that all of us must face before we die. Our moderator is Harvard Law Professor Arthur Miller.

MILLER: Panelists, I want to welcome you to Centerville. Centerville is a medium size community somewhere in the center of the United States, and a good deal of the life of Centerville is centered around a bookstore called "The Browser's Bookstore."

And in the course of our conversation, we're going to meet a number of people who hang out at Browser's Bookstore. The first person we're going to meet doesn't happen to be in the bookstore today. It's Cathleen Johnson. Cathleen Johnson is married, two lovely young children, but today, she's in the hospital. As a matter of fact, Dr. Nuland, she's with you. What's happened is that Cathleen has a primary care physician, and some time ago, the physician ordered a biopsy. And the biopsy revealed that there was some cancer. And that required surgery, and you've now looked at all the pathology reports and—they are not too positive.

Indeed, they show locally advanced breast cancer—cancer in the axillary lymph nodes, and Anna, you're Cathleen. You knew there was some cancer, but you certainly didn't know it was this serious. Dr. Nuland, talk to Cathleen.

DR. SHERWIN NULAND: Cathleen, we've got to talk about the results of your biopsy. It hasn't turned out the way I had hoped it would turn out. There is serious disease in it. It is malignant. In other words, it is cancerous. There are many things that we can do for this particular kind of cancer and for the stage at which it's at. But we have to face the other side of it too. We have to face the other possibility. That our treatment will not be successful.

Now, the important thing to realize in that situation is that if our treatment isn't successful, it's not as though it will fail next week or next month. It will fail a year or two down the line.

ANNA QUINDLEN: Well, Doctor, I—I love the way you doctors talk. You're— You're saying the treatment might fail in a year or a year and a half? I mean, are you, basically, saying to me, "You've got advanced breast cancer Cathleen and

continued

you're probably gonna die?" Is—Is that really what you're saying? If you divest it of all of the euphemisms that you guys like to use?

DR. NULAND: My guess is that if this cancer proves to be nowhere beyond the lymph nodes, there's a very good chance that not only will you not die in this very short period of time you're probably worried about. But that you will survive without any significant problems for some period of years. Those are the things we have to focus on.

MILLER: Karen Stanley, appraise Dr. Nuland's discussion with Cathleen.

KAREN STANLEY, RN, AOCN: I see a woman who is scared silly with good reason and a very kind physician who is trying, inasmuch as is possible, to say hard things in a kind way.

MILLER: Are doctors very good at this?

STANLEY: No. It's very painful to give hard news, I think it is. And sometimes—in our efforts—to remove ourselves from the painful situation, we blurt it out, and then leave the room. The physician could've come in and said, "You have meta-static breast cancer. There's not much I can do. I'll send the oncologist in and be gone."

MILLER: Will Gaylin, why would doctors not be all Charlton Hestons at this?

DR. WILL GAYLIN: The typical surgeon is not necessarily trained, not trained, but also not by inclination or temperament, the kind of guy who is gonna like to be a cuddly-up and get into emotions. Most guys aren't. Most men aren't.

A typical surgeon is still a man today. And as I say, of all the physicians, he does less of it. He's really seeing bodies for the most part. He's in and out quick. Big bucks are at stake here. You've gotta brain surgeon or a breast surgeon and he goes in, he does his thing and he's superb at it. And I don't know and with the economy of medicine going the way it is, you really want an HMO that's gonna spend time—spend money for his time there and even if you did, so everything is in concert, in a sense, for this to be a bad scene, let alone the fact it's a failure. It just is failure, even though it isn't. Doctors don't like to see failures any more than anybody else does.

MILLER: Dr. Fegan, how do you react?

DR. CLAUDIA FEGAN: It's painful. Physicians who do it poorly are physicians who have not had to come to grip with their own mortality, who don't ha—who are not comfortable with death and dying.

And they often will extricate themselves. They'll give a diagnosis and leave the room quickly. The important thing here is that most patients after you say the word cancer, don't hear anything else. And—And to go on and talk about the

continued

other information which he gave, which was very good information, is gone. She won't remember that tomorrow.

DR. NULAND: Well, let me tell you something you haven't taken, perhaps, into consideration. I don't know this woman. We are about to begin a long journey together. The journey may end with her death. I know nothing about her spiritual values. I know very little about her family.

Even if she has a primary physician, the way we work in America, is that from here on in, I am responsible for this woman. So I have to create for her two things, optimism and the sense, which I think I didn't do very well, that I will be with her throughout the process, that—

MILLER: And you think it's appropriate that the primary care physician has sorta handed her off to you and you can deliver this news, even though you, yourself say you don't know her.

DR. NULAND: I don't know what's appropriate. This whole thing is so irrational. Cancer is irrational, the setting in which we treat it is irrational. It was pointed out a moment ago the mu—the moment that word appears in the vocabulary of the two people talking, bingo, the rest of the conversation is shut off and it's been my experience that it's sometimes shut off just before that word. Remember what we're talking about. We are talking about the prime instinct of living, human things. To stay alive. And someone has just said, "You may not stay alive." And everything shuts off.

MILLER: Let me—Let me move the clock a bit.—Cathleen has a radical mastectomy, radiation, chemotherapy. She comes out of it all beautifully. It's—It's miraculous. For about a year. And then a reversal sets in. And, if anything, she's worse and she's going through chemotherapy again. Dr. Payne, now you—you do this, but it's not working. You reach the point where you are confident, bad word, I suppose, it's not worth it. It's just not worth it. Tell her.

DR. RICHARD PAYNE: Cathleen, we've—you've had several courses of chemotherapy. You are really not much better. You've—been getting sick. You're not feeling well. We have objective evidence that—the cancer really hasn't responded. I would recommend that—you not have any further chemotherapy. And that, at this point, we really—emphasize—treating pain and other symptoms.

MILLER: Now, by nature, you are a fighter. Indeed, the whole family wears buttons and the buttons say, "Failure is not an option." Now, Art Caplan is your brother. You two have a conversation with Dr. Payne.

ART CAPLAN, PHD: You tell 'em, sis.

QUINDLEN: Well, Dr. Payne, this conversation reminds me of the conversation I had with Dr. Nuland when I first came out of surgery. What—emphasizing other aspects, do you, basically, mean you're giving up on me?

continued

DR. PAYNE: No. At this point, the best possible treatment is not to—persist with more chemotherapy, but really to—to persist in—in treating your symptoms.

QUINDLEN: Well, let me tell you what I want to persist in. I have a 14-year-old daughter. I wanna make sure I'm at her high school graduation. You tell me how I can do that.

DR. PAYNE: It—unfortunately,—I'm not certain that I can guarantee that.—I would very much like to—, but—your cancer hasn't really responded to the treatments that we've—provided. There are other possible experimental treatments that—could be tried.

CAPLAN: That's what we wanna hear about, Doc.

QUINDLEN: That's—

CAPLAN: What—What are you talkin' about? I've read, actually, you know, in the supermarket, recently, about an experimental treatment, something having to do with lasers, I think it was.

DR. PAYNE: The issue here is whether—it is in your best interest to pursue these experimental treatments which are experimental because we don't know if they work.

CAPLAN: Of course it's in her best interest, if that's all she's got.

DR. PAYNE: Because the treatments may make you sicker without really treating your cancer.

CAPLAN: Doctor, I—I just have to tell you somethin' about my sister. For as long as we've been a family, she has been a fighter. She is not a person to give up. We wanna take this anyplace, anywhere.

QUINDLEN: Wait a minute. But what I think he's tryin' to tell me is I can be a real mother to my kids for a certain period of time, or I can be an invalid mother to my children for a longer period of time—

CAPLAN: Sis, don't even talk that way. Don't even talk that way.

QUINDLEN: If I take—. Well, that's what he—that's what he's saying. Wait, wait, wait. Who's cancer is this anyhow? This is what the doctor is saying to me. And I've gotta make a decision whether I wanna really be there for them or be there in a haze.

CAPLAN: You— You know what Mom and Pop said, though. We fight. We're a family of fighters.

DR. PAYNE: And we will continue to fight. And we will continue to fight to give you the best possible—life you can have—

MILLER: Doctor, is it her decision or your decision?

continued

DR. PAYNE:—It is her decision.—Hopefully, with me, informing her of—her options and alternatives . . .

The program continues to consider several more perspectives, but you likely get the gist of the exercise, so now use the "Four Principles Approach" table to analyze each role player's response to the ethical issues/decisions in the case. Please weight the four ethical principles from each of the roles in the case. After weighting the ethical principles for each role, answer the following questions in your notebook.

1. Based on your Four Principles Approach to analyzing the case, who approached the issues/decisions in the case most ethically? Why?

2. Did you find analyzing the case using this approach enlightening? Why or why not?

In addition to the ethical principles or moral obligations espoused by the Hippocratic Oath and the Four Principles Approach in health care environments, there are several ethical orientations that need to be considered to further understand how and why health care providers, practitioners, patients, and the public may think and behave in the ways they do.

Ethical Orientations

In this section on ethical orientations to health communication, we broadly categorize the various approaches to ethical issues and dilemmas into traditional, shared religious, legalistic, and contemporary orientations. For each ethical orientation, we provide a description and examples. As you read through the ethical orientations, try to determine which orientation or combination of orientations best describes the way you believe health-related situations should be approached and handled. Keep in mind, according to Redding (1992), all behavior has ethical overtones and each person develops a general ethical approach to behavior which shapes his or her actions and communication. Consequently if two people are involved in an ethical dilemma, their ethical orientation shapes their side of the argument and informs their behavior.

Traditional Orientations to Ethics

Since the Middle Ages, questions of medical ethics have been discussed from within two broad philosophical frameworks that form the traditional orientations to ethics.

Consequentialism/Utilitarianism

For the purposes of our discussion, we incorporate two closely related ethical perspectives into one traditional ethical orientation:

◆ Consequentialism
◆ Utilitarianism

Within this traditional orientation to ethical situations, the consequences or outcomes of actions are the main concern. Basically, *consequentialism* asserts that the right way to act in any circumstance is the action that produces the best overall result. And the best overall result or the result that is considered to have value is a result that emphasizes the well-being of the individuals involved in terms of freedom, happiness, pleasure, fulfillment, knowledge, health, and such.

The primary ethical principle within this orientation is the principle of utility. The principle of utility, which forms the basis of *utilitarianism*, maintains that people ought to always produce the maximal balance of positive value over negative value. Therefore, actions are considered to be right or wrong according to the balance of good over bad consequences. In making moral decisions from this perspective, people essentially perform a cost/benefit analysis asking themselves could negative consequences such as harm or injury to one or a few individuals outweigh gains for the many or the larger group?

Another ethical principle within this traditional orientation is the requirement to do the "greatest good for the greatest number." This principle was coined by philosophers Jeremy Bentham (Baumgardt, 1952) and John Stuart Mill (2002). These philosophers put forth that moral behavior involves doing the most good for the most people. Hearn (as cited in DeGeorge, 1986) rephrased the same principle this way: "Do the most good or select the option that benefits the most persons" (p. 93). So, for example, in the choice between donating $50 to help a local child buy a motorized wheelchair or sending the money overseas to feed 10 children for a week, the latter option would be the more ethical choice because the $50 would help more children.

Consequentialism/Utilitarianism—pursuit of happiness by doing the greatest good for the greatest number of people is the main concern in making ethical decisions.

Example—performing a medical experiment to test a new cancer drug during which some may suffer adverse consequences, including death, is appropriate because when the drug is perfected, it will save many people.

Can you think of another example of an ethical decision from this ethical orientation?

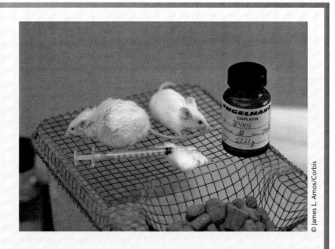

© James L. Amos/Corbis

Counterarguments to Consequentialism/Utilitarianism

Although this famous principle has been widely accepted and applied because of its emphasis on equality and a universal sense of fair play, some have argued that it promotes two ethical principles simultaneously—greatest happiness and greatest number (Griffin, 1986, 2008; Scarre, 1996). Which principle takes precedence or is more important? Generally, the greatest happiness standard supersedes the greatest number standard. This ordering is based on the assumption that happiness is considered greater when it is spread across more people. However, there may be times when these two standards conflict. There may be times when people have to choose a course of action that promotes greater happiness for a few people and less happiness for a larger number of people.

For example, the "Prosthetic Parity" movement being promoted by the Amputee Coalition of America (2009) advocates for the passage of legislation that provides equal coverage for prosthetic limbs across health insurance plans. Few would disagree that people with limb loss or limb differences deserve to have their prosthetic devices covered by their health insurance plans. So providing this coverage can be valued as a "greatest good." However, given that people with limb loss and limb differences constitute less than 10% of the United States population, some might question whether the "greatest number" standard is applicable, especially given that the costs associated with prosthetic devices would essentially be shared among all the members of each health insurance plan.

Although this traditional ethical orientation of consequentialism/utilitarianism has mass appeal, there is another major concern that must be considered. As Christians (2007) explained, this seemingly straightforward approach to moral questions depends on the ability of people to predict both short-term and long-term consequences of actions and to weigh costs and benefits. However, such predictions about the future and costs versus benefits are difficult and often imperfect. Another concern Christians pointed out is that utilitarianism places too much emphasis on future consequences that obscure what's been learned from decisions made in the past. DeGeorge (1999) added another concern that in emphasizing the greatest good for the greatest number, the value of the individual and justice for the individual may be denied. This paves the way into the other traditional orientation to ethics which in many ways is the opposite of consequentialism/utilitarianism.

Deontology/Nonconsequentialism

Again, for the purposes of our discussion, we incorporate two closely related ethical perspectives into the second traditional ethical orientation:

- ◆ Deontology
- ◆ Nonconsequentialism

Within this traditional orientation to ethical situations, the central question is: What makes humans essentially human? In this orientation, this essential element is humans' rational capacity or ability to reason (Veatch, 1974). In other words, as humans we are conscious of what we are doing and choosing to do, which makes us unique from animals. Because of our ability to reason, humans have a moral obligation or duty to do what is intrinsically right or good regardless of the consequences of that right or good action. Basically, *deontology* and *nonconsequentialism* claim that some features of actions other than or in addition to consequences make actions right or wrong (Darwell, 2002).

Immanuel Kant is the philosopher most often associated with this ethical orientation. From the Kantian viewpoint, morality is grounded in reason because it is humans' rational powers that motivate them morally and allow them to prescribe moral rules. Rules provide the moral reason that justifies action (Kant, 1964). Further, humans should rest moral judgments on reasons that also apply to all other persons who are similarly situated (Wood, 2001). In other words Kantian deontology is an ethic of respect for people and is rule governed.

For Kant, the supreme principle of morality, from which all duties derive, is the categorical imperative. When a moral imperative is considered categorical, it means that it must be followed without exception. There are a few formulations of the categorical imperative, but the one most relevant in health care and for health communication will be singled out. The *categorical imperative* is a moral principle which states: "Act in such a way that you always treat humanity, whether in your own person or in the person of any other, never simply as a means, but always at the same time as an end" (Kant, 1964, p. 96). In other words, humans are not means to an end but ends themselves. Humans deserve respect regardless of who they are and what they are doing. Therefore, any action or behavior that is dehumanizing is unethical.

Deontology/Nonconsequentialism—The goal of right or good action should be to enhance human potential rather than be dehumanizing. Humans are not means to an end but ends themselves, which is the main concern in making ethical decisions.

Example—although euthanasia was illegal, Dr. Jack Kevorkian performed physician-assisted suicides because he was a proponent of terminally ill patients' right to die with dignity and on their own terms.

Can you think of another example of an ethical decision from this ethical orientation?

© Rob Kim./Retna Ltd./Corbis

Whether health communication is considered dehumanizing is based on determining the intent of the person, the means used to communicate, and the circumstances. The notion of an ideal speech situation can assist in making a determination about whether communication is dehumanizing. According to Habermas (1990), an *ideal speech situation* is concerned with notions of fair play in dialogue. There are five assumptions of fair play in an ideal speech situation:

◆ Equal opportunity
◆ Comprehendibility
◆ Truth
◆ Sincerity
◆ Harmony with social values and rules

The first assumption of an ideal speech or communication situation is that every individual should have an *equal opportunity* to participate in the discourse and express opinions, desires, and needs. Perhaps this promotion of equal opportunity is why deontology has been referred to as the ethic of equal opportunity. For example, in the health care reform debate of the 2009–2010 congressional legislative session, members of the Senate and House of Representatives held town hall meetings in their districts, perhaps as a deontological turn to give their constituents the opportunity to participate in the discourse about the health care reform debate and express their opinions. Unfortunately, when so many town hall meetings became uncivil shouting matches that offended legislators, many future meetings were conducted by teleconference.

The second assumption of an ideal speech situation is that the communication is *comprehendible,* meaning that the communication is understandable by the audience. So in our previous example, this assumption of deontology was violated

© Ted Soqui/Corbis

when many town hall meeting attendees around the country became so incensed about health care reform proposals that their shouting was not comprehendible and their statements and arguments could not be openly analyzed by others.

The third assumption of an ideal speech situation is that the communication is *true*, meaning that it is based on factual information. In our ongoing example, although some of the arguments and evidence posed by irate town hall meeting attendees were accurate, other claims seemed to lack veracity and supporting evidence. An originally unidentified protestor in Virginia, for instance, held up a sign which featured President Obama in Joker's makeup and read "Organizing for National Socialist Health Care: The Final Solution" (Zahn, 2009). Do you think this message meets the third assumption of an ideal speech act? Why or why not?

The fourth assumption of an ideal speech situation is that the communication is *sincere* or presented in a manner that is genuine. The fifth assumption of the ideal speech situation has the most obvious link to deontology because it assumes that the communication is *harmonious with social values and rules,* meaning that the communication is consistent with the values of the culture and follows the rules of that culture. Returning to our example of the town hall meetings on health care reform, this assumption was violated in many of the meetings because people did not conform to the rules of civility and meeting procedure. This may explain, in part, why many legislators and other meeting facilitators became frustrated and in a few cases ended the meetings or changed the venue of future town hall meetings to a less open context.

Counterarguments to Deontology/Nonconsequentialism

Although it may seem difficult to argue with an ethical perspective that values humanity and considers each person uniquely human and worthy of ethical treatment for being human, there are a couple of counterarguments or concerns with this ethical stance that merit mention. The first counterargument asks the question, what if moral obligations conflict? By claiming that all moral rules are imperative, no space or guidance exists in cases of conflicting moral obligations. For example, according to Kant (Paton, 1948), one of our moral obligations is to keep our promises. But what if one promise breaks another promise? For example, what if you promised to take your mother to all her health care appointments since her cancer diagnosis but you also made a pact (a type of promise) with your best friend that you'd get in shape together by taking an aerobics class at the gym? This week those two promises conflict because your mother has an appointment with her oncologist at the same time as your aerobics class. This ethical perspective does not offer a viable solution but instead seems to suggest that you are expected to accomplish the impossible and keep both promises.

The second counterargument suggests that slavish devotion to absolute moral imperatives tends to overemphasize rules and underemphasize relationships. Ironically, as Beauchamp and Childress (2009) pointed out, although it was attention to maintaining relationships that formed the basis of many laws, formal rules, and contracts, we do not ordinarily use contracts and formal rules when interacting with family and friends. So perhaps this ethical perspective is better suited for interaction among strangers and professional colleagues rather than family and close friends.

The third counterargument involves the disregard this ethical perspective has for emotions having value or moral worth. Although Kant and others within deontology do not completely disallow emotions, they believe there is no place for emotions in determining moral action. According to this ethical perspective, can a health care provider act ethically for a patient out of both a sense of duty and obligation to fulfill the terms of the job but also out of deep concern for the patient and the patient's family? Deontology/nonconsequentialism does not allow for this duality of motives.

The transition from these two broad traditional orientations to ethics into shared religious perspectives is fairly straightforward because the various religious philosophies on ethics also are rooted in tradition with many of the ethical principles associated with shared religious perspectives corresponding with one or more of the traditional orientations.

Shared Religious Orientations to Ethics

Rather than attempting to distinguish between the many religious perspectives on ethics that are relevant to health communication, we follow Jensen (1997) in discussing shared religious orientations toward communication ethics.

Obviously Eastern and Western religions, including Hinduism, Buddhism, Taoism, Confucianism, Judaism, Christianity, and Islam, have significant differences in their core values, and in health communication these differences in values may cause serious challenges if not realized, understood, and attended to. For a pertinent example, Fadiman (1998) presented a compelling account of the "collision" between how the Hmong symbolize belief in the Spirit—tying a string around a finger—and the American medical establishment's strivings for sterility and cleanliness. However, these religions have similar or shared views concerning communication ethics and stress individual responsibility.

According to Jensen (1997) there are six ethical standards for communication that permeate these shared religious perspectives on ethics:

- ◆ Tell the truth and avoid lies.
  - ❖ Be open with intentions and be accurate.
  - ❖ Be honest when responding and giving feedback.
- ◆ Do not slander or injure others through communication.
- ◆ Do not blame, dishonor, and profane sacred persons, symbols or rituals central to the religion.
- ◆ Avoid communication that demeans other persons or life forms.
- ◆ Model ethical virtues.
- ◆ Show people how close to excellence humans can become and enhance the lives of those people.

Although these ethical standards were generated from the study of several religions, Jensen (1997) emphasized that a person does not need to be religious to learn from and follow these standards, which emerge from "human beings' centuries-old struggle toward ethical communication as part of their coping with life in all its dimensions" (p. 20). Now, take a few minutes to practice applying these ethical standards by completing Health Communication Nexus 2.3.

Can you apply Jensen's (1997) standards for communication ethics from the shared religious perspectives? Read the following ethical dilemmas—posed by students in Professor Mattson's health communication ethics class. Answer the questions posed for each ethical dilemma in your notebook.

A nurse brings a patient the wrong medication. The patient realizes the mistake and refuses to take the medication. The nurse insists that he double-checked (but did not) and brought the correct medication and that the patient "is confused" and should trust the nurse, who "knows better."

- Which of Jensen's shared religious standards for ethical communication is this nurse violating and why?

- How could this nurse have avoided unethical communication?

An abortion clinic is on fire and a devout Catholic firefighter is sent to the scene. When this firefighter arrives at the scene, she refuses to fight the fire on religious grounds—Catholicism teaches that abortion is morally wrong.

- Is the firefighter violating any of Jensen's shared religious standards for ethical communication, and if so why?

- Could the firefighter have responded to the situation differently according to the shared religious standards for ethical communication?

Another orientation to ethics which follows closely from the traditional orientations already discussed is a legalistic orientation, which is guided by existing laws.

Legalistic Orientation to Ethics

Legalistic orientations to ethics take the stance that any behavior that is illegal is unethical or put another way every behavior that is legal is ethical. Those with a legalistic perspective on ethics behave consistently within two basic formulas:

- ◆ Legal = ethical
- ◆ Illegal = unethical

The major benefit of a legalistic perspective on ethics is that following these formulas allows for a simple approach to ethical decisions. We only need to measure communication acts or techniques against current laws to determine whether those communication acts or techniques are ethical or unethical. In essence, illegal and unethical become synonymous and legal and ethical become synonymous.

Several concerns with a legalistic perspective on human communication ethics were identified by Johannesen, Valde, and Whedbee (2008). We highlight those concerns that are most relevant to health communication and use the example of needle exchange programs to reduce HIV infection rates to illustrate these concerns. The first concern is that oversimplified and superficial judgments may arise from complex situations. The second concern is that individuals will feel less free to speak their minds for fear of legal action. The third concern is that legal regulation tends to focus responsibility on the communicator and minimizes audience responsibility and does not recognize shared responsibility. The fourth concern is that illegal actions may be justifiable on moral grounds because morality is broader than legality.

The legality and morality of needle exchange programs is a pertinent example to illustrate some of the concerns with a strictly legalistic approach to ethics. The goal of needle exchange programs is to provide safe sites where illegal drug users can exchange used, dirty needles for new, clean needles in order to reduce the spread of HIV (Watters, Estilo, & Clark, 1994). Sharing used needles for drug use is a common way that HIV is spread because infected blood may transfer from a used needle to an uninfected individual. At needle exchange sites, illegal drug users do not have to worry about being arrested because law enforcement agencies agree not to make arrests at designated needle exchange sites. In addition, at these sites visitors are given other HIV-prevention information and strategies, including supplies to clean needles and condoms to promote safer sex.

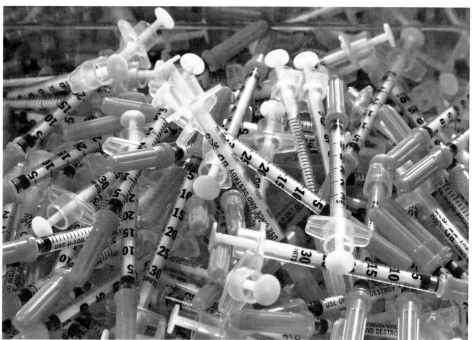

© 2011, Steve Heap, Shutterstock, Inc.

Discarded needles at a needle exchange site. HIV-prevention strategies provided at needle exchange sites include new needles, bleach to clean needles, prevention information, and condoms.

Critics of needle exchange programs often use a legalistic perspective on ethics to argue against offering such programs by simply stating that taking illicit drugs is illegal and therefore needle exchange programs should not be permissible. Some even argue that needle exchange programs promote drug use. An argument against needle exchange programs strictly because they are illegal may be too simplistic because it does not recognize that drug use is a complex problem and needle exchange programs have been effective in decreasing the spread of HIV among both illicit drug users and non-drug users. Illicit drug users take advantage of needle exchange programs because at these sites they are free to act safely and responsibly within their drug-use habit and because they can avoid the added fear of being arrested for breaking the law.

Taking a legalistic perspective on the ethicality of needle exchange programs also does not recognize the shared responsibility that we all have in our communities for the antecedents of drug use that include complicated issues such as social inequality. Instead, it is easier to blame illicit drug use on drug users and seek to arrest them for not obeying laws rather than assist them in keeping themselves and others safe even if they continue to use drugs. Given the evidence of effectiveness, perhaps needle exchange sites that skirt laws regarding illicit drug use are ethical because the morality of helping both drug users and their friends and families be safer and healthier in the fight against HIV supersedes laws (Stryker & Smith, 1993). So what do you think about needle exchange programs? Should they be allowed? Should they be discontinued?

The following more contemporary orientations to ethics would view needle exchange programs in a very different light than legalistic orientations because these perspectives take a more inductive approach to ethical issues and dilemmas. That is, building from the particulars of the individual situation toward the decision, which then may be applied to decision making in other cases.

Contemporary Orientations to Ethics

Ethic of Care

Grounded in the experiences of women and emphasizing affective aspects of moral life, the central concern of an *ethic of care* orientation is the virtue or value of caring, which is manifested in a genuine concern for the well-being of others (Gilligan, 1982; Groenhout, 1998; Veatch, 1998). Further, an ethic of care counters traditional orientations to ethics in health care that favor objective detachment from patients and promotion of moral universals rather than the practical, contextual qualities of an individual's unique and often quite precarious health situation (Enomoto, 1997; Liddell, Halpin, & Halpin, 1992; Tong, 1998).

Consistent with the Hippocratic Oath and the implicit goals of health care, an ethic of care perspective privileges the patient-provider relationship and highlights systemic forces that support committed relationships. "True care," according to Carse (1995), involves "attunement to the reality of other people and to the actual relational contexts we find ourselves in" (p. 243). Care, then, is grounded in the relationship and facilitates altruism, trust, reciprocity, and empathy.

One ethic of care value that is especially pertinent in the health care context and health communication is the value of voice. Voice involves "the ability both to construct and articulate knowledge and to make choices and act in situations" (Mattson & Buzzanell, 1999, p. 64). It is through genuine voice that patients become empowered. For example, Brann and Mattson (2004) analyzed confidentiality breaches in health care from an ethic of care perspective. They discovered that although confidentiality should be a fundamental right of patients in a health care setting, health care providers who take an oath to uphold confidentiality often neglect this basic patient right. In the health care context, confidentiality focuses on the issue of patients' privacy. *Confidentiality* is defined as private information shared by patients with their health care providers that should be kept confidential. A *breach of confidentiality* describes a situation in which a health care provider intentionally or unintentionally does not keep a patient's private information confidential. Based on interviews with 51 patients and observations of health care providers in a hospital setting, a typology of confidentiality breaches emerged. From this typology, several practical *suggestions for avoiding confidentiality breaches* were offered, including:

◆ Only relevant information should be authorized and discussed with individuals vital to patients' care and with the patients' knowledge.
◆ Renovate less than private areas to foster private discussion and exchange of information. For example, eliminate open space that allows for easy access to confidential information.
◆ Improve confidentiality-protection policies. For example, streamline the process of patient registration to reduce the number of employees and visitors who may have access to or overhear confidential information.
◆ Conduct telephone calls in private locations.
◆ Sign confidentiality agreements.
◆ Ensure thorough and recurrent training in maintaining confidentiality for health care providers.
◆ Discuss confidential information with necessary health care providers or care-seeking patients in private, audibly secure locations.
◆ Patients have mutual responsibility with health care providers to maintain confidential information.
◆ Educate patients on what defines a confidentiality breach and what they need to do to help prevent breaches.
◆ Report confidentiality breaches.

Another contemporary orientation to ethics focuses specifically on the individual and the individual's unique case or situation to make decisions about the ethical way to proceed.

Casuistry/Case-Based Ethics

As we did previously, for simplicity we again group two rather distinct yet similar perspectives into one orientation to ethics. Although this perspective on ethics in health care was influential in medieval philosophy, it has been revised and has again gained prominence in modern ethics (Arras, 1991). *Casuistry* is defined as a pragmatic theory in which previous value-laden decisions are examined with reference to their factual and cultural context, with an objective of aiding future decisions. Differences in facts and cultural context across the case are noted and then reflection is undertaken on whether the departures vary so significantly from the previous context that the past decision can or cannot be relied on for guidance.

Case-based ethics refers to the use of case comparison in search of maxims from exemplar cases to reach moral conclusions or make moral decisions (Wells, 2002). This approach is founded on the premise that no one ethical theory can capture the complexity of moral ideas and practical experience is needed to judge and determine the right course of action in complex situations. Priority is given to practice over theory. Pence's (2008) book, *Medical Ethics: Accounts of the Cases that Shaped and Define Medical Ethics,* provides exemplar medical cases that have served as models for decision making in similar subsequent cases. Examples include classic cases about the ethical controversies and related decisions surrounding death and dying when the patient is in a coma, such as Karen Quinlan, Nancy Cruzan, and Terri Schiavo.

Casuistry and case-based ethics are consistent with *experiential ethics,* in which experience is considered the starting point of ethics rather than abstract principles or absolute rules determining how to respond to an individual situation. Similar cases are collected for comparison, and previous knowledge is considered, but the focus remains on the particulars and experience of the case in making decisions about care and treatment (Reich, 1988).

In the practice of case-based ethics, those making decisions in an individual case always begin and end with the individual case. As many details as possible are sought out, including aspects of the patient's values and life. To acquire details

Casuistry/Case-Based Ethics—use of patient's immediate environment and culture along with comparison cases is the main concern in making ethical decisions.

Example—in each episode of the television drama *House*, Dr. House and his medical team crack unique and nearly impossible cases by employing ethically controversial investigations not only into patients' physical symptoms of disease or illness but also into their culture and environment. Often they compare the current case with previous medical cases to establish similarities and differences that can assist them in diagnosing and treating the patients.

Can you think of another example of an ethical decision from this ethical orientation?

© Fox/Photofest

beyond medical information, the patient's perspective or story is highlighted. The patient's case is then compared with as many other similar cases as possible to add further insight on ethically-appropriate courses of action.

For example, in their conversation analysis of HIV-test counseling sessions, Mattson and Roberts (2001) discovered that in certain cases HIV-test counselors suggested to a client the strategy of deception with a primary sexual partner as a way of keeping that partner safe while the client waited for HIV-test results. The clients agreed to attempt the deception strategy so they would not have to reveal to their primary partner that they had sex outside the relationship. Considering the particulars of the case, especially that these clients would not otherwise practice safer sex with their primary partner, the HIV-test counselors deemed the deception strategy appropriate, and previous cases suggested it was an effective strategy.

PROFILE

Belief and Practice of Case-Based Ethics

Robert Taylor, MD—
Neurologist in Hospice Care and Professor of Ethics

"A man's ethical behavior should be based effectively on sympathy, education, and social relationships . . . "

Albert Einstein

Dr. Robert Taylor decided to specialize his medical career in neurology because of his fascination with neuro anatomy. He discovered that working with the brain was an exciting and unique challenge, almost like detective work. While working in neurology he became very interested in the ethical issues that arise while practicing medicine, especially those concerning death and dying. As a neurologist, he was frequently called in to consult on cases involving strokes, brain infections, and brain injury. These cases often led to conversations with a family about ending life support which brought up questions about the meaning of "brain dead" and what is meant by "quality of life."

Often he faced situations when patients were admitted to the intensive care unit (ICU) after going into cardiac arrest. Patients would be in a coma and showing minimal brain stem activity and decisions would need to be made about how treatment should proceed such as inserting a feeding tube or performing a tracheotomy. In these situations it was often up to the family to decide which treatments to continue and physicians did not have the right to deny treatment. Dr. Taylor saw his role in these situations as making sure that families had the information and understanding needed to make reasonable decisions. He feels that many physicians have trouble really listening to families and taking the time needed to ensure their understanding.

His experiences in neurology led him to working in the hospice setting and to the faculty of Ohio State University where he teaches courses on medical ethics. Patients admitted to the hospice are there to receive palliative care until they die. Palliative care is care to relieve pain or other problems without treating the underlying health issue directly. Dr. Taylor's role as a physician is to work with families and patients to develop treatment plans. Generally, the primary goal of these treatment plans is pain management and patient comfort. He feels that almost every decision that is made has ethical dimensions to it. He takes a casuistry or case-based ethics approach to patient care, meaning he evaluates each case on an individual basis. He also refers to Beauchamp and Childress' principles of ethics which require that ethical decisions protect patient autonomy, are beneficent, are free from malfeasance, and promote justice.

For many the mere thought of working in an environment with only terminally-ill patients is scary and depressing. Taylor says that he actually finds it very rewarding as every interaction with a patient and his or her family can be successful. In this situation, death does not represent failure, so decisions that allow a person to die in a dignified manner count as success.

As the examples we used to illustrate traditional, shared religious, legalistic, and contemporary orientations to ethics imply, ethics is inextricably linked to health communication. Next we discuss specific linkages between ethics and health communication.

Health Communication and Ethics

By definition health communication often involves a purposeful attempt to influence people's views about health or to adopt health recommendations (Guttman, 2003). This intersection of the health communicator and the audience can and often does initiate value conflicts which form ethical issues and dilemmas. Ethics always involves value conflicts. And the conflicting values can be located in three communication aspects within the situation:

◆ Topics chosen for attention
◆ Decision arguments
◆ Stylized language

One communication aspect that can lead to value conflicts and ethical dilemmas involves the *topics chosen for attention* because focusing on certain topics over others accentuates certain interests while suppressing or provoking competing interests. For example, when a physician chooses to focus on a patient's physical symptoms rather than how those symptoms are affecting the patient's personal life, the values of the health care provider and the patient may be in conflict. More specifically, the physician's goal to treat the patient's high blood pressure with medication may be in conflict with the patient's concerns including skepticism about medications and his ability to afford the medication due to the loss of a job and health insurance benefits, which may, ironically, be causing the high blood pressure.

Or, as discussed further in Chapter 11, "Linking Health Communication with Media," *Agenda-Setting Theory* suggests that the topics the media industry chooses to cover influence the public agenda or what the public thinks about. Further, *Media Framing Theory* argues that not only does the media industry set the public agenda by selecting certain topics for attention but the media industry also influences the way the public thinks about those topics. Let's revisit an example we've expanded on throughout this chapter. When health care reform was being discussed with constituents during Congress' August recess in 2009, the topic of a "public health insurance option" was debated at town hall meetings (Levey, 2009). The media's choice to cover the town hall meetings at which the most raucous crowds attended and spoke out against a public health insurance option likely influenced President Obama's decision to back down from his initial commitment to offer a public option paid for by the government and instead champion a health insurance co-op option that would not be directly funded by the United States government (Brown, 2009).

Relatedly, the *decision arguments* used to convey the way health topics are discussed and debated are influenced by values and can instigate value conflicts and ethical dilemmas. Argumentation refers to the reasoning used to convey an opinion, a decision or an approach. Ideally, arguments are rational (logos), recognize the credibility of the arguer (ethos), and appeal to the emotions of the audience (pathos). How we form our arguments reflects our values and may conflict with how another or others form their arguments.

For example, you and your sister may adamantly disagree on whether health care reform in the United States should include a "public health insurance option" funded by the government. Your argument that everyone living in the United States should have equal access to health care services through either private or public health insurance may seem logical, credible, and emotionally appropriate to you given your firm belief in the value of equality and your experience with the health care system. However, your sister may strongly disagree, arguing that the United States is based on the values of capitalism and competition and if the government becomes more involved in health care access, it will stifle competition and allow the government too large a role in our daily lives. From her perspective and given the public's reaction to health care reform, this argument is more logical, credible, and emotionally appropriate. Consequently, the ethical dilemma between you and your sister centers around the role of the government in health care. After arguing for awhile, one of you may persuade the other through compelling arguments or you both may eventually agree to disagree so your relationship is not compromised.

A third way that value conflicts can arise in communication is through the use of stylized language. *Stylized language* is the specialized language or jargon that is conventionally used in a particular context. As Schiappa (2003) explained, much like our use of language more generally to classify and categorize our experiences into manageable pieces, these specialized or technical vocabularies form to talk about the world in specific ways that meet the needs and interests of the discourse communities that use the specialized vocabularies. In the health care context, stylized language or jargon used by health care providers exhibits the values of their profession as credible and important. However, this technical language may not be understood by patients or their family members, who tend to prefer less jargon-laden language because they value lay understandings during their encounters with health care providers.

For example, during an episode of the television show *The Doctors* (2009), Fran Drescher, actress and women's health activist, discussed her battle with uterine cancer that went undiagnosed for two years. Based on her experience, one of the tips she suggested for being better health care consumers is to ask your physicians or other health care providers how to spell medical terms so that you can better understand those terms and look them up later or use the terms for future reference. By doing this, you alert your health care providers that an unfamiliar term is being used but you are willing to take an active role to gain mutual understanding of that term and its meaning for your health.

Although value conflicts and ethical issues and dilemmas are inevitable, there are practical strategies for creating and maintaining ethical health communication.

Practical Strategies for Ethical Health Communication

As you've been reading about the orientations to ethics and thinking about which orientation best corresponds with your values, you may have been wondering, how do I avoid an ethical dilemma or what do I do if I am facing an ethical dilemma? Although a few strategies were included within the previous discussions of particular ethical orientations, in this section we provide some useful communication strategies that seem to cut across the ethical orientations.

Following Jensen's (1981) lead and with confirmation from Hope's (2004) ethics toolbox, we begin this section by presenting a series of guidelines, including ethical obligations to the immediate audience and ethical obligations toward others not in the immediate audience. Then we discuss guidelines from professional codes of ethics.

Ethical Guidelines toward Those in the Immediate Audience

Often those in the immediate audience or context are most affected by the ethicality of a health communicator's messages or behaviors. For example, during surgery, a surgeon's immediate audience is the patient and the surgery team, which may include nurses and an anesthesiologist. Therefore, there is a fairly long list of ethical commitments to your immediate audience to pay attention to and follow:

- Benevolence—respect the dignity of each person in your audience through sensitivity and tactfulness.
- Honesty—in always telling the truth also be accurate and complete in the information provided.
- Relevance—do not include irrelevant content to deceive, mislead, or distract.
- Openness—present both sides of an argument.
- Understandability—provide information, claims, and recommendations at an appropriate level to aid understanding and avoid confusion.
- Reason—appeal to logic first to promote thought about the issue and supplement with emotional appeals to counter apathy.
- Social utility—consider short-term and long-term survival of the group but also the ramifications for individuals.

Although exceptions to these commitments may be justified within a specific situation or because a personal ethical orientation may warrant it, any exception should be very carefully considered in advance.

Ethical Guidelines Toward Others Not in Immediate Audience

Although those in your immediate audience or context may be your major concern as a health communicator, you also must be cognizant of ethical commitments to primary and secondary groups, to society, and to yourself. The following list provides guidance in addressing each of these non-immediate audiences:

- Maintain respect for primary and secondary groups—do not act or communicate in such a way that dishonors the primary (for example, family, coworkers, community organizations) and secondary groups (for example, professional associations) you affiliate or associate with.
- Preserve and expand values of society—avoid injuring or harming fellow citizens of the culture or society by upholding and advancing shared values of that culture or society through your health communication.
- Respect self in communication with others—in order to ethically interact with others you must respect yourself and maintain personal integrity.

For example, when lawmakers in California questioned Leslie Margolin, president of Anthem Blue Cross, one of the largest health insurance companies in the United States, to testify about her company's proposed plan to increase individual insurance premiums by 39% for approximately 700,000 customers, lawmakers had an ethical obligation to appeal to the needs of their immediate audience, including other lawmakers, and the company president. In addition, they had an ethical obligation to those not in their immediate audience, including citizens in their districts who complained about increased health insurance costs. The Associated Press (Hindery, 2010) reported that lawmakers showed unusual bipartisan unity in being extremely critical of Margolin and her company for raising premiums amidst an economic downturn, and at one point a lawmaker asked Margolin, "Have you no shame?" According to the ethical guidelines just provided, do you think this question was appropriate? Why or why not?

Ethical Guidelines from Professional Codes of Ethics

Another source of ethical guidelines is professional associations' or organizations' codes of ethics. A *professional code of ethics* is defined as an "expression of principles, rules, ideals, and values of a specific professional group, creating responsibility to strive for states, ideals, and goals, and to uphold certain rules, in each member professional's conduct" (Berglund, 2007, p. 18). In addition to guiding you on how to act, a code of ethics socializes you into what is appropriate behavior within your profession. It also implies shared responsibility for ethical conduct between you and the other members of your profession. According to Knultgen (1988), the purpose of a professional code of ethics is threefold: to promote a sense of community within the profession, to regulate or discipline behavior within the profession, and to instill public trust in the profession's actions.

To be most effective, codes of ethics need to provide detailed guidance rather than general principles. A code of ethics should be revisited on a regular basis to encourage personal reflection on the code and to consider code revisions. In addition, it is not enough simply to have a code of ethics—there must be organizational mechanisms in place to systematically share the code, enforce the code, and update the code. How do you think an organization could share its code of ethics? Perhaps through orientation programs and/or its Web site. How do you think an organization could enforce its code of ethics? Perhaps through corresponding terms written into a contract. How do you think an organization could update a code of ethics? Perhaps through a biennial code of ethics review and revision committee. To familiarize yourself with applying a code of ethics, please complete Health Communication Nexus Interlude 2.4.

For this interlude, complete the following steps.

- Step 1: Find the code of ethics for Emergency Medical Technicians (EMTs). You likely can find the professional code of ethics by going to the Web site of a professional association for members of this profession.

- Step 2: Read the following ethical dilemma. As you may recall, this situation is part of the critical incident that was included in the first chapter of this book and was revisited in the introduction to this chapter.

After colliding with a semi truck while riding her motorcycle and losing her left leg above the knee upon impact, Professor Mattson was flown via helicopter to a level one trauma center. She found out several days later that during the helicopter flight she was given a blood substitute which is artificial blood to replace blood she lost because of the accident. She was told this by her surgeon and was asked if it was OK. Her husband later mentioned to her that the surgeon also told him about the blood substitute a few days after she arrived at the hospital. Although she was grateful that the blood substitute helped keep her alive, she wondered why she wasn't asked for her permission to use the blood substitute instead of human blood considering she was conscious during the helicopter flight. Several months later she read in a newspaper that the hospital she was flown to was participating in a research study of blood substitutes that was somewhat controversial because trauma patients were given blood substitutes without their knowledge or consent to participate in the research study.

- Step 3: Review the principles from the EMT code of ethics you found. Based on the principles in the code, answer the following questions. Jot down your answers in your notebook.

  - According to their code of ethics, do you think the EMTs acted ethically in administering blood substitute to Professor Mattson? Why or why not?

  - According to their code of ethics, how might the EMTs have handled the situation with the blood substitute differently and perhaps more ethically?

  - How do you think Professor Mattson should respond? Why?

For more information about the blood substitute research studies, refer to an online newspaper article by Davis (2008).

Ethical Analysis for
Health Communication Campaigns

As we discussed throughout this chapter, considering ethics in health communication is important, and there are a variety of orientations to ethics that may vary by individual or situation. However, applying abstract ethical principles in practice can be difficult. So in this service-learning application, we provide a practical ethical analysis technique called MORT analysis and explain how we use this technique to assess our ongoing health communication campaign—the Motorcycle Safety at Purdue (MS@P) campaign. Using this example as a guide, you should be able to perform a MORT analysis on any health communication campaign or project associated with a health communication campaign. This application specifically addresses the Partnership standard for effective service-learning practice because it emphasizes the importance of collaboration and communication among the MS@P campaign, the class working on a campaign project, and community partners (Corporation for National & Community Service, 2010).

MORT Analysis

When working on a health campaign, four ethical considerations can help health campaign practitioners avoid mistrust by the community within which the campaign is embedded. The acronym of these four ethical considerations form the basis of a MORT analysis—Money, Ownership, Rigor, Time (adapted from Kegeles, Hays, & Coates, 1996).

◆ Money—if the campaign is seeking funding, carefully consider who or what organizations will seek funding from and be open about how the funding will be used within the campaign and by whom.

◆ Ownership—clearly designate who owns or has the rights to campaign materials and findings from any research associated with the campaign.

◆ Rigor—determine and be consistent about what methods will be employed to conduct the campaign.

◆ Time—identify and communicate if the goal of the campaign will include short-term and/or long-term benefits.

As an example to illustrate how to conduct a MORT analysis, let's consider the MS@P campaign.

Overview of MS@P

As the campaign team likes to ironically emphasize, the Motorcycle Safety at Purdue (MS@P) campaign came about literally by accident. Almost a year after their professor, Marifran Mattson, was seriously injured in a motorcycle accident, a group of graduate students enrolled in Professor Mattson's campaign evaluation class suspected a need to advocate for

motorcycle safety in their community. Upon convincing their professor to change the trajectory of the class to conducting a needs assessment, they determined that a health communication campaign was warranted and MS@P (www.It InvolvesYou.com) was born.

The goal of this campus campaign is to make the roads safer for everyone. The campaign aims to accomplish this goal in three ways and by addressing three target audiences.

1. Encourage *motorcyclists* to engage in safety practices such as wearing proper safety gear, becoming properly licensed, and obeying traffic laws.

2. Encourage *drivers of cars and trucks* to be aware of motorcycles and to avoid aggressive driving.

3. Encourage *friends and family* of motorcyclists to talk about motorcycle safety.

MORT Analysis of MS@P

The MS@P campaign receives funding from a variety of sources, including service-learning grants through Purdue University and Indiana Campus Compact, the Motorcycle Safety Foundation (MSF), and small community donations. In pitching potential funding organizations, a written proposal is submitted to relevant organizations whose goals are consistent with the campaign, and the proposal clearly states what the *money* will be used for and by whom. For example, a grant proposal was submitted to Purdue University's Office of Engagement by a class of undergraduate students working on a service-learning project to develop a new campaign message and buy a sign and space for the sign on the back of a city bus which travels around campus.

In the funding proposal, it clearly states that *ownership* or rights to materials created as part of the funded project will be shared between the funder and the MS@P campaign. For example, MSF provided funds to MS@P to develop a community guide for designing, implementing, and evaluating a motorcycle safety campaign. The rights to the Community Guide to Motorcycle Safety are jointly held by Motorcycle Safety at Purdue and the Motorcycle Safety Foundation, and the guide is available through both organizations.

For all aspects of the MS@P campaign, the *rigor* or methods used to conduct the campaign or answer research questions for the campaign are clearly described. In addition, participants in any research projects are fully informed about the project before their consent to participate is requested and confirmed in writing. For example, before the MS@P campaign evaluation survey is administered each academic year, approval from an Institutional Review Board is secured, the survey is fully explained to participants, and their consent is requested and recorded.

Regarding *time*, for each project associated with the MS@P campaign both short-term and long-term goals are communicated and reiterated. For example, a class of undergraduate students partnered with the City of West Lafayette's Mayor's Office—Purdue University is in West Lafayette, Indiana—to create a public service announcement (PSA). The mayor is an avid motorcyclist and agreed to be a spokesperson for the campaign. The project proposal to the mayor's office included a timeline with the semester-long goal of a PSA and included short-term goals or milestones throughout the semester to achieve the longer-term goal such as deadlines for script drafting and approval and draft video production and approval. This way, the mayor and his staff would know the timeframe up front and could plan accordingly. The PSA can be seen at the MS@P campaign Web site.

A MORT analysis can be used with any campaign or component of a campaign. This ethical analysis exercise benefits the campaign by helping the campaign practitioners make sure they are addressing important aspects of the campaign and campaign projects, including money, ownership, rigor, and time. In addition, the community of the campaign benefits because if these issues are addressed by the campaign, the community can feel more confident in the campaign's goals and practices.

Chapter Summary

In this chapter we emphasized the importance of ethics in health communication. After considering an example of an ethical dilemma regarding whether or not to sue someone after an accident, we presented the criteria for what constitutes an ethical dilemma. Next we defined key concepts, including values, morals, and ethics, and considered how these concepts are interrelated. We then discussed why people believe that unethical behavior is common. To link ethics specifically with health care, we presented the Hippocratic Oath and discussed how this long-standing oath formed the basis of bioethics and the Four Principles Approach to ethical analysis. This was followed by a summary of traditional and contemporary orientations to ethics and the implications of these orientations for health communication situations. Based on these orientations to ethics, several strategies and guidelines for ethical health communication emerged, including professional codes of ethics. The chapter concluded with a service-learning application that offered an ethical analysis tool for health communication campaigns and included specific examples from an existing campaign.

References

Amputee Coalition of America (2009). Issues: Prosthetic parity. Retrieved August 26, 2009, from http://www.amputee-coalition.org.

Arras, J. D. (1991). Getting down to cases: The revival of casuistry in bioethics. *Journal of Medicine and Philosophy, 16*, 29–51.

Baumgardt, D. (1952). *Bentham and the ethics of today.* Princeton, NJ: University Press.

Beauchamp, T. L., & Childress, J. F. (2009). *Principles of biomedical ethics* (6th ed.). New York: Oxford University Press.

Berenson, A. (2005, April 24). Evidence in Vioxx suits shows intervention by Merck officials. *New York Times,* p. 1. Retrieved August 3, 2009, from www.nytimes.com.

Berglund, C. (2007). *Ethics for health care* (3rd ed.). South Melbourne, Australia: Oxford University Press.

Bok, S. (1989a). *Lying: Moral choice in public and private life.* New York: Vintage.

Bok, S. (1989b). *Secrets: On the ethics of concealment and revelation.* New York: Vintage.

Brann, M., & Mattson, M. (2004). Toward a typology of confidentiality breaches in health care communication: An ethic of care analysis of provider practices and patient perceptions. *Health Communication, 16*, 229–251.

Brown, C. B. (2009). White House backs away from public health care option. Retrieved August 16, 2009, from http://www.politico.com/news/stories/0809/26158.html

Callahan, D. (2004). *The cheating culture: Why more Americans are doing wrong to get ahead.* Orlando, FL: Harcourt.

Carse, A. L. (1995). Qualified particularism and affiliative virtue: Emphasis of a recent trend in ethics. *Revista Medica de Chile, 123*, 241–249.

Cheney, G. (2004). Bringing ethics in from the margins. *Australian Journal of Communication, 31*, 35–40.

Cheney, G. (2009). *Just a job?: Communication, ethics, and professional life.* New York: Oxford University Press.

Chopra, D. (2008, May 9). Politicians and the cycle of lying. *The Washington Post.* Retrieved June 3, 2009, from www.washingtonpost.com.

Christians, C. G. (2007). Utilitarianism in media ethics and its discontents. *Journal of Mass Media Ethics, 22*, 113–131.

Corporation for National & Community Service (2010). Learn and Serve: America's National Service–Learning Clearinghouse. Retrieved January 12, 2010, from www.servicelearning.org.

Darwell, S. (Ed.). (2002). *Deontology.* Malden, MA: Blackwell.

Davis, R. (2008, April 28). Study: Blood substitute increases risk of death. *USA Today.* Retrieved June 5, 2009, from www.usatoday.com.

DeGeorge, R. T. (1986). *Business ethics* (2nd ed.). New York: Macmillan.

DeGeorge, R. T. (1999). *Business ethics* (5th ed.). Upper Saddle River, NJ: Prentice Hall.

Enomoto, E. K. (1997). Negotiating the ethics of care and justice. *Educational Administration Quarterly, 33*, 351–370.

Fadiman, A. (1998). *The spirit catches you and you fall down.* New York: Farrar, Straus and Giroux.

Ganguzza, M. (Writer) (1996). Before I die: Medical care and personal choices [Television]. A. Schatz (Producer). USA: Public Broadcasting Service.

Gert, B. (Ed.) (2008). *The Stanford encyclopedia of philosophy* (Fall ed.).

Gilligan, C. (1982). *In a different voice: Psychological theory and women's development.* Cambridge, MA: Harvard University Press.

Graham, D. (2000). Revisiting Hippocrates: Does the oath really matter? *Journal of the American Medical Association, 284*, 2841–2842.

Gray, P. (1992, October 5). Lies, lies, lies. *Time,* 32–39.

Griffin, J. (1986). *Well-being: Its meaning, measurement and moral importance.* Oxford, UK: Clarendon Press.

Griffin, J. (2008). *On human rights.* Oxford, UK: Oxford University Press.

Groenhout, R. (1998). Care theory and the ideal of neutrality in public moral discourse. *Journal of Medicine and Philosophy, 23,* 170–189.

Guttman, N. (2003). Ethics in health communication interventions. In T. L. Thompson, A. Dorsey, M., K. I. Miller & R. Parrott (Eds.), *Handbook of health communication* (pp. 651–679). Mahwah, NJ: Lawrence Erlbaum Associates.

Habermas, J. (1990). *Moral consciousness and communicative action* (C. Lenhardt & S. Weber, Trans.). Cambridge, MA: MIT Press.

Hindery, R. (2010, February 24). "Have you no shame?" *AP News.* Retrieved February 25, 2010, from www.ap.org.

Hope, T. (2004). *Medical ethics: A very short introduction.* New York: Oxford University Press.

Jensen, J. V. (1981). *Argumentation: Reasoning in communication.* New York: D. Van Nostrand Company.

Jensen, J. V. (1997). *Ethical issues in the communication process.* Mahwah, NJ: Lawrence Erlbaum Associates.

Johannesen, R. L., Valde, K. S., & Whedbee, K. E. (2008). *Ethics in human communication.* Long Grove, IL: Waveland.

Josephson Institute (2008). *The ethics of American youth—2008 summary.* Los Angeles, CA: Author.

Kant, I. (1964). *Groundwork of the metaphysics of morals* (H. J. Paton, Trans.). New York: Harper & Row.

Kegeles, S. M., Hays, R. B., & Coates, T. J. (1996). The Mpowerment project: A community-level HIV prevention intervention for young gay men. *American Journal of Public Health, 86,* 1129–1136.

KidsHealth (2009). KidsHealth for parents: Steroids. Retrieved January 9, 2009, from www.kidshealth.org/parent.

Knultgen, J. (1988). *Ethics and professionalism.* Philadelphia: University of Pennsylvania Press.

Lerner, M. (1992, May 14). Looters were living out the cynical American ethos—We don't care to acknowledge that our social system is ravishing the Earth. *Los Angeles Times.* Retrieved August 4, 2009, from http://articles.latimes.com/1992-05-14/local.

Levey, N. N. (2009, May 10). Public debate over "public option" for healthcare. *Los Angeles Times.* Retrieved August 17, 2009, from http://articles.latimes.com/2009/may/10/nation/na-healthcare10.

Liddell, D. L., Halpin, G., & Halpin, W. G. (1992). The measure of moral orientation: Measuring the ethics of care and justice. *Journal of College Student Development, 33,* 325–330.

Lyon, A. (2007). "Putting patients first": Systematically distorted communication and Merck's marketing of Vioxx. *Journal of Applied Communication Research, 35,* 376–398.

Mattson, M., & Buzzanell, P. M. (1999). Traditional and feminist organizational communication ethical analyses of messages and issues surrounding an actual job loss case. *Journal of Applied Communication Research, 27,* 49–72.

Mattson, M., & Roberts, F. (2001). Overcoming truth telling as an obstacle to initiating safer sex: Discussing deception in pre-HIV test counseling sessions. *Health Communication, 13,* 343–362.

Mill, J. S. (2002). *The basic writings of John Stuart Mill: On liberty, the subjection of women, and utilitarianism.* New York: Modern Books.

Mitchell, T. R., & Silver, W. S. (1990). Individual and group goals when workers are interdependent: Effects on task strategies and performance. *Journal of Applied Psychology, 75*, 185–193.

Orr, R. D., Pang, N., Pellegrino, E. D., & Siegler, M. (1997). Use of the Hippocratic Oath: A review of twentieth century practices and a content analysis of oaths administered in medical schools in the US and Canada in 1993. *Journal of Clinical Ethics, 8*, 377–388.

Paton, H. J. (1948). *The categorical imperative: A study in Kant's moral philosophy*. Chicago: University of Chicago Press.

Pence, G. E. (2008). *Medical ethics: Accounts of the cases that shaped and define medical ethics*. Boston: McGraw-Hill.

Redding, W. C. (1992). *Ethics and the study of organizational communication: When will we wake up?* Paper presented at the Center for the Study of Ethics in Society.

Reich, W. T. (1988). Experiential ethics as a foundation for dialogue between health communication and health-care ethics. *Journal of Applied Communication Research, 16*, 16–28.

Rosenberg, M. (2009). Population growth rates: Population growth rates and doubling time. Retrieved October 30, 2009, from www.ask.com.

Ross, J. S., Hill, K. P., Egilman, D. S., & Krumholz, H. M. (2008). Guest authorship and ghostwriting in publications related to rofecoxib: A case study of industry documents from rofecoxib litigation. *Journal of the American Medical Association, 299*, 1800–1812.

Saad, L. (2008). *Nurses shine, bankers slump in ethics ratings: Annual honesty and ethics poll ranks nurses best of 21 professions*. Princeton, NJ: Gallup.

Scarre, G. (1996). *Utilitarianism*. London: Routledge.

Schiappa, E. (2003). *Defining reality: Definitions and the politics of meaning*. Carbondale: Southern Illinois University Press.

Stryker, J., & Smith, M. D. (Eds.). (1993). *Needle exchange*. Menlo Park, CA: Sage.

The Doctors. (2009). Take control of your body [Television]. Retrieved February 28, 2009, from www.thedoctorstv.com.

Tong, R. (1998). The ethics of care: A feminist virtue ethics of care for healthcare practitioners. *Journal of Medicine and Philosophy, 23*, 131–152.

United States Anti-Doping Agency (2009). Clean sport and you. Retrieved January 9, 2009, from usantidoping.org

Veatch, R. M. (1974). *Aristotle: A contemporary approach*. Bloomington, IN: Indiana University Press.

Veatch, R. M. (1998). The place of care in ethical theory. *Journal of Medicine and Philosophy, 23*, 210–224.

Watters, J. K., Estilo, M. J., & Clark, G. L. (1994). Syringe and needle exchange as HIV/AIDS prevention for injecting drug users. *Journal of the American Medical Association, 271*, 115–120.

Weaver, P. H. (1998). *News and the culture of lying*. New York: Free Press.

Wells, K. (Ed.). (2002). *The Gale encyclopedia of nursing and allied health* (Vol. 3). Detroit: Gale Group.

Wexler, M. (2000). *Confronting moral worlds*. Scarborough, Ontario: Prentice Hall.

Wood, A. W. (Ed.). (2001). *Basic writings of Kant*. New York: Modern Library.

Zahn, D. (2009, August 28). Town-hall clash! Arrest threat over Obama "Joker" poster. Retrieved November 30, 2010, from *WorldNetDaily.com*.

Theories Informed by Health Communication

Chapter Learning Objectives

◆ Define theory and list the purposes of theory
◆ Compare and contrast four health communication theories
◆ Explain the importance of incorporating theory into health communication practices and programs
◆ Highlight examples of health communication theory within applied projects
◆ Review suggestions for integrating theories into service-learning or other health communication projects

Chapter Preview

In this chapter, we discuss the role of theory in health communication and highlight four theories that are uniquely situated within health communication philosophies and practices. We first offer a few definitions of theory and establish a preferred working definition of theory. Next we discuss the benefits of incorporating theory into health communication practices and programs. Third, we describe in detail four prominent theories in health communication by explaining the basic concepts of each theory, and then considering some examples of how these theories have been applied to health communication projects. The theories we cover include the Extended Parallel Processing Model, the Reconceptualized Health Belief Model, Diffusion of Innovations, and Harm Reduction Theory. We conclude the chapter with a service-learning application about how theories were used in the design and implementation of a health communication campaign that provides students with an applied learning experience linked to course curriculum.

THERE'S AN INDESCRIBABLE FEELING YOU GET
FROM RIDING AFTER A COUPLE DRINKS.

SUCH AS FLESH BEING TORN FROM YOUR LIMBS AS YOUR BONES SNAP LIKE TWIGS.

National Highway Transportation Safety Administration

DON'T WRECK YOUR MOTORCYCLE AND YOUR LIFE. RIDE SMART. RIDE SOBER.

What is your gut reaction to this public service announcement (PSA)? When you see this image and read the words, how does it make you feel? Are you afraid, sad, or disgusted? Is the message too graphic for you? Does it make you want to look away? What will you remember from this PSA? Is this message relevant to you? Does this PSA convince you that you should not ride a motorcycle after drinking alcohol? If you ride a motorcycle, are you less likely to drink and ride now that you've seen this message?

The public service announcement (PSA) that begins this chapter is a good example of using a fear appeal in an attempt to change the public's behavior. The design of messages such as this is guided in part by health communication theories. These theories help campaign practitioners craft messages that are more likely to be persuasive and bring about the desired attitude or behavior change. In fact, one of the most important assets that health communication specialists can bring to the field of health communication and related health fields is a working knowledge of theories uniquely informed by a health communication perspective. These theories offer practitioners guides for designing health-related messages, health interventions, and health campaigns.

Defining Theory

In order to learn about some of the influential theories uniquely informed by a health communication perspective, we must first define the term *theory* and understand its purposes. To prepare yourself to learn about theory, please complete Health Communication Nexus Interlude 3.1.

Read the following scenario.

J.J. and Nick are playing a game of one-on-one basketball. As J.J. attempts to make a lay-up, Nick defends him by slapping down the ball. Suddenly J.J. is lying on the court yelping in pain and clutching his hand. Nick rushes over to help him and after taking a closer look suggests that they go over to the health center so that J.J. can get checked out by a doctor.

What do you suppose happened to J.J? In your notebook write an explanation for what likely happened to J.J. in this scenario.

Naive Theory

Your proposed explanation for what happened in the scenario in Health Communication Nexus Interlude 3.1 is an example of a *naive theory,* meaning a common-sense explanation or understanding based on experience and/or intuition. You provided an explanation for what happened based on the facts you were given about the situation as well as your general knowledge about how the world works. Not everyone's theory of this scenario will be the same. Some might have written that the ball Nick slapped down hit J.J.'s finger and broke or sprained it. There are other possible explanations though. It could be that J.J. is allergic to bees, got stung during the game, and is having an allergic reaction. It may be that someone in the area was playing catch and an errant throw hit J.J. You cannot be 100% certain of what occurred given the facts provided, but you may feel fairly certain of your explanation based on your knowledge of basketball, gravity, and common sports injuries.

We began with Health Communication Nexus Interlude 3.1 so that you would be comfortable and not intimidated by the idea of theory. Although the theories in this chapter may be more refined and detailed than your explanation of how J.J.'s injury likely occurred, at the core all theories are proposed explanations or understandings of naturally occurring phenomena or situations. Also keep in mind that theories are just abstractions, meaning that the theory is not the phenomenon, behavior, or the communication itself. It is a set of ideas that help make sense of the phenomenon, behavior, or communication.

Formal Definitions of Theory

Now, let's consider some more formal definitions of theory. Donohew and Palmgreen, two professors in the discipline of communication, defined theory in the following way:

> A *theory* is a tentative explanation invented to assist in understanding some small or large part of the "reality" around us. . . . Ideally, the concepts within a theory are measurable and its propositions testable and therefore subject

to refutation. A theory comes into prominence when it is noticed and pursued by the scientific community and it passes into history when better explanations are found (Donohew & Palmgreen, 1981, p. 29; 2003).

This very traditional definition of theory presents one way of thinking about theory and is consistent with a classic definition of theory from Kerlinger and Lee, (2000), who defined theory in the following way:

> A *theory* is a set of interrelated constructs (concepts), definitions, and propositions that present a systematic view of phenomena by specifying relations among variables, with the purpose of explaining and predicting the phenomena (p. 11).

What are some of the words that seem especially important within these definitions of theory? Perhaps one or more of the following key words seemed important to you too:

◆ Explanation
◆ Concepts/variables
◆ Measurable
◆ Proposition
◆ Prediction
◆ Testable
◆ Systematic
◆ Refutation

In essence these definitions argue that theories are essentially designed to explain a phenomenon by creating systematic propositions of predictable or expected relationships between concepts or variables. The propositions must be measurable and testable and open to being refuted or proven wrong through research.

Let's further boil down the definition of theory and return to our basketball scenario. The two formal definitions of theory presented thus far contain three primary concepts: explanation, testable, and prediction. As we discussed, a theory is used to *explain* the connections or relationships among events or ideas. In the case of J.J. and Nick playing basketball, you tried to make connections between the actions during the game and J.J.'s injury. The next concept, *testable*, refers to the idea that theories are tested and studied over time through research. You likely based your explanation of J.J.'s injury on your or others' past experiences. The final concept is that a theory is used to make predictions. *Predictive* power means that you can use the theory to predict future behaviors and actions. In your theory about what happened to J.J., for example, did you make predictions about what would happen in the future for either J.J. or others who sustain a similar injury? So, according to this boiled down definition of theory as an explanation based on predictions that have been tested, is your explanation of what happened to J.J. a theory or just a potential explanation of an occurrence? Why? Would the authors of the two traditional definitions of theory consider your explanation of what happened to J.J. a theory? Why or why not?

Although we recognize and appreciate the benefits of a traditional definition of theory that carefully limits the boundaries of what is and what is not considered theory, we prefer a broader definition that may allow for a wider understanding of social phenomena, and may promote creative thinking about theory. For this reason, our preferred definition of *theory* is: a "consciously elaborated, justified, and uncertain understanding" (Babrow & Mattson, 2003, p. 36). At first glance this definition may seem short and simple compared with the other definitions of theory we presented, but closer inspection shows that it contains some powerful ideas.

What are some of the words that seem especially important within this definition of theory? Perhaps one or more of the following key words seemed important to you too:

◆ Consciously elaborated
◆ Justified
◆ Uncertain understanding

First, a theory must be *consciously elaborated,* meaning that the theory has been thought about and is specifically communicated. Next, a theory is *justified,* meaning that reason and evidence support the theory. In the case of your theory of what happened to J.J., you relied on your knowledge of how injuries occur as well as your previous experience with basketball. This knowledge allowed you to justify your explanation. Justification is important because it ensures that theories are reasonable and supported.

Finally, this definition emphasizes that every theory is an uncertain understanding. As we previously discussed, theories are fundamentally explanations for or understandings about what occurs in the world around us. Because all is not known about the phenomena, there always is a degree of *uncertainty in the understanding* a theory promotes. When you were devising an explanation for what occurred on the basketball court, there was no way to be completely certain that you were correct. Some theories have less uncertainty than others as more justification for some theories is available, but there is always an element of the unknown.

So, according to this definition of theory which emphasizes understanding, is your explanation of what happened to J.J. while playing basketball with Nick a theory? Why or why not? No matter what definition of theory you prefer, theory is important to health communication for several reasons.

Importance of Theory

As you probably realized while we were defining theory, even though definitions of theory and the theories themselves can be challenging to grasp, there are a number of benefits of incorporating theory into our health communication practices and programs. Theories provide a common language, practical tools, and assist practitioners in moving beyond their intuition and experiences toward designing and evaluating health communication messages and programs that are based on established understandings about human behavior. Also, knowing the array of theories that exist to shed light on health communication and health behaviors allows practitioners to think creatively and work innovatively in addressing specific situations. Theory provides a road map to studying a problem, developing appropriate interventions, and evaluating those interventions to understand both successes and failures. In this way, theory informs practice. However, the practice of health communication also informs theory by supporting theory or calling into question the assumptions or concepts of a theory (Babrow & Mattson, 2003; Corman, 1995). Also, it is important to keep in mind that health communication problems often require input from more than one theory, so a combination of theories may need to be employed to understand and/or address the situation. This especially may be the case with large-scale health campaigns such as those we discuss in Chapter 7, "Linking Health Communication with Health Campaign Theories," and Chapter 8, "Linking Health Communication with Health Campaign Practice."

PROFILE

Developing and Applying Problematic Integration Theory

Austin Babrow, PhD—Professor, Ohio University

Austin Babrow began his academic studies at the University of Illinois at Champaign-Urbana. While studying persuasion, he became interested in communication, uncertainty, and values, and specifically in how uncertainty is socially constructed. This interest and exploration of associated issues lead to the creation of the Theory of Problematic Integration, or PI Theory, which was first introduced in 1992. PI Theory continues to be refined based on further thinking and research by Babrow and others.

The basic idea behind PI Theory is that we go through life making judgments based on the likelihood of events occurring or our expectations that those events will occur which form our probabilistic orientations. We also form evaluative orientations, which are our beliefs as to whether those events are good or bad. Typically we integrate our probabilistic orientations and our evaluative orientations without much thought. There are times, however, when our expectations and desires do not mesh. For example, we value something highly, such as being healthy, but our expectations for that outcome are low. In these situations we must work to integrate our conflicting feelings. In some cases this means decreasing our uncertainty as to the likelihood of an event occurring whereas in other cases, increased uncertainty may lead to hope. Communication plays an integral role in either creating PI or in helping to resolve it.

As Babrow continued to work on PI Theory he became more and more interested in how his theory could apply to health situations given the magnitude of uncertainty that is associated with health. Some of the health issues he has applied PI Theory to and considered the role of uncertainty in include dialysis, breast cancer, pregnancy, and bioterrorism. As he explains it, health, illness, and disease all are laden with values and expectations that are created and resolved through communication.

As a scholar, Babrow's primary goal is to investigate questions and problems that will create a greater understanding of how communication works to help us make sense of our lives. As he continues developing his ideas regarding PI and uncertainty, Babrow aspires to work outside his comfort zone and do more applied research. He says he admires fellow colleagues who go out into the community and use their expertise to enact change. For him theory is meant to explain and provide understanding, but it also should be applied to make the human experience better. In other words, he feels a responsibility to study issues such as health that are so central to the human condition and experience.

Now that we have a better appreciation for different ideas about theory and why theories are important, we turn our attention to a set of theories we consider to be uniquely informed by the field of health communication.

Health Communication Theories

Rationale

Although there are several theories that inform and have been informed by health communication practices and the work of health communication scholars, specialists, and health campaign practitioners, in this chapter we focus on four theories that we consider uniquely informed by health communication. The four theories are:

- ◆ Extended Parallel Process Model
- ◆ Reconceptualized Health Belief Model
- ◆ Diffusion of Innovations
- ◆ Harm Reduction Theory

Each of these theories fits our definition of theory because it is consciously elaborated, justified by research and observation, and provides an uncertain understanding of human behavior and health communication.

Extended Parallel Process Model

Fear appeals have frequently been used as a persuasive tool to encourage people to avoid behaviors or to motivate behavior change. Think of advertisements with blackened and diseased lungs you have seen, or images similar to the one in the introduction to this chapter with mangled vehicles and debris from horrific accidents. These images are intended to frighten you into not smoking and being safer on the roads. The basic idea behind using a fear appeal is that after seeing an image of a wrecked motorcycle, for example, the viewer will think twice before riding a motorcycle after drinking alcohol. However, fear appeals do not have a 100% success rate. You may know someone who still smokes even though he or she has seen the images of diseased lungs and is aware of the health risks of smoking. You might also know someone who has driven under the influence of alcohol or drugs despite being knowledgeable about the many risks of drunk driving, including death. The question then is why do people continue to engage in risky health

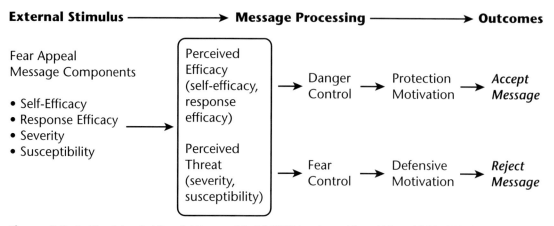

Figure 3.1 ◆ *The Extended Parallel Process Model (EPPM; adapted from Witte, 1992, 1994)*

behaviors even after being presented with frightening messages about the consequences? The *Extended Parallel Process Model* (EPPM, Figure 3.1) is a health communication theory developed by Witte (1992, 1994) to explain why some fear appeals are successful and others are not.

As you can see in Figure 3.1, the EPPM assumes individuals conduct two major appraisals when processing a fear appeal message; the appraisal of the threat and the appraisal of efficacy. If an individual does not find the threat to be personally relevant, then that individual will cease to process the message. If the threat is personally relevant, though, the individual will engage in one of two types of responses; a fear control response where the individual acts to alleviate the fear, or a danger control response where the individual acts to alleviate the danger. The EPPM seeks to explain why some individuals fail to recognize a personal threat and it seeks to explain why individuals have different reactions to threat messages.

This EPPM incorporates several key concepts:

- ◆ Appraisal of threat
  - ❖ Perceived severity
  - ❖ Perceived susceptibility
- ◆ Danger control
- ◆ Fear control
- ◆ Appraisal of efficacy
  - ❖ Response efficacy
  - ❖ Self-efficacy

Appraisal of Threat

Let's first consider the appraisal of threat process. According to the EPPM, when confronted with a threat, an individual performs an *appraisal of the threat* or evaluates both the *perceived severity* of the threat and that individual's *perceived susceptibility* or vulnerability to the threat. A threat must be perceived as severe and the individual must feel susceptible to the threat in order for the threat to effectively arouse feelings of fear. In the case of a motorcycle crash caused by drunken riding, the threat of an accident that could lead to serious injury or death would likely be perceived as highly severe. In other situations, such as walking to class for example, the potential threats, such as being struck by a car, truck, or bicycle may not seem severe. In situations that contain non-severe threats, a message about pedestrian safety, like in the walking to class example, would not be effective in arousing fear.

Other examples of non-severe threats might include getting a hangover from drinking too much alcohol or being jittery from consuming too much caffeine. It is difficult to raise fear in individuals about threats they consider to be minor. When presented with minor threats such as these, individuals usually cease paying attention to health messages about these risky behaviors. A fear appeal needs to arouse enough fear in the message recipient to motivate that individual to act in response to that fear.

Those faced with the motorcycle safety PSA at the beginning of this chapter also would have to assess their susceptibility to the threat, meaning their feelings of vulnerability to the threat. If you have never ridden a motorcycle or do not plan to ride one, you likely would feel that the threat is not relevant to you or that you were not susceptible to the threat of a motorcycle crash, since you do not ride. Even if you rated the threat as highly severe, you would not be too concerned because you would not feel as if the threat would affect you. At this point you would no longer attend to the message about motorcycle safety. If you do ride motorcycles, the threat of a crash becomes more personally relevant and you might feel more susceptible to the threat. There are other factors that could influence your susceptibility assessment, though. You might not drink alcohol, or you might feel that you are a good rider and could avoid a crash. Some people may feel as if they are invincible or that motorcycle accidents are something that happen to other people, which also would lead to a low perception of susceptibility. On the other hand, if you felt that you were susceptible to the threat because you drink and ride, you would be more likely to attend to the message about motorcycle safety.

The key aspects to remember about the EPPM are that in order for individuals to fully process a fear message, they must consider the threat to be severe and feel personally susceptible to the threat. The challenge for those designing health messages is to convince the audience that the threat is severe and that target audience members are susceptible to the threat. In Health Communication Nexus Interlude 3.2, you explore the challenging process of presenting a threat as severe and relevant to the audience.

For this interlude, imagine that you are trying to raise awareness among college students about the various threats associated with chronic stress. Jot down in your notebook ideas of messages you would create in order to raise perceptions of severity and susceptibility about chronic stress in your target audience of college students.

Danger and Fear Control Responses

Once an individual is convinced that the threat in a message is worth attending to, that individual engages in one of two reactions. One possible reaction is a danger control response, which is the desired reaction. When an individual is engaging in a *danger control* response to a message, that individual is taking actions to control the danger or minimize the threat. In the case of riding a motorcycle while intoxicated, a danger control response to a PSA message would be not riding a motorcycle after drinking alcohol. In this scenario, the viewer of the motorcycle safety message was frightened enough by the message to adapt his or her behavior in order to avoid the threat of injury or death.

The other possible reaction is a fear control response, which is the undesirable reaction. Rather than working to minimize the threat, in a *fear control* response the individual works to minimize or alleviate the fear aroused by the message. Ways of doing this include on one end of the continuum ignoring or avoiding the message and on the other end of the continuum becoming defensive or having an angry response to the message. Fear control responses address the immediate negative feelings, but do not address the actual threat and risk.

For the motorcycle safety PSA at the beginning of this chapter, ideally viewers of the PSA are frightened by the message and uncomfortable enough with that fear that they will try to find a way to minimize their risk by not riding a motorcycle after drinking alcohol. On the other hand, after viewing the motorcycle safety PSA, some individuals might engage in fear control by looking away from the message or becoming angry and insulted by it. More specifically, some might call the message unrealistic or tell themselves that the message designers are clueless and do not understand anything about riding motorcycles. Individuals also can be overly frightened and become paralyzed with fear which leaves them unable to act in response to the message.

As another example, during times when there is a public health crisis such as an outbreak of meningitis, some may become so frightened that they stay in their homes and avoid interacting with people in the outside world for fear of contracting the disease, even if certain interactions would help protect them against the threat, such as visiting a health clinic to get a meningitis vaccine. What then determines what kind of reaction someone has to a fear appeal? Why are some individuals motivated to control the danger and others are motivated to control the fear? The answer lies in the other appraisal process within the EPPM.

Appraisal of Efficacy

When those faced with a fear appeal determine the threat is both severe and personally relevant, they engage in a second appraisal process of perceived efficacy. The *appraisal of efficacy* process comprises two components, *response efficacy* and *self-efficacy*.

Efficacy is defined by Witte (1994) as pertaining to the "effectiveness, feasibility, and ease with which a recommended response impedes or averts a threat" (p. 114). There are two dimensions that underlie efficacy, including response efficacy and self-efficacy. *Response efficacy* refers to the belief that the recommended action will bring about the desired result or it will stop the threat. In the motorcycle safety PSA example, individuals would evaluate whether refraining from riding while intoxicated would prevent the individual from being involved in a crash. If viewers of the message strongly believe that not riding while intoxicated would alleviate the risk of a crash, then they would have a high perception of response efficacy.

In some situations, individuals may not feel that taking a recommended action will bring about the desired result. For example, a campaign to curb the rising level of obesity in children might have to convince the children and their parents that limiting the amount of television time each day will lead to weight loss and prevent the obesity rate from rising. However, not everyone would see the link between television watching and weight and therefore would not think that watching less television would lead to weight loss. According to the EPPM, if individuals do not have a high perception of response efficacy, they will engage in a fear control response and reject the message.

In addition to believing that a recommended action can achieve its purpose, individuals must have *self-efficacy*, or a belief that they are capable of performing the recommended actions. For example, individuals can fully believe that eating fewer calories will lead to weight loss but lack a belief in their personal ability to eat healthier and eliminate sugary and fatty snacks from their diet. In the case of motorcycle riding while intoxicated, self-efficacy would refer to riders' beliefs in their ability to avoid drinking alcohol and riding. Self-efficacy in these cases comprises the physical ability to perform the task as well as the psychological ability to resist temptation and instead make healthy choices. In the case of not drinking and riding there may be some individuals, such as alcoholics, who may not be able to physically refrain from drinking. If drinking is a part of the individuals' social activities, the riders must be able to socialize without drinking and must be able to resist any pressure to drink alcohol. Further, if individuals consume alcohol they must have the ability to find an alternative means of transportation. Those with a low perception of self-efficacy will engage in a fear control response rather than a danger control response and reject the message. Those with a high perception of self-efficacy are more likely to engage in a danger control response and accept the message due to their confidence in their ability to protect themselves.

Influence of the EPPM on Health Communication

So what does all this mean and how does it influence the design of health messages and health campaigns? Refer again to the PSA with the crashed motorcycle at the beginning of this chapter. After choosing to use a fear appeal to address the issue of drunken riding, the first step for the message designers was to create a message in which the threat of being in a crash is considered to be severe and those viewing the message will feel susceptible to the threat. The next step for message designers is to balance that threat with messages that provide a clear way to avoid that threat—response efficacy—along with affirmation that an individual can perform those actions—self-efficacy. So, based on what you now know about the EPPM, how effective do you think this fear appeal PSA is? Are there any messages that need to be added to the PSA? Are there any components of the EPPM that still need to be addressed within this PSA?

The concepts of the EPPM have been used in the formation of health messages related to a variety of health issues, including breast cancer (Hubbell, 2006; Kline, 2000), HIV/AIDS (Roberto et al., 2007), firearm safety (Roberto, Meyer, Johnson, & Atkin, 2000), and alcohol abuse (Moscato et al., 2001). Do you think you could design an effective PSA for a health issue of concern to you given what you know about the EPPM? Why or why not?

To further illustrate how the EPPM has been used to guide message design and evaluation, let's consider the development of brochures intended to increase hearing protection use among agricultural and landscape workers (Smith et al., 2008). Hearing loss is a pervasive problem, particularly among those who work in the agricultural and landscaping sectors. Despite the fact that the noise generated by equipment and machinery used in the fields and in landscaping frequently exceeds recommended decibel levels, few workers wear hearing protection, such as earplugs or earmuffs. Hearing loss also makes workers more susceptible to other work-related injuries, making hearing loss an even greater threat.

In order to promote the use of hearing protection, health communication specialists working with health issue experts designed two brochures. One brochure was targeted to farmers and one to landscape workers. The first goal of the brochures was to raise awareness about the problem of noise-induced hearing loss (NIHL). Following the guidelines of the EPPM, the brochure designers included messages that would present the problem as serious and highlighted workers' susceptibility to hearing loss. Severity messages included the statement "Hearing loss is permanent and irreversible" with a list of consequences of hearing loss, such as constant ringing in the ears, isolation, and depression.

To increase perceptions of susceptibility, the brochures reported how common NIHL is among agricultural and landscape workers by including statements such as, "Did you know that farmers suffer more hearing loss than any other occupational group?" and "Lawn care workers are at a high risk for hearing loss!" These statements were accompanied by images of commonly used equipment and the decibels each piece of equipment was capable of producing. By seeing equipment they regularly use, farmers and landscape workers would be more likely to recognize a personal threat.

Because they were using a fear appeal and were guided by the EPPM, the message designers recognized the need to promote a danger control rather than a fear control response. To do this, the brochures included several efficacy messages. To increase feelings of response efficacy, the brochures included pictures of foam earplugs and plastic earmuffs and explained that NIHL is a farm hazard that is easy to protect against. Messages addressing self-efficacy included directions on how simple the safety precautions are to use and directly told readers that "you can begin saving your hearing today."

The brochures were disseminated to argricultural and landscape workers at local meetings, and follow-up surveys indicated that the brochures were effective in raising workers' intentions to wear protective hearing equipment. These brochures illustrate that designing successful fear appeal messages is a process and health communication specialists must ensure that all of the components in the theory or model are addressed. Go to this book's Web site to view the hearing protection brochures.

The EPPM focuses specifically on fear-arousing messages, so its use is limited to situations in which fear appeals are appropriate. Because of its focus on messages, the EPPM directly emphasizes communication aspects of health-related behavior. The next theory we consider, the Reconceptualized Health Belief Model, is a broader model that considers multiple factors that contribute to an individual's health-related behavior.

Reconceptualized Health Belief Model

In the early 1950s, Rosenstock and his colleagues at the United States Public Health Service (Rosenstock, 1966, 1974a, 1974b; Rosenstock, Strecher, & Becker, 1988) developed the original Health Belief Model (HBM) to help explain why people were not using a free tuberculosis (TB) screening program. The program used mobile units that traveled around communities offering free TB screening X-rays. Despite the convenience of these mobile units, they were not widely utilized, leading researchers to investigate why.

Later, other psychologists expanded research with the HBM to include people's responses to symptoms (Kirscht, 1974), behaviors in response to diagnosed diseases, and compliance with prescribed medical treatments (Becker, 1974; Becker, Drachman, & Kirscht, 1974; Janz & Becker, 1984). Basically, the HBM describes factors that influence an individual's health behaviors and choices. Since its inception, the HBM has become one of the most widely used frameworks to promote a variety of health-related recommendations, including immunizations (Szilagyi, Rodewald, Savageau, Yoos, & Doane, 1992), condoms to prevent sexually transmitted diseases (STDs) (Mattson, 1999; Rose, 1996), and seatbelt use (Simsekoglu & Lajunen, 2008; Webb, Sanson-Fisher, & Bowman, 1988).

The original HBM consisted of four components or concepts:

◆ Perceived susceptibility
◆ Perceived severity
◆ Perceived benefits
◆ Perceived barriers

Some of these concepts may already be familiar to you from the EPPM. Next we consider each of these components more closely to understand how they influence individuals' decisions about health behavior. Before we delve into these concepts, however, please complete Health Communication Nexus Interlude 3.3.

Health Communication Nexus Interlude 3.3

For the next few minutes imagine that you are going to spend the day at the outdoor swimming pool with your friends. Also think about using sunscreen with at least SPF15 to protect yourself against skin cancer. Now, in your notebook jot down your answers to the following questions.

- What is the likelihood that cancer will personally affect you? How likely do you think you are to develop skin cancer?

- How serious do you think skin cancer is? What happens to someone with skin cancer? Can you survive skin cancer?

- What are the benefits of using sunscreen? What are the immediate or short-term benefits? What are the long-term benefits?

- What are the financial costs of using sunscreen? What are the time costs of using sunscreen? Can you think of any other costs associated with using sunscreen?

- Based on your answers to the previous questions, how likely do you think you are to use sunscreen at the outdoor swimming pool? Why or why not?

Keep your responses to all these questions available as we work through the components of the original Health Belief Model and later the Reconceptualized Health Belief Model.

Let's first consider the component or concept of *perceived susceptibility,* which refers to an individual's perception of how vulnerable that individual is to a particular health threat. In Health Communication Nexus Interlude 3.3, you were asked to assess your own perceived susceptibility to the threat of cancer in general and skin cancer in specific. Your susceptibility could be either immediate or longer term. You might not believe that you will develop skin cancer tomorrow, but you might be concerned that prolonged sun exposure could lead to skin cancer later in life. Various factors influence your ideas about your susceptibility. For example, individuals with fair skin and blue eyes are at greater risk for developing skin cancer than those with dark skin. In addition, those with a family history of skin cancer or even other kinds of cancer may consider themselves more susceptible. Age also can figure into your perceptions of susceptibility. Some might consider themselves too young to develop cancer, even though recent reports have shown that skin cancer rates are rapidly increasing among those in their 20s (Ries et al., 2007).

An individual's perceptions of susceptibility to a threat influence that individual's behavior to avoid or alleviate the threat. Those who believe they are highly susceptible to a threat are most likely take action to prevent that threat and conversely, those who feel less susceptible to a threat are less likely to take preventive action against that threat.

The next concept is *perceived severity,* which also relates to assessment of a threat and refers to perceptions about the seriousness of a health threat. In addition to an individual deciding how likely a threat is to be personally harmful, individuals also have perceptions about how serious that threat is. Health threats run the gamut of seriousness from minor discomfort to death. Threats do not have to be specifically health related. Other threats include financial strain such as paying for skin cancer treatment costs, or cosmetic threats such as imagining yourself with spotted and damaged skin. When you were thinking about skin cancer during Health Communication Nexus Interlude 3.3, did you rate skin cancer as a highly severe threat due to the possibility of death? Or did you rate skin cancer as a lesser threat because the majority of cases are treatable? Logically, if you deem a threat to be more severe, you are more likely to take actions to avoid that threat than a threat that does not concern you. A less serious threat, although unpleasant, may not be enough to deter you from an unhealthy behavior.

It also is important to remember that all the components in the original HBM and the RHBM are considered in relation to each other. For example, you may consider the severity of the threat of anthrax poisoning to be very high, as it can result in death, but feel that your personal susceptibility is extremely low because you live in a rural area or in a small town or city. In this case, even though anthrax exposure is a severe threat, you would not be very motivated to protect yourself against an anthrax attack. On the other hand, you may feel extremely susceptible to catching the flu during flu season, but also perceive that catching the flu is a mildly severe risk resulting in discomfort for a few days. Consequently, you take only minimal precautions to avoid catching the flu, such as avoiding obviously infected people, but not going as far as getting a flu shot.

The other two concepts in the original HBM, perceived benefits and perceived barriers, refer to an individual's perceptions about the advantages and disadvantages of the recommended health actions. And keep in mind that the recommended health actions can be tangible products such as sunscreen, behaviors such as eating five servings of fruits and vegetables each day or getting thirty minutes of exercise, or medical tests and procedures such as yearly mammograms or monthly breast self-exams.

Perceived benefits are an individual's perceptions regarding the benefits or advantages of using a recommended health action, including the perception that the behavior will be successful in preventing the health threat. In Health Communication Nexus Interlude 3.3 about using sunscreen at an outdoor swimming pool, you possibly listed protection against skin cancer as a benefit. If you were not sure that sunscreen really did protect against skin cancer, then you would not be as inclined to use it. Cancer protection may not be the only benefit you listed though. You also may have included protection against sunburn or protecting your skin from aging. Although you may not have listed it, another possible benefit of using sunscreen is approval of others. If you are with a group of sun-conscious friends, you might be more likely to use sunscreen because you know your friends will approve of your protective actions.

Perceived barriers are an individual's perceptions about the costs associated with adopting the recommended health behavior. When you think of the term *cost*, you probably think of financial costs. In the case of skin cancer protection, the cost of a bottle of sunscreen is approximately $8.00, which may be prohibitive for some individuals. Not all costs are financial though. In the case of how the original HBM was developed by researching a TB testing program, even though the tests were free, there still may have been costs to those who used the program, such as being inconvenienced to travel to and receive the test. One important cost is time. Putting on sunscreen takes just a minute or two, but other health behaviors, such as exercising regularly, require substantial time commitments. Costs also can be emotional or psychological. For some people, for example, there may be fear associated with medical procedures or with knowing the results of medical procedures. There also may be a fear of disapproval by others. If you are with a group of friends who regularly sunbathe to get a tan so they smear on baby oil, you may feel embarrassed to slather on sunscreen in front of them or fear their negative reactions to your healthy behavior.

As we discussed previously, your perceptions about all of these factors are weighed against each other. In deciding whether or not to adopt a recommended health behavior, you must first feel that there is a serious enough health threat that you are susceptible to. You will then weigh the benefits of the healthy solution versus the barriers or costs of that solution. You may think that sunscreen is good protection against skin cancer, but the hassle of remembering to bring it and put it on is too much of a barrier or cost for you, so you choose not to use it. Others may think that the cost of not looking tanned is not worth the benefit of protecting their skin. The most important idea to take away is that effective health interventions and messages must take all of the factors within the HBM into account.

In 1988, *self-efficacy* was added to the HBM as another moderating factor to help explain why individuals were generally unsuccessful changing their chronic unhealthy behaviors such as smoking or overeating (Rosenstock, Strecher, & Becker, 1988). As we discussed previously in this chapter, *self-efficacy* is your belief in your personal ability to adopt a recommended health behavior. If you are not confident that you can perform certain necessary actions, then you are less likely to try. This explains why many individuals continue to smoke cigarettes despite knowing that it is bad for their health and quitting could significantly improve their health. In the case of skin cancer prevention, you need to feel confident that you can effectively use sunscreen to protect yourself.

As more and more health interventions were designed using the HBM as a framework, the concept of *cues to action* was added to the model. *Cues to action* are stimuli that encourage an individual to adopt a recommended health behavior. Cues to action can be either internal or external. *Internal cues to action* are stimuli from within the individual. An example of an internal cue to action is having a physical symptom, such as being short of breath when walking up stairs, which could be a cue to start exercising more to avoid heart disease. *External cues to action* are stimuli or messages from outside the individual and can come from a variety of sources, such as the media, coworkers, family, friends, and health care providers. If you are glancing through a magazine while lounging at the pool and see an ad recommending that you wear sunscreen, this could cue you to put on your own sunscreen. A regular visit to your physician in which she reminds you to use adequate sun protection could also be a cue to action. Cues to action serve to enhance one or more of the other components of the HBM, such as perceived threat, benefits, and barriers, which increase the likelihood that the recommended health behavior will be adopted.

Mattson and others have argued that the HBM needs to account for more of the social influences that contribute to health perceptions. Specifically, Mattson (1999) argued that cues to action need to be given a more central place in the model, as interpersonal and other forms of communication often are the cues that spur preventive actions or recommended health behaviors. Mattson's study of HIV-test counseling sessions found that persuasive messages to clients provided by the HIV-test counselors served a pivotal role in changing clients' safer-sex behaviors. Generally, when clients visit a health care clinic for an HIV test, they meet with a counselor to discuss any concerns as well as any behaviors that are putting them at risk for contracting HIV. In Mattson's research, frequently HIV-test counselors made suggestions to clients for ways to have safer sex, which spurred the clients' intentions to engage in safer-sex practices such as wearing condoms or abstaining from sex until their HIV-test results were determined to be negative. Based on this research, Mattson proposed the Reconceptualized Health Belief Model (RHBM).

HIV-Test Counseling

HIV testing is an important way for individuals who are sexually active to either ensure that they are disease free or learn that they have contracted the virus as soon as possible. Early treatment of HIV can help an individual maintain better health, and knowledge of one's HIV status also can prevent transmission of HIV to that individual's sexual partners.

In addition to getting a blood test, those who have an HIV test frequently participate in some form of counseling. Prior to taking a blood test, counselors discuss how the test is done, why the clients feel they are at risk and in need of an HIV test, explain methods of protecting themselves and others against HIV, and what the impact of potential test results might be.

In many places, HIV-test results are not immediate and individuals must wait an average of one week to receive results, which are provided by counselors. If the HIV test is positive, counselors answer any questions and provide any needed emotional support. Additionally counselors will stress the importance of contacting any sexual partners who may have been exposed to HIV. Regardless of the results, counselors provide information about safer sex and other HIV-prevention practices.

Figure 3.2 depicts how the components of the Health Belief Model (HBM) work together to predict whether an individual will take the preventive action or adopt the recommended health behavior. Figure 3.2 also compares the components of the original HBM and Mattson's Reconceptualized Health Belief Model (RHBM). What is the main difference in the RHBM?

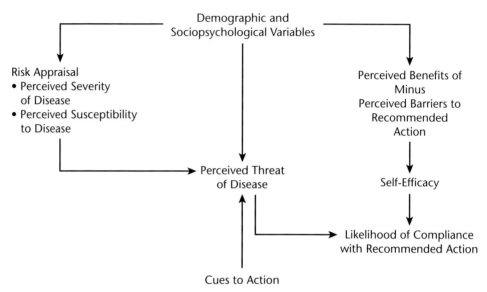

The Health Belief Model (HBM) adapted from Janz and Becker (1984) and Becker (1990)

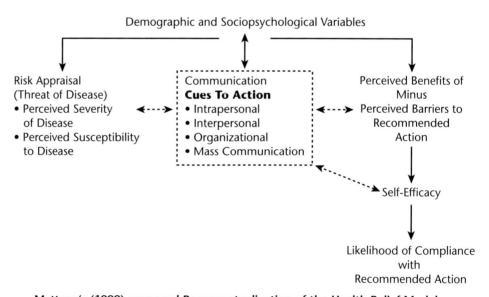

Mattson's (1999) proposed Reconceptualization of the Health Belief Model

Figure 3.2 ◆ *Comparison of the Health Belief Model (HBM) and the Reconceptualized Health Belief Model (RHBM)*

Now that you understand the components of the model, let's consider an example health intervention based on the RHBM. One pressing problem in the United States is a high level of inactivity. Engaging in just moderate physical activity, such as walking for at least 30 minutes five times a week, can reduce the risk of heart disease, stroke, colon cancer, diabetes, and high blood pressure. To promote increased physical activity among residents of St. Joseph, Missouri, the *Walk Missouri* campaign was launched (Wray, Jupka, & Ludwig-Bell, 2005). Integrating a mass media initiative with community-based programs, the campaign attempted to increase residents' weekly minutes of walking. Can you identify components of the RHBM in the campaign message in Figure 3.3?

Figure 3.3 ◆ *Poster from* Walk Missouri *campaign*

While planning and developing the campaign messages, campaign organizers met with members of the community to identify what their perceived benefits of and barriers to walking were as well as potential cues to action. Based on the community's responses, it was determined that messages should be focused on short-term benefits of walking rather than long-term health benefits, and the community also desired messages that provided strategies for overcoming the barriers to walking. These findings lead to the creation of messages that touted several short-term benefits of walking, such as weight loss, spending time with family and friends while walking, and having fun while walking. Messages also provided tips for how to incorporate walking into a daily routine.

The campaign was implemented May through September and messages were distributed via billboards, newspaper, posters, and radio advertisements. The campaign also partnered with the existing *Get Movin' St. Joe* coalition to sponsor community walks and promote walking trails and walking paths around the town. An evaluation of the campaign revealed that those who were exposed to campaign messages had more positive beliefs about the benefits of walking and perceived fewer barriers to walking. Follow-up evaluation also found an increase in the number of citizens who were walking during the week.

This is just one example of a campaign developed around the components of the RHBM. One of the reasons the RHBM is effective is because it focuses on individuals and individual change. The next theory we consider, Diffusion of Innovations, focuses on larger populations.

Diffusion of Innovations

Diffusion of Innovations (DOI) is unique from the other two theories covered so far because its focus is not on message design or communication as a cue to action for individuals, but instead DOI attempts to explain how ideas and behaviors spread among people. Are you one of those people who is among the first to try something new, or are you one of the last to catch on to a new trend? For example, when a new video game system comes out, are you someone who camps out overnight to be sure that you get your hands on one, or are you still enjoying your original Nintendo? Perhaps you are somewhere in the middle of this continuum. DOI describes what type of consumer you are and what influences the decisions you make about adopting innovations.

The initial development of DOI is credited to French sociologist Gabriel Tarde, who mapped the rate of diffusion of new technologies using an S-shaped curve. He argued that there are those who rapidly adopt a new product or service on one end of the curve, those who moderately adopt, which is most people and creates a bulge in the middle of the curve, and at the other end of the curve are those who are the slowest to adopt (Figure 3.4). Using these ideas, researchers at the University of Iowa studied how the use of hybrid corn seed, a new technology at the time, spread among Iowa farmers, and specifically looked at the farmers' rates of adoption.

In 1962, one of these researchers, Everett Rogers, published his book *Diffusion of Innovations*. In this book, Rogers argued for a generalized diffusion model that could be applied to public health. In this section we review several key concepts associated with the theory and provide a sense of the innovation adoption process that this theory seeks to describe and explain.

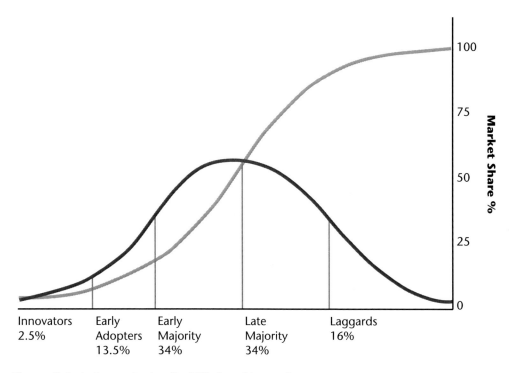

Figure 3.4 ◆ *S-curve to describe Diffusion of Innovations*

Diffusion is defined as the process through which an *innovation*, an idea perceived as new, spreads via certain communication channels over time among the members of a social system. This definition contains four key components:

◆ Innovation
◆ Communication channels
◆ Social system
◆ Time

Most of us probably are very familiar with technological innovations; you may even have one with you right now, such as an iPhone or an iPod. We live in a technological age where technologies are constantly improving and being upgraded. According to this theory, though, an *innovation* does not have to be a tangible product but also can be a new idea, behavior, or service. For example, although recycling might be second nature to many of us today, the idea of recycling paper and aluminum cans was once an innovation. An innovation also can be a behavior such as performing a breast self-exam to detect cancerous lumps. When you think about other innovations in health and disease prevention, what may come to mind are behaviors, products, and services such as using condoms to prevent sexually transmitted diseases, Gardasil the vaccine against cervical cancer, and DNA testing.

As we learned during our discussion of the communication model in Chapter 1, "Introducing Health as Communication Nexus," *communication channels* are the ways that messages are disseminated. Examples of communication channels include television, the internet, e-mail, the telephone, and interpersonal conversation. The *social system* is the group of people the idea is being spread among. This can be as broad as the entire population of a country, or it can be more targeted to members of a specific community such as college students or Chinese immigrants in the United States. The concept of *time* recognizes that change is a process and occurs over time. The rate of adoption can vary widely, over weeks, months, or even years.

Diffusion of Innovation Phases and Attributes

DOI identifies five phases in the adoption process, including knowledge, persuasion, decision, implementation, and adoption. Table 3.1 defines each of these phases. To better understand how an individual moves through these phases, let's use receiving a flu shot to protect yourself against the flu as a primary example. Unlike other routine vaccines you may have received as a child, such as the measles, mumps, and rubella (MMR) vaccine or a tetanus shot, a flu vaccine is voluntary and must be administered each year to protect against strains of the virus in the current flu season.

Table 3.1 ◆ *Phases in the Diffusion of Innovations process*

Knowledge	awareness of the innovation, knowledge of how to use the innovation properly
Persuasion	an attitude about the innovation is developed
Decision	a decision is made to accept or reject the innovation
Implementation	the innovation is used
Adoption	the innovation is regularly used

Considering yourself as an example, explain how the health innovation of a flu shot went through the diffusion of innovations process? Remember to refer to the definitions of the phases provided in Table 3.1.

A few attributes of an innovation influence individuals' attitudes about it and the likelihood that the innovation will be adopted. These attributes can be either positive or negative factors and include:

- ◆ Relative advantage
- ◆ Compatibility
- ◆ Complexity
- ◆ Trialability
- ◆ Observability

One important attribute of an innovation is its *relative advantage*, meaning the "degree to which an innovation is perceived as better than the idea it supersedes" (Bertrand, 2004, p. 118). In other words, the innovation must be perceived as better than the existing options. In the case of the flu shot, the question is, is it better than existing options for avoiding the flu, such as avoiding infected persons or engaging in frequent hand washing?

A second attribute is the innovation's *compatibility,* which is "the degree to which an innovation is perceived to be consistent with existing values, past experiences, and needs of potential adopters" (Bertrand, 2004, p. 118). An innovation must fit into an individual's life and worldview as well as meet a need. For example, if you have never been vaccinated or do not plan on vaccinating your children due to either religious or other personal beliefs, you most likely would not get a flu shot either. A third attribute is the *complexity* of the innovation. More complex innovations are those that are more difficult to understand or use. A flu shot, for example, is relatively low in complexity and is relatively easy to obtain. It requires a small shot in the arm and only one dose is needed each year, as opposed to a daily pill regimen or multiple shots over a period of time. Understanding how the vaccine works to prevent the flu, however, may be more difficult to comprehend.

A fourth attribute is the innovation's *trialability,* which refers to an individual's ability to try an innovation. Various factors influence trialability, including cost, time, and commitment. If an innovation is expensive it may be difficult to try because the price is a deterrent. For example, flu shots generally cost between $10 and $15. For some, this is relatively inexpensive, but for others this cost may be prohibitive. Time also is a valuable resource. If using or learning to use an innovation takes an extensive time commitment, this could deter individuals from trying it. Some innovations require a long-term commitment in order to work. For example, Gardasil, the vaccine that protects against certain strands of the human papilloma virus (HPV), requires three injections administered over a six-month period. In contrast, with a flu shot individuals have the option to try it one year and experience the results before deciding whether or not to get a flu shot the next year.

The fifth attribute is the innovation's *observability,* which is the extent to which others can see the results of using the innovation. If others can see the innovation being used and particularly if they can see positive results, they are more inclined to form favorable attitudes toward the innovation. Some results are easily observable, such as noticing a coworker wearing a pedometer and seeing the coworker using the stairs rather than the elevator. Upon seeing this, you may make the connection that the pedometer measuring your coworker's steps may be encouraging that coworker to walk more during the day. Observing the positive effects of the innovation also can spark conversation. This communication could influence your attitudes toward the innovation as well as persuade you to try using a pedometer and walking more yourself.

Results of using other innovations are more difficult to observe and imitate, especially when the innovation is designed for use in a private setting. An example of an innovation that is difficult to observe is the female condom, an alternative to the male condom for protecting women against pregnancy and sexually transmitted infections (STIs) and diseases (STDs). Generally, women are unable to observe other women using this form of protection and as a result are unable to directly connect the benefits of lack of pregnancy and STIs and STDs to female condom use. Also, it is difficult to directly observe the results of receiving a flu shot. However, individuals may talk about getting the flu shot, any side effects, and their good health during the flu season, which provide information to others who are considering a flu shot.

In order to better understand how these attributes influence potential innovation adoption, please complete Health Communication Nexus Interlude 3.4.

Health Communication Nexus Interlude 3.4

For this interlude, consider the health innovation of spray-on sunscreen. This product protects like traditional sunscreen but comes in a can rather than a tube or bottle. To apply, you spray yourself with a fine mist, much like you would apply bug spray. The advantages of spray-on sunscreen are that it is easier to apply and is a sheer mist with no white, messy lotion to rub in. Its cost is equivalent to that of traditional sunscreen lotion. Now in your notebook rate this spray-on sunscreen innovation on the five attributes that we discussed by indicating whether it is low or high on each of these attributes. Also, briefly note a reason for your rating.

Relative advantage: Rating—Low 1 2 3 4 5 High Reason _____

Compatibility: Rating—Low 1 2 3 4 5 High Reason _____

Complexity: Rating—Low 1 2 3 4 5 High Reason _____

Trialability: Rating—Low 1 2 3 4 5 High Reason _____

Observability: Rating—Low 1 2 3 4 5 High Reason _____

Keep these ratings and reasons in mind as you think about why some innovations are adopted while others are not.

So far we discussed the definition of diffusion and examined the attributes of innovations that contribute to likelihood of adoption. The model also considers the rate of adoption across a population by identifying five *categories of adopters*:

◆ Innovators
◆ Early adopters
◆ Early majority
◆ Late majority
◆ Laggards

Innovators are those who most quickly adopt an innovation, or to be exact, the first 2.5% of individuals in the population who adopt an innovation. These are the people who have a new gadget before many others have even heard of it or are the first to try out the latest craze. Innovators generally have significant financial resources that allow them to acquire expensive new technologies. For example, in 1984 the first commercially sold cell phones cost almost $4,000. Innovators also are able to manage a high level of uncertainty. Innovations are new and unknown and innovators are willing to take risks to try something new. Innovators also are critical in the diffusion process because they bring new ideas into their social systems for others to observe, discuss, and consider adopting.

The next category of adopters, *early adopters*, adopt innovations quickly but are less on the cutting edge than innovators. Early adopters tend to be well-respected members of the social system and serve as role models to others. They are not considered as far out as innovators, and therefore other members of their social system can more easily relate to them and will copy their choices. The *early majority* is a large group who adopt new innovations just prior to the average person. These are individuals who appreciate and accept new technologies but tend not to be leaders in change. Early majority members make thoughtful and deliberate choices about the innovations they adopt. They wait long enough to be sure that the innovation works and any initial bugs or quirks are resolved.

The *late majority* includes individuals who adopt an innovation just after the average person. Late majority members tend to be highly cautious and skeptical of new ideas and products. Adoption often is the result of peer pressure and takes place after most others in the social system. For example, late majority members may have been reluctant to purchase a cell phone but did so after friends and family complained that they were difficult to contact. This group often has limited resources, which makes them more cautious about trying new innovations.

The last category, *laggards*, are the very last to adopt an innovation. When making decisions, laggards look to the past as their point of reference. Highly suspicious of change and change agents, laggards prefer to do things the way they have always been done. A laggard still might refuse to carry a cell phone, believing that a land-line telephone is a perfectly acceptable and often a better means of communication. Laggards also have little communication with the broader social system about new innovations.

Additionally, the model includes *opinion leaders,* who are individuals considered to be experts or whose opinions are highly valued. For example, Dr. Oz, a physician with a daily television program, is considered an extremely powerful opinion leader. His opinion is valued by many on everything from what books to read, how to raise healthy children, and what diet and exercise plan to follow. Opinion leaders can play a significant role in encouraging others to try and eventually adopt an innovation. Members of a social system look to opinion leaders for their take on new ideas. One challenge for campaign designers is to identify the opinion leaders within a community and persuade them to use or endorse a health innovation.

Diffusion of Innovations Examples

Now that we have explored this complex theory, let's consider how Diffusion of Innovations has been used in the health communication process. In the early

1980s HIV and AIDS were rapidly spreading among the gay male population in San Francisco. The STOP AIDS project (www.stopaids.org) worked to promote safer-sex practices, including condom use among gay males. Project workers and volunteers planned community outreach activities and conducted information sessions with small groups of men. The hope was that the men in these sessions would spread the ideas to other members in their social networks. The project also incorporated the use of opinion leaders by identifying highly-respected men in the gay community and asking them to endorse safer-sex practices. STOP AIDS was very successful in its mission. In 1983, the number of new HIV cases was 8,000 and by 1985 it dropped to 650. STOP AIDS continues to fight the spread of HIV/AIDS using similar tactics of community outreach, small group workshops, and community forums.

Diffusion of Innovations also has been used to promote family planning in developing countries (Murphy, 2004). Prior to the diffusion of family planning practices, population rates in developing countries were skyrocketing. These large populations placed a strain on the environment and increased national poverty levels. Recognizing the disadvantages of high population rates, in the early 1960s, governments around the world began to develop initiatives to promote modern family-planning methods, and curb population growth rates in developing countries. Programs worked to educate individuals about clinical and nonclinical family-planning methods, including contraceptive pills, periodic abstinence, and injections. Programs also made various forms of contraceptives easily available, including condoms, spermicidal gels, and foams.

The ideas and behaviors these programs sought to advance were disseminated through a variety of communication channels, including pamphlets, interpersonal communication, and fertility clinics. Messages about the importance of family planning were written into popular radio dramas and puppet shows with family-planning themes that were performed in local villages.

Prior to family-planning information being disseminated to the public, program organizers worked with national and local government officials to obtain both approval for the programs as well as their endorsement of the health ideas being promoted. By first obtaining buy-in from governments, program developers were able to use endorsements by opinion leaders to spread their message to local leaders. After local leaders accepted the importance of family planning, the ideas spread in earnest through local communities.

These programs, which were influenced by the DOI process, were very successful and are credited with increasing the use of modern family-planning methods in developing countries and decreasing the fertility rate by nearly 45% (Murphy, 2004).

The next theory, Harm Reduction Theory, is more of a philosophy of how to approach health problems. Like DOI, it does not explain how to specifically craft messages, but instead provides guidance as to what the general goals of a campaign or other health care intervention should be and offers insight into how to reduce the harm of engaging in unsafe and risky health behaviors.

Harm Reduction Theory

Harm Reduction Theory is one of the more controversial approaches in health communication and public health, especially in the United States. *Harm Reduction Theory* (HRT) is defined as an approach to health with the overall goal to "reduce the problematic effects of unhealthy behaviors and can include techniques ranging from prevention to intervention to maintenance" (Logan & Marlatt, 2010, p. 203). HRT emphasizes a pragmatic, nonjudgmental approach and supports any steps taken in the direction toward healthy behavior (Marlatt, 1998). The primary intention of harm reduction is to reduce harm to individuals who are engaging in risky health behaviors. Health care providers utilizing an HRT approach recognize the challenges individuals face in completely stopping or preventing risky health behaviors. And although stopping the behavior is the best possible and most desirable outcome, harm reduction advocates take a more realistic and practical approach by attempting to help those individuals engaging in risky behaviors and their immediate communities be as safe as possible.

In order to get yourself into a Harm Reduction Theory mindset, please complete Health Communication Nexus Interlude 3.5.

Health Communication Nexus Interlude 3.5

Imagine you are the director of the Student Wellness Center at a college or university. One of the campus initiatives this semester is to curb the problem of underage drinking on campus, and specifically the problem of binge drinking. *Binge drinking* is defined as drinking four or more drinks in about two hours for women and five or more drinks in about two hours for men. You believe that it would be almost impossible to stop all student drinking, so your focus is on making students as safe as possible. Using the following diagram as a guide, take a few minutes to think about and jot down notes in your notebook about programs you could offer, messages you would send to students, and behaviors you would recommend students engage in from this harm reduction perspective.

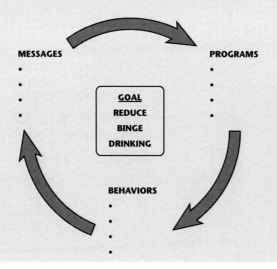

Let's consider some of the suggestions you wrote down during Health Communication Nexus Interlude 3.5. Maybe some of your suggestions included promoting alcohol-free events on campus or providing alternatives to drinking, such as midnight basketball or movies. The intent of these suggestions is to stop drinking altogether, so although these may be good ideas, they are not considered harm reduction approaches. Perhaps you wrote that you would encourage students to consume fewer drinks in an evening. You might have suggested that students keep track of how many drinks they are having by holding on to bottle caps. These recommendations are not telling students to stop drinking alcohol, but instead are trying to minimize the harm they may encounter by encouraging them to drink less. These ideas would qualify as HRT approaches. Maybe you made some programming suggestions such as starting a sober-driver program or a free-ride service. These programs would not stop students from drinking, but they potentially would keep intoxicated students from driving and putting themselves and others in danger. So a sober-rider program also is an HRT approach to the risks of binge drinking. Remember HRT promotes reducing harm for individuals and those in their immediate communities, including family, friends, and neighbors.

Now specifically consider the ideas you developed that did not focus on completely ending the risky behavior of binge drinking, but instead tried to lessen the potential harms of drinking too much alcohol. What kinds of objections to these suggestions might you face from the college or university administration, parents, the media, or even students? What sort of criticisms could be levied against your ideas? Some people might argue that your ideas are not doing enough to stop drinking. Others might argue that you simply are making it easier for students to participate in heavy drinking by providing a way for them to get to and from drinking venues. Some might even say that you are condoning alcohol use by minors because you are not explicitly coming out against underage drinking. Keep these criticisms in mind as we more specifically discuss how HRT is being used in health communication initiatives and why it is such a controversial approach.

Harm Reduction Coalition

In the United States, the harm reduction approach most notably has been applied to illicit drug use and risky sexual behaviors. In 1993, the Harm Reduction Coalition (HRC) was formed to assist individuals and communities affected by drug use. Still operating today, the HRC "advances policies and programs that help people address the adverse effects of drug use, including overdose, HIV, hepatitis C, addiction, and incarceration" (www.harmreduction.org). Fundamental to the HRC's philosophy are the beliefs that social inequalities contribute to drug abuse and that all people have a right to health and well-being.

The HRC defines harm reduction as "a set of practical strategies that reduce negative consequences of drug use, incorporating a spectrum of strategies from

Ethics Touchstone

Refer to our preferred definition of health presented in Chapter 1, "Introducing Health as Communication Nexus," and answer the following questions.

Ideally, health is a state of complete physical, mental, and social well-being. However, health is more commonly experienced as the absence of physical, mental, or social disease or illness and should be considered a basic, universal human right.

◆ Does Harm Reduction Theory promote this definition of health? Why or why not?

◆ Do people who participate in harm reduction programs personify this definition of health?

◆ Based on what you learned about health communication ethics in Chapter 2, "Linking Health Communication with Ethics," do you think a harm reduction approach to health issues is ethical? Why or why not?

safer use, to managed use, to abstinence." Members of the HRC work with drug users "where they're at." Homeless heroin addicts may not be ready or even able to stop using drugs, but the HRC works with these addicts to make their drug use as safe as possible. Ultimately those who work with drug users hope that as time passes, addicts may reach a point where they can begin using less and possibly even quit using illicit drugs altogether. For example, members of the HRC may provide addicts with clean needles to reduce their risk of infections, such as HIV, which can be acquired by sharing used needles that contain infected blood. HRC workers also may counsel addicts by encouraging them to resist sharing needles with other drug users. These actions do not end addicts' drug use but help keep addicts and others interacting with them safer. In reaching out to illicit drug users, the HRC applies the following principles:

◆ Illicit drug use is a part of the world, and the HRC prefers to try to minimize the harmful effects of drug use rather than condemn or ignore drug users.

◆ Drug use encompasses a continuum of behaviors, from severe drug abuse to abstinence from drug use.

◆ Some ways of using drugs are safer than others.

◆ Quality of community and individual life is the ultimate measure of successful interventions, not necessarily abstinence.

◆ Services are provided in a nonjudgmental and noncoercive way.

◆ Drug users have a voice in creating programs and policies that affect them and their communities.

◆ Drug users are recognized as powerful change agents and are empowered to help themselves and others.

◆ The harm or danger of illicit drug use is not minimized or ignored.

Needle Exchange as Health Communication

In addition to the harmful effects of illicit drug use itself, intravenous drug users are at an increased risk for contracting HIV and hepatitis C due to the common practice within the drug-using culture of reusing and sharing needles. According to the HRC, approximately 1/3 of HIV cases in the United States are a result of injection drug use, and each year 15,000 people are infected with hepatitis C. One major initiative of the HRC and similar agencies is to provide drug users with unused, clean needles through *needle-exchange programs* which allow drug users to go to a safe site to exchange their used needles for new ones. Drug users then are able to inject with clean needles, which greatly reduces their risk of infection. Another benefit of needle-exchange programs is that used and dirty needles are properly disposed of, which eliminates the possibility of other users finding and using them, becoming infected, and possibly infecting others. It also reduces the possibility that non-drug users will become infected by accidentally coming in contact with improperly disposed of used needles.

Needle-exchange sites also are places where drug users can receive additional support and education. HRC workers are able to talk with drug users about their drug use and suggest safer behaviors. Users are offered support for reducing or possibly even stopping their drug use. HRC believes that any step toward decreasing drug use is a positive step and consequently advances programs that support any positive change including the use of methadone as a substitute for heroin.

Needle-exchange programs face tremendous opposition in the United States. Currently there is a federal ban on needle-exchange programs, which means that states cannot use any federal funds to support needle-exchange programs, leaving all funding responsibilities to state and local governments. Individual communities have resisted having needle-exchange or methadone clinics due to the belief that these programs attract dangerous drug users to the community. Many have opposed the programs because they believe they ultimately encourage drug use by not actively condemning it. Others are opposed to the idea of assisting drug addicts with their habit by providing drug paraphernalia and providing a place for drug

---

Needle-Exchange Programs

The purpose of needle-exchange programs is to provide intravenous drug users with clean needles as well as properly dispose of used needles. Based on the tenets of Harm Reduction Theory, needle exchange programs seek to limit the harm of intravenous drug use. Using dirty needles to inject drugs increases the risk of contracting a blood-borne infection such as HIV or hepatitis. Generally, a needle-exchange program site allows drug users to exchange used needles for new, clean needles free from fear of being arrested for drug use and often the service is free of charge. Oftentimes, needle-exchange sites also offer information on how to prevent the spread of disease. Needle-exchange programs are criticized as promoting drug use by making it easier and safer to use drugs.

users to inject. Programs also have been considered havens for those who are engaging in illegal activities.

As a specific example, despite having one of the highest HIV-infection rates in the United States, Washington DC banned the use of local monies to fund needle-exchange programs. When the ban was passed, the existing needle-exchange program in the area, the Whitman-Walker clinic, was forced to close. To fill the gap in services created by the closing of this clinic, PreventionWorks!, a program funded entirely by private donations, was implemented. PreventionWorks! operates as a mobile unit and travels around the Washington DC area to reach clients. Go to this book's Web site to see a photo of PreventionWorks.

Services provided by PreventionWorks! include one-for-one needle exchange for registered clients, HIV testing, drug treatment referrals, and overdose prevention. Although the program is small, with just two full-time employees, it has been very effective reaching out to the drug-using community. In 2007, PreventionWorks! worked with over 1,800 clients, distributed 178,891 sterile needles, properly disposed of 177,111 used syringes, had 10,499 conversations about drug treatment, and administered 97 HIV tests. Since the ban on needle-exchange programs was lifted in Washington DC, PreventionWorks! has received minimal funding from the government and continues to rely on the generosity of private donors.

The following article provides more information about the situation. What is your reaction to the perspectives presented in the following articles?

Dearth of District Needle Programs Challenges City*

Washington Business Journal—by Jonathan O'Connell
Staff Reporter

A federal spending bill last year lifted a ban that prevented the District from funding needle-exchange services, and a feeling of relief spread among the city's AIDS-fighting organizations. Yet there may be an absence of viable programs to seek some of the new money.

Dirty needles are blamed for about one-fifth of HIV infections in D.C., according to a November report from the D.C. Department of Health. Needle exchanges can reduce the spread of HIV by at least 30 percent and do not increase injection drug use, the National Institutes of Health says.

In needle exchanges, service providers hand out clean needles and collect and destroy potentially infected ones.

After the ban was lifted late last year, Mayor Adrian Fenty announced on Jan. 2 he was making $650,000 available for exchange programs.

However, the nine-year ban has left D.C. with only one needle-exchange operation. There is no indication yet that other nonprofits are prepared and able to start new ones.

Almost half the new money will go to expand the one exchange, **PreventionWorks!**, on 14th Street NW.

The city intends to split the remaining $350,000 among no more than four providers, which should already be offering services to drug users and homeless people, according to a Jan. 25 request for applications.

"We're specifically looking at organizations with existing social and medical infrastructure," said Health Department spokeswoman LaSHon Seastrunk, not "for someone to build new infrastructure altogether."

Conversations with AIDS activists unveiled no obvious candidates. A key financial backer of HIV prevention—and of the ban's removal—is worried whether the right service provider is out there now that the money has finally become available.

"I'm hoping there are going to be [other organizations that can establish programs], but these aren't typically easy to start up and do correctly," said Nancy Mahon, executive director of the New York-based MAC AIDS Fund.

The charity, funded by MAC Cosmetics, gave $100,000 to PreventionWorks! to buy a second recreation vehicle for the exchanges. It also gave $100,000 to help fight the ban.

Even the most obvious candidate might not be interested. Whitman-Walker Clinic, which provides more HIV-AIDS services than any other local organization and operated a needle exchange before the funding ban, is noncommittal about restarting the program, said spokesman Chip Lewis.

Another HIV service provider, The Washington Free Clinic, closed in June after 39 years of service and moved its staff to Whitman-Walker.

Ken Vail, executive director of PreventionWorks!, said he isn't sure which nonprofits might apply.

"I think what [the city] wants to do is incorporate syringe exchange programs into existing services, but it will be interesting to see how many applicants they get," Vail said.

The District Health Department reported about 12,500 residents were known to be living with HIV-AIDS in 2006, more than nine times the national average.

The deadline for applications for city money for a needle exchange is Feb. 29.

Alone in a City's AIDS Battle, Hoping for Backup*

The nation's capital is the only city in the country barred by federal law from using local tax money to finance needle exchange programs. It is also the city with the fastest-growing number of new AIDS cases.

These two facts keep Ron Daniels on the move, tirelessly driving his rickety Winnebago from drug corner to drug corner across the rougher parts of this city, counseling the addicted and swapping clean needles for dirty ones.

Faced with an AIDS problem growing here at a rate 10 times the national average, Mr. Daniels, the director of PreventionWorks!, the city's only needle exchange program, is armed with a shoestring budget of $385,000 in private donations, a small fraction of what programs in other major cities receive in state and local money.

Since Washington is not part of a state, Congress controls the city's local system of government, and for nearly a decade members of the House, citing concerns about worsening drug abuse, have inserted language in the bill approving the city's budget to prohibit financing such programs.

That may soon change.

"This city's situation is totally improper," said Representative José E. Serrano, Democrat of New York and chairman of the subcommittee responsible for the District of Columbia appropriations bill, "It's politically obscene to have Congress tell the District of Columbia that it can't use local funds for something like needle exchange programs, which have been proven to have a major effect on fighting a deadly disease."

Calling the matter both a public health concern and a basic political right of home rule, Mr. Serrano said he planned to make it a priority to remove the language that prevents the city from financing such programs. The city's mayor, Adrian M. Fenty, has said he will provide city money as soon as Congress takes such action.

Washington was among the first cities nationally to create an AIDS monitoring office after the virus first appeared in the United States more than 20 years ago. But it has slid backward in its fight against the disease, which is commonly spread by intravenous drug users sharing needles.

"For every person I help, there're seven more I can't reach," said Mr. Daniels, 49, who describes his program as providing a thin wall between the city's drug and AIDS epidemics. "But I'd be reaching a lot more if my hands weren't tied."

Critics of needle exchange programs argue that rather than reducing the suffering of drug users and preventing them from spreading diseases, the programs foster further drug use.

"We need to fight drugs, not show people that they can be used in a safe manner," Representative Sam Graves, Republican of Missouri, said last year during House floor debate about drug policy.

Mr. Daniels said fighting drugs was exactly what his program did.

"The needle is just an enticement, really," he said, looking through the screen door of his van at a line of about 10 people who gathered within minutes of his arrival at a corner on the city's grittier Northeast side.

He said his program, which reaches about one third of Washington's estimated 9,700 intravenous drug users, relied on clean syringes to attract users so he and his staff of four could counsel them about drug rehabilitation and testing for HIV, the virus that causes AIDS.

"Want ointment? Alcohol pads?" asks Mr. Daniels, running down his checklist as he prepares supplies for a heroin addict who counts a week's worth of used needles, dropping them in a plastic bucket. "Need food? Condoms?" Mr. Daniels asks.

One by one, they file in: a security guard sick of hiding his addiction from his wife, a carpenter looking for methadone, a prostitute with a bad case of the shakes. Many are rail thin. Most have sores.

Teefari Mallory sits at the laptop entering data on each user. Three other staff members go into the neighborhood to talk about safe sex and AIDS prevention.

"Give me 5 apples, 10 blues and 2 groins," says a man named Bernard after dropping 17 used syringes, a week's supply, into the bucket.

"Apples" and "blues" are syringes used by addicts who have been taking drugs for shorter periods. "Groins are what you use when all your other veins collapse," said Mr. Daniels, who used to be known on the streets as Boo when he sold drugs and needed four hits of heroin a day to get by.

In Washington, with just over half a million residents, one in 20 are HIV positive.

And the number of people with AIDS is growing. The city's rate of new AIDS cases was 128.4 per 100,000 people in 2005, compared with a national average of 13.7 per 100,000, according to the most recent data available from the Federal Centers for Disease Control and Prevention, which compares the district with states rather than other cities.

What's the Point?*

President Bush tries to revive a ban on needle-exchange programs in the District.

President Bush's 2009 budget proposal is the resurrection of a provision, dumped by Congress last year, that prohibits the District from using its own money to fund needle-exchange programs. This is unconscionable, especially since intravenous drug use is helping to fuel the HIV-AIDS crisis gripping the city. That Mr. Bush would do this in a budget that will take effect after he's left Washington strikes us as gratuitous and shortsighted.

The restriction was attached to the District's appropriations bill by Rep. Todd Tiahrt (R-Kan.) in 1998. Mr Bush has supported the prohibition every year of his administration. Despite plenty of evidence to the contrary, he and Mr. Taihrt are part of the head-in-the-sand crowd that believes swapping addicts' dirty needles for clean ones encourages drug use. Never mind that there are more than 210 syringe-swapping programs in 36 states. Every attempt to excise the harmful provision failed—until last year. Del. Eleanor Holmes Norton (D-D.C.) and Rep. José E.

Serrano (D-N.Y.) used the new democratic majority in the House to finally strip it from legislation.

Mayor Adrian M. Fenty (D) wasted no time once the District's federal appropriation was finalized late last year. He immediately pumped $300,000 into PreventionWorks!, the city's only needle-exchange program, to expand its services. He hopes to fund four more organizations that do similar work. The deadline to answer a request for proposals is Feb. 29. The awards will be made in April. The help can't come soon enough. Fourteen percent of District residents who became HIV-positive did so through intravenous drug use. Overall, AIDS is devastating the city, with 128.4 AIDS cases per 100,000 people. This is higher than the rates in Baltimore, New York and Philadelphia.

Mr. Bush's attempt to reinstate the ban on local funding of needle-exchange programs will not affect Mr. Fenty's current plans. Still, he will have to fight anew to ensure that the prohibition does not make it into the final appropriation that will go into effect next year. But we take heart in one thing: While the president can make budget proposals, Congress will actually write the bill. Congress would do the District a good deed and potentially save lives if it ignored Mr. Bush on this issue.

Programs such as PreventionWorks! are actively operating in over 30 states to help illicit drug users address their drug habits and reduce the number of HIV cases and other infections caused by sharing used needles. Proponents of these programs adamantly insist they do not encourage or support drug use and often are more successful in eliminating drug use than other measures such as incarceration. They also argue the harm reduction approach is more effective because it works to improve the entire community not just individual illicit drug users.

Expanding HRT to Other Health Issues

Mattson (2000) argued for applying the principles of Harm Reduction Theory to other health issues besides drug use. She suggested that HRT is a more realistic approach to unhealthy behaviors because it emphasizes reducing harm rather than totally eliminating unhealthy behaviors. Further, harm reduction occurs primarily through health communication, so incorporating the principles of HRT may positively influence health communication efforts. Consistent with the principles outlined by the Harm Reduction Coalition and presented previously, Mattson adapted the traditional principles of HRT to include:

◆ All individuals deserve to be treated with respect, dignity, and compassion.
◆ Inevitably, most people will practice some unhealthy behavior.
◆ Unhealthy behavior is not necessarily the problem but likely is a symptom or a coping mechanism for dealing with other complex issues (e.g., low self-esteem, abuse, relationship problems).
◆ Unhealthy behaviors can result in harm to individuals who practice them, to their loved ones, and to their communities.
◆ Harm from unhealthy behavior can result in personal, social, political, and economic hardship.
◆ Individuals can make reasonable, informed choices to reduce harm to themselves and others.

- Health care providers and health communication practitioners need to recognize, through training and self-reflexivity, that they may have personal biases and make judgments about individuals who practice unhealthy behaviors. After recognizing these biases, they need to consciously alleviate their impact on counseling and assisting individuals.

- Prevention strategies to address unhealthy behaviors must be relevant to and practical for individuals.

- The emphases of prevention strategies to address unhealthy behaviors need to be on attainable, short-term, personalized results over idealistic and often impractical long-term goals.

- Individuals need to be offered a hierarchy of choices—not just abstinence from unhealthy behaviors—in their quest for healthier behaviors.

- Most importantly, the agenda for practicing healthy behaviors belongs to the individuals. Health care providers and health communication practitioners facilitate dialogue about healthier behaviors rather than thrusting a predetermined health behavior agenda upon individuals.

To support her argument for applying HRT to other health issues, Mattson used HIV test counseling as a case study. The counseling that accompanies HIV testing can be an important prevention tool for encouraging individuals to practice safer sex to avoid contracting HIV/AIDS. If HIV test counseling is performed in a way that is consistent with HRT, it encourages agency-promoting and empowering dialogue. From the case of HIV test counseling, Mattson recommended that HRT be used as a health communication heuristic and a practical health communication training and evaluation strategy.

ETHICAL DILEMMA ◆ What Would You Do?

A recent National Public Radio news story reported on the request by some veterans with post-traumatic stress disorder (PTSD) to have medical marijuana prescribed to them by physicians working for the Veterans Administration (VA). Currently medical marijuana is illegal under federal law, so the VA cannot prescribe it to veterans. Considering this issue from a Harm Reduction Theory perspective, answer the following questions:

- If you were a veteran suffering from PTSD, would you join those working to change the current VA policy on medical marijuana? Why or why not?

- If you were a physician at the VA treating patients with PTSD, would you help your patients get medical marijuana elsewhere? Why or why not?

- If you were the family member or a friend of a veteran suffering from PTSD, would you assist that veteran to acquire marijuana to ease the symptoms of PTSD? Why or why not?

Now that we covered definitions of theory, the role of theory in health communication, and four theories that are situated within health communication, including several examples to illustrate these theories in action, we present a service-learning application about applying theory to health communication practice while linking the service-learning project to course content.

SERVICE-LEARNING APPLICATION

Extending Course into Real-World Health Issue

One of the main reasons to learn theories is to apply the ideas and concepts of those theories to practical problems. Service-learning projects provide an excellent way to bridge the gap between learning and applying theories. There are two primary benefits of applying theories within service-learning projects. One benefit is that you gain valuable experience using theory and applying theory. A second benefit is that applying theory to service-learning projects often makes those projects more effective.

However, to realize these benefits, we need to emphasize one of the key components of any service-learning project—link to curriculum. *Link to curriculum* means that the service-learning project is purposely integrated into the course by the instructor to meet the learning goals of the course and the course helps students transfer knowledge and skills from one setting to another (Corporation for National & Community Service, 2010). So if two of the learning goals of a course are to learn relevant theories and understand how those theories apply to community health issues, a service-learning project could be designed in which students partner with a community health organization, together identify a community health issue, and then incorporate theory learned in the course to address that health issue.

Let's consider an example of how an introductory health communication theory course that had these same two learning goals outlined in the syllabus incorporated a service-learning project to apply theoretical principles to a real-world health issue. For this example, let's again turn to the Motorcycle Safety at Purdue (MS@P) campaign (www.ItInvolvesYou.com) and how theory was used to conceptualize and plan the details of the campaign from the very beginning. The first step the students took to address the relevance of theory for MS@P was to research what the goals of a motorcycle safety campaign should be for the target audience of motorcyclists. After interviewing motorcyclists and reviewing the literature and statistics about motorcycle safety, some goals for reaching motorcyclists emerged, including:

◆ Decrease the number of individuals who choose to start riding motorcycles.

◆ Encourage people to stop riding motorcycles.

◆ Raise awareness about the risks of riding a motorcycle.

◆ Encourage motorcyclists to take a rider education course.

◆ Encourage motorcyclists to become properly licensed.

◆ Increase the use of protective gear while riding a motorcycle, including boots, pants, jacket, helmet, and gloves.

◆ Increase the knowledge of drivers of other vehicles as to how to safely share the road with motorcycles.

As you can see, the goals covered a wide spectrum of outcomes, everything from completely abstaining from motorcycle riding to taking the small step of wearing gloves while riding to protect the hands. As members of the health communication theory course debated what the focus of the motorcycle safety campaign for the target audience of motorcyclists should be, the idea of using a harm reduction approach to design the campaign was considered along with other theories. After learning the principles of Harm Reduction Theory in class, the students wondered if this theory could be used to guide MS@P. After all, motorcycle safety is a health issue, and rather than promote abstinence from riding, the students wondered if an HRT approach to the campaign would be more appropriate and effective. Although some class members strongly believed that any form of motorcycle riding was extremely dangerous, all the students recognized that persuading those entrenched in motorcycle riding and the motorcycle culture to stop riding would be extremely difficult if not impossible. The students also believed that the issue of whether or not to ride a motorcycle was one of personal choice and preferred to respect that choice. After much discussion, the students decided to adopt an HRT approach to MS@P.

In taking a harm reduction approach, the campaign team determined that the best strategy would be to follow a key principle of the theory and meet motorcyclists "where they are at." This meant that the campaign would focus on providing information and services in a nonjudgmental way to all types of motorcyclists and those considering taking up motorcycle riding. If motorcyclists were committed to riding, they would not be asked to stop riding, but they would be encouraged to adopt safer riding habits such as wearing a helmet or always obeying the speed limit while riding. Even small measures such as these would make their motorcycle riding safer. The students also worked to establish relationships with those within the motorcycle community, believing that change would most likely occur from inside the target audience and their community.

As plans and messages for MS@P were developed, the student campaign team settled on the idea of offering a hierarchy of choices that motorcyclists and potential motorcyclists could make. These choices ranged from deciding not to ride a motorcycle to taking a rider safety course to wearing some versus all motorcycle safety gear. Because of its emphasis on HRT, one of the major goals of the campaign became educating the motorcyclist audience so they could make choices based on solid, factual information. The campaign team also tried to make safely riding motorcycles easier by offering motorcyclists training courses on campus and at a reduced cost in addition to providing information for enrolling in other local courses.

As students worked to make the motorcycle riding community safer, they had to strike a careful balance between meeting motorcyclists where they were at and engaging in activities that may seem to be promoting risky motorcycle riding. For example, the student campaign team was approached by motorcycle rider organizations about the possibility of sponsoring motorcycle rides to raise awareness about motorcycle safety. The campaign team felt that even if wearing all motorcycle safety gear was promoted at such an event, the lack of a helmet law in the state might encourage some to ride without a helmet which would strongly contradict and be inconsistent with the campaign's overall safety goals. In addition, the fear and risk of a motorcycle crash during a motorcycle ride sponsored by the MS@P campaign was too much of a concern to be ignored.

As this example illustrates, the principles of HRT served as a guide while planning the MS@P service-learning project. When team members struggled to decide what messages they wanted to send or what events should be offered, they also referred back to the theory to see what it would suggest. If a message or activity was not consistent with the ideas of harm reduction it was not included in the campaign.

Now that you know how theory played an integral role in a service-learning project, consider the following tips as you work to implement theories into your own service-learning or other health communication projects.

◆ Identify aspects of your project in which theory could be applied. Not every aspect of a project may need a theory, but activities involving message design and implementation are excellent opportunities to apply your theoretical knowledge.

◆ Decide on a theory or theories that you would like to use during the beginning stages of your project. This will allow you to integrate that theory or theoretical ideas into all phases of your project.

◆ Be sure to address all components of the theory or model. For example, if you chose to use the tenets of the Extended Parallel Process Model (EPPM) to guide message design, messages must address both severity and efficacy.

◆ Always check with your intended audience as you are identifying the various components of a model. For example, do not assume that you know what the perceived barriers to an intervention are. You must go to the target audience and ask.

◆ Continually go back to the theory or model throughout your project to be sure that you are on track.

◆ Look to examples of other projects that have used theories. We can always learn from the successes and mistakes of other projects.

◆ You may want to use *Theory at a Glance,* available from the National Institutes of Health at www.cancer.gov/.

Careers in health communication offer abundant opportunities to use theories in planning, implementing, and evaluating communication strategies and initiatives. Also, keep in mind that you may need to employ more than one theory in your health communication efforts especially in large-scale campaigns.

Chapter Summary

In this chapter, we discussed the role of theory in health communication and highlighted four theories that are uniquely situated within health communication philosophies and practices. First, we offered informal and formal definitions of theory and established our preference for a definition that is broad and may allow for a wider understanding of health. Next, we discussed the benefits of incorporating theory into health communication interactions and programs. Third, we described four prominent theories in health communication by explaining the basic concepts of each theory and providing examples to illustrate how these theories were incorporated into health communication projects and practices. We concluded the chapter with a service-learning application about how a theory was used in the design and implementation of a health communication campaign which also taught students to link theories with course content.

References

Babrow, A., & Mattson, M. (2003). Theorizing about health communication. In T. Thompson, A. Dorsey, K. I. Miller, & R. Parrot (Eds.), *Handbook of health communication* (pp. 35–61). Mahwah, NJ: Lawrence Erlbaum.

Becker, M. H. (1974). The health belief model and personal health behavior. *Health Education Monographs, 2*, 236–473.

Becker, M. H. (1990). Theoretical models of adherence and strategies for improving adherence. In S. Shumaker, E. B. Schron, & J. K. Ockerene (Eds.), *The handbook of health behavior change*. New York: Springer.

Becker, M. H., Drachman, R. H., & Kirscht, J. P. (1974). A new approach to explaining sick-role behavior in low-income populations. *American Journal of Public Health, 64*, 205–216.

Bertrand, J. T. (2004). Diffusion of innovations and HIV/AIDS. *Journal of Health Communication, 9*, 113–121.

Corman, S. R. (1995). That works fine in theory but . . . In S. R. Corman, S. P. Banks, C. R. Bantz, & M. E. Mayer (Eds.), *Foundations of organizational communication: A reader* (pp. 3–10). New York: Longman.

Corporation for National & Community Service (2010). Learn and Serve America's National Service-Learning Clearinghouse. Retrieved January 12, 2010, from www.servicelearning.org.

Donohew, L., & Palmgreen, P. (1981). Conceptualization and theory building. In G. H. Stempel, & B. H. Westley (Eds.), *Research methods in mass communication* (pp. 29–47). Englewood Cliffs, NJ: Prentice-Hall.

Donohew, L., & Palmgreen, P. (2003). Constructing theory. In G. H. Stempel, D. H. Weaver, & G. C. Wilholt (Eds.), *Mass communication theory and research* (pp. 111–128). New York: Allyn & Bacon.

Hubbell, A. P. (2006). Mexican American women in rural areas and barriers to their ability to enact protective behaviors against behavior cancer. *Health Communication, 2*, 35–44.

Janz, N., & Becker, M. (1984). The health belief model: A decade later. *Health Education Quarterly, 11*, 1–47.

Kerlinger, F. N., & Lee, H. B. (2000). *Foundations of behavioral research* (4th ed.). Fort Worth, TX: Harcourt.

Kirscht, J. P. (1974). The health belief model and illness behavior. *Health Education Monographs, 2*, 2387–2408.

Kline, K. I. (2000). Breast self-examination pamphlets: A content analysis grounded in fear appeal research. *Health Communication, 12*, 1–21.

Logan, D. E., & Marlatt, G. A. (2010). Harm reduction therapy: A practice-friendly review of research. *Journal of Clinical Psychology, 66*, 201–214.

Marlatt, G. A. (1998). *Harm reduction: Pragmatic strategies for managing high-risk behaviors.* New York: Guilford Press.

Mattson, M. (1999). Reconceptualizing communication cues to action in the health belief model: HIV test counseling. *Communication Monographs, 66*, 240–265.

Mattson, M. (2000). Empowerment through agency-promoting dialogue: An explicit application of harm reduction theory to reframe HIV test counseling. *Journal of Health Communication, 5*, 333–347.

Moscato, S., Black, D. R., Blue, C. L., Mattson, M., Galer-Unti, R. A., & Coster, D. C. (2001). Evaluating a fear appeal message to reduce alcohol use among "Greeks." *American Journal of Health Behavior, 25*, 481–491.

Murphy, E. (2004). Diffusion of innovations: Family planning in developing countries. *Journal of Health Communication, 9*(Supplement 1), 123–129.

Ries, L. A. G., Melbert, D., Krapcho, M., Stinchcomb, D. G., Howlader, N., Horner, M. J., et al. (2007). *SEER Cancer Statistics Review, 1975–2005*. Bethesda, MD: National Cancer Institute.

Roberto, A. J., Meyer, G., Johnson, A. J., & Atkin, C. K. (2000). Using the extended parallel process model to prevent firearm injury and death: Field experiment results of a video-based intervention. *Journal of Communication, 50*, 157–175.

Roberto, A. J., Zimmerman, R. S., Carlyle, K. E., Abner, E. L., Cupp, P. K., & Hansen, G. L. (2007). The effects of a computer-based pregnancy, STD, and HIV prevention intervention: A nine-school trial. *Health Communication, 21*, 115–124.

Rose, M. (1996). Effect of an AIDS education program for older adults. *Journal of Community Health Nursing, 13*, 141.

Rosenstock, I. M. (1966). Why people use health services. *Milbank Memorial Fund Quarterly, 3*, 94–127.

Rosenstock, I. M. (1974a). Historical origins of the health belief model. *Health Education Monographs, 2*, 328–335.

Rosenstock, I. M. (1974b). The health belief model: Origins and correlates. *Health Education Monographs, 2*, 336–353.

Rosenstock, I. M., Strecher, V. J., & Becker, M. H. (1988). Social learning theory and the health belief model. *Health Education & Behavior, 15*, 175–183.

Simsekoglu, O., & Lajunen, T. (2008). Social psychology of seat belt use: A comparison of theory of planned behavior and health belief model. *Traffic Psychology and Behaviour, 11*, 181–191.

Smith, S. W., Rosenman, K. D., Kotowski, M. R., Glazer, E., McFeters, C., Keesecker, N. M., et al. (2008). Using the EPPM to create and evaluate the effectiveness of brochures to increase the use of hearing protection in farmers and landscape workers. *Journal of Applied Communication Research, 36*, 200–218.

Szilagyi, P., Rodewald, L., Savageau, J., Yoos, L., & Doane, C. (1992). Improving influenza vaccination rates in children with asthma: A test of a computerized reminder system and an analysis of factors predicting vaccination compliance. *Pediatrics, 90*, 871–875.

Webb, G. R., Sanson-Fisher, R. W., & Bowman, J. A. (1988). Psychosocial factors related to parental restraint of pre-school children in motor vehicles. *Accident Analysis & Prevention, 20*, 87–94.

Witte, K. (1992). Putting the fear back into fear appeals: The extended parallel process model. *Communication Monographs, 59*, 329–349.

Witte, K. (1994). Fear control and danger control: A test of the extended parallel process model (EPPM). *Communication Monographs, 61*, 113–134.

Wray, R. J., Jupka, K., & Ludwig-Bell, C. (2005). A community-wide media campaign to promote walking in a Missouri town. *Preventing Chronic Disease, 2*(4). Retrieved July 14, 2008, from http://www.cdc.gov/pcd/issues/2005/oct/05_0010.htm.

Patient Interaction

Chapter Learning Objectives

◆ Review history of patient/health care provider interaction
◆ Discuss micro-level and macro-level influences on patient/health care provider interaction
◆ Understand patient rights of informed decision making and informed consent
◆ Recognize what constitutes patient-centered communication and care
◆ Identify skills patients need to fully participate in patient-centered communication
◆ Compare patient-centered communication with traditional approaches to health care interaction
◆ Explore developing conversation starters for health-related interactions

Chapter Preview

In this chapter we consider the complex dynamics of patient/health care provider interaction from the patient's perspective. We begin by defining our meaning and use of the term patient. This is followed by reviewing an abridged history of the health care provider/patient relationship which formed the basis for later study of more general patient/health care provider interaction. Next we address several micro-level and macro-level influences on patient/health care provider relationships. This is followed by an explanation of the principles of informed decision making and informed consent, so that these important aspects are not ignored or misunderstood in your patient/health care provider interactions. The intricacies of patient-centered communication, the current model for patient/health care provider interaction, are discussed next. Following this model, the skills patients need to have effective interactions with their health care providers are outlined. Ultimately, we acknowledge and explain some patients' preference for a traditional, more paternalistic approach to health care communication. We conclude the chapter by emphasizing how to engage participants in meaningful and personally relevant service-learning by developing conversation starters to instigate health communication about health issues.

Questions about Starting NuvaRing®

☐ How to Use NuvaRing®

☐ When can I start using NuvaRing®?

☐ How do I insert and remove NuvaRing®?

☐ Can NuvaRing® fall out or get lost inside me?

NuvaRing® and Sexual Intercourse

☐ Do I need to remove NuvaRing® before sexual intercourse?

☐ Will my partner or I be able to feel NuvaRing®?

How Will NuvaRing® Affect Your Body?

☐ Will NuvaRing® affect my weight?

☐ How will NuvaRing® affect my periods?

NuvaRing® and Other Methods of Birth Control

☐ What makes NuvaRing® different from other types of birth control?

☐ Is NuvaRing® right for me?

Notes:

This conversation starter is designed by the manufacturer (www.nuvaring.com) to help women talk with their physicians about the possibility of using the NuvaRing® as a form of birth control. NuvaRing® is a form of hormonal birth control. Because of the personal nature of birth control, a woman may be uncomfortable talking with her physician about her birth control options. However, even if a woman is comfortable having this discussion, she may not know what questions to ask in order to make an informed decision. This is just one example of an attempt to empower patients as they talk with their health care providers.

Patient Defined

Although we refer to patients in the title and throughout this chapter, we broadly define the term *patient* across this book as anyone who receives health-related services. So, for our purposes, in addition to patients who receive medical services, we also may be referring to audience members of nonmedical services, such as clients of public health services, target audience members of health campaigns, and individuals who surf the internet for health information. Now that we've clarified our meaning and use of the term patient, let's consider an abridged history of the relationship between health care providers and patients.

Abridged History of the Health Care Provider/Patient Relationship

To understand how patients and health care providers predominantly interact, specifically in the United States, it is helpful to know how this unique relationship developed and evolved over time. Historical records and artifacts indicate that medicine, in some form or another, has been practiced since the prehistoric era. Early health practitioners, sometimes referred to as medicine men or shamans, used a combination of herbs, minerals, animal parts, and spiritual practices to heal patients. Hippocrates, known as the father of modern medicine and for whom the Hippocratic Oath is named, argued for a more rational approach to medicine than his predecessors. The Greeks of Hippocrates' time believed that the body was composed of four humors: black bile, yellow bile, phlegm, and blood. Illness was believed to be the result of an imbalance in the humors, so physicians' goals were to bring those elements into balance (Nutton, 2004). With no medical tests, physicians or medicine men had to rely primarily on patients' explanations of their symptoms to determine the problem.

As the study of medicine progressed, understanding of the human body, disease, and illness remained relatively simple. Medical treatments were based primarily on home and herbal remedies. Physicians were very limited in what they could offer patients, although there is evidence that basic surgeries were performed by ancient tribes. The majority of physicians made house calls and met with patients in the privacy and comfort of patients' homes. This system of practice meant that physicians knew patients and their families on a personal level.

It was not until the late 1800s that a major shift occurred in the Western Hemisphere regarding roles of health care providers and patients. In 1880, Robert Koch discovered the link between bacteria and illness, which led to the discovery of antibiotics in the early 1900s. This was the beginning of the biomedical era, when diagnoses could be made using tests and other scientific innovations. It also was during the 1800s that physicians began using instruments such as stethoscopes and thermometers in their examinations. These instruments provided physicians information about patients' bodies that previously patients could not provide to their physicians. This situation left patients in a fairly passive role within health care encounters as physicians relied on their instruments rather than patients' accounts of symptoms.

Another key change in the health care system that strongly influenced patient/health care provider interaction was the spread of hospitals. Up until the 1930s, physicians primarily made house calls. After the 1930s, hospitals were built across the country and health care moved out of the home and into medical buildings. A specific example of this is the process of childbirth in the United States. In 1900, less than 5% of women gave birth in hospitals; 95% gave birth at home and often were tended to by a midwife. By the 1920s, nearly 40% of women gave birth in hospitals, and by 1950 that number was up to 88%. Today, less than 1% of women give birth at home. Through time, childbirth became a medical condition that required medical expertise and intervention. This shift into hospitals and away from homes means that women deliver their babies in more unfamiliar environments, and their birthing experiences are controlled by the policies and regulations of where they deliver and the medical personnel who are assisting them. Generally, movement of patient and health care provider interactions into medical institutions gives patients less control over these encounters, as they no longer are seen in their own space. Instead of meeting with health care providers at home, patients are seen in examining rooms, asked to disrobe, and often are asked to lie on an examining table.

Brief Chronology of Health Care Provider/Patient Relationship

(adapted from Gonzalez-Crussi, 2007; Nutton, 2004)

- Prehistoric Era
  - Medicine men and shamans used herbs, minerals, animal parts, and spiritual practices to heal patients
- Hippocrates (460–377 BC)
  - Argued for more rational approach to medicine
  - Imbalance of four humors caused illness
  - Patients' explanations key to diagnoses
- Pre-1800s
  - Simple understanding of human body and treatment
  - House calls
- Late 1800s
  - Shift in emphases from patients and patients' experiences to medicine and health care providers
  - 1880: Koch discovered link between bacteria and illness
  - Physicians began using instruments
- Biomedical Era—Early 1900s
  - Discovery of antibiotics
  - Building of hospitals and medical institutions—movement away from house calls
  - Formalized medical training
- Contemporary Health Care
  - Emphasis on medical specialties
  - Health care teams
  - Patient-centered care

Also during this historical period, medical training became more formalized, and advanced degrees and licensure were required, offering health care providers greater status and prestige. In other words, during this time period there was a shift in medicine from a personal focus on patients in their own environments to the biomedical model of illness and medical care offered in institutions (Zook, 1994).

This brings us to the current time in medicine and its corresponding health care climate. As research and scientific knowledge have advanced, so too has the field of medicine and health care. Today there are numerous medical specialties, including oncology, radiology, internists, physical therapists, occupational therapists, and orthopedics. Medical costs are skyrocketing and health care costs and health care insurance are challenging issues that almost everyone must address. These historical changes in medicine also have created pressures and challenges for patient/health care provider communication. Now that we basically understand how the patient/physician relationship evolved over time, let's consider what typically influences and occurs during health care interactions.

Micro-Level and Macro-Level Influences on Health Care Interactions

A basic theme repeated throughout this book is that health and health communication are complex concepts. Additionally, perceptions of what constitutes health and effective health communication are affected by both micro-level and macro-level influences in the social context. *Micro-level influences* on patient/health care provider interaction are localized influences within the immediate context of the interaction. *Macro-level influences* on patient/health care provider interaction are larger-scale or broader influences outside the immediate context of the interaction. Micro-level and macro-level influences on patient/health care provider communication include:

◆ Patient/health care provider goals
◆ Interpersonal influences
◆ Cultural influences
◆ Power dynamics
◆ Organizational influences
◆ Media influences
◆ Health literacy

Based on our definition of micro-level and macro-level influences on patient/health care provider interaction, which of the influences listed would you consider micro-level and which would you consider macro-level? If you responded that patient/health care provider goals, interpersonal influences, cultural influences, and power dynamics are the micro-level influences, you are correct! We'll discuss each of these influences, and power dynamics and then move on to discuss the macro-level influences on patient/health care provider interaction. We begin with the micro-level influences because from most patients' perspectives, these more localized influences likely are of more immediate concern to their interactions with health care providers.

Micro-Level Influences on Health Care Interactions

As a reminder, micro-level influences are localized influences within the immediate health care provider/patient context that affect the interaction.

Patient/Health Care Provider Goals

In any health care encounter, patients and health care providers have a set of three goals that influence their interaction (Beck, 1997) including:

- Relational goals
- Educational goals
- Medical goals

The first type of goals, *relational goals*, pertain to how individuals in health care interactions wish to be perceived and how individuals position themselves within the interaction. Relational goals are related to Goffman's (1963) and Brown and Levinson's (1978) concept of *facework*, which posits that we adjust our behavior and communication in order to present our best self or our best face. For a more detailed discussion of facework, refer to Chapter 6, "Linking Health Communication with Social Support."

During medical interactions with patients, health care providers may have the relational goals of appearing to their patients as both expert and trustworthy. Health care providers' relational goals may compete with the relational goals of patients. In order to meet their relational goals, health care providers may want to use technical terms to establish expertise, but the technical language may be off-putting to patients and interfere with development of rapport and trust. For their part, patients may have the relational goals of wanting to appear knowledgeable and responsible to the health care providers treating them. Whatever individual relationship goals health care providers and patients have in medical encounters, those goals influence how the parties interact with each other.

The second type of goals, *educational goals*, involve exchange of information. Both patients and health care providers have educational goals related to sharing and seeking information. Often an educational goal for patients is uncertainty reduction (Babrow, Kasch, & Ford, 1998). Patients may not know what is causing their symptoms and they are looking to health care providers for answers or diagnoses. To accomplish uncertainty reduction, patients must provide information regarding their symptoms, medical history, and lifestyle to their health care providers in the hopes of gaining accurate diagnoses and treatment options.

Health care providers also have educational goals. They attempt to accomplish these goals by obtaining information from patients that assists them in determining diagnoses and/or treatment plans. When providing information about diagnoses and treatment plans to patients, a major goal of health care providers is patient compliance. *Patient compliance* is the extent to which patients follow health care providers' directives concerning preventive behaviors, medications, and other treatments (DiMatteo, 1994; DiMatteo & Lepper, 1998; Vermeire, Hearnshaw, VanRoyen, & Denekens, 2001). Examples of patient compliance behaviors are a patient completing a regimen of antibiotics or refraining from smoking based on a physician's advice.

The third type of goals, *medical goals*, are goals that patients and health care providers have for outcomes related to patients' health problems. Patients' medical goals usually involve feeling better or being diagnosed and cured of their current illnesses or health problems. Health care providers' medical goals usually involve attempting to understand and diagnose what is troubling their patients and to prescribe effective treatments. Difficulties may arise when patients' medical goals conflict with health care providers' medical goals. A current example of this is parents desiring antibiotics for their children. Although antibiotics have no benefits in treating the common cold or other viruses, some parents believe that antibiotics are needed even when physicians diagnose their children with colds. During medical visits, parents may so strongly desire a prescription that they either alter their communication to obtain an antibiotic or feel dissatisfied if an antibiotic is not prescribed (Mangione-Smith et al., 2004; Stivers, 2002).

Difficulties may arise when any of the goals of the patient and health care provider conflict or when the parties inaccurately assume they share similar goals. Contemplate, for example, a patient who is diagnosed with stage IV cancer. The patient's goal may be to maintain as high a quality of life as possible by enjoying his remaining time before death. On the other hand, his oncologist, physician with a specialty in cancer, may have the goal of using medical treatments to offer the patient as much time as possible before death. This extra time could be obtained through aggressive treatment, but treatment that also would have serious side effects. In this case, the patient and oncologist may both assume that the other has similar goals and will proceed to act as if this is so. These mistaken assumptions can lead to frustration and dissatisfaction on both sides as the patient resists treatments and is annoyed by the oncologist offering those treatments while the oncologist doesn't understand the reasons for the patient's resistance. This example illustrates why goals need to be openly discussed in order for patients and health care providers to align their goals and find treatment plans that are mutually acceptable.

Now that we reviewed the types of goals that patients and health care providers bring to health care interactions, let's consider the role of interpersonal influences on how health care interactions progress.

Interpersonal Influences

Another set of micro-level influences that affects patient/health care provider interaction consists of interpersonal influences. *Interpersonal influences* are defined as attributes of the participating individuals that affect the interaction or conversation. Research in the field of health communication has examined a variety of interpersonal influences on patient/health care provider interaction. Patient attributes that influence this interaction include:

◆ Education level—those with higher education levels tend to be more active in medical conversations (Florin, Ehrenberg, & Ehnfors, 2008).

- ◆ Age—older adults tend to be more passive and treat medical personnel as authorities (Degner & Sloan, 1992).
- ◆ Health status—sicker individuals tend to be more passive and less satisfied with care (Shadmi et al., 2006).
- ◆ Gender—women tend to talk more about emotions and feelings, men tend to be focused on the specific health issue (Bertakis, 2009).
- ◆ Socioeconomic status (SES)—those with a lower SES tend to be more passive during medical encounters (Manderbacka, 2005).

Cultural Influences

There are many cultural influences that shape patient/health care provider interactions. *Cultural influences* are broadly defined as patterns of thinking, beliefs, values, behavioral norms, linguistic expression, and styles of communication possessed by a group of people and transmitted to others in the group over time (Jandt, 2009). Culture often is equated with race or ethnicity and although racial and ethnic groups can and do have distinct and very strong cultural influences, so do many other aspects of culture, including age, religion, or even geographical region. Just as each culture has a unique understanding of health and disease, so too do cultures have unique understandings of the roles of patients and health care providers (Geist-Martin, Ray, & Sharf, 2003). Some cultures may promote a more passive role for patients in health care interactions, whereas other cultures may encourage more collaborative relationships between patients and health care providers.

Although we stressed that race and ethnicity are not the only forms of culture, these important aspects of patients' and health care providers' cultures have been shown to influence health care interactions. In the most basic way, for example, a difference in language can greatly impede patients and health care providers from communicating effectively. Although most hospitals have language interpreters on staff, adding an interpreter to the interaction between patients and health care providers changes the dynamics and flow of the interaction. Different ethnicities also have different communication styles and preferences (Jandt, 2009). For example, people from collectivistic cultures, such as Asian countries, tend to be more indirect in their speech while relying more on cues in the situational context and they tend to have greater respect for authority, such as the medical authority of physicians, whereas those from more individualistic cultures, such as the United States, tend to use a more direct communication style and have the perception of a smaller power distance between physicians and patients.

Culture also influences patients' understandings and beliefs about health. For example, some cultures, such as Chinese, tend to have a more fatalistic perception of health. *Fatalism* is the belief that health is a result of fate, and because it is predetermined, nothing can be done to alter it. A study of Chinese immigrants in the United States found that their fatalistic attitudes created a barrier to breast cancer screening, as they believed that if they were going to get cancer and die, it was meant to be (Lim, Yi, & Zebrack, 2008). Other cultures have ideas about what causes sickness. For example, in many Hispanic and Latino cultures, illness is thought to be the result of an overall imbalance in one's emotional state. Beliefs such as these could influence how patients respond to health care providers' questions and suggestions.

Power Dynamics

In discussing the various influences on patient/health care provider interaction, we cannot ignore the influence of power. In interpersonal interactions, *power* is defined as an attribute of a relationship during which persons, by virtue of their position or by withholding rewards or inflicting punishments, have the ability to impose their wills on others despite resistance (Berger, 1994). It is important to keep in mind that in any interaction, including health care interactions, the power that each party has wields enormous influence on how that interaction plays out. Emanuel and Emanuel (1992) explained that there are three indicators in health care encounters that specifically exhibit power dynamics including:

◆ Who sets the goals and agenda
◆ Role of patients' values
◆ Functional role of health care providers

The first indicator of power, *who sets the goals and agenda*, refers to whether health care providers control the flow, outcome, and plan for the health care interaction, or whether patients and health care providers work together to determine the flow, outcome, and plan. In situations when health care providers assert more power, they direct the conversation, make diagnoses, and suggest treatment plans without much consultation with patients. For example, a physician who is rushed and makes it clear to the patient that she has little time uses her power to direct the conversation.

Another indicator of power is the *role patients' values* or ideals play in the interaction. Many times patients' values are not explored or health care providers may assume they know patients' values or that their values are mutually shared. In other situations, when patients are co-participants in health care interactions, health care providers inquire about patients' values and incorporate those values into treatment plans. For example, when Professor Mattson was going through physical therapy to learn how to use a prosthetic leg, her physical therapist inquired about her values regarding physical activity and incorporated specific range-of-motion exercises to help her return to participating in sports such as bicycling.

The third indicator of power, the *functional role of health care providers,* which is discussed more thoroughly in Chapter 5, "Linking Health Communication with Health Care Provider Interaction," refers to the ways health care providers approach their patients. The functional role of a health care provider may be that of a guardian, an advisor, or a consultant. In other words, does the health care provider's communication imply that the patient is inferior, relatively equal, or a health care customer?

Your first instinct might be to think that the more power the patient has, the better. This is not entirely the case, though. Although some power within the patient's role is good, it is not ideal for all the power within the patient/health care provider relationship to reside with the patient. Health care providers, who have medical expertise, need to have power to make diagnoses and give treatment recommendations. When patients exert too much power, there can be situations where medications and treatments are prescribed that are not medically necessary. For example, as discussed previously, when antibiotics are prescribed unnecessarily for children because their parents demand these prescriptions from their health care providers.

PROFILE

Exploring Micro-Level and Macro-Level Influences in Health Communication

Rebecca Cline, PhD—Professor, Kent State University

A common thread running through Rebecca Cline's career is an interest in how everyday interpersonal communication influences the health and well-being of individuals. This interest led her to conduct research about self-disclosure, HIV/AIDS, death and dying, and health care providers/patient interaction. Her decision to study and work in health communication came about from her long-standing interests in communication and medical science. Health communication allows her to combine her passions and participate in projects that help improve the well-being of others. She accomplishes this through educating students and medical practitioners about how to communicate with those experiencing health issues.

One of Cline's current research interests is studying the effects of slow-motion technological disasters and how to more effectively communicate during these situations. The majority of research on natural disasters has focused on rapid onset natural disasters such as a hurricane or an earthquake where the damage is almost instantaneous and there is no control over the cause of the disaster. Slow-moving technological disasters occur over several years and often there is someone or a group or agency to blame.

An example of a slow-motion disaster is toxic waste leakage that may have been contaminating water and soil for years. Cline explains that people have different reactions to these types of disasters so the current best practices for dealing with disasters do not always apply. Specifically, Cline has been studying the town of Libby, Montana which is the site of a former vermiculite mine. Residents of the town and workers in the mine were unknowingly exposed to a naturally-occurring form of asbestos that was released as a result of the mining process. Exposure to asbestos can lead to serious and often fatal lung conditions. The asbestos disaster has been detrimental to the health of the community as there have been over 200 deaths attributed to asbestos exposure and countless illnesses. The situation also has devastated the local economy and caused disagreements among community members about how to handle the situation. Cline and her research team are studying the effects of the disaster on residents and trying to determine what communication response strategies might be most helpful in this situation and other slow-moving technological disasters (Cline et al., 2010).

For Cline, health communication is an important area of study because effective communication leads to better outcomes for both health care providers and patients or consumers. Communication also is unique because it can resolve larger issues related to health such as health disparities, problems with health care delivery, and social stigma.

Macro-Level Influences on Health Care Interactions

As a reminder, macro-level influences are broader influences outside the immediate patient/health care provider context that affect the interaction.

Organizational Influences

Organizational influences refer to aspects of the organizational context or environment that shape patient/health care provider communication including:

- Physical facility
- Rules and regulations
- Managed care and insurance plans

Some of the organizational influences derive from the *physical facility* where health care providers are employed, which includes the way the built environment is organized. For example, if a neighborhood pharmacy does not have an enclosed, private space other than the public counter to discuss questions and concerns about a medication such as Viagra, it is difficult if not impossible to have a confidential consultation, and instead patients may decide to remain silent about their questions and concerns.

In addition, health care organizations such as hospitals, medical clinics, and health care provider offices have *rules and regulations* that guide communication practices, meaning that the health care organization or the industry imposes procedures or laws that govern conduct or actions. For example, if you go to see a physical therapist following surgery on an injured knee and the clinic schedules patient appointments in 30-minute time periods, your time with your physical therapist will be limited to this timeframe, which may constrain your communication.

Another organizational influence is the managed care system. *Managed care* is a health care system with administrative control over primary health care services within a medical group practice that serves prepaid subscribers. The intention of managed care organizations is to eliminate redundant facilities and services and reduce costs. Managed care organizations take many forms, with two of the most common being health maintenance organizations (HMOs) and preferred provider organizations (PPOs). HMOs and PPOs utilize primary care physicians to provide comprehensive care to patients and limit unnecessary services by controlling access to specialists unless the primary care physician provides a referral. Managed care organizations aim to control medical costs and streamline processes for efficiency (Mosby, 2009). Because one of the primary ways managed care organizations control costs is by using primary care physicians as gatekeepers to medical specialists and other health care services, the existence of a managed care system can severely limit the power and control of patients when it comes to selecting their health care providers, deciding what specialists and tests they prefer to pursue, and preserving the privacy of their health care information.

For example, Mattson and Brann (2002) discovered that a managed care organization could release the details of a patient's urological problems in a lawsuit debated in open court even though the patient was not involved in the lawsuit and did not know that his information could be released once he revealed it to his physician. As a result of their communication boundary management analysis, these researchers suggested that patients become fully aware of who may have access to their health care information in managed care environments by reading consent forms and asking questions of their health care providers.

A parallel organizational influence relates to the trust patients have in their health care providers. Employers frequently search out and switch insurance providers and *insurance plans* in attempts to find the most affordable option for the organization and its employees. As insurance plans change, so too do the health care providers patients are covered to visit by those health insurance plans. Health care providers are members of different health insurance networks and it costs less for patients to visit health care providers who are in the network their insurance plan offers. Changing insurance plans, therefore, can cause patients to switch health care providers, leading to breaks in the continuity of communication and care. Because trust in health care providers develops over time and positive experiences, when patients frequently change health care providers it is difficult to develop and maintain trust. In addition, with limited time to spend with patients within the managed care system, as previously mentioned, it can be difficult for new health care providers to establish and maintain trust with patients (Servellen, 2009).

Another issue that influences the development of trust in the patient/health care provider relationship is that patients can become suspicious of primary care physicians' motivations for referrals to specialists and other health care services. When patients suspect that their primary care physicians are being controlled by a managed care system or that physicians are recommending health care specialists or medical tests to make a profit, trust decreases between patients and health care providers. In other words, patients may question the motives for primary care physicians making referrals to specialists or recommending tests that they may worry are not necessarily in patients' best interests but instead the recommendations or referrals are being made to generate business among medical colleagues.

Media Influences

Media influences refer to the increasingly important role that various forms of media have in shaping patient/health care provider interaction. There are three primary ways media influence health care interactions including:

- ◆ Fictional portrayals of medical situations
- ◆ Vast array of medical information available
- ◆ New technologies

However, before we proceed with this discussion, please take a break to complete Health Communication Nexus Interlude 4.1.

For this interlude take a few minutes to think of any television shows or movies you have watched that were set in a hospital. Based on the characters in these shows or movies, write down a list of adjectives you would use to describe the patients and health care providers you watched.

As you think about the adjectives you listed, how do you think these adjectives might influence or have influenced the ways you communicate with people in a hospital? In what ways do they promote stereotypes of patients? In what ways do these shows promote stereotypes of health care providers?

One way media influences patient/health care provider interaction is through *fictional portrayals of medical situations.* Think about the abundance of television dramas and comedies that feature health-related topics. Examples include *ER, Grey's Anatomy, Scrubs, Chicago Hope,* and *House.* Although these programs contain fictionalized accounts, viewers are given an intimate look into the interactions between health care providers, including physicians, nurses, medical technicians, and patients and their families and friends. From the stories depicted in these programs, we begin to develop expectations about how health care providers should or should not behave, as well as how patients should or should not respond in various situations. CNN reported on what some physicians have referred to as the *"House Effect,"* which is the phenomenon of patients expecting a battery of expensive tests whenever they may have a health problem. Some worry that this phenomenon is one of the factors driving up the cost of health care, as patients can be insistent about the tests and procedures they believe they need based on what they have observed on television (Weaver, 2008).

A second way media influences health care interactions is through the *vast array of medical information available* to patients. Primarily via access to the internet, patients search for information about diseases, symptoms, and treatments. For example, Web sites such as WebMD.com offer symptom checkers so individuals can self-diagnose their perceived health problems. How does this influence health care encounters? Due to all the medical information available through media, health care providers are confronting a more informed clientele. This can be a positive influence because patients can be more actively involved in their health and in health-related discussions (Kivits, 2006). In fact, some health care providers refer patients to internet sites for more information (Podichetty, Booher, Whitfield, & Biscup, 2006). However, more information also can be a negative influence because not all health information available in the media is accurate. Even if the information is accurate, patients without medical training may have difficulty understanding and applying the health information they obtain. In addition, some health care providers may feel threatened by patients who believe or act as if their knowledge obtained from the media is equal to or surpasses health care providers' expertise.

The third way media influences patient/health care provider interaction is through *new technologies* that have altered the channels through which patients and health care providers communicate. As examples, you may have called a physician's office or clinic to report your symptoms and discuss with a triage nurse what you can do next. Medical forms and prescriptions are routinely faxed. Some health care providers even use e-mail and the internet to communicate with patients. For more on the influence of technology on health communication, refer to Chapter 12, "Linking Health Communication with e-Health."

Health Literacy

An important macro-level influence on patient/health care provider interaction is health literacy. The U.S. Department of Health and Human Services (2009) defined *health literacy* as "the degree to which individuals have the capacity to obtain, process, and understand basic health information and services needed to make appropriate health decisions" (p. 2.1). More specifically, health literacy is an individual's capability to understand a variety of health-related materials and situations, such as:

- Directions on prescription bottles
- Medical education brochures
- Consent forms
- Calculation of health-related numbers such as blood sugar and medication dosages
- Hospital discharge instructions
- Complex health care systems

It is important to reiterate that health literacy is not just the ability to read health-related information but also includes the ability to apply analytical and decision-making skills to health situations and health information in the media (Bernhardt & Cameron, 2003). For example, individuals may be able to read a consent form, but if they do not fully understand the risks they are agreeing to, they are not considered to be health literate. In addition, individuals must have a certain level of numerical competency, as the previous list indicates. As examples, if individuals cannot measure out medication or comprehend what the numbers on a blood-pressure monitor readout mean, they are not considered to be health literate.

Certain populations are more vulnerable to low health literacy including:

- Those age 65 and older
- Minorities
- Immigrants
- Low-income individuals

There are a multitude of reasons for the low health literacy levels in these populations. Those age 65 and older may have trouble following complex instructions and may become confused by complicated medical regimens. Minorities and immigrants may face language barriers if information is not conveyed in their primary language or if medical professionals do not speak a common language. For example, the book *The Spirit Catches You and You Fall Down* (Fadiman, 1998) documented the life of a young Hmong child with a serious case of epilepsy. Lia's parents were immigrants from Laos and spoke minimal English. Their daughter's condition required a complex treatment plan involving several medications taken at different times throughout the day. Unable to understand English instructions or read prescription labels, her parents struggled to keep up with her complex medical condition and her subsequent health needs.

Those in the low-income category may have less access to quality education and other crucial resources. Evidence suggests that approximately half of all Medicaid and Medicare recipients read at 5th grade level or below (U.S. Department of Health and Human Services, 2009), limiting their ability to comprehend complex medical explanations and medical jargon.

So what happens when individuals, groups, or populations have a low level of health literacy? One immediate consequence of low literacy is increased hospitalizations and increased visits to emergency rooms (Baker et al., 2002). When individuals do not comprehend the basic techniques of caring for themselves, they are more likely to make mistakes in their self-treatments, leading to greater levels of illness and slower recoveries. The National Academy on an Aging Society (1999) estimated that additional costs for low health care literacy were $73 billion due to additional hospital visits and extended treatment plans.

Now that you've been exposed to various micro-level and macro-level influences that affect patient/health care provider interaction, we turn to a few issues of specific interest to patients.

Patient Rights in Health Care Interactions

When patients and health care providers interact, there are certain rights patients possess, which they should be aware of and exercise. The majority of patient rights are not prescribed by law, but instead are basic rights that health care providers have agreed to confer upon patients. In 1995, the Association of American Physicians and Surgeons (www.aapsonline.org) adopted the Patients' Bill of Rights. Similarly, the American Hospital Association (www.aha.org) developed a list of patient rights. Patients' rights include:

- ◆ To consult with the physician of their choice
- ◆ To be treated confidentially
- ◆ To use their own resources to purchase care
- ◆ To refuse treatment
- ◆ To be informed about their care
- ◆ To make decisions regarding their care

- ◆ To receive full disclosure from their insurance plans regarding coverage
- ◆ To be informed of hospital policies pertaining to care

Although health care providers and health care organizations have a responsibility to respect patient rights, as we discussed when defining communication in Chapter 1, "Introducing Health as Communication Nexus," patients also need to make sure that their rights are being respected and ask questions when their rights as patients may be compromised.

Regarding confidentiality, patients do have legal rights under the Health Insurance Portability and Accountability Act (HIPAA; www.hhs.gov), which became law in 1996. The purpose of HIPAA is to ensure privacy of patients' written, oral, and electronic health information and to limit access to patients' health information. Under HIPAA, patients have the right to see all their health records, receive notification when health records are shared, and give permission for sharing or using any of their health information. This means patients can control their health information and decide who can have access to their files and learn about their health history. The legal protection offered by HIPAA restricts health care providers from sharing with others your health status and even whether you were a patient.

Now that you have a better understanding of the complex relationship between patients and their health care providers, including the many factors that influence how patients and health care providers communicate, including basic patient rights, we discuss the specific communication rights of informed decision making and informed consent.

Informed Decision Making

Throughout this chapter we have referred to the importance of patients being involved in making decisions about their health care. In this section we discuss some of the factors involved in informed decision making by patients. Often patients may feel ill-equipped to make important health care decisions when they do not have medical training and/or an extensive discussion with their health care providers about aspects of the decision (Braddock, Edwards, Hasenberg, Laidley, & Levenson, 1999) including:

- ◆ Nature of the decision
- ◆ Benefits of options
- ◆ Risks of options
- ◆ Alternative options
- ◆ Uncertainties about the options

As you can see from the list, patients need a lot of information to make genuinely informed decisions. For example, let's consider patients deciding on whether to have gastric bypass procedure, which is a surgery that decreases stomach size in order to facilitate weight loss. Patients seeking this procedure may be desperate to lose weight and may have heard about others who lost large amounts of weight with the procedure, such as NBC weatherman Al Roker. This procedure has several risks, though, and in order for patients to make an informed decision about the procedure, they need to thoroughly understand the facts, in addition to their emotional desire to lose weight.

First, patients need to understand the *nature of the decision,* meaning the influence the decision would have on all aspects of their lives. In our example of gastric bypass procedure, the decision to have or not have the surgery would impact all aspects of the patient's life. The surgery itself is a major procedure. It also changes how a person can eat and drink. The procedure is considered permanent, although it can be reversed with another major surgery. Patients need to be sure they comprehend the gravity of their situation and the lasting consequences that go along with the decision.

Second, patients need to understand the *benefits of options,* meaning the merits or advantages of the options they are considering in their decision. In the case of gastric bypass procedure, the benefits of the procedure are the reduction of appetite, which leads to weight loss and weight-loss maintenance.

Third, patients need to understand the *risks of options* they are considering, meaning their level of exposure to the possibility of injury or loss. Patients considering gastric bypass surgery need to assess several risks. One area of risk involves their current condition of obesity. Risks associated with obesity include diabetes, high blood pressure, heart disease, depression, and sleep apnea. Another area of risk revolves around the gastric bypass procedure. Because this procedure involves major surgery, there are several risks involved, including internal bleeding, blood clots, infections, cardiac problems, and even death. In making a decision, patients need to weigh the risks of their current condition against the risks associated with the procedure.

Patients also need to know about *alternative options,* meaning any other previously unexplored choices. In the case of deciding whether or not to have gastric bypass surgery, alternative options include achieving weight loss through strict diet and exercise regimes, appetite suppressants, or hypnotism.

Fifth, patients need to be aware of *uncertainties about the options,* meaning unknown, doubtful, or incomplete information about the options. In our example of gastric bypass procedure, if health care providers do not have exact statistics regarding how many patients suffer from each negative side effect, or if a treatment is experimental, these uncertainties need to be shared with patients.

For decision making to be genuinely informed, it is not enough for health care providers to simply discuss the previous aspects of health care decisions with patients. Health care providers also must ensure that patients understand the discussion. This means thoroughly explaining medical procedures and risks in terms that patients comprehend. As is evident from our example of gastric bypass procedure, there are numerous factors to consider and evaluate. Ideally patients will have time to consider their options and/or talk over those options with others whom they also want to inform about their decision.

Although health care providers may have strong opinions about the best decisions for patients, they need to respect patients' decision-making processes and preferences. When health care providers' and patients' opinions drastically differ as to the best decision and course of treatment, it can be a source of tension and concern within the patient/health care provider relationship. In some cases, patients must sign an *Against Medical Advice (AMA) document* stating that they understand that they are going against the medical advice of their health care providers. For example, following the birth of a child a woman may decide to immediately leave the hospital despite her physician's opinion that she should stay at least 24 hours for monitoring. Before leaving the hospital against her physician's advice, she may be asked to sign an AMA.

Prior to the emphasis on informed decision making by patients, there were serious breaches to patient safety, which led to the widespread adoption of the principle of informed consent. In the next section we discuss this principle, including its history and current practices.

Informed Consent

Informed consent stipulates that "decisions about the medical care a person will receive, if any, are to be made in a collaborative manner between patient and physician" (Appelbaum, Lidz, & Meisel, 1987, p. 12). *Informed consent* refers to patients' acknowledgment that they knowledgably and willingly agree to a medical procedure or test. You may be familiar with consent forms if you have ever been admitted to a hospital or health care clinic for a medical procedure or test. Upon being admitted to the hospital or clinic, in addition to your medical history, often you are asked to sign a form that indicates you are consenting to the medical services being performed, such as surgery or magnetic resonance imaging (MRI).

The principle of informed consent arose out of the Nuremberg Trials of the 1940s, which prosecuted members of the Nazi regime for war crimes. Among the defendants were Nazi physicians who forced prisoners to participate in a variety of horrific medical experiments. One of the outcomes of the trials was the creation of informed consent documents for individuals participating in medical experiments, tests, or procedures. By signing informed consent forms, individuals acknowledge the potential risks and benefits of experiments, tests, or procedures and agree to participate.

Today, the process of acquiring and documenting informed consent for experiments and other methods of research involving humans is monitored by universities and the United States government (Olufowote, 2008). Similarly, patients are asked to sign a consent form whenever they undergo medical procedures that involve risk. For example, patients who undergo surgery sign a consent form that states they acknowledge the risks involved with the surgery, the anesthetic being used, and any forms of sedation.

One of the ongoing concerns with informed consent involves whether the majority of patients who sign the forms actually are informed or aware of what they are consenting to. Throughout this chapter we have been emphasizing the importance of ensuring that patients are involved in their health care. However, without a general level of health literacy, are patients really capable of consenting to medical tests and procedures, especially in high-stress or emergency situations when they do not have much time to think about their options or seek outside information or advice?

ETHICAL DILEMMA ◆ What Would You Do?

Suppose you had elective cosmetic laser surgery to remove a tattoo you got while on vacation. After recovering from the surgery, you realized that you have some very unattractive scarring. Although you signed the consent form, your surgeon assured you that there would be no scarring from the most current laser method available.

◆ Would you ever consider suing the surgeon for causing the scarring? Why or why not?

◆ What role would informed consent play in your decision whether or not to sue?

Deriving from both the principles of informed decision-making and informed consent, in the next section we focus on the currently popular approach to health care referred to as patient-centered communication.

Patient-Centered Communication

Patient-centered communication is described by the National Institutes of Health (Epstein & Street, 2007) as communication that accomplishes the following:

◆ Elicits, understands, and validates the patient's perspective
◆ Tries to understand patient within patient's context
◆ Reaches mutual understanding about problem and treatment
◆ Offers patient meaningful involvement in decisions relating to patient's health

In other words, patient-centered communication attempts to treat each patient as an individual rather than just another person with symptoms in need of diagnosis and treatment. *Patient-centered communication* is defined as interaction in which health care providers allow patients to lead whenever possible while trying to identify patients' major concerns rather than focusing only on health care providers' concerns and interests. An underlying assumption of patient-centered communication is that what patients have to say matters and patients are a valuable source of information in their medical evaluation and treatment processes.

As we learned when we discussed the definition of health communication, communication comprises both verbal and nonverbal interaction. To better understand what is involved in patient-centered communication, refer to Table 4.1 that lists both verbal and nonverbal interaction behaviors used in patient-centered communication.

Patient-Centered Communication

Verbal Behaviors   avoiding interrupting, establishing purpose of health care visit, asking about patient's beliefs, values, and preferences, eliciting and validating patient's emotions, discussing family, discussing social context, providing information about all aspects of care, avoiding medical jargon, checking for understanding, providing reassurance, offering encouragement, offering support

Nonverbal Behaviors   eye contact, leaning toward patient, nodding to indicate understanding, avoiding distracting behaviors, sitting at patient level whenever possible

It is important to note, though, that every health care provider should be sensitive to the patient and adapt their behaviors accordingly. For example, in some cultures, direct eye contact is offensive and could alienate the patient.

(adapted from Epstein & Street, 2007)

Table 4.1 ◆ *Verbal and nonverbal behaviors in patient-centered communication*

The verbal and nonverbal communication behaviors represented in Table 4.1 may seem simple, such as avoiding interruptions, but even engaging in these small actions can drastically alter health care conversations.

To illustrate, consider the following two scenarios. In the first scenario, the physician does not use patient-centered communication whereas in the second scenario, the physician does practice patient-centered communication.

Sarah's Injured Knee

Sarah is a 28-year-old female who twisted her knee while playing soccer with her friends. She treated the sore knee at home with ice and a pain reliever for the past two days but the pain increased and she noticed some swelling. Sarah is a manager at a local clothing store. This job requires her to be on her feet multiple hours per day. Because of the increased pain, difficulty maneuvering around the house, and her concerns about being able to perform her job, Sarah makes an appointment with a local physician.

Health Care Communication Scenario 1

When Sarah arrives at the health clinic for her appointment with the doctor, she is asked to take a seat in the waiting room until her name is called. After waiting for about 30 minutes, Sarah's name is called and she is shown into an examine room. A nurse comes into the room and instructs Sarah to undress, put on a paper gown, and wait on the exam table. After about 20 minutes, the doctor enters. He quickly introduces himself and asks Sarah where the pain is. She tells him it is in her knee and begins to explain how the injury occurred. The doctor interrupts her and asks if the pain is sharp or achy. She replies that the pain is achy and then starts to clarify that the pain becomes sharper when applying ice. The doctor does not respond to her statement although he continues to look at and move her leg. He then walks over to a desk in the room and begins to scribble words onto his prescription pad. "I think you just strained it," he tells her and gives her prescriptions for an anti-inflammatory medication and a pain medication. "Please follow up in a week or so if the pain continues," he advises Sarah. As the doctor reaches to open the door, Sarah says, "I was wondering," but she stops when the doctor tells her he will send in his nurse to answer any questions. With that the doctor leaves the room. Sarah is given a diagnosis of knee strain and is given a treatment plan of medication.

Was the communication in Health Care Communication Scenario 1 effective? Did Sarah seem to have issues and concerns that were not addressed by the physician? Why was this scenario not an example of patient-centered communication?

Now let's consider another scenario with Sarah seeing a different physician for her knee pain.

Health Care Communication Scenario 2

When Sarah arrives at the health clinic for her appointment with the physician, she is asked to take a seat in the waiting room until her name is called. After just a few minutes of waiting, a nurse who escorts her to an exam room calls Sarah's name. The nurse asks Sarah to sit in a chair and wait for the doctor to come in. Ten minutes later the doctor comes in and introduces himself to Sarah. He asks her why she came to the clinic. Sarah tells the doctor about injuring her knee during a soccer game, she describes her symptoms, and explains how she has been treating the injury at home. As Sarah talks, the doctor maintains eye contact and listens without speaking. When Sarah is finished the doctor asks her some questions about the intensity of the pain. At this point the doctor asks Sarah to sit on the exam table and roll up her pant leg. The doctor proceeds to do a physical exam on Sarah's knee asking her how she is feeling as he progresses with the exam. Following the physical exam the doctor asks Sarah about her job and her level of physical activity. He then tells her that he believes the knee is just sprained and writes prescriptions for a pain medication and an anti-inflammatory medication. The doctor explains how to take the medications properly and also reviews the potential side effects of the medications. He then talks with her about the environment at her job and about resting her knee as much as possible. Before leaving he asks Sarah if she has any additional questions. She answers no and he reminds her that she can call his office with any questions or issues that arise.

Why is Health Care Communication Scenario 2 an example of patient-centered communication? Some may consider the outcomes of the two scenarios virtually identical. Sarah received the same diagnosis and the same prescriptions for medications. Although the major difference may seem to be that the second physician spent more time talking with Sarah, there are more differences. Because the second physician took time to inquire about Sarah's personal life, he discovered that her job requirements would put additional strain on her knee and talked with her about how to handle her job situation. Beginning the meeting by sitting across from Sarah rather than standing over her while she was sitting or lying on the exam table in a paper robe, likely caused Sarah to feel less anxious. In addition, the physician's explanation of the prescriptions and their side effects likely made Sarah feel confident she could easily follow her prescription regimen.

As illustrated in the previous two scenarios, the communication style exhibited by each physician was drastically different. Table 4.2 highlights some of the key communication differences between a patient-centered and a healthcare provider-centered approach. These differences also were illustrated in the contrasting health care communication scenarios of Sarah's injured knee.

PATIENT-CENTERED	HEALTH CARE PROVIDER-CENTERED
• Asks open-ended questions (e.g., "How would you describe your pain?")	• Asks closed-ended questions (e.g., "Does your knee hurt?")
• Requests opinions (e.g., "Would you be willing to work with a physical therapist? Why or why not?")	• Issues directives (e.g., "You will go to physical therapy twice a week.")
• Acts as counselor focusing on emotional concerns of patient (e.g., "Do you feel like this is putting you under added stress?")	• Focuses on physical factors (i.e., does not probe into emotional concerns of patient)
• Offers support (e.g., "This type of injury is challenging but I'm confident you can get through it.")	• Interrupts patient

Table 4.2 ◆ *Patient-centered vs. health care provider-centered communication*

Patient Benefits of Patient-Centered Communication

As you may have ascertained from the description of patient-centered communication and the previous example scenarios, patient-centered communication may take more time and effort for both health care providers and patients. This increase in time commitment warrants two questions: Why is there so much emphasis on patient-centered communication? and, Are the time costs associated with patient-centered communication offset by the benefits of patient-centered communication? The answers to these questions are intertwined. There is so much emphasis on patient-centered communication because there are proven benefits for both patients and health care providers that definitely offset the costs associated with patient-centered communication.

The benefits of patient-centered communication for patients (Brown, Stewart, & Ryan, 2003) may seem obvious but include:

◆ Perception of genuine concern
◆ Increased satisfaction with health care encounters
◆ Decreased stress and anxiety
◆ Improved health outcomes

One benefit of patient-centered communication is that patients *perceive genuine concern* on the part of health care providers. This perception of concern is key to patients experiencing the other benefits of patient-centered communication.

Another benefit of patient-centered communication is that patients tend to report *increased satisfaction with health care encounters* when they feel they are treated as unique individuals because the health care providers treating them also sincerely care about them. Because patients' concerns are addressed and discussed during patient-centered communication, patients often report *decreased stress and anxiety,* which is a third benefit of patient-centered communication for patients.

The fourth benefit of patient-centered communication is that patients tend to have *improved health outcomes* because they are more likely to adhere to health care providers' advice and treatment plans. One potential reason for this is that patients feel more involved in the process of their health care and feel more responsibility for following through on their treatment plans. Patients also may have a better understanding of what the treatment plan is due to patient-centered communication. Improved health outcomes also may be attributed to better diagnoses, as health care providers often are able to get more complete information from patients during patient-centered interactions.

Patient Skills for Patient-Centered Communication

Patients need a certain skill set to effectively work with their health care providers. Patients skilled in patient-centered communication also can achieve the most from their communication with health care providers, even if the health care providers are not practicing patient-centered communication.

Skills patients need to communicate effectively with their health care providers include:

◆ Information seeking
◆ Information provision
◆ Information verifying

We discuss each of these skills and the specific behaviors patients need to learn and practice when interacting with their health care providers.

Information Seeking

Information seeking involves patients gathering information from health care providers about aspects of their health conditions from diagnosis to treatment. The primary skill in information seeking is asking questions. You may think this is a relatively easy skill, as most people know how to ask questions such as, "How much do I owe for this visit to the clinic?" However, in health care settings, many patients struggle to ask questions, especially relevant questions that provide information they need to understand their health conditions and treatments.

Research has shown that the majority of patients do not ask many questions and not because they know all of the information. On the contrary, there are several possible reasons why patients hesitate to ask questions (Parrott, Duncan, & Duggan, 2000) including:

◆ Feeling intimidated by health care providers
◆ Limited time
◆ Needing time to process information
◆ Not knowing what to ask
◆ Not realizing information is misunderstood until trying to follow treatment plan

In health care settings, one reason patients do not ask questions is because they may *feel intimidated by health care providers* and feel uncomfortable because they fear their questions make them seem unintelligent or annoying to their health care providers. Patients often perceive their health care providers as too busy, so patients do not want to bother them with seemingly unnecessary questions.

Another reason that contributes to the lack of patients' questions is the issue of *limited time,* which can be real but more often is perceived as real by patients. When patients sense that the health care setting is crowded or that health care providers are rushing to get to the next patient, they may not believe there is enough time to ask questions. Also, during briefly scheduled health care consultations or exams, there may not be enough time for patients to listen to their health care providers, process the information, and formulate and ask questions.

A third reason that patients do not readily ask questions is because many people *need time to process complex information* before they are able to formulate appropriate questions. Imagine, for example, a patient named John whose physician came into the exam room and told him that his lab results indicated that he has type 2 diabetes. Type 2 diabetes is a serious health condition during which the body does not produce enough insulin, the chemical that enables the body to break down and convert glucose to energy (www.diabetes.org). The news comes as a shock to John and is stressful to comprehend, as diabetes is a lifelong condition with potential for serious side effects, including blindness and limb loss. The physician begins to talk to John about some of the treatment possibilities, such as medication and diet change. John just nods as the physician talks because John is trying to absorb everything he is hearing. His mind is so busy trying to make sense of the news he just heard that he is unable to think of a question he should ask.

In health care situations, patients often do *not know what kinds of questions they need to ask.* If you refer back to the conversation starter for the NuvaRing® at the beginning of this chapter, you see that it contains a list of potential questions to ask a physician about a potential medication. Without such a list of questions, patients may not be sure what needs to be discussed about diagnoses or treatment plans.

A fifth reason patients do not ask questions is because sometimes they may *not realize they misunderstand information until they try to follow a treatment plan.* In other words, the misunderstanding does not occur to them until they try to put recommendations given to them by their health care providers into action. For example, following John's diagnosis of type 2 diabetes he sets up an appointment with a diabetes educator to learn more about testing his blood sugars, tracking his diet, and using his medication. Throughout the appointment he listens carefully and feels confident that he can manage his diabetes care. At home that night, though, John struggles to test his blood sugar, as he is not sure how to insert the testing strip. And when trying to track his eating habits, he struggles to read and understand food labels. At home he realizes he is confused and now has several questions he would like to ask his health care providers.

The confidence and assertiveness of patients also contributes to how many questions they ask. More passive and shy patients may not be as comfortable speaking up and pressing health care providers for answers. Also, as acknowledged throughout this book, if patients do not have at least a basic level of health literacy, they likely will not be able to equally participate in conversations with their health care providers. However, regardless of personality differences and health literacy levels, patients must be willing to ask questions and get answers even when their health care providers appear to be rushed and busy.

Asking Questions Effectively

So, how can patients become more effective at asking questions? Many experts and organizations, including AARP (formerly known as the American Association for Retired Persons; www.aarp.org), suggest that patients bring a list of questions to their health care appointments. Having a list of questions to refer to can help patients who feel tense and/or may forget their questions.

When asking questions, it might be helpful for patients to take notes because they likely will be trying to process and remember a lot of information that is offered in responses to their questions. For example, information about the number of times a day a medication needs to be taken might not be easily remembered and written notes can be helpful later when patients are unsure about something discussed during their appointment.

Another suggestion is to bring someone to the health care appointment who can serve as a health advocate. The health advocate should be a family member or friend the patient feels comfortable in the presence of while discussing health care issues. The health advocate can serve several purposes. Even if the advocate never speaks, he or she can serve as an extra set of ears to understand and remember what is said at the appointment. A health advocate who is close to the patient or is involved in patient care also can participate in asking questions. Studies have shown that older adults who bring an advocate to health care appointments generally are more satisfied with their care (Wolff & Roter, 2008). In addition, patients need to feel confident in their ability to ask follow-up questions after their appointments. As examples, asking follow-up questions could involve calling an information desk or leaving a message for the physician to return a call.

Information Provision

Another important patient skill to promote patient-centered communication is the provision of information. *Information provision* refers to the act or process of giving information to health care providers. There are two challenges to information provision: providing relevant and accurate information and telling the truth. Both of these challenges to the provision of information by patients are discussed in the following sections. However, before we more closely consider information provision, take a few minutes to complete Health Communication Nexus Interlude 4.2.

Health Communication Nexus Interlude 4.2

For this interlude, consider the following questions and answer as many as possible.

- What is the date of your last tetanus shot?
- List the names of any prescription drugs you are taking and the dosage.
- List the names of any over-the-counter medications you have taken in the past week.
- What is the date of your last medical exam?
- What is your blood type?
- Name any family members with a history of heart disease.

Did you have trouble answering any of the questions? Were there any questions for which you needed to look up the information or were there questions for which you were unsure of the answer? Keep any difficulties you had with providing answers to these questions in mind as we consider some of the reasons that many patients struggle to provide information to their health care providers.

Relevant and Accurate Information

In order for health care providers to make accurate diagnoses and develop effective treatment plans, they often need information from patients about their symptoms and medical history. It may seem like an easy task to provide information about yourself, but in reality, many patients struggle to provide health care providers with relevant and accurate information. To explain, we highlight a personal example experienced by the second author of this book, Lecturer Hall:

"When one of my triplet daughters was 18 months old she was referred to a developmental pediatrician due to some delays in walking and talking. I was told when I made the appointment to arrive about 15 minutes early to fill out some paperwork. "No problem," I thought, "I've filled out plenty of paperwork over the years." When I arrived for the appointment, I was handed a pen and a stack of paper attached to a clipboard. I sat down and began writing. The first blanks were easy to fill in; birth date, weight at birth, weeks gestation. Then I moved on to a section that asked me to list the medications I had taken while I was pregnant with her. Due to my very high-risk pregnancy, the list of medications was quite long and I wrote down what I remembered, but I left several off the list because I could not remember. I then moved on to a checklist of developmental milestones such as rolling over and sitting independently. In addition to checking the milestones my daughter had met I was supposed to indicate at what age she had met them. Now I felt as though I was really at a loss. My daughter is a triplet, so not only is her first year very blurry, but it is hard to remember which of the three babies did what and when. I felt bad about not knowing when she had first rolled over in addition to the other milestones so I filled out the list with my best estimates. When I was done with all the paperwork I handed my papers to the nurse and worried that my lack of an accurate medical history would impede the doctor in correctly evaluating my daughter."

This example illustrates that knowing or remembering all necessary medical details may be difficult, if not impossible, especially in situations when patients are seriously ill or injured. Even during seemingly mundane health care interactions, providing relevant and accurate information may be challenging. During a routine exam, for example, a patient might forget to mention a troubling symptom or incident because he or she is anxious to get through the exam.

Regardless of the challenges, providing relevant and accurate information is very important. The Agency for Healthcare Research and Quality (2009) offered these suggestions for how patients can be better information providers:

◆ Write down a list of symptoms and concerns
◆ Bring current medical history to appointment
◆ Bring list with family medical history
◆ Bring list of all medications and dosages

By following these few suggestions, patients can be better prepared and more likely to offer relevant and accurate information to aid in their health care.

Truth Telling

Another challenge for patients in information provision is telling the truth to health care providers. Even though patients are going to health care providers to seek help for health issues or wellness check-ups, a surprising number of patients either intentionally deceive health care providers or inadvertently omit pertinent information. Although this may seem counterintuitive, consider the following situation. You are at a dentist's office to have your teeth cleaned. The dentist asks if you floss frequently. Perhaps you are an avid flosser and can honestly reply that you floss once per day. However, what if your flossing behavior is more sporadic? Would you be tempted to lie to the dentist about your flossing habits or exaggerate about how often you floss in order to avoid judgment? Chances are many people would answer "Yes!" to this question.

Flossing your teeth may seem like a relatively minor health issue to lie about, but this is just one example of the behaviors that patients don't tell the truth about to their health care providers. Patients withhold or fail to volunteer all kinds of information that may relate to their health conditions. Why do patients do this? Parrott (2009) identified a few typical reasons patients withhold medical information:

- ◆ Threats to self-identity
- ◆ Worry about confidentiality due to team care
- ◆ Cultural differences
- ◆ Personal characteristics

The concept of self-identity relates to the relational goals we discussed previously in this chapter. Generally, patients want to present themselves or their self-identities in positive ways to health care providers. They want health care providers to see their best face. Revealing personal or embarrassing health-related information could pose a *threat to their self-identity* and a threat to their face. For example, telling a physician that you drink alcohol at least three nights per week or that you smoke cigarettes may cast you in a negative light. Or some of your health behaviors may be embarrassing to share, such as your number of sexual partners or your use of safer-sex practices.

As a related reason, patients may be reluctant to share personal or embarrassing health information because they *worry about confidentiality due to team care*, meaning they are concerned that the information they provide will spread to others in the health care team. In many health care situations, such as hospitalization, a team of health care providers oversees patient care. This health care team may include physicians, nurses, various therapists, dieticians, and medical technicians. Patients may be concerned about such a large number of people knowing about and discussing their personal information.

Also, often because of *cultural differences* and/or *personal characteristics* some individuals are more likely than others to be deceptive or to withhold information. Some patients are more concerned with saving face than others, and some people are more willing to self-disclose than others. Some patients may want to be considered model patients and are eager to please their health care providers, which leads them to being deceptive about what they are or are not doing. For example, a study at Johns Hopkins University found that 73% of asthmatic patients told physicians they used their inhalers three times a day, yet only 15% were actually using their inhalers that often. The study also found that 14% of patients actually emptied their inhalers before a health care appointment so it would appear as if they were using their inhalers as often as prescribed (Simmons, Nides, Rand, Wise, & Tashkin, 2009).

Cultural issues also may inhibit full honesty and disclosure. In some cultures, women may be uncomfortable discussing their health with a male physician and therefore may omit symptoms. For example, in the Islamic culture, women do not discuss their personal health with the opposite sex. Similarly, in some cultures, men may not trust or feel confident with female physicians and will not divulge all of their symptoms and concerns. In some countries in the Middle East, for example, hospitals are divided into male and female units to avoid these issues.

When patients deceive their health care providers or withhold pertinent information, there can be serious negative health consequences. Physicians may not be able to make correct diagnoses if they are making diagnoses based on incomplete or inaccurate information. Also, if patients are not honest about the medications they are taking, they could risk serious drug interactions.

Information Verifying

The third skill essential for patients to achieve the most from their health care is information verifying. *Information verifying* refers to the abilities of patients to confirm the information they receive from health care providers (Cegala & Broz, 2003). In other words, information verifying is the process of patients making sure they understand what is being communicated to them. For example, if a nurse or a respiratory therapist gives a patient instructions on how to use an inhaler, the patient needs to confirm with the nurse or therapist that he or she understands the instructions and can perform the inhaler routine correctly. A common problem in health care is patients who are unable to follow instructions due to lack of understanding. In many cases, patients may think they are following directions when actually they are not. Failure to verify medical information could lead to delays in healing or have more dire and even life-threatening consequences. The wrong doses of insulin for a diabetic, for example, could be extremely dangerous and even cause death from diabetic shock.

Patients need to be encouraged to verify all health care information they receive. Simple strategies such as taking notes or bringing home literature from health care providers can assist in the information verification process.

Now that you better understand the patient skills needed to facilitate patient-centered communication, the question is, how can patients learn the skills they need to be active and informed participants in their health care? The broad answer is patient skills training, which is discussed in the next section.

Patient Skills Training

Patient skills training teaches patients the communication skills they need to be involved participants in their health care. There are several patient skills training options. Some of the options include holding face-to-face training, providing literature such as brochures or materials on Web sites, watching video-taped skills training sessions, viewing a model illustrating a patient skill, and/or having the ability to practice communication techniques. Research shows that interventions during which individuals are able to model and practice skills are the most effective approaches to skills training (Cegala & Broz, 2003).

However, there are challenges to providing patient skills training. Costs in time and qualified personnel to model and interact with participants and provide feedback can be prohibitive (Cegala & Broz, 2003). To address this challenge, the internet offers many opportunities for patient skills training. Not only can potential patients read about better patient communication, they also can watch online videos that model effective communication techniques. Patients tend to learn more when they can imitate behavior they have seen. One disadvantage of relying on the internet is that not all potential patients have access to this technology to participate in skills training.

Although we argued for the benefits of patient-centered communication and discussed both the health care provider skills and patient skills needed to practice patient-centered communication, we must not ignore that some patients do not prefer this approach to their health care.

Preference for Traditional Approach to Health Care Communication

Throughout this chapter we've been focusing on the many benefits of patient-centered communication, including greater satisfaction for patients. However, like most issues in communication, there is rarely a style or concept that is always preferred or best. Some patients may not desire to be active participants in health care communication or decision making. There may be patients who prefer a more traditional model of patient/health care provider interaction, in which health care providers are paternalistic and tell patients how they should and should not behave. Some patients may feel uncomfortable making health care decisions because they have not had extensive medical training. Relatedly, as discussed previously, aspects of culture may influence these preferences. For example, older patients often prefer to take a more passive role in medical encounters. They may prefer a more paternalistic style because they have experience with it and, therefore, are more comfortable with this style of care.

In the service-learning application, we return to discussing how conversation starters can be developed to be effective tools of interpersonal communication. This activity can provide a meaningful experience both for the developers and the target audience members while maximizing the effectiveness of the conversation starters.

SERVICE-LEARNING APPLICATION

Developing Conversation Starters for Health Campaigns

Remember the conversation starter that began this chapter? In this service-learning application, we focus on immersing campaign team members and target audience members of campaigns into the process of developing conversation starters. *Engaging participants in meaningful and personally relevant service-learning activities* also is an important quality standard of effective service-learning practice (Corporation for National & Community Service, 2010), which we emphasize in this application.

Within the realm of health communication, *conversation starters* are defined as written materials that provide suggestions for beginning and sustaining a conversation about a given health topic. Currently these tools come in many formats, including brochures, booklets, downloadable documents, and postcards (Kosmoski, 2009; McAllister, Matarasso, Dixon, & Shepperd, 2004).

To develop a conversation starter, follow these steps:

◆ Choose a health topic that is personally relevant to your campaign team members and that you think would benefit from the inclusion of a conversation starter. Think about what your team's goal would be in developing a conversation starter. What audience would you target and with whom would that audience use the conversation starter?

◆ Research existing campaigns about your chosen health topic to determine if a conversation starter already exists. If a conversation starter already exists, consider revising it to meet the needs of your target audience(s). Be sure to give credit to the source of the original conversation starter. If a conversation starter does not exist for your chosen health topic, consider drafting one.

Determine which health communication theories/models may guide your team in revising or drafting a conversation starter. For example, you may want to consider the Reconceptualized Health Belief Model (Mattson, 1999) or the Message Design Tool (Mattson & Basu, 2010). For more information on health communication theories and models, refer to Chapter 3, "Linking Health Communication with Theories Informed by Health Communication."

◆ Before revising or drafting a conversation starter, interview target audience members either individually or in focus groups to collect their responses to the following questions:
  ○ Do they think a conversation starter for this health topic is necessary? Why or why not?
  ○ What would they suggest including in a conversation starter for this health topic?
  ○ Would they use a conversation starter for this health topic? Why or why not?

◆ Based on the results of the interviews and your other research, revise or draft the conversation starter. Consider the following communication components and the health communication theories/models you chose as you revise or draft the conversation starter.
  ○ Format
    – Usability
    – Quality
    – Cost-effectiveness
  ○ Written content and images
    – Attention-getting and relevant
    – Motivating
    – Culturally consistent
  ○ Readability level appropriate for health literacy of target audience

◆ Conduct focus groups with target audience members to gather feedback about your draft conversation starter.

◆ Revise draft conversation starter based on focus group feedback.

◆ Distribute conversation starter and evaluate use.

To illustrate the process of developing a conversation starter, let's turn to the Motorcycle Safety at Purdue (MS@P) campaign. A service-learning project team of graduate students working on the MS@P campaign designed a series of four conversation starters to address the target audience of friends and family of motorcyclists. These conversation starters were developed in response to findings from the needs assessment. For more information on needs assessments refer to Chapter 8, "Linking Health Communication with

Health Campaign Practice." According to the needs assessment survey, 80% supported their friend or family members' motorcycle riding, but they wanted them to ride more safely. This data exposed an integral way to reach motorcyclists through their loved ones who wanted them to wear safety gear and ride safely. The needs assessment also revealed that although friends and family members felt comfortable talking with the motorcyclists they knew, they did not believe that the conversation would bring about behavior change and instead they were concerned it might jeopardize their relationships. These were indications that this target audience not only needed techniques for successfully persuading their friends or family members who ride motorcycles, but also self-efficacy messages that helped them feel capable of having effective conversations (Kosmoski, Mattson, & Hall, 2007).

The MS@P campaign project team was intricately involved in all aspects of developing these conversation starters. First the students drafted conversation starters by incorporating information they knew about motorcycle safety from their own experience and research. Next, during focus groups, they asked family and friends of motorcyclists to provide feedback about the draft conversation starters. Then they revised the draft conversation starters and sought additional input until target audience members were comfortable using the conversation starters. These conversation starters are available at all events the campaign participates in and through the campaign Web site (www.ItInvolvesYou.com).

Another example of a conversation starter was developed by CDC's DES Update (www.cdc.gov/des/consumers/do/questions.html) to help target audience members start discussions about possible exposure to the drug diethylstilbestrol (DES). DES was formerly prescribed during pregnancy to prevent miscarriages or premature deliveries. Target audience members are encouraged to take these conversation starter questions to their health care provider or share it with family and friends.

Based on the steps to developing conversation starters for health issues and the example conversation starters from other campaigns, your service-learning campaign project team is ready to begin developing conversation starters that are meaningful and personally relevant to you and your target audiences' health needs.

Chapter Summary

The overarching theme of this chapter was the complex dynamics of patient/health care provider interaction from the patient's perspective. We began by defining the term patient and explaining our use of this term. This was followed by an abridged history of the physician/patient relationship. Next we addressed several micro-level and macro-level influences that shape patient/health care provider interactions. This was followed by explaining patient rights and the principles of informed decision making and informed consent. Next, patient-centered communication was discussed including skills patients need to be involved in patient-centered care. We also acknowledged that some patients prefer a more traditional, paternalistic approach to health care interactions. We concluded the chapter with a service-learning application emphasizing how to engage participants in meaningful and personally relevant service-learning by developing health-related conversation starters.

References

AARP (2009). How to talk to your doctor. Retrieved August 29, 2009, from www.AARP.org.

Agency for Healthcare Research and Quality (2009). *Quick tips when talking with your doctor*. Retrieved September 30, 2009, from http://www.ahrq.gov/consumer/quicktips/doctalk.pdf.

Appelbaum, P. S., Lidz, C. W., & Meisel, A. (1987). *Informed consent: Legal theory and clinical practice*. New York: Oxford University Press.

Babrow, A. S., Kasch, C. R., & Ford, L. A. (1998). The many meanings of "uncertainty" in illness: Toward a systematic accounting. *Health Communication, 10,* 1–23.

Baker, D. W., Gazmararian, J. A., Williams, M. V., Scott, T., Parker, R. M., Green, D., et al. (2002). Functional health literacy and the risk of hospital admission among Medicare managed care enrollees. *American Journal of Public Health, 92,* 1278–1283.

Beck, C. S. (1997). *Partnerships for health: Building relationships between women and health care providers.* Mahwah, NJ: Lawrence Erlbaum.

Berger, C. R. (1994). Power, dominance, and social interaction. In M. L. Knapp & G. R. Miller (Eds.), *Handbook of interpersonal communication* (2nd ed., pp. 450–507). Thousand Oaks, CA: Sage.

Bernhardt, J. M., & Cameron, K. A. (2003). Accessing, understanding, and applying health communication messages: The challenge of health literacy. In T. L. Thompson, A. M. Dorsey, K. I. Miller, & R. Parrott (Eds.), *Handbook of health communication* (pp. 583–605). Mahwah, NJ: Lawrence Erlbaum.

Bertakis, K. D. (2009). The influence of gender on the doctor-patient interaction. *Patient Education & Counseling, 76,* 356–360.

Braddock, C. H., Edwards, K. A., Hasenberg, N. M., Laidley, T. L., & Levenson, W. (1999). Informed decision making in outpatient practice: Time to get back to the basics. *Journal of the American Medical Association, 282,* 2313–2320.

Brown, J. B., Stewart, M., & Ryan, B. L. (2003). Outcomes of patient-provider interaction. In T. L. Thompson, A. M. Dorsey, K. I. Miller, & R. Parrott (Eds.), *Handbook of health communication* (pp. 141–161). Mahwah, NJ: Lawrence Erlbaum.

Brown, P., & Levinson, S. (1978). *Politeness: Some universals in language usuage.* Cambridge, MA: Cambridge University Press.

Cegala, D. J., & Broz, S. L. (2003). Provider and patient communication skills training. In T. L. Thompson, A. M. Dorsey, K. I. Miller, & R. Parrott (Eds.), *Handbook of health communication* (pp. 95–119). Mahwah, NJ: Lawrence Erlbaum.

Cline, R. J. W., Orom, H., Berry-Bobovski, L., Hernandez, T., Brad, B. C., Schwartz, A. G., & Ruckdeschel, J. C. (2010). Community-level social support responses in a slow-motion technological disaster: The case of Libby, Montana. *American Journal of Community Psychology, 46,* 1–18.

Corporation for National & Community Service (2010). Learn and serve: America's national service-learning clearinghouse. Retrieved January 12, 2010, from www.servicelearning.org.

Degner, L. F., & Sloan, J. A. (1992). Decision making during serious illness: What role do patients really want to play? *Journal of Clinical Epidemiology, 45,* 941–950.

DiMatteo, M. R. (1994). Enhancing patient adherence to medical recommendations. *Journal of the American Medical Association, 271,* 79–83.

DiMatteo, M. R., & Lepper, H. S. (1998). Promoting adherence to courses of treatment: Mutual collaboration in physician-patient relationships. In L. D. Jackson & B. K. Duffy (Eds.), *Health communication research: A guide to developments and directions* (pp. 75–86). Westport, CT: Greenwood Press.

Emanuel, E. J., & Emanuel, L. L. (1992). Four models of the physician-patient relationship. *Journal of the American Medical Association, 267,* 2221–2226.

Epstein, R. M., & Street, R. L. (2007). *Patient-centered communication in cancer care: Promoting healing and reducing suffering.* Bethesda, MD: National Cancer Institute. Available at http://www.outcomes.cancer.gov/areas/pcc/communication/pcc_monograph.pdf.

Fadiman, A. (1998). *The spirit catches you and you fall down: A Hmong child, her American doctors, and the collision of two cultures.* New York: Farrar, Straus and Giroux.

Florin, J., Ehrenberg, A., & Ehnfors, M. (2008). Clinical decision making: Predictors of patient participation in nursing care. *Journal of Clinical Nursing, 17,* 2935–2944.

Geist-Martin, P., Ray, E. B., & Sharf, B. F. (2003). *Communicating health: Personal, cultural, and political complexities*. Belmont, CA: Wadsworth.

Goffman, E. (1963). *Behavior in public places: Notes on the social organization of gatherings*. New York: Free Press.

Gonzalez-Crussi, F. (2007). *A short history of medicine*. New York: Modern Library.

Jandt, F. E. (2009). *An introduction to intercultural communication: Identities in a global community* (6th ed.). Thousand Oaks, CA: Sage.

Kivits, J. L. (2006). Informed patients and the internet: A mediated context for consultations with health professionals. *Journal of Health Psychology, 11*, 269–282.

Kosmoski, C. L. (2009). *Breaking the ice: Toward a conversation starter tool for use in conversations about direct-to-consumer advertised prescriptions between patients and health care providers*. Unpublished Dissertation, Purdue University, West Lafayette, Indiana.

Kosmoski, C. L., Mattson, M., & Hall, J. (2007). Reconsidering motorcycle safety at Purdue: A case study integrating campaign theory and practice. *Cases in Public Health Communication & Marketing, 1*. Available at http://www.gwumc.edu/sphhs/departments/pch/phcm/casesjournal/volume1/peer-reviewed/cases_1_07.cfm.

Lim, J., Yi, J., & Zebrack, B. (2008). Acculturation, social support, and quality of life for Korean immigrant breast and gynecological cancer survivors. *Ethnicity & Health, 13*, 243–260.

Manderbacka, K. (2005). Exploring gender and socioeconomic differences in treatment of coronary heart disease. *European Journal of Public Health, 15*, 634–639.

Mangione-Smith, R., Elliott, M. N., Stivers, T., McDonald, L., Heritage, J., & McGlynn, E. A. (2004). Racial/ethnic variation in parent expectations for antibiotics: Implications for public health campaigns. *Pediatrics, 113*, 385–394.

Mattson, M. (1999). Reconceptualizing communication cues to action in the health belief model: HIV test counseling. *Communication Monographs, 66*, 240–265.

Mattson, M., & Basu, A. (2010). Centers for Disease Control's DES Update: A case for effective operationlization of messaging in social marketing practice. *Health Promotion Practice, 11*, 580–588.

Mattson, M., & Brann, M. (2002). Managed care and the paradox of patient confidentiality: A case study analysis from a communication boundary management perspective. *Communication Studies, 53*, 337–357.

McAllister, M., Matarasso, B., Dixon, B., & Shepperd, C. (2004). Conversation starters: Reexamining and reconstructing first encounters within the therapeutic relationship. *Journal of Psychiatric and Mental Health Nursing, 11*, 575–582.

Mosby (2009). *Mosby's medical dictionary* (8th ed.). St. Louis: Mosby/Elsevier.

National Academy on an Aging Society (1999). Fact sheet: Low health literacy skills increase annual health care expenditures by $73 billion. Retrieved May 18, 2009, from http://www.agingsociety.org/agingsociety/publications/fact/fact_low.html.

Nutton, V. (2004). *Ancient medicine*. New York: Routledge.

Olufowote, J. O. (2008). A structurational analysis of informed consent to treatment: Societal evolution, contradiction, and reproductions in medical practice. *Health Communication, 23*, 292–303.

Parrott, R. (2009). *Talking about health: Why communication matters*. Malden, MA: Wiley-Blackwell.

Parrott, R., Duncan, V., & Duggan, A. (2000). Promoting full and honest disclosure during conversations with health care providers. In S. Petronio (Ed.), *Balancing the secrets of private disclosures* (pp. 137–148). Mahwah, NJ: Lawrence Erlbaum.

Podichetty, V. K., Booher, J., Whitfield, M., & Biscup, R. S. (2006). Assessment of internet use and effects among healthcare professionals: A cross sectional survey. *Postgraduate Medical Journal, 82*, 274–279.

Servellen, G. V. (2009). *Communication skills for the healthcare professional: Concepts, practice, and evidence* (2nd ed.). Boston, MA: Jones and Bartlett.

Shadmi, E., Boyd, C. M., Hsiao, C., Sylvia, M., Schuster, A. B., & Boult, C. (2006). Morbidity and older persons' perceptions of the quality of their primary care. *Journal of the American Geriatrics Society, 54,* 330–334.

Simmons, M. S., Nides, M. A., Rand, C. S., Wise, R. A., & Tashkin, D. P. (2009). Unpredictability of deception of compliance with physician-prescribed bronchodilator inhaler use in clinical trials. *Chest, 118,* 290–295.

Stivers, T. (2002). Presenting the problem in pediatric encounters: "Symptoms only" versus "candidate diagnosis" presentations. *Health Communication, 14,* 299–338.

U.S. Department of Health and Human Services (2009). Quick guide to health literacy: Fact sheet. Retrieved February 15, 2009, from http://www.health.gov/communication/literacy/quickguide.

Vermeire, E., Hearnshaw, H., VanRoyen, P., & Denekens, J. (2001). Patient adherence to treatment: Three decades of research. A comprehensive review. *Journal of Clinical Pharmacy & Therapeutics, 26,* 331–342.

Weaver, C. (2008, September 8). Do TV shows drive up medical costs? *The Seattle Times.* Retrieved May 21, 2009, from www.seattletimes.nwsource.com.

Wolff, J. L., & Roter, D. L. (2008). Medical visit companions as a resource for vulnerable older adults. *Archives of Internal Medicine, 168,* 1409–1415.

Zook, E. G. (1994). Embodied health and constitutive communication: Toward an authentic conceptualization of health communication. In S. Deetz (Ed.), *Communication yearbook 17* (pp. 344–377). Thousand Oaks, CA: Sage.

Health Care Provider Interaction

Chapter Learning Objectives

◆ Understand the many influences on health care provider/patient interaction
◆ Become familiar with the benefits of patient-centered communication for health care providers
◆ Identify skills health care providers need to practice patient-centered communication
◆ Explain techniques for improving patients' health literacy

Chapter Preview

In this chapter we continue to consider the complex dynamics of patient/health care provider interaction, but from the health care provider's perspective. We begin by defining the term health care provider. Next, we address several macro-level and micro-level contextual influences on how health care providers communicate with patients including organizational, interpersonal, cultural, and power. The chapter progresses with a discussion of patient-centered communication, including the benefits to health care providers of using patient-centered communication and an explanation of the skills health care providers need to adopt a patient-centered approach to communication and care. The next section of the chapter attends to the issue of health literacy and provides strategies for how health care providers and practitioners can enhance the health literacy of patients, clients, or target audiences. We conclude the chapter by exploring an example service-learning project and discussing the important role of training to create an audience-centered approach to diversity within a health communication campaign.

This cartoon pokes fun at one of the common critiques of the ways health care providers and health care institutions think about and treat their patients. In this chapter we focus on the health care provider's role in patient/health care provider interaction and consider communication skills that can help health care providers treat patients as individuals and not just as numbers.

Health Care Provider Defined

Before addressing several factors that influence health care providers and their communication with patients, it is important to explain who we mean by health care providers. For our purposes, the term *health care providers* refers to anyone who offers health-related services to patients or clients. This includes physicians, nurses, therapists, medical technicians, public health practitioners, campaign workers, nutritionists, and health educators, to name a few. Now that we understand who we mean by the term health care providers, let's consider macro-level and micro-level influences on health care provider communication with patients.

Macro-Level and Micro-Level Influences on Health Care Provider Communication

Just as we discussed in Chapter 4, "Linking Health Communication with Patient Interaction," there are several macro-level and micro-level factors that influence health care provider communication. *Macro-level influences* on health care provider communication are broad or large-scale factors from outside the immediate context of the health care provider/patient interaction. *Micro-level influences* on health care provider communication are localized influences within the immediate context of the health care provider/patient interaction. Macro-level and micro-level influences on health care provider communication include:

- ◆ Organizational influences
- ◆ Interpersonal influences
- ◆ Cultural influences
- ◆ Power dynamics

Based on our definition of macro-level and micro-level influences on health care provider/patient interaction, which of the influences listed would you consider macro-level influences and which would you consider micro-level influences? If you responded that organizational influences are macro-level influences and that interpersonal influences, cultural influences, and power dynamics are micro-level influences, you are correct! We'll discuss each of the macro-level and micro-level influences in turn. We begin with macro-level influences because from most health care providers' perspectives, these broader influences are less within their locus of control but nevertheless permeate their interactions with patients.

Macro-Level Influences on Health Care Provider Communication

As a reminder, macro-level influences are broader influences outside the immediate health care provider/patient context that affect the interaction.

Organizational Influences

Most health care providers, whether they are medical personnel or public health practitioners, work in an organizational setting and must function within the rules and confines of that organization as well as the other organizations with which they interact. In this section we explore some organizational influences on how health care providers communicate with patients including:

- ◆ Managed care
- ◆ Organizational culture
- ◆ Organizational rules and guidelines

Managed care is a health care system with administrative control over primary health care services within a medical group practice that serves prepaid subscribers. The intention of managed care organizations is to eliminate redundant facilities and services and reduce costs. Managed care organizations take many forms with two of the most common being health maintenance organizations (HMOs) and preferred provider organizations (PPOs). HMOs and PPOs utilize primary care physicians to provide comprehensive care to patients and limit unnecessary services by controlling access to specialists unless the primary care physician provides a referral. Managed care organizations aim to control medical costs and streamline processes for efficiency (Mosby, 2009).

In Chapter 4, "Linking Health Communication with Patient Interaction," we discussed how the managed care system places constraints on patients and their abilities to communicate with health care providers. Managed care also places constraints on health care providers and influences their communication with patients (Lammers & Geist, 1997). One of the outcomes of managed care is an even greater power shift to the health care provider. Primary care physicians are given the power by managed care organizations to control referrals to specialists and other health care services, such as medical tests. In addition, physicians often are under pressure to see as many patients as possible each day, which limits the amount of time they can interact with each patient. A recent study estimated that the average time a physician spends with a patient in the office is 18 minutes (Mechanic, McAlpine, & Rosenthal, 2001). Because of time constraints, physicians attempt to control their encounters with patients by strictly keeping conversations to what they deem relevant to the current health issue. Health care providers may also be limited in the services they can offer and suggest based on patients' health insurance, their level of coverage, and what they can afford.

Another organizational influence is the organizational culture within which the health care provider practices. *Organizational culture* is defined as "actions, ways of thinking, practices, stories, and artifacts that characterize a particular organization" (Eisenberg, Goodall, & Trethewey, 2007, p. 127). Some organizational cultures in the health care industry promote patient-centered communication and care, whereas other organizational cultures promote efficiency and accuracy rather than developing strong relationships with patients. Most often health care providers conform to the organizational culture and communication norms within their work environments.

An example of how organizational culture influences health care provider communication can be found at Bronson Methodist Hospital located in Kalamazoo, Michigan. Bronson Methodist Hospital is focused on achieving excellence by providing patient-centered care and involves all of its medical staff and employees in the process. In order to promote a patient-centered organizational culture and socialize employees accordingly, Bronson leadership distributes a one-page list of expectations to all new employees and has routine reviews and communication with employees to ensure the list of expectations are attended to and achieved.

Bronson also created a family advisory council to provide input on employee behaviors and communication that are most beneficial to families. Bronson Methodist Hospital's organizational culture is steeped in patient-centered communication and care.

There also are organizational rules and guidelines that influence health care provider/patient communication. *Rules and guidelines* are defined as explicit or understood regulations that guide behavior within a particular environment. For example, some health care organizations have rules about health care providers interacting with patients outside the professional setting. Health care providers may be discouraged from forming personal relationships with patients in order to maintain professional relationships. Health care providers also may be required to follow rules or guidelines that limit the amount of personal information they reveal about themselves so that the focus of their interactions remains on patients.

The *Health Information Privacy Accountability Act (HIPAA)* also places constraints on the ways health care providers communicate about and share their patients' health information. The purpose of HIPAA is to ensure privacy of patients' written, oral, and electronic health information and to limit access to patients' health information. Entities covered by this law include health care providers, health insurance providers, and health care organizations and agencies. Under HIPAA, health care providers and health care organizations must actively protect patients' privacy by getting consent to share health information, even with family members, and they must take reasonable actions to maintain patient privacy.

For example, patients can request to not be contacted at home or to have bills sent in unmarked envelopes. In health care settings, health care providers are required to take reasonable actions to protect patients' privacy. If you have ever been waiting in line at the pharmacy and seen a sign asking you to wait a certain distance away from the counter, you have seen HIPAA in action. In addition, many health care providers make it personal practice not to approach or interact with patients outside health care organizations or in public to respect their privacy.

Micro-Level Influences on Health Care Provider Communication

As a reminder, micro-level influences are localized influences within the immediate health care provider/patient context that affect the interaction.

Interpersonal Influences

Interpersonal influences are defined as attributes of the participating individuals that affect the interaction. Research in health communication shows that there are several personal attributes or practice-style differences of health care providers that influence the interpersonal nature of health care provider/patient interaction including:

◆ Gender—female physicians tend to have longer, less technical, and more patient-centered consultations than male physicians (Bertakis, 2009; Lurie et al., 1993).

- *Specialty*—health care providers from different areas of medical care (e.g., physicians versus nurses) interact with patients differently (Ruiz-Moral, Podriguez, de Torres, & de la Torre, 2006).
- *Age*—older health care providers trained in more traditional methods may favor a more paternalistic approach to health care but they also may be perceived as more knowledgeable and experienced (Buller & Buller, 1987; Waitzkin, 1984, 1985)
- *Communication style*—some health care providers have a more direct and open communication style, while others are more reserved (Bertakis, 2009; Zachariae et al., 2003).

Cultural Influences

In the previous chapter, we considered some of the cultural influences on patients and their communication with health care providers. Similarly, health care providers' cultural backgrounds influence the ways they communicate with patients. *Cultural influences* are broadly defined as systems of beliefs, attitudes, and values that shape how we live and communicate. Health care providers bring their cultural conceptions of power, health, time, and appropriate verbal and nonverbal communication to interactions with patients. For example, a Native American physician might find it difficult to maintain eye contact with patients because in many Native American cultures this is a sign of disrespect. Patients unaware of this norm within their physician's culture may be offended by the lack of eye contact or perceive the physician as incompetent or dishonest.

In addition to health care providers' cultural backgrounds influencing their communication style, the culture of the patient also can influence health care providers' communication style. When patients' culture, race, or ethnicity varies from their health care providers' culture, race, or ethnicity it is more likely there will be difficulties communicating and creating relationships. For example, some studies found that White health care providers interact and communicate differently with African American patients than they do with White patients, and usually this communication is rated as less effective (Johnson, Roter, Powe, & Cooper, 2004; Street, Gordon, & Haidet, 2007). These variations in communication might be a result of health care provider discomfort with cultural differences or simply because health care providers lack the communication skills needed to bridge cultural gaps.

Power Dynamics

Power is defined as an attribute of a relationship during which persons, by virtue of their position or by withholding rewards or inflicting punishments, have the ability to impose their wills on others despite resistance (Berger, 1994). The power of each party involved in the interaction influences what is said and how it is said. Power dynamics often determine who controls the conversation and whose agenda is achieved. Another way to conceptualize or think about power dynamics within health care interactions is depicted in Table 5.1, which displays the different relational styles that can result from differences in power between patients and health care providers (Roter & McNeilis, 2003).

		HEALTH CARE PROVIDER POWER	
		LOW	HIGH
PATIENT POWER	Low	Default	Paternalism
	High	Consumerism	Mutuality

Table 5.1 ◆ *Intersection of health care provider and patient power dynamics*

The two quadrants on the left side in Table 5.1, default and consumerism, likely are the least productive to effective health care communication. The top left quadrant, *default*, represents a relationship between health care providers and patients that lacks direction and may come to a standstill because their expectations of the interaction are at odds and they cannot seem to renegotiate those expectations. In the lower left quadrant, *consumerism*, the traditional health care provider/patient relationship is reversed such that patients seek information and services based solely on their preferences, and health care providers comply. Examples of consumer-based medicine may be elective cosmetic plastic surgery such as liposuction, eye lifts, or breast augmentation. Patients wanting elective cosmetic surgery do not have a medical need but go to plastic surgeons to purchase the procedures they prefer. Generally, consumerism is not a desired relationship style, as patients do not always have the medical expertise needed to control decisions regarding diagnosis and treatment.

The two quadrants on the right side in Table 5.1, paternalism and mutuality, are recognized as more effective approaches to health care communication, with mutuality being the ideal relational style. The top right quadrant, *paternalism*, represents the most traditional view of patient/health care provider interaction in which health care providers are considered authorities who take care of patients. In this traditional mode of interaction, health care providers are the experts and the suppliers of information to patients. Paternalistic communication minimizes the role of patients and does not involve them any more than necessary. This relationship style is sometimes referred to as provider-centered communication. The lower right quadrant, *mutuality*, represents a more current perspective in which both patients and health care providers share power in information provision and decision making. This relationship style also is referred to as patient-centered communication or patient-centered care and often is considered ideal.

Now that you have a better understanding of the complex relationship between health care providers and patients from health care providers' perspectives, including the macro-level and micro-level influences on health care providers' interaction with patients, let's turn our attention to patient-centered communication from the perspective of health care providers.

Patient-Centered Communication from Perspective of Health Care Providers

As described in Chapter 4, "Linking Health Communication with Patient Interaction," *patient-centered communication* is communication that maximizes involvement of patients in the health care provider/patient relationship, which is beneficial for patients. However, in addition to being beneficial for patients patient-centered communication has several benefits for health care providers.

Benefits of Patient-Centered Communication

Even though patient-centered communication is focused on patients rather than health care providers, there also are benefits of patient-centered communication for health care providers. However, the benefits of patient-centered care for health care providers may not seem as obvious because this approach may take more time, effort, and skill on the part of health care providers. Health care providers have to continually be aware of patients' needs and adapt their communication accordingly. The three benefits of patient-centered communication for health care providers (Brown, Stewart, & Ryan, 2003) are:

◆ Increased patient compliance
◆ Fewer malpractice claims
◆ Greater patient satisfaction

One major benefit of patient-centered communication for health care providers is *increased patient compliance,* which means patients are more likely to follow what their health care providers direct them to do. When patients feel ownership in, a sense of responsibility for, and clear understanding of the treatment plans, they are more likely to follow the treatment routine (Robinson, Callister, Berry, & Dearing, 2008; Schoenthaler et al., 2009). When patients comply with health care providers' orders, it also increases health care providers' sense of accomplishment because their patients are more likely to have improved health outcomes.

The second benefit of patient-centered communication for health care providers is *fewer malpractice claims*. Patients who are involved in patient-centered care are less likely to sue health care providers for mistreatment because they feel a connection with their health care providers, believe their health care providers have their best interests in mind, and realize better health outcomes. Also, health care providers incorporating patient-centered communication are more likely to understand the complexity of patients' conditions and can treat their health issues more efficiently.

The third benefit of patient-centered communication for health care providers is *greater patient satisfaction*, which means patients feel more content with their health care. When patients feel that health care providers listen to them, seriously consider their concerns, and work with them to find solutions, they are generally more satisfied with their health care providers (Uitterhoeve et al., 2009; Venetis, Robinson, Turkiewicz, & Allen, 2009). This also benefits health care providers in that patients are more likely to become repeat patients. Patients also are less likely to file complaints against their health care providers when they are satisfied with their care.

Using patient-centered communication provides benefits for health care providers, but incorporating this approach into health care also can be challenging because it requires developing an array of communication skills. In the next section, we discuss some of the skills health care providers need to practice patient-centered communication.

Ethics Touchstone

Return to the *Before I Die* transcript presented in Chapter 2, "Linking Health Communication with Ethics," to address the following:

◆ Did any of the health care providers practice patient-centered communication? Provide an example from the dialogue in the transcript to support your answer.

◆ Choose a section of dialogue from the transcript that is not very patient-centered and rewrite that dialogue to represent a more patient-centered approach.

◆ With which ethical orientation does patient-centered communication and care align? Why?

Health Care Provider Skills for Patient-Centered Communication

Skills that health care providers need to practice patient-centered communication include:

◆ Active listening
◆ Therapeutic interviewing
◆ Advice giving
◆ Empathy
◆ Bad news delivery

A primary skill health care providers need to practice patient-centered communication is active listening. As discussed previously, a patient-centered approach values what patients have to say and encourages patients to communicate as much pertinent information as possible with their health care providers. For health care providers this means they must be good at listening. Even more specifically, health care providers need to be skilled in *active listening,* which involves focusing attention on their patients by suspending their own frames of reference and judgment. Statements are paraphrased back to patients to clarify and check perceptions. Feedback ensues until mutual understanding between health care provider and patient occurs (Brownell, 2006; Schultz, 2003). In other words, active listening requires genuinely listening to what patients are saying and if necessary encouraging patients to talk more. There are three steps or skills involved in active listening.

An important skill for active listening is listening to patients without interrupting. Health care providers also need to indicate their focus on patients and to what patients are saying by maintaining eye contact, avoiding distracting gestures, and using encouraging nonverbals and verbals such as nodding or murmuring phrases such as "Yes" or "I see." Health care providers who ask questions of patients but then appear to be busy with other tasks when patients are responding may not be considered to be actively listening. Instead, giving positive responses to patients may encourage them to talk about their symptoms and concerns. An actively listening health care provider also helps patients feel more comfortable when talking about sensitive medical issues.

Other active listening skills include listening both to what patients say and to what they do not say. An active listener must be in tune with patients' tone and body language to determine if they may be withholding something (Moss, 2008). For example, patients may deny that they are experiencing pain but if that denial is spoken with an unsure tone or with an anguished facial expression, it may be a cue to health care providers to probe further about symptoms. In addition, health care providers may need to repeat and clarify to aid patients in more fully understanding their communication. Paraphrasing and summarizing patients' words are additional techniques for fact checking and helping patients feel heard and listened to.

A second skill health care providers need to practice patient-centered communication is therapeutic interviewing. A common activity in any health care setting is performing a basic interview. During this interview information is gathered about patients' current health issues as well as their medical histories. *Therapeutic interviewing* in health care communication involves "an interpersonal exchange, using verbal and nonverbal messages that culminates in someone's being helped" (van Servellen, 2009, p. 169).

Therapeutic interviewing has several potential goals including:

◆ Obtaining full descriptions of patients' conditions and concerns
◆ Reducing patients' emotional distress
◆ Offering support
◆ Listing primary and secondary health problems
◆ Establishing collaborative relationship

Given the goals of therapeutic interviewing, what are the specific behaviors and skills that can help health care providers and patients meet those goals? There are two key interviewing skills that health care providers need to develop therapeutic interviewing which are:

◆ Question asking
  ❖ Closed-ended questions
  ❖ Open-ended questions

- ❖ Clarifying questions
- ❖ Probing questions
- ◆ Common language

Often when we think of interviewing, we immediately think of the significance of questions, as *question asking* is a principal way to gather information. Generally, health care providers have two broad types of questions available to use; closed-ended questions and open-ended questions. *Closed-ended questions* are questions that can be answered with a "yes" or a "no," such as "are you having any pain in your leg?" *Open-ended questions* are questions that cannot be answered with yes or no, such as "How would you describe the pain in your leg?" Health care providers need to be skilled in using both types of questions. Open-ended questions tend to elicit the most information so open-ended questions are encouraged in patient-centered communication. However, closed-ended questions are useful when health care providers need to obtain specific details.

Health care providers also must become skilled at asking clarifying and probing questions. *Clarifying questions* are questions of fact that ensure health care providers understand what patients are saying. *Probing questions* are used to determine additional information and ask patients to expand on what they said. For example, a patient may simply volunteer that she has been feeling extremely fatigued. The health care provider needs to ask some probing questions to determine the extent of the fatigue, including questions about lifestyle issues that may be influencing the level of fatigue and other symptoms related to fatigue.

In addition to being skilled at asking questions, another challenge to effective therapeutic interviewing is that health care providers and patients often do not share a common language. To begin grasping a sense of this challenge, please take a few minutes to complete Health Communication Nexus Interlude 5.1.

Health Communication Nexus Interlude 5.1

For this interlude think about all of the words you can use to describe a pain you are currently having or a pain you've had in the past. Take a few minutes to jot down all of your ideas in your notebook.

Keep this list of your adjectives to describe a pain nearby as you continue to read and think about the difficulties health care providers and patients may have in gaining mutual understanding.

Now imagine a scenario in which, due to persistent knee pain, a patient makes an appointment with a physician. The physician asks the patient about the severity of the pain by questioning, "How severe is the pain you've been feeling in your knee?" This simple question raises an important issue. The health care provider and patient may have very different conceptions or definitions of what constitutes severe pain, which may cause misunderstanding and possibly misdiagnosis and mistreatment. The physician then asks the patient to describe the pain by questioning, "So how would you describe the pain you are feeling in your knee?" Refer back to the list of pain terms you wrote down during Health Communication Nexus Interlude 5.1. Just as you did, the patient in this scenario could describe the pain in a variety of ways, perhaps it is "a dull pain," or "an aching pain," or "a stabbing pain," or "a sharp pain." The challenge for the health care provider and patient is to come to a mutual understanding of what kind of pain the patient is experiencing so diagnosis and treatment can be as accurate and helpful as possible.

The challenges of finding a common language are even more difficult when patients and health care providers speak different languages. Most hospitals and many medical practices have interpreters on staff to assist health care providers and patients in their communication. However, the use of interpreters can make communication difficult because there is a delay in sending and receiving messages, some words from each language may not have direct translations, and health care providers may struggle to build rapport with the patients (Rosenberg, Leanza, & Seller, 2007). When professional interpreters are not available, family members sometimes serve as translators. This can be problematic as family members may be more likely to interject their own opinions and concerns into the conversation rather than directly translating.

A third skill that health care providers need to practice patient-centered communication is advice giving. Often we think of health care providers issuing orders or giving patients directives such as "Take this medication for the next week" or "Try to get a lot of rest." However, because ultimately patients have freedom to make their own health care decisions, what health care providers really are doing is giving patients advice about diagnoses and how to proceed with treatment. *Advice giving* is defined as "the act of disclosing what one thinks or feels about another's experience, namely, what you think they should do, think, or feel" (van Servellen, 2009, p. 169).

There are times when patients may request advice from health care providers on how to handle a medical situation or on how to live a healthier lifestyle. When patients ask for advice from their health care providers, they tend to be more receptive to the advice they receive. When advice is given without being requested, patients may be less receptive to health care providers' advice. In particular, advice may not be well received by patients if they sense their health care providers are trying to be dominating or controlling.

Therefore, health care providers need to be sensitive when giving unsolicited advice to patients. Advice should be coupled with logical reasons and potential outcomes from following the advice. Unsolicited advice also can be softened with opening phrases such as, "You might want to consider . . ." or "An option you could take would be to . . ." These phrases provide an element of choice or agency for the patient, making the advice more likely to be accepted and potentially followed.

The fourth essential skill needed by health care providers to practice patient-centered communication is empathy. *Empathy* is defined as identification with or vicariously experiencing the feelings or thoughts of another. Health care providers are empathetic and are able to express this when they feel sympathy for patients and understand where patients are coming from. Empathy occurs when health care providers come to understand patients' situations and the struggles patients face. For example, a physician may be seeing an overweight patient to treat his high blood pressure. An empathetic physician seeks to discover and understand the myriad of reasons for the patient's weight problem and tries to develop feasible strategies to help the patient manage his high blood pressure while working also to help him reduce his weight.

Empathy is a challenging concept for many health care providers because they may be concerned about maintaining professional boundaries while showing genuine concern for patients. Getting too emotionally involved with patients also can be draining for health care providers, so they need to strike a balance between being concerned about patients and not becoming emotionally consumed. Miller, Birkholt, Scott, and Stage (1995) referred to this issue when they explained the difference between emotional contagion and empathetic concern. *Emotional contagion* is having an affective response that consists of parallel emotions to another or "feeling *with* another" (p. 126; author's italics). *Empathetic concern* is having an affective response that consists of nonparallel emotions to another or "feeling *for* another" (p. 126; author's italics). Empathetic concern is the more communicatively effective stance for health care providers to take with patients. For example, if a nurse in the trauma unit struggles to perform his duties because he becomes physically nauseous when patients report extreme pain, he may be experiencing an emotionally contagious response to his patients, which is negatively affecting his performance.

Empathy also can be a difficult patient-centered communication skill to teach as it involves adjusting health care providers' thought processes, not just their communication behaviors. To become more empathetic, often health care providers must adjust their cognitive energy from remaining relatively detached and only concerned about diagnoses and treatments toward being more interested in patients' relevant feelings and experiences. One way for health care providers to learn to express empathy is to practice active listening in order to gain insight into patients' situations. Other ways to use empathetic communication include acknowledging patients' experiences or feelings, agreeing with patients, and conveying positive feelings.

A fifth skill health care providers need to practice patient-centered communication is delivering bad news. *Bad news delivery* is defined as the process of health care providers presenting unfavorable medical information or diagnoses to patients and/or their families that likely is unwelcome or disturbing. Perhaps one of the most challenging situations for health care providers is to communicate bad news to patients or patients' families. For example, some of the most extreme situations during which health care providers need to talk with patients and patients' families about bad news include the diagnosis of a terminal illness and/or the death of

PROFILE

An Exemplar of Patient-Centered Care

Mark D'Amico, Certified Prosthetist—Amputee Care Center

Mark D'Amico is a certified prosthetist (CP) in Indianapolis, Indiana. As a prosthetist he works with patients who are missing limbs due either to amputations or birth defects. His job includes creating and fitting prosthetic limbs, rehabilitation, and gait analysis. His primary goal is to help amputees reach their full potential with the assistance of adaptive devices. As a CP he can easily relate to his patients as he too is an amputee. At age three he was involved in a lawn mower accident and lost his leg above the knee. He was fortunate to become involved in testing state of the art prosthetic devices and also participates in a variety of sports including cycling, skiing, and swimming. In 1992 and 1998 he represented the United States at the Paralympic Games. His loss of a limb never holds him back.

D'Amico's positive experiences with adaptive devices led to his current career. The driving force in his career is patient satisfaction and success rather than monetary gains. He believes that effective and sufficient communication with his patients is essential for them to get the most out of their adaptive devices. This means making himself available to his patients and giving them the time they need to discuss their concerns and ask their questions. He knows that in a profit-driven medical world this can be difficult to do as there is pressure to book more and more clients in order to generate revenue. To resist this pressure, D'Amico keeps the overhead, or costs of doing business, as low as possible.

One of the greatest challenges D'Amico faces in communicating with his patients is making sure that he and his patients fully understand each other. A patient may describe something as uncomfortable or painful, but uncomfortable and painful may have different meanings to different patients. Another challenge he faces is adapting his communication style to the variety of patients. Some patients simply want to be told what to do and what is going to be done whereas other patients like to approach the situation more as a team and make decisions and treatment plans together. As a health care provider D'Amico has to get to know each patient fairly quickly and determine what communication style is going to help that patient have the best possible outcomes.

Now, based on this profile, answer these questions:

◆ How is Mark D'Amico an exemplar of a health care provider who uses patient-centered communication and care? Give two examples from his profile to support your answer.

◆ What new aspect of patient-centered care did you learn about from this profile?

◆ What is one suggestion you would give a health care provider about patient-centered care?

a patient. Most often, scant formal training is offered to health care providers in how to effectively and empathetically deliver bad news. Consequently, most health care providers learn from trial and error or from other health care providers the most effective and ineffective ways to convey bad news. In general, though, delivering bad news is a very unpleasant task and one that makes many health care providers uncomfortable and anxious.

To effectively deliver bad news, health care providers must be honest with patients. Although health care providers may feel compelled to withhold some

ETHICAL DILEMMA ◆ What Would You Do?

Imagine you are an oncologist and you just learned through testing that one of your patients has terminal cancer. The patient's family asked that you not tell the patient if the tests come back with life-threatening news.

◆ Would you tell the patient? Why or why not?
◆ What would you say to the patient?
◆ What would you say to the patient's family?

---

information from patients in order to protect them or their families or to give them a sense of hope, medical ethics and legal requirements mandate honesty. These ethical and legal mandates require health care providers to offer patients full information so they can make informed decisions. Patients or patients' families should not be given false hope, but instead must be presented with accurate and truthful information. For more on health communication and ethics, please refer to Chapter 2, "Linking Health Communication with Ethics." Next we present a technique for delivering bad news.

To assist health care providers in the difficult task of delivering bad news, the SPIKES method was developed, which provides a six-phase process to guide bad news message delivery (Buckman, 1992). SPIKES is an acronym that stands for:

◆ **S**etting
◆ **P**erceptions of health status
◆ **I**nvitation
◆ **K**nowledge
◆ **E**motions/empathy
◆ **S**ummary/strategy

The first phase in the SPIKES method is setting. *Setting* refers to the environment of the health communication exchange and creating a maximally conducive situation for the delivery of bad news. An important initial consideration is the location of the conversation during which bad news is given. If possible a quiet location such as a private office or small conference room is ideal. During these conversations, health care providers should strive to be at eye level with patients and/or patients' families to promote a sense of relaxation and equality. Health care providers also should not appear to be rushed and if possible should block out potential interruptions such as ringing telephones or beeping pagers. Subtle nonverbal gestures such as sustained eye contact or a touch on the arm can create rapport and help soothe patients and/or their families.

The second phase in the SPIKES method is for health care providers to determine patients' or patients' families' current assessment or perceptions of their health status. *Perceptions of health status* refer to feelings about the state of an individual's own health or the health of another. Simple questions posed by health care providers such as "What is your understanding of your condition?" can help gauge patients' and/or their families' perceptions of patients' health. Determining perceptions of health status allows health care providers to correct any false information and provide needed explanations. This phase also may reveal patients' and/or their families' technical knowledge of their health situation as well as their emotional condition.

During the third phase in the SPIKES method, *invitation*, health care providers talk with patients and/or their families about how much information and in how much detail they would like to know about their health and by what means they would prefer to receive that information. Some patients may desire a general overview of their diagnoses and treatment plans, although others may want specific details such as the names of medications and dosages. This phase respects that patients and their families are unique and have different informational needs and desires.

The fourth phase in the SPIKES method is *knowledge,* which is when the bad news is told to patients and/or their families. Health care providers can begin this phase by providing patients and/or their families with some kind of warning that bad news is about to be presented. Preemptive statements may include, "I am sorry to have to tell you . . ." or "Unfortunately . . ." In addition, when giving medical details, health care providers need to consider the medical knowledge of patients and use terms that are easily understood. Also, it is helpful to provide information to patients and their families in small chunks and between providing these chunks of information check for receivers' level of understanding and emotional status. Health care providers should try to avoid being excessively blunt, such as beginning the conversation with, "You have cancer and have three months to live." Taking longer to facilitate the conversation can ease the blow of the bad news for patients and/or their families.

The fifth phase in the SPIKES method of bad news delivery is to address and respond to patients' and/or their families' emotions while expressing empathy. This phase can be especially difficult and uncomfortable for health care providers, in particular when emotional reactions by patients and/or their families involve crying, anger, or disbelief. The SPIKES method includes a four-step technique for *responding to emotions and providing an empathetic response*. First, health care providers must be aware of patients' and/or their families' emotional responses whether overt, such as crying, or more introverted, such as silence. Second, health care providers need to name or identify the emotions expressed to themselves. If health care providers are unsure of what emotions are being expressed it is best to ask patients and/or their families. Third, health care providers should identify reasons for the emotions. For example, "My patient is scared because the radiation did not shrink the tumor." Fourth, health care providers should voice an empathetic response that names and validates patients' and/or their families' emotions. For example, "I understand that you are feeling frightened because of the poor test results."

The fifth phase in the SPIKES method is to provide a *summary* of the information provided and present a *strategy* for future treatment. Although health care providers may be uncomfortable presenting plans when there are few medical options for treatment left to consider, they need to focus on creating a mutual plan for making the patients and/or their families as comfortable and contented as possible. Do you think the health care providers, patient, and her family depicted in the *Before I Die* transcript presented in Chapter 2, "Linking Health Communication with Ethics," could have benefitted from using the SPIKES method?

Skills Training in Patient-Centered Communication

With such a wide variety of skills needed for health care providers to practice patient-centered communication, it is reasonable to assume that these skills may not come naturally to most health care providers. If health care providers do not naturally possess these skills, they need to learn patient-centered communication skills. This raises the question of how communication skills are incorporated into the curriculum of education programs attended by future health care providers.

Some may argue that health care providers learn patient-centered communication skills not through formal training in communication classes but through the socialization process of working with other health care professionals in their area of specialty. During their education health care providers participate in a number of situations during which health care professionals closely monitor their work. For example, consider a physician's internship and residency. While in the field for these portions of their education, medical school students observe and often model the communication behaviors of those health care providers around them. If the health care providers that students are observing are not using patient-centered communication techniques, but instead are using more of a health care provider-centered approach, students likely will adopt relatively the same communication style.

Based on this concern about using only a socialization and/or modeling approach to training health care providers in health communication, some medical schools and other health care training programs have incorporated more formal communication training into their curriculums. For example, the Ohio State University Medical School requires a two-year ongoing course sequence about patient-centered care that focuses on many aspects of communication. Other health care provider training programs incorporate communication elements into existing courses (Batalden, Leach, Swing, Dreyfus, & Dreyfus, 2002).

Health Literacy

In Chapter 4, "Linking Health Communication with Patient Interaction," we discussed how patients' health literacy influences their communication, as well as their health status. Consequently, health care providers need to take steps to improve their patients' and/or clients' health literacy in order to improve overall well-being. Before we further describe techniques for accomplishing this, please take a minute to complete Health Communication Nexus Interlude 5.2.

To complete this interlude read the following statement describing a health risk to an organization's employees.

"Employees who fit into the following categories should be aware of an increased susceptibility to contracting *methicillin-resistant Staphylococcus aureus (MRSA)*:

• Use invasive devices

• Have been treated with fluoroquinolones (ciprofloxacin, ofloxacin or levofloxacin) or cephalosporin

• Weakened immune system

• Have been a resident at a health-related facility for a duration of fourteen or more days"

As you read this statement again, jot down in your notebook what you think this message means. Were you able to decipher the message? What suggestions would you give for making this message more accessible to employees at the organization?

Techniques for Improving Health Literacy

Healthy People 2010 identified improving health literacy as one of its goals (U.S. Department of Health and Human Services, 2010). The question is, how can health literacy be improved? Many of the techniques to improve health literacy involve adapting and changing health messages to be easily understood by the audience. Generally, these strategies place the onus on the health communicator whether it be a nurse, physician, or the designer of a pamphlet or Web site. Suggested techniques for increasing health literacy include:

◆ Acknowledge and adapt to cultural differences
◆ Use clear communication
  ❖ Main or key points first
  ❖ Four or fewer main or key points
  ❖ Manageable chunks of information
  ❖ Common vocabulary
  ❖ Active voice
  ❖ Short sentences
  ❖ Text written in easy-to-read fonts
  ❖ High-contrast colors
  ❖ Supplement instructions with images
◆ Focus on behavior
◆ Pretest messages and promotional materials

Now that you have read this list, review your notes from Health Communication Nexus Interlude 5.2. Did you incorporate any of the suggested techniques to increase health literacy as you tried to make the message easier to understand? Here is one example of how the message in Health Communication Nexus Interlude 5.2 could be rewritten:

> Employees who fit into the following categories should be aware that they are more likely to contract MRSA (a drug-resistant staph infection):
>
> ◆ Individuals who are on dialysis or have a catheter or a feeding tube
> ◆ Individuals who have recently been on an antibiotic
> ◆ Individuals who have a weakened immune system due to HIV/AIDS or other immune-compromising condition
> ◆ Individuals who have had a recent hospital stay over two weeks long

Incorporating more familiar language and fewer technical terms makes the message more accessible to the audience and easier to understand and act upon.

Let's further consider the specific techniques for improving health literacy. *Acknowledge and adapt to cultural differences* refers to understanding the culture of your target audience or audiences and then creating or adapting health messages that are culturally sensitive and appropriate. For example, when Professor Mattson was working on CDC's DES Update (Centers for Disease Control and Prevention, 2009), the campaign team learned through telephone focus groups with target audience members from across the United States that the initial design for the promotional materials, particularly the photos, were not culturally sensitive. The uncopyrighted photos initially chosen depicted only White people who were smiling. Focus group members wondered why other races were not depicted given that exposure to DES did not have strict racial boundaries. They also wondered why all the people in the photos were smiling considering they were representing exposure to DES, which is known to have serious negative health effects. Based on their feedback, the campaign team changed the photos on the promotional materials to better represent the variety of people exposed to DES. According to Airhihenbuwa (1995), to be culturally consistent, involvement of community members is essential when planning health interventions. This example from CDC's DES Update also addresses the importance of *pretesting messages and promotional materials* with target audience members before those materials are mass produced.

Generally, the other techniques listed to improve health literacy are self-explanatory and can be subsumed within the more general technique of using clear communication. *Using clear communication* means writing or speaking in ways that are straightforward and easy to understand. When delivering health-related information, health communicators need to put the *main or key points first* and use *four or fewer main or key points*. People may lose interest or become distracted over time so you want them first to see or hear the most essential elements of your message. Breaking a complex message up into four or fewer main or key points also is a good strategy so those points are easier to understand and remember.

For example, a complex medical procedure may need to be explained in more than one key point. Although many have heard of or know someone who has had laser-assisted in-situ keratomileusis, or LASIK, eye surgery, the details about the surgery including the risks, costs, benefits, and details of the actual procedure need to be explained separately and may even require more than one office visit. LASIK is a type of refractive laser eye surgery that patients choose instead of wearing corrective lenses (Mayo Clinic, 2009). LASIK basically involves an eye surgeon using a laser to reshape the cornea and correct focusing problems in the eyes. The thought of a laser touching an eye can be emotional or challenging for some who may require more time to receive and understand all the necessary aspects of this procedure, including making a decision on whether or not to have the surgery.

Relatedly, in an effort to use clear communication, it is important to divide the main or key points and the information contained within each key point into *manageable chunks of information*. In our LASIK eye surgery example, this means grouping similar concepts and/or procedures together into the separate key points of risks, costs, benefits, and details about the procedure. As another example, a patient just diagnosed with diabetes requires much information about testing sugar levels, diet, and medication. Instead of explaining all of these topics at once or in one appointment, which may be confusing and overwhelming for the patient, it would be best to cover each topic thoroughly with the patient before moving to the next topic. For some patients covering each topic in a separate appointment may be appropriate.

Clear communication also means using *common vocabulary* to explain technical concepts and terms. In Health Communication Nexus Interlude 5.2 about those at risk of contracting MRSA, you witnessed how technical language can be confusing and limit an individual's ability to understand the message. Keeping that example in mind, if you were tasked with creating a brochure about the risks of contracting a disease or illness you would want to define any terms that may not be understood by an average person or that may have multiple meanings for an average person. In your brochure, for example, if you list a fever as one of the symptoms a patient needs to watch for, it is best to include a specific temperature, such as over 100.5 degrees Fahrenheit.

Clear communication should *use active voice* rather than passive voice. For example, instead of writing or saying, "Your temperature will be taken by the nurse," you want to write, "The nurse will take your temperature." Writing or speaking in passive voice, even for brief periods of space or time, can make words seem more tedious, can be confusing, and can decrease the sense of urgency in your message. Using active voice more clearly explains who is doing or feeling something. For similar reasons, use *short sentences* that are clear and concise. This helps the message flow more smoothly and prevents the audience from becoming confused, as they might when trying to follow long, complex sentences.

In addition, an important aspect of health literacy involves making sure the design of health messages does not hamper individuals' abilities to read or view, the messages. This means, in part, that *text is written in easy-to-read fonts*. A clear font type in a large enough size, for example, can be especially important in messages intended for older adults who may have failing eyesight. *High-contrast colors* also should be used to increase readability such as white text on a dark background or dark text on a light background. Whenever possible, *supplement verbal or written instructions with images*, such as photographs or simple line diagrams. Instructions that involve complex movements, such as directions for exercises, or multiple steps, such as instructions for programming a medical device, can be difficult to understand when explained only with words. An accompanying illustration provides visual elements to complement the words and is especially useful for those who are visual rather than auditory learners.

Consider, for example, the following instructions for stretching the neck muscles of an infant suffering from a stiff neck:

"When the infant's head is tilted to the left side you will need to gently rotate the head to the left while stretching the head and neck to the right."

It may be difficult for an individual reading these instructions to determine exactly how the neck muscle stretches are to be accomplished. When accompanied by graphic illustrations of the instructed movements, these instructions become much easier to follow.

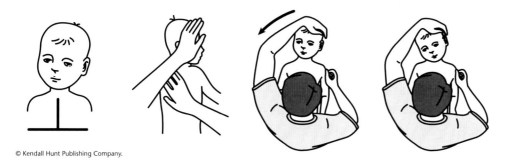

© Kendall Hunt Publishing Company.

"As in the above diagrams, when the infant's head is tilted to the left side you will need to gently rotate the head to the left while stretching the head and neck to the right."

In addition, when instructions are verbal and/or are accompanied by a demonstration it is a good idea to have a printed illustration that individuals can take with them and refer to later.

Another important technique is to *focus on behavior* because ultimately the goal of health messages is to persuade the target audience to behave in certain ways that promote their health. So messages need to explicitly tell the audience how you want them to behave to avoid or control injury and disease and maintain their health. For example, the poster in Figure 5.1 initially stated: "Every year more than 1,500 college-age adults DIE in motorcycle accidents." However, we learned during the testing of this message that we needed to tell those who saw it what they can do in response to this statistic. So we added, "Watch for motorcycles!" to include a call to action that is behavior focused and specifically tells viewers what they can do to decrease the risk of motorcycle accidents.

As another example of the importance of focusing on behavior rather than the underlying health principles, a brochure about preventing diabetes in older

Figure 5.1 ◆ *Poster from Motorcycle Safety at Purdue campaign*

adults should explain the behaviors an individual can enact that help prevent diabetes, such as exercising regularly and maintaining a healthy body weight, rather than devoting a lot of attention to explaining the particulars of how diabetes develops in the body. By focusing on behaviors, audience members more readily receive information about what actions to take to care for themselves or others.

As mentioned previously, it is necessary to *pretest messages and promotional materials* with a sample of audience members prior to those messages being publicly distributed or aired in the media. Pretesting allows message designers to gauge audience reactions to messages and expose errors or problems with the materials in addition to unintended consequences that the messages may generate. Although message designers may favor a particular message or think a message is easy to understand, the audience may be turned off by the message or find the message confusing and difficult to follow. Focus groups are an excellent research method to gather the opinions of a small group of target audience members (Krueger, 1998) before a message is mass produced, distributed, and later determined to be ineffective.

It also is important to note that as technologies continue to develop and change, there are more and more ways to distribute health information. For example, when using the internet as a channel to distribute health information, it is important to ensure that the information posted to Web sites is easily accessible and understandable. Simple strategies such as having clearly marked buttons or links to navigate the Web site and a search engine within the Web site can aid viewers in processing information contained on the Web site. Again, pretesting or usability testing with target audience members to determine how easy a Web site is to navigate and understand is important prior to launching the Web site.

The role of health communication in promoting higher health literacy rates is in creating messages that are easily accessible and comprehendible by target audience members. In addition, as the guidelines for improving health literacy emphasize, draft messages and proposed channels for distribution must always be pretested with target audience members to determine if the messages and channels meet their health information and behavior needs.

In our service-learning application, we consider how communication skills training is used in the Motorcycle Safety at Purdue campaign (MS@P) and how the issue of diversity is incorporated into this training.

SERVICE-LEARNING APPLICATION

Celebrating Diversity in Health Campaigns

In this service-learning application, we focus on incorporating, appreciating, and reaching out to the diverse audience that exists in the community you are serving as a health care provider or a health communication practitioner. Diversity also should be a key component in any service-learning activity or project so this application specifically addresses the *diversity standard for effective service-learning practice* because it promotes understanding of diversity and mutual respect among all participants (Corporation for National & Community Service, 2010).

One of the activities of the Motorcycle Safety at Purdue (MS@P) campaign is setting up a booth at campus events to distribute information and campaign materials and to talk with audience members. While working at the booth, campaign team members engage in conversations with diverse audience members that include motorcyclists, drivers of cars and trucks, and friends and family of motorcyclists. Audience members also come from different age groups, races, and cultural backgrounds, which presents challenges for campaign team members as they try to engage visitors to the booth in meaningful conversations. Based on team members' concerns about these challenges, a training manual and video was created to provide tips and teach team members how to best interact with various audience members.

The training materials contain basic hints and steps for taking an audience-centered approach to communication with audience members. Similar to the patient-centered approach discussed in this chapter, an audience-centered approach encourages campaign team members to listen to the audience and act in ways that make them comfortable. The training materials also give suggestions for questions or comments that could spark conversations. Another important component of the training materials is facts about motorcycles, motorcycle riding, and motorcycle safety. In order for campaign members to talk comfortably and intelligently with different audience members, they need a basic level of knowledge about the issues. Go to this book's Web site to view the MS@P training materials.

As you can see from this example, although you may be excited to reach a diverse audience with your service-learning project, working with individuals and groups who are different than you can present challenges as your team tries to reach out to diverse audiences and help diverse communities. Here are some suggestions for tailoring your service-learning projects and your communication to overcome these challenges:

◆ Identify diverse elements within your audience or community—if you do not recognize diversity, you will not be able to address diversity.

◆ Talk with members of different communities—learn firsthand what they want and need.

◆ In any communication materials, be sure to be sensitive to diversity by using inclusive language and inclusive images.

◆ If possible, recruit people to your service-learning team who represent the diversities in your target audience.

Chapter Summary

In this chapter we continued to consider the complex dynamics of patient/health care provider interaction, but from the health care provider's perspective. We began by defining the term health care provider keeping in mind that our use of this term extends beyond typical medical settings to include health educators and other health communication and public health practitioners. Next, we addressed several macro-level and micro-level contextual influences on how health care providers communicate with patients including organizational, interpersonal, cultural, and power. The chapter progressed with a discussion of patient-centered communication including the benefits to health care providers and an explanation of the skills health care providers need to adopt a patient-centered approach to communication and care. The next section of the chapter attended to the issue of health literacy and provided strategies for how health care providers and practitioners can enhance the health literacy of patients, clients, or target audiences. We concluded the chapter by exploring an example service-learning project and discussing the important role of training to create an audience-centered approach to diversity within a health communication campaign.

References

Airhihenbuwa, C. O. (1995). *Health and culture: Beyond the Western paradigm*. Thousand Oaks, CA: Sage.

Batalden, P., Leach, D., Swing, S., Dreyfus, H., & Dreyfus, S. (2002). General competencies and accreditation in graduate medical education. *Health Affairs, 21*, 103–111.

Berger, C. R. (1994). Power, dominance, and social interaction. In M. L. Knapp & G. R. Miller (Eds.), *Handbook of interpersonal communication* (2nd ed., pp. 450–507). Thousand Oaks, CA: Sage.

Bertakis, K. D. (2009). The influence of gender on the doctor-patient interaction. *Patient Education and Counseling, 76*, 356–360.

Brown, J. B., Stewart, M., & Ryan, B. L. (2003). Outcomes of patient-provider interaction. In T. L. Thompson, A. M. Dorsey, K. I. Miller, & R. Parrott (Eds.), *Handbook of health communication* (pp. 141–161). Mahwah, NJ: Lawrence Erlbaum.

Brownell, J. (2006). *Listening: Attitudes, principles, and skills* (3rd ed.). Boston, MA: Allyn & Bacon.

Buckman, R. (1992). *How to break bad news: A guide for healthcare professionals*. Baltimore, MD: Johns Hopkins University Press.

Buller, M. K., & Buller, D. B. (1987). Physicians' communication style and patient satisfaction. *Journal of Health and Social Behavior, 28*, 375–388.

Centers for Disease Control and Prevention (2009). CDC's DES Update. Retrieved May 11, 2009, from www.cdc.gov/des.

Corporation for National & Community Service (2010). Learn and Serve America's National Service-Learning Clearinghouse. Retrieved January 12, 2010, from www.servicelearning.org.

Eisenberg, E. M., Goodall, H. L., & Trethewey, A. (2007). *Organizational communication: Balancing creativity and constraint* (5th ed.). Boston: Bedford/St. Martin's.

Johnson, R. L., Roter, D., Powe, N. R., & Cooper, L. A. (2004). Patient race/ethnicity and quality of patient-physician communication during medical visits. *American Journal of Public Health, 94*, 2084–2090.

Krueger, R. A. (1998). *Focus group kit.* Thousand Oaks, CA: Sage.

Lammers, J. C., & Geist, P. (1997). The transformation of caring in the light and shadow of "managed care." *Health Communication, 9,* 45–60.

Lurie, N., Slater, J., McGovern, P., Ekstrum, J., Quam, L., & Margolis, K. (1993). Preventive care for women: Does the sex of the physician matter? *New England Journal of Medicine, 329,* 478–482.

Mayo Clinic (2009). LASIK surgery: Is it right for you? Retrieved May 11, 2009, from http://www.mayoclinic.com/health/lasik-surgery/MY00375.

Mechanic, D., McAlpine, D., & Rosenthal, M. (2001). Are patients' office visits with physicians getting shorter? *New England Journal of Medicine, 334,* 198–204.

Miller, K. I., Birkholt, M., Scott, C., & Stage, C. (1995). Empathy and burnout in human service work: An extension of a communication model. *Communication Research, 22,* 123–147.

Mosby (2009). *Mosby's medical dictionary* (8th ed.). St. Louis: Mosby/Elsevier.

Moss, B. (2008). *Communication skills for health and social care.* Los Angeles: Sage.

Robinson, J. H., Callister, L. C., Berry, J. A., & Dearing, K. A. (2008). Patient-centered care and adherence: Definitions and applications to improve outcomes. *Journal of American Academy of Nurse Practitioners, 20,* 600–607.

Rosenberg, E., Leanza, Y., & Seller, R. (2007). Doctor-patient communication in primary care with an interpreter: Physician perceptions of professional and family interpreters. *Patient Education & Counseling, 67,* 286–292.

Roter, D., & McNeilis, K. S. (2003). The nature of the therapeutic relationship and the assessment of its discourse in routine medical visits. In T. L. Thompson, A. M. Dorsey, K. I. Miller, & R. Parrott (Eds.), *Handbook of health communication* (pp. 121–140). Mahwah, NJ: Lawrence Erlbaum.

Ruiz-Moral, R., Podriguez, E. P., de Torres, L. A. P., & de la Torre, J. (2006). Physician-patient communication: A study on the observed behaviours of specialty physicians and the ways their patients perceive them. *Patient Education & Counseling, 64,* 242–248.

Schoenthaler, A., Chaplin, W. F., Allegrante, J. P., Fernandez, S., Diaz-Gloster, M., Tobin, J. N., & Ogedegbe, G. (2009). Provider communication effects medication adherence in hypertensive African Americans. *Patient Education & Counseling, 75,* 185–191.

Schultz, K. (2003). *Listening: A framework for teaching across differences.* New York: Teachers College Press.

Street, R. L., Gordon, H., & Haidet, P. (2007). Physicians' communication and perceptions of patients: Is it how they look, how they talk, or just the doctor? *Social Science & Medicine, 65,* 586–598.

U.S. Department of Health and Human Services (2010). *Healthy People 2010.* Retrieved January 21, 2010, from www.healthypeople.gov.

Uitterhoeve, R., Bensing, J., Dilven, E., Donders, R., deMulder, P., & van Achterberg, T. (2009). Nurse and patient communication in cancer care: Does responding to patient's cues predict patient satisfaction with communication. *Psycho-Oncology, 18,* 1060–1068.

van Servellen, G. (2009). *Communication skills for the health care professional: Concepts, practice, and evidence.* Sudbury, MA: Jones and Bartlett.

Venetis, M. K., Robinson, J. D., Turkiewicz, K. L., & Allen, M. (2009). An evidence base for patient-centered cancer care: A meta-analysis of studies of observed communication between cancer specialistes and their patients. *Patient Education & Counseling, 77,* 379–383.

Waitzkin, H. (1984). Doctor-patient communication: Clinical implications of social scientific research. *Journal of the American Medical Association, 252,* 2441–2446.

Waitzkin, H. (1985). Information giving in medical care. *Journal of Health and Social Behavior, 26,* 81–101.

Zachariae, R., Pedersen, C. G., Jensen, A. B., Ehrnrooth, E., Rossen, P. B., & von der Maase, H. (2003). Association of perceived physician communication style with patient satisfaction, distress, cancer-related self-efficacy, and perceived control over the disease. *British Journal of Cancer, 88,* 658–665

Social Support

Chapter Learning Objectives

◆ Define social support and its components
◆ Identify and define the types of social support
◆ Understand the health benefits of social support
◆ Discuss key aspects of supportive communication
◆ Recognize individual differences in support-seeking behaviors
◆ Explain the differences between an in-person and an online support group
◆ Compare the benefits and drawbacks of social support groups

Chapter Preview

In this chapter we examine the concept of social support as it relates to health and well-being, highlighting how health communication can create a sense of social support. We begin by defining social support, emphasizing the connection between social support and communication. Next, we present the various types of social support. Because the health benefits of social support should not be taken for granted, we explain the link between social support and health. This is followed by a consideration of supportive communication and the factors that make socially supportive communication more or less effective. We then reflect on the idea of social networks and the role networks play in the social support process. We also consider the role of individual differences such as culture and gender in the process of seeking social support. We then delve into the more formal function of support groups in providing social support. We conclude the chapter with a service-learning application that provides an example of how to start a support group while accentuating the importance of partnerships.

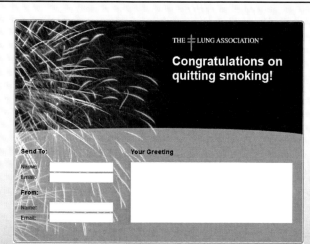

© 2009 Canadian Lung Association. All Rights Reserved.

These images are example e-cards you can send to a friend or family member who is trying to quit smoking. This is an easy, quick, and free way to encourage someone and let them know you support their decision. Would you be likely to send an e-card like these to someone you know? Why or why not? If you were trying to quit smoking how would you respond to receiving an e-card?

These e-cards are one way to provide social support. Thanks to advances in technology, it is now easier than ever to let someone know you are thinking about them or to offer them encouragement.

Defining Social Support

In order to discuss the role of social support in health, we must first define social support and identify key features of social support. We present a few definitions to give you a sense of the varying perspectives on the concept of social support. Albrecht and Adelman (1987) defined social support as "verbal and nonverbal communication between recipients and providers that reduces uncertainty about the situation, the self, the other, or the relationship, and functions to enhance a perception of personal control in one's life experience" (p. 19). In this definition, the key features of social support are:

◆ Communication
◆ Uncertainty reduction
◆ Enhanced control

According to this definition, social support is any type of communication that helps individuals feel more certain about a situation and therefore feel as if they have control over the situation. For example, a nurse is with a patient who is feeling nervous about a blood test. The nurse explains the exact procedure for the test, how much blood is taken, and what level of pain the patient is likely to feel. Additionally, the nurse provides information about what the meaning of the results may be and what steps are taken after the results are determined. This information could help ease some of the uncertainty the patient is feeling about the test, and therefore ease some of the patient's concern which enhances the patient's sense of control over the blood test.

This definition is somewhat limited because it states that supportive communication must reduce uncertainty. This might leave out other communication that would be supportive, but not necessarily reduce uncertainty about a health-related issue. For example, if you hug a friend after being told that one of his parents died, you are providing a form of social support, even if that hug does not lessen the uncertainty and lack of control your friend is feeling.

The National Cancer Institute (www.cancer.gov/dictionary) offers this definition of social support: "a network of family, friends, neighbors, and community members that is available in times of need to give psychological, physical, and financial help." The key features of this definition of social support are:

◆ Network
◆ Psychological help
◆ Physical help
◆ Financial help

Unlike the first definition of social support, which emphasizes the preferred outcomes of the social support process, this definition accentuates the network of typical people who are available to provide support. This definition also delineates the types of assistance that can be provided by the network, including psychological support (e.g., a listening ear), physical support (e.g., a ride to the physician's office), and financial assistance (e.g., a short-term loan to pay a health insurance copayment). One of the advantages of this definition is the recognition of the multiple types of support that can be offered.

Gottlieb (2000) defined social support more broadly as the "process of interaction in relationships which improves coping, esteem, belonging, and competence through actual or perceived exchanges of physical or psychosocial resources" (p. 28). In this definition the key features of social support are:

◆ Interaction
◆ Coping
◆ Esteem
◆ Belonging
◆ Competence
◆ Exchange

This definition of social support is unique compared with the other two definitions offered because the emphasis is on communication by indicating that social support is an interactive process. The idea that communication creates the relationship as effectively supportive and satisfying through the interaction of the individuals involved in the situation is consistent with the attributes of communication we discussed in Chapter 1, "Introducing Health as Communication Nexus." This broader definition also includes outcomes suggesting that social support can lead to improvement in several areas of health and well-being. Communication that helps people cope with a situation, makes them feel better about themselves by raising their sense of self-esteem, reaffirms their association or sense of belonging to a group, or improves their ability or competence to perform needed tasks all are considered forms of social support. The communication that leads to these supportive outcomes occurs through an exchange of physical or psychological resources between at least two individuals. This means that those involved in a social support interaction exchange something with each other, such as money to pay an overdue bill or helpful advice.

Although all three of the previous definitions emphasized different features of social support, none of these definitions encompassed all of the aspects that we consider necessary when defining social support. Borrowing components from each of the three definitions we define *social support* as a transactional communicative process, including verbal and/or nonverbal communication, that aims to improve an individual's feelings of coping, competence, belonging, and/or esteem.

In defining social support we also must think about actual versus perceived social support. *Actual support* is the support that an individual receives in terms of what is said, what is given, and what is done for that individual. However, much more significant than actual support is an individual's perception of the availability of support. *Perceived support* refers to an individual's belief that social support is available, is generally considered positive or negative, and provides what is considered needed by that individual (Norris & Kaniasty, 1996; Sarason, Sarason, & Pierce, 1990).

For example, McDowell and Serovich (2007) conducted a survey to compare the ways perceived and actual social support affect the mental health of men and women living with HIV/AIDS. Results suggested that for all those involved in the study, perceived social support predicted positive mental health, while the effect of actual social support on their mental health was minimal.

You may wonder why perceived support is sometimes more important than actual support. Take a minute to consider the following scenario. Ed, a junior majoring in engineering, just learned that he has mononucleosis. He is very upset about the diagnosis and calls his parents to tell them and seek support. His mom answers the phone and expresses how sorry she feels for him, offers to call the pharmacy about the prescription medications he needs, and goes on to advise that he must eat properly, drink plenty of fluids, and get a lot of rest. Ed hangs up the phone and complains to his roommate that although his mom answered the phone, she was not helpful at all and the only thing she did was tell him what to do.

What happened in this situation? Although Ed's mom was available to talk and provided several forms of social support, including listening to him, offering to perform a task for him, and giving him information, Ed's communication with his roommate revealed that he didn't feel as if he received any support from his mom. His perception of her support was negative based on his mother's verbal and nonverbal communication. Consequently, Ed did not consider the interaction with his mother supportive.

In addition to an individual's general perception of social support, perception of support includes an individual's feeling that the support provided was adequate or that it was the support that was needed in the given situation. In our example with Ed, he may have wanted something specific from his parents, such as an offer to pay for the visit to urgent care and his prescriptions or he may have wanted his mom to simply sympathize with him and not give him so much advice. When he did not feel as if his mom was responding in the ways that he wanted or needed, he may have perceived or recognized that she was attempting to offer support but he did not regard the support as being adequate.

Now that you understand many dimensions of social support from the various definitions, in the next section we further delineate the various types of social support.

Types of Social Support

One of the aspects we stressed in our definition of social support is that support can be either verbal or nonverbal communication. This is just one way to categorize the many types of social support. Before we delve into the various types of social support, please complete Health Communication Nexus Interlude 6.1.

Health Communication Nexus Interlude 6.1

For this interlude, imagine that your friend was recently in a car accident and broke a leg. It is February and in the middle of the school term. Your friend is in considerable pain, has trouble getting around because of the cast, and is feeling stressed about the schoolwork she needs to make up. Take a minute to brainstorm and jot down the many ways that you could reach out and help your friend.

After completing your list, consider all the ways you could categorize or organize the ideas you have to help your friend. How many different ways and categories did you think of to support your friend? Keep this list nearby as you read on to determine whether the ways you categorized your support ideas are similar to how scholars categorize types of social support.

Schaefer, Coyne, and Lazarus (1981) described five types of social support:

◆ Emotional support
◆ Esteem support
◆ Network support
◆ Information support
◆ Tangible support

The first type of social support, *emotional support*, is communication that meets an individual's emotional or affective needs. These are expressions of care and concern, such as telling someone, "I feel bad for you" or "I just want you to know how much you mean to me." This type of support is what we most often think of when we hear the term social support. Expressions of emotional support do not try to directly solve a problem but serve to elevate an individual's mood. For example, in Health Communication Nexus Interlude 6.1 you may have written that you could send a get-well card or a text message with something like, "hope you are feeling better." These expressions would be considered emotional support.

The next type of social support, *esteem support*, is communication that bolsters an individuals' self-esteem or beliefs in their ability to handle a problem or perform a needed task. This type of support refers to encouraging individuals to take needed actions and convincing them that they have the ability to confront difficult problems. For example, you may have a friend who is slightly overweight and wants to start a new exercise routine. Knowing that he is not entirely confident in his ability to lose weight you might say to him, "I know you can do it because you're always good at sticking to a schedule." In Health Communication Nexus Interlude 6.1 you may have written that you would remind your friend with a broken leg what a good student she is and therefore should have no problem making up the schoolwork. This reminder to your friend would be an effort to increase your friend's confidence and decrease her feelings of stress.

Unlike the first two types of social support, *network support* does not focus on emotions or self-concept, but instead refers to communication that affirms individuals' belonging to a network or reminds them of support available from the network. In other words, network support is communication that reminds people that they are not alone in whatever situation they are facing. Members of a network may offer many types of support but the concept of network support emphasizes that a network is available to provide social support. In Health Communication Nexus Interlude 6.1 you may have thought to remind your friend that she has lots of friends willing to drive her to class and to go to the store for her. These reminders to your friend are examples of communicating network support.

Another type of social support, *information support*, is communication that provides useful or needed information. When facing any challenging situation, often information is needed in order to make decisions. Not knowing the details of what one is facing or about the different options available can be a source of upset and stress. An individual just diagnosed with an illness or health problem often needs more information about their condition and treatment options and can be supported by those who provide useful information. In Health Communication Nexus Interlude 6.1 if you wrote that you would support your friend with a broken leg by communicating with each of her professors to determine schoolwork that was missed and needed to be made up, this would be an example of information support.

The fifth type of social support is *tangible support,* which is any physical assistance provided by others. This can range from making a meal for someone who is sick to driving that person to a doctor's appointment. In some situations, individuals need material goods or actions to help them in challenging situations. In

Health Communication Nexus Interlude 6.1 you may have thought of driving your friend to and from class or offering to take her to the doctor, which would be considered tangible support. Other forms of tangible support could be doing laundry or straightening up your friend's apartment. We sometimes do not think of tangible support as communication because often either very few or no words are exchanged during the provision of this type of support. However, often tangible support is a form of nonverbal communication. As the familiar expression emphasizes, there are times when "actions speak louder than words."

Considering the various types of social support leads to an important question, which type of social support is best? Revisit the list you created for Health Communication Nexus Interlude 6.1. Which of the supportive ideas you listed do you think would be most beneficial to your friend with a broken leg? Why did you pick these strategies? Some answers to these questions can be found in matching models of social support such as the Theory of Optimal Matching (Cutrona & Russell, 1990). The *Theory of Optimal Matching* hypothesizes that the best type of social support is support that matches an individual's needs. For example, if you feel you need esteem support after flunking a quiz because you were sick and someone offers to bring you dinner, a form of tangible support, this support would not be very effective because it does not match or meet your needs. Also remember our previous example of Ed, the engineering student with mononucleosis, who did not feel supported by his mother on the telephone because she provided support that did not match his needs.

Although the matching model of type of support with need for support makes intuitive sense, matching models are criticized for being overly simplistic because they suggest that upon identifying a person's need there is a corresponding type of support that can address that need (Barrera, 1986). However, human beings are complex and have multiple needs. As the previous example of Ed illustrated, although he may have had many issues that needed attention, his mother did not seem to respond to his most pressing need or needs. Another criticism of matching models is that the same supportive action can fulfill multiple needs. If a member of your church or faith community brings you a meal when you are recovering from surgery, this could meet your tangible need for food, remind you of the network of support your faith community provides, and help you feel cared for. Despite these criticisms, matching models of support serve an important role in our understanding of how support is provided and received.

For example, let's consider research that investigated social support for victims of domestic violence. The researchers (Few, 2005; Levendosky et al., 2004; Trotter & Allen, 2009) found that women in abusive relationships had multiple needs for social support, including information about local shelters, advice about how to handle the problem, and tangible aid such as housing, child care, and transportation, as well as emotional and esteem support. Depending on their situations, some types of support were more needed by some women than other women. Having all of their social support needs met was a crucial factor in their ability to cope with the violence and trauma as well as their ability to leave the abusive relationship and become self-supporting. Without a place to stay, some women were forced to return to the home of their abuser as they had no other options for housing. Other women struggled with the emotional aspects of leaving their abuser, and those who lacked emotional support and reassurance that they were doing the right thing felt guilt about breaking their marriage vows and were more likely to return home. Those whose friends and family assured them that they were doing the right thing felt supported and were more likely to stay away from their abusers.

Now that we identified and defined the various types of social support, let's consider the many health benefits of social support.

Health Benefits of Social Support

Social support not only helps us feel better or helps us cope with challenges; it also leads to improved health, including physical health, psychological health, and overall well-being. This means that having access to adequate social support is essential to a healthy life. Much research links social support to several health outcomes (Albrecht & Goldsmith, 2003; Cobb, 1976; Lyyra & Heikkinen, 2006; Motl, McAuley, Snook, & Gliottoni, 2009; Schaefer, Coyne, & Lazarus, 1981). Some of the many health outcomes of social support include:

- ◆ Psychological adjustment
- ◆ Improved efficacy
- ◆ Better coping with upsetting events
- ◆ Resistance to disease
- ◆ Recovery from disease
- ◆ Reduced mortality

For example, researchers studied the effects of social support on an elderly individual's recovery from a hip fracture. Those who had less social contact and support were five times more likely to die within five years of fracture than those with more social contact and support (Mortimore et al., 2008). Another study found that people with the highest levels of social support had the highest levels of self-efficacy in choosing and preparing the most nutritional foods. The support of friends and family gave them both information about eating healthier and the confidence that they could choose healthy over unhealthy foods (Anderson, Winett, & Wojcik, 2007).

There are several theories as to why social support is so beneficial to physical health. A basic explanation is that better mental and emotional health is related to better physical health. According to the *stress-buffering hypothesis*, stress is associated with several negative health effects and social support can be effective in shielding individuals from stress (Cassel, 1976; Cobb, 1976; Cohen & Willis, 1985). Some of the physiological symptoms of stress include headache, back pain, heart disease, high blood pressure, decreased immunity, and disrupted sleep. Those experiencing high levels of stress are more likely to overeat, under eat, use drugs or alcohol, or smoke. So if social support can minimize stress, the physical side effects and related unhealthy behaviors also could be minimized or eliminated.

A related explanation for the benefits of social support is that if people have a support network, they have access to the tangible support needed to stay healthy or recover from illness. For example, cancer patients need reliable transportation to and from treatments. And those recovering from surgery need assistance taking care of basic tasks, including cooking and house cleaning, in order to get the rest they need. In other words, those lacking access to tangible support may not be able to fully comply with medical recommendations regarding treatment and rest.

Communication is a primary way that social support is provided but providing communication that actually is supportive often is very challenging. In the next section we discuss the complexities of supportive communication and offer suggestions for providing and accepting supportive communication.

Supportive Communication

Have you ever been in a situation when you did not know what to say to someone who had just suffered a loss or received bad news? Has there ever been a time when you were upset and a friend tried but was unable to say anything that was helpful? If you answered yes to either of these questions you also may have wondered what makes some communication supportive and other communication unsupportive. In this section we examine the features that make communication more or less supportive and suggest ways for crafting supportive messages.

Supportive communication is verbal and/or nonverbal communication that intends to provide assistance to others who are perceived to be in need. When considering supportive communication from a health communication perspective we acknowledge communication as central to improving the well-being of individuals in need of assistance. This is different than other perspectives that consider communication as either providing a buffer for individuals so they can better handle stress or a conduit that promotes better coping techniques, which reduce upset.

ETHICAL DILEMMA ◆ What Would You Do?

Suppose you are enlisted in the United States Army and you recently returned from an overseas tour of duty fighting in a war. You are finding it very difficult to readjust to noncombat life. You visit the nearest Veterans Administration (VA) Medical Center and are diagnosed with post-traumatic stress disorder (PTSD). However, you are denied a referral to the PTSD support group. Without the referral, you cannot attend the support group.

◆ Would you continue to seek a referral to a support group or other counseling through the VA? If yes, why? How would you continue to seek a referral?

◆ According to your understanding of ethical dilemmas from Chapter 2, "Linking Health Communication with Ethics," does this situation constitute an ethical dilemma? Why or why not?

◆ Do you think the VA owes you social support? Why or why not?

◆ Would you seek a support group elsewhere? Why or why not? If yes, how would you seek out a support group? If you found a support group, what questions would you ask to make sure the support is legitimate and helpful?

This situation is based on a true story (Gildea, 2010).

Neither of these other perspectives view communication as the essential element that improves individuals' health and well-being.

From a health communication perspective, however, it is the interaction and the verbal and nonverbal messages that are primarily responsible for individuals' perceptions of support and for making them feel better. Think back to our review of the nature of communication and our definition of health communication presented in Chapter 1, "Introducing Health as Communication Nexus," and keep in mind it is communication that creates relationships as supportive. Before we proceed to discuss supportive messages, please take a moment to complete Health Communication Nexus Interlude 6.2.

Health Communication Nexus Interlude 6.2

For this interlude, consider the following situation. You just learned that your close friend's parent died from a heart attack. This death was very unexpected and your friend is distraught over the news. Take a few moments to think about and jot down in your notebook some ideas of what you would say or do for this friend. Keep your responses in mind as we continue to consider supportive communication.

During Health Communication Nexus Interlude 6.2, was it difficult for you to think of what you would say to your friend who just lost a parent? If so, this is not unusual as many people feel incompetent when it comes to providing support after a death. Did you wonder if anything you could do or say would provide any comfort or be of any help? Did you jot down that you would deliver food? Did you write down any generic expressions of concern such as "Your Dad is in a better place now," or "It was meant to be"? Keep in mind your thoughts in response to these questions as we further discuss supportive communication.

Emotionally supportive or comforting messages express care and concern. Not all messages are equally supportive and some emotional support or comforting messages are more effective than others. Additionally, a message that helps one person feel substantially better may have no effect on another person. Why is this so?

Person-Centered Communication

Person-centered communication occurs when messages reflect an awareness of the situation requiring social support. This includes an awareness of the subjective, relational, and affective aspects of the situation (Jones, 2004). In other words, person-centered communication adapts to the receiver of the messages.

The level of person-centeredness in a supportive or comforting message can be rated on a continuum from low to high as illustrated in Figure 6.1.

Person-Centered Communication

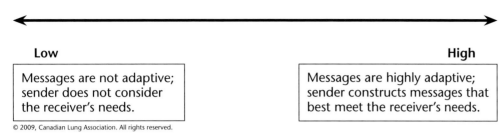

Figure 6.1 ◆ *Rating Person-Centered Communication*

As Figure 6.1 illustrates, at one end of the continuum are messages that are highly person-centered. These messages are adapted by the sender to meet the needs of the individual who needs social support. To appropriately adapt supportive messages, individuals must consider their relationship to the person in distress, the situation or extent of the problem, how much control the person has over the situation, and the emotional undertones of the situation (MacGeorge, Clark, & Gillihan, 2002).

The emphasis of person-centered communication is on helping the individual process and make sense of the situation and his or her feelings about the situation (Jones, 2004). This involves asking probing questions to encourage the individual to think about the situation, taking the perspective of the individual, and representing competing perspectives to further the individual's understanding of the situation. Person-centered support also involves a fair amount of active listening. This means asking questions that clarify, encouraging the person to elaborate, and nonverbally communicating to indicate genuine interest and concern, such as nodding and making eye contact.

At the opposite end of the continuum illustrated in Figure 6.1 are messages that are low in person-centeredness. These messages do not take into account the specifics of a situation and are not intended to assist the individual in making sense of the situation and his or her feelings about the situation (Jones, 2004). Often, low person-centered messages attempt to negate the feelings of the individual needing support. For example, you might want to tell a friend to "get over it" or that "this is not a big deal," but messages like these rarely are helpful in making a person feel better and do not allow the person to process and work through any negative feelings about the distressing situation. Even though the support giver may believe that an individual is overreacting to a situation, this may not be the message that the individual needs to receive in order to feel social support.

Additionally, in intensely stressful situations, like the situation depicted in Health Communication Nexus Interlude 6.2, support givers often feel uncomfortable and are unsure of what to say and as a result choose generic expressions of concern or sympathy. These feelings of uncomfortableness and not knowing what to say also are often the case in novel situations when people have little background knowledge about the subject (Egbert, 2003). In general, generic expressions of concern are not considered to be effective because they lack person-centeredness.

Let's revisit Health Communication Nexus Interlude 6.2 regarding the death of a close friend's parent. Previously, it may have been difficult to think of what to say because of the extreme situation. Some research has explored individuals' reactions to grief-related messages. A study by Rack, Burleson, Bodie, Holmstrom, and Servaty-Seib (2008) found that high person-centered messages were deemed more effective in providing support and improving the emotional well-being of bereaved young adults. High person-centered messages included messages that stated one was there for the other person, identified with the individual's feelings, or offered to listen or talk. On the other hand, low person-centered messages such as stating it was for the best or encouraging the griever to move on were not helpful, and at times were considered offensive. Now, reconsider the ideas or messages you wrote to support your friend who lost a parent in Health Communication Nexus Interlude 6.2. How would you rate your ideas or messages in terms of their person-centeredness? Would you add or take away any ideas or messages given what you've just learned about person-centered communication? Next we'll discuss advice giving, which is another aspect of supportive communication.

Advice Giving

Another common response when a person needs support is to offer advice. Unlike most messages designed to provide emotional support, advice-giving messages generally receive even more mixed reviews in terms of effectiveness. Think of a time when you were frustrated because you felt like you were coming down with an illness and all you wanted to do was vent to your friend or family member. As you began complaining about your situation, your friend or family member interrupted with suggestions for how you could suppress your oncoming illness. You may have appreciated that your friend or family member was trying to help, but you were not looking for advice, only a sympathetic ear, and besides the advice did not seem to help.

Think of another time when you had a health problem and were not sure what to do. As you talked over the problem with your friend, you gladly welcomed suggestions for how to handle the problem and afterward chose to implement some of the suggestions. In this situation, advice was exactly what you needed and it helped you cope with your distress. Why is it that sometimes advice is unwanted and unhelpful and at other times seems to be exactly what is needed? One answer to this question lies in Goffman's (1963) conception of facework, which was expanded on in *Politeness Theory* (Brown & Levinson, 1978). *Facework* refers to actions individuals take to protect their public image. In other words, it involves actions individuals engage in so they can present a positive face, or self, to others in an effort to save face. There are two types of facework:

◆ Positive facework
◆ Negative facework

PROFILE

Merging Personal and Professional in the Realm of Supportive Communication

Erina MacGeorge, PhD—Associate Professor, Purdue University

Have you ever wondered what to say to a friend who has just broken up with his girlfriend or how to help a friend who is failing a class? How do you comfort them and what kind of advice should you give them? Erina MacGeorge has made a career of researching what makes advice and social support more or less helpful. Her interest in studying social support began during her graduate years as she worked closely with her advisor and mentor, Daena Goldsmith. MacGeorge has studied many aspects of advice giving, including gender, emotion, and knowledge.

Her research became more personal after having a miscarriage. As she struggled to cope with her loss and experienced social support, she became interested in how other women who have experienced miscarriages felt about the social support they received. Research showed that women who received quality social support after a miscarriage were less likely to suffer from depression and anxiety than those who received poor support. MacGeorge, with graduate student Kristi Wilcomb, set out to discover what made women feel more or less supported in these situations and to determine the dimensions of quality support.

The initial findings from their interviews with women found that often people would say things that were perceived as insensitive by the women. For example, in an attempt to support a woman, a person might tell her that the baby was probably deformed and that is why she lost the baby. Those who had previous experience with miscarriage, either directly or indirectly, were less likely to say something insensitive. They also discovered that the quality of support declined over time as others were ready to move on sooner than the women who experienced a miscarriage.

Another interesting area MacGeorge's research is exploring is use of internet support groups. When women cannot find the support they need in their existing relationships, they often turn to online forums for support and information. Most physicians, however, are reluctant to direct patients to the internet because they have concerns about the accuracy of the information provided there. To address this issue, MacGeorge is coding the advice and medical information on Web sites, to determine those with accurate and helpful advice so that physicians can feel more comfortable directing patients to these Web sites.

MacGeorge is especially proud of this work, as it merges theory and scholarship with practical application. The findings of this line of research potentially will help countless women and allow MacGeorge to integrate her personal life experience with her professional interests.

Positive facework is defined as actions that protect individuals' desires to be evaluated positively in response to others. We want others to see us as good and capable. *Negative facework* is defined as actions that attempt to free individuals from any constraint or opposition. Negative facework arises from the desire to be independent and make our own choices.

Advice poses a threat to both positive and negative facework. When individuals offer advice, it can feel as if they are questioning our competence or ability to handle a situation, which threatens our positive facework. Advice also can feel constraining to our independence, as if we're being told what to do, which threatens our negative facework. In either situation, we feel defensive because our face is being threatened.

For example, consider, a woman named Jasmine. She is slightly overweight and decides to start a new fitness and diet regimen. She mentions to her coworkers at lunch how difficult it is for her to get motivated to go to the gym and to resist snacking at night. Her coworkers quickly respond with all sorts of advice on how to eat healthier and lose weight. Jasmine is looking for some sympathy and support when she brought up her troubles with her coworkers. Instead, all of their advice makes her feel as if she is not a capable person and something is wrong with her because losing weight is so challenging for her. Because her coworkers are so ready to offer advice, she feels they must not struggle like she does to eat healthy and exercise. She regrets bringing up her weight problem and exercise and eating concerns and hopes this line of conversation ends soon. In this example, the advice threatened Jasmine's positive facework by questioning her ability to follow a weight-loss regimen and maintain her own health.

Now, let's consider an example of how advice can threaten someone's negative facework, or desire to be autonomous. Let's again consider Jasmine who is trying to lose weight. On the weekend, she meets up with a small group of friends for lunch and proudly announces her new commitment to weight loss. Immediately her friends respond with all kinds of advice, including different diets they have read or heard about. One friend tells her to avoid carbohydrates, while another swears by drinking at least ten glasses of water per day. Another friend gives Jasmine suggestions as to which gym she should join. Jasmine feels as if the flood of advice is dictatorial and confining and feels controlled by the pointed nature of her friends' advice. Once again she is eager to change the topic. In this situation, the eager advice of her friends makes Jasmine feel as if she is being controlled. As each person offers specific suggestions about what to eat and how much to eat, Jasmine feels uncomfortable making her own food choices in front of her friends. Her friends' advice infringes on Jasmine's perception of independence.

Techniques for Offering Supportive Advice

Now that we understand why advice can be less than helpful, there are times when advice is very helpful and an excellent form of social support. If someone directly asks for advice, it may be better received. Also, there are ways that the advice giver can soften the threat to face that advice may present. Three techniques to offer supportive advice are:

- ◆ Offer an expression of solidarity
- ◆ Include an expression of uncertainty or deferment
- ◆ Give advice off-record

One technique for providing supportive advice is to *offer an expression of solidarity*, which helps advice recipients feel as if they are not the only ones who struggle with a problem. In Jasmine's situation, her coworkers and friends could have offered their same advice but started with expressions of solidarity such as, "When I was trying to lose weight," or "I know how hard it is to get started." When messages begin like this, the advice seems to come from experience.

Another technique is to *include an expression of uncertainty or deferment*, which serves to lessen the sense that advice givers are presenting themselves as experts. Jasmine's coworkers and friends could have cushioned their advice by including expressions of uncertainty or deferment such as, "I am not sure if this would work," or, "It's not as if I am an expert, but . . ."

A third technique for providing supportive advice is to *give advice in an off-record way*, which means that rather than giving advice in a direct manner, advice is given in an indirect way, such as telling a story about someone else or mentioning something seen on television or read in a magazine. By doing this, the advice is considered as general information that may contain helpful ideas or strategies. For example, one of Jasmine's friends could tell her a story about someone who lost weight following a certain diet plan. By couching the advice in a story, it is less threatening to Jasmine.

The key suggestion to remember in trying to provide supportive communication is to always consider the person you are trying to support. Also, it is important to keep in mind that the intentions behind supportive communication often are as important as what is said. If message recipients recognize attempts to be supportive, they often appreciate the attempts and feel supported even if the message itself is not very helpful.

Social Networks

Much of the supportive communication we receive comes from our *social networks*. This is another integral concept to our discussion of social support. Before we consider the concept of social networks further, please complete Health Communication Nexus Interlude 6.3.

Imagine you are working at a local homeless shelter as a case manager. You are working with one of your clients, George, a 45-year-old man who has been unemployed for the past five years. Prior to being unemployed, he worked as the night stocker at the local grocery store until an injury prevented him from being able to lift more than 20 pounds. He mentions family that lives in town, including some grown children. You know he is a religious man but also learn that he is known to stay too late at the local bar. He has been in and out of the shelter for the past five years and is very friendly with the other clients, staff, and volunteers. You are trying to help him find a job and a place to live. You want to work with him on identifying the various places and people he could turn to for support. Start by writing down in your notebook a list of the potential people and organizations that could be in George's social network.

After completing your preliminary list, consider and jot down which potential social network members might be most helpful to George. Are there any members who might harm George and his attempts at putting his life back together? Can you identify any major gaps in his social network? Keep your responses nearby as we further explore the concept of social networks.

The study of social networks is fundamental to the study of social support. In some disciplines other than communication, the measure of an individual's social network is a measure of their social support. For example, from the disciplinary perspective of sociology, the larger individuals' social networks, the more social support they possess. In other words, the longer your list of people or groups generated in Health Communication Nexus Interlude 6.3, the more social support George possesses. This is because the more people or groups in George's social network, the more social support is potentially available to him from these people or groups. However, as is addressed later in this chapter, a communication perspective on social networks argues that the connection between an individual's social network and that individual's perceptions of support is a more complex process and varies depending on the quality of interactions with members of the social network as well as the quality of the members within the social network.

Social Network Integration

The foundations of social network research are rooted in Durkheim's (1951) study of social conditions and suicide in the late 1800s. He discovered that those with fewer social ties or social connections and smaller social networks were more likely to commit suicide than those with a greater number of social ties and larger social networks. From this seminal work, the concept of social integration was created as other researchers began the practice of measuring the size of social networks and the number of social ties. *Social integration* is the extent to which an individual participates in a broad range of social relationships including:

- Family
- Spouse/significant other
- Friends
- Formal organizations (e.g., clubs, religious groups, jobs)

The more social relationships or social ties individuals have, the more integrated they are in social networks.

Look back at the list you created for George's social network in Health Communication Nexus Interlude 6.3. Did you list people from a variety of places? Did George have a number of potential individuals and organizations on your list, or was the list fairly limited? In theory, the broader your list is, the more socially integrated George is. Another key concept in social networks is network ties. *Network ties* are the connections between individuals in a network. George has a unique tie or connection to each of the individuals and groups on your list of his social network.

How does a social network relate to and influence health, and why are larger social networks associated with better physical and mental health? The most obvious answer to these questions is that when individuals are connected to other individuals or groups, they have social support available. Additionally, when we are in a social network, we are exposed to normative influences on our behavior. If members of our network engage in healthy behaviors such as exercise or eating a variety of fruits and vegetables, we are influenced to engage in similar behaviors. Members of our social network also may avoid or look down upon unhealthy behaviors such as illicit drug use or excessive alcohol consumption. In addition to influencing us with their actions, members of our social networks also verbally encourage us to engage in healthy and safer behaviors, such as urging us to obey the speed limit or reminding us to take our medications. So how do we measure the level of our integration in our social network?

Measuring Social Network Integration

If we consider social integration a positive factor influencing health, we become interested in measuring the extent to which we are integrated in our social network. The most basic form of social network measurement is to calculate the size of your network by counting the number of people and organizations in your social network. Originally, this was the sole method used by researchers to assess social network integration. If you wanted to measure the size of George's potential network, you would count how many people, groups, and/or organizations were on the list you created during Health Communication Nexus Interlude 6.3.

However, this method of social network integration is criticized for being too simplistic and not accurately measuring the amount of social support available to an individual. A person may be in your social network but he or she may only be a casual acquaintance whom you would not turn to to discuss a health problem. Or there may be others in your social network with whom you have a close relationship but they are not very reliable. For example, perhaps you have an older brother who is well intentioned but fails to follow through on promises such as driving you to doctors' appointments and often doesn't respond to phone messages. So, due to his familial relationship with you, you have a seemingly strong tie to your brother in your social network but it is not a very reliable tie and therefore may actually be a weak social tie even though he is your brother. Consequently, to more accurately measure social network integration, other more complex and descriptive methods were developed (Stohl, 1995) including:

◆ Network density
◆ Reciprocity
◆ Network ties

One more current measure of social network integration is network density. *Network density* is a measure of how interconnected the members of a social network are with each other. In a dense network many of the individuals have relationships with one another. On the other hand, an individual may have a large network but the members of the network may not interact or have relationships with each other, which would characterize a less dense social network. In denser networks there is more potential for support because individuals in the social network can work together to support a person in need.

Another measure of social network integration is reciprocity. *Reciprocity* is a measure of the degree of exchange between network members. In a reciprocal relationship, both parties give relatively equally to each other. All relationships are not reciprocal, however, or at least not equally reciprocal. You may be in a social relationship in which one individual consistently gives more than the other individual. Take, for example, the student/teacher relationship. In most cases teachers provide instruction and support for their students. At times this support may involve issues outside the classroom, such as talking to a teacher about a personal illness that resulted in late homework. Although students come to class and participate, it is rare that students provide support to teachers regarding issues outside the classroom. You also may have personal relationships in which it seems as though you are consistently giving much more support and assistance compared with other individuals' level of support and assistance given to you. In both of these instances, there is no or low reciprocity between social network members.

A third measure of social network integration is the strength of network ties between members. Network ties can be classified as either strong or weak. *Strong network ties* exist between network individuals with a strong connection to one another and a great deal of reciprocity. Examples of strong network ties may be mothers or fathers and their children or spouses or significant others. When a strong network tie exists, there is a high likelihood that these individuals provide social support to each other when necessary.

Other network ties may be classified as weak ties. *Weak network ties* are loose connections between individuals in a social network. When a network tie is loose, individuals do not feel a strong sense of obligation to each other and are less likely to provide substantial or meaningful social support to one another. If you made a list of people and groups in your social network, you may include a classmate whom you are friendly with in class but do not have a relationship with outside of the classroom. You may like the classmate, but not turn to him or her when social support is needed for issues that do not pertain to the class. When the class is over at the end of the term, your relationship with this classmate may even end. So, based on the number of people and groups on your social network list, you may have a large network, but if it is constructed primarily of weak ties, like the tie with this classmate, and less quality social support is available to you.

Another way to consider social network ties is to determine if they are obligatory or voluntary. *Obligatory network ties* are based on required relationships due to structural features of our lives and our communities. Examples of obligatory network ties are family relationships, coworker associations, and classmate interactions. These ties are with people we may not choose to know or relate to but do because they share our environment. *Voluntary network ties* form when we elect to have a relationship with someone. Examples of voluntary network ties are our friends or members of organizations we join such as faith communities and recreational teams. Generally, voluntary network relationships tend to bring more satisfaction than obligatory network relationships. In voluntary network relationships, both parties choose to be in the relationship, so it is more likely that these individuals like each other and have commonalities that bring them together. However, this is not to say that obligatory ties cannot be satisfactory, and frequently family and other obligatory ties are a valuable source of all types of social support.

Now that you understand what a social network is and the many ways that it can be measured, let's consider an example that illustrates why having a strong social network is so important to health and well-being. In October 2007, Lecturer Hall, the second author of this book, found out she was pregnant with triplets. This is her story of social support:

"I had not used any fertility medication or procedures, so the news that I was pregnant with triplets came as quite a shock to my husband, our 18-month-old daughter, and me. I was 18 weeks pregnant when we learned the news and was told that I would need to go on complete bed rest at 24 weeks. The hope was that I could hold off delivery until at least 34 weeks, but undoubtedly the babies would be born very premature. In the next few days, as we attempted to absorb the news, our minds turned to the question of how we could prepare for the addition of three babies to our family as well as how we could possibly take care of them once they were born and came home from the hospital. The list of equipment and clothing we would need was staggering; two more cribs, car seats, high chairs. In addition, we were uncertain as to how to take care of our daughter and keep our house running smoothly while I was confined to bed and my husband was working full-time.

continued

The situation was especially difficult due to the lack of immediate family in the area where we lived. It was during this time that I learned just how important a strong social network is. Over the next year, during my pregnancy and after the babies were born, we were overwhelmed by the amount of support and assistance we received from a variety of people, groups, and organizations.

One vital source of support was my husband's coworkers. He is a fifth-grade teacher, and during my pregnancy his fellow teachers organized a large shower for us, found us a used chest freezer, stocked it with frozen meals, and frequently watched our daughter while I was in the hospital. Our friends also had a shower for us, came and visited me while I was on bed rest, and took over teaching my classes at the university. A good friend with twins became an important source of information. The moms' support group I belonged to organized fresh meals to be delivered to our home and held a diaper and wipes drive. Even though our family lived further away, they sent gifts, money, and came to visit.

When the babies were born, countless people came to help hold them, feed them, and change diapers. People gave us gently-used clothing and wherever we went an extra pair of hands always seemed to appear to carry a baby or hold open a door.

Needless to say, the support of our social network was invaluable in helping us not only survive a difficult time, but to help us persevere, and at times even help us thrive. One of the advantages of having such a large support network was that no one person or group had an excessive burden placed on them by offering to help us. Having such a large support network also provided us with connections to others we did not know personally, but who had knowledge, advice, and tangible goods that we needed. For example, through my moms' support group I learned of a community organization that provides formula and other basics for babies and their families."

As this example illustrates, often the majority of the social support we need comes from our support network, including friends, family and coworkers. However, there are situations when individuals lack a large enough social support network to meet all their needs. One group that routinely reports having limited social networks is immigrants. There are several reasons for the relative isolation of immigrant populations. In moving to a new country, many immigrants become separated from family and friends and lose those close social network ties, which can lead to feelings of isolation. Immigrants who do not effectively speak the language of their adopted country also feel alienated from community members and organizations and often have restricted knowledge about community resources. Some studies found that because of their limited social networks, immigrants rely more heavily on the existing family they have in their new locations, which can place a heavy strain on network members (Almeida, Molnar, Kawachi, & Subramanian, 2009).

Another important factor that relates to the size of the social network and the level of social support is immigrants' level of acculturation or assimilation into a new culture. A study of Asian immigrants found that those who were more acculturated and had more positive attitudes about acculturation, meaning they spoke English better and had more friends who spoke English, had higher levels of general social support (Choi & Thomas, 2009). Another study explored the social network sizes of Korean immigrants with breast cancer and found that more acculturated women had larger social networks and in turn had better social support (Lim, Yi, & Zebrack, 2008).

So far in this chapter we focused on defining social support, emphasized ways to provide effective social support, and discussed the role of support networks. Another side of social support involves times when people have a problem and actively seek social support.

Social Support Seeking

There are two primary questions to consider regarding social support seeking. First, what kinds of behaviors or support-seeking strategies do individuals use in attempts to get the social support they need? Second, who is most likely to seek social support?

Social Support-Seeking Behaviors

Barbee and Cunningham (1995) created a typology of social support-seeking behaviors, which is illustrated in Table 6.1. As you can see in Table 6.1, there are both verbal and nonverbal ways as well as direct and indirect ways to elicit support. Direct methods of support elicitation, such as giving details of the problem, are more likely to result in helpful support because those providing support are made fully aware of the problem and what is needed to provide support. Indirect methods of support elicitation, such as sighing, can be misunderstood or ignored because these are subtle ways to let someone know there is a problem. There also are individuals who do not actively seek help and try not to let others know when problems exist.

	DIRECT	INDIRECT
Verbal	Asking for help Giving details of the problem	Hinting about problem Complaining
Nonverbal	Crying	Pouting Sighing Fidgeting

Table 6.1 ◆ *Typology of Social Support-Seeking Behaviors*

Risks of Seeking Social Support

You may be wondering why people would use indirect methods of support elicitation if these methods may not be effective or why some people do not try to find support, despite the effectiveness of social support in improving health. One of the major reasons individuals are reluctant to directly ask for support is because of the risks involved in seeking social support. One risk of seeking social support is *worry about being a burden* to others in terms of time, resources, and emotional energy. Have you ever been sick with a bad cold and been reluctant to ask a friend to pick up some cold medicine, as you knew that friend was busy and you did not want to be a bother? Your reluctance to bother your friend prevented you from asking for the tangible support you needed.

Another risk of seeking social support is the *risk of losing face*. As discussed previously in this chapter, individuals want to present their best face. By asking for assistance, individuals acknowledge they cannot do something independently or that they are struggling. Asking for support also could reveal intimate and sometimes embarrassing details regarding individuals' physical, mental, and emotional health. In order for individuals to be willing to admit their weaknesses, they typically need to have a strong sense of interpersonal trust with those they are asking for support.

Individual and Cultural Factors

Research has explored individual and cultural factors that contribute to individuals' likelihood to seek social support. These factors include:

◆ Perceptions of trustworthiness
◆ Stigma attached to the issue
◆ Proximity to sources of support
◆ Availability of support
◆ Gender norms
◆ Cultural norms

There are two relevant *perceptions of trustworthiness* that influence individuals' likelihood of seeking social support. The first perception of trustworthiness was mentioned previously, that is that individuals are more likely to show their weaknesses to those they perceive to be trustworthy. The second perception of trustworthiness is that individuals are more likely to seek support from those they have confidence in to follow through with support. These perceptions of trust in those we seek help from are necessary for both individuals and organizations. For example, individuals who abuse illicit drugs would be reluctant to turn to community programs, such as drug treatment programs, if they feared program staff might report them to the police. Also, to feel comfortable asking for the different forms of support they need, individuals need to believe their health care providers are trustworthy.

Another factor that contributes to individuals' likelihood to seek social support is *stigma attached to the issue* requiring support, meaning that when individuals perceive they may be stigmatized for their problem, they are less likely to

Ethics Touchstone

Amy is working as a volunteer at the crisis hotline in her town. Her job is to answer calls that come in during her shift, talk with the callers, offer support, and encourage callers to utilize support services. She knows it is important for callers to trust her so they keep talking and she can get them connected with the help they need.

Sometimes during her shift she gets calls from minors who have been sexually assaulted. During volunteer training for the crisis hotline, she learned that the law requires her to report any suspected cases of sexual abuse or assault to law enforcement authorities. She receives a call from a 16-year-old girl who has been raped by her mother's boyfriend. The caller is very afraid and begs Amy not to tell anyone about their conversation. Amy agrees to keep the conversation private and proceeds to get more information from the girl so that she can make a full report and have the girl removed from her home. Think about this situation and answer these questions:

◆ Was Amy justified in lying to the girl to provide social support? Why or why not?

◆ On which ethical orientation from Chapter 2, "Linking Health Communication with Ethics," do you base your answer to the previous question?

directly seek help. For example, a study of low-income women found that they used more indirect methods to solicit support because they feared that divulging the details of their precarious financial situations would vilify them. The same study also considered a subset of the women who were victims of domestic violence and found they also used indirect methods, as they were embarrassed by their situations and feared judgment by those from whom they were seeking help (Williams & Mickelson, 2008).

The next two factors that contribute to individuals' likelihood to seek social support, *proximity to sources of support* and *availability of support*, are related because individuals are more likely to turn to sources of support that are near them and that are readily available. Advances in technology have changed our definitions of proximity and availability, primarily because the internet and mobile phones have made it possible to reach out and connect with others almost anywhere and at any time. Social networking tools such as Facebook and Twitter make it easy for individuals to share their problems with many people and get supportive comments and offers for help. An article in the online version of *Business Week* magazine noted that many professionals who were struggling due to the economic downturn in 2008 turned to their Facebook communities for social support. Men and women who typically were reluctant to share bad news found comfort in the Facebook format and used their connections in that community to cope with their difficulties (MacMillan, 2008).

In addition to the individual factors just discussed, there also are cultural or normative influences of support-seeking behavior. *Gender norms* refer to what society considers to be appropriate behaviors for males and females and the strong influence these norms have on support-seeking behaviors (Barker, 2007). In many cultures, males are socialized to be in control and not talk about their emotions. Therefore, many males prefer to handle problems themselves and are reluctant to seek support. Generally females are socialized that it is acceptable to be emotional and talk about their problems and therefore are more likely to seek help. In some cultures, though, women are restricted from many activities and are taught to feel shame regarding their bodies and health issues and therefore are less likely to seek help from external organizations.

Research also has found *cultural norms* or differences in support-seeking based on what is considered appropriate behavior within a culture to be a factor in individuals' likelihood to seek support. For example, people from Asian cultures, which tend to have a more collectivist orientation, are less likely to seek help than their European and American counterparts (Mortenson, 2009; Taylor, et al., 2004). One explanation for this is that Asian cultures typically discourage the expression of unpleasant emotions or sharing emotional distress, as members of these cultures do not want to disrupt relational harmony. In Western cultures, however, it is considered more normative and appropriate to express distress. Also, being more individualistic, Western individuals tend to be more concerned with remedying their physical or emotional pain.

Now that we've considered aspects of informal support seeking, let's turn our attention to more formal ways that people seek social support.

Support Groups

Support groups are one of the more formal ways that social support can be given and received. In this discussion we define the term support group, discuss the benefits and limitations of participating in a support group, and contemplate the advantages and limitations of online support groups.

Defining Support Group

A *support group* consists of individuals who share a common life stressor and come together to provide mutual support and information (Miller, 1998). Examples of common life stressors include having the same disease, disability, relationship challenge, unique life experience, or loss. In general, the more homogeneous or similar the group members are in terms of the life stressor they are facing, the more effective the support group is. More similar group members tend to relate better to one another and provide relevant information and support. This is why support groups form for very specific conditions, such as a particular type of cancer or diabetes. There is not a definitive rule as to how many members a support group should have, but a range of between six and twelve tends to be best. If the group is too large, it is difficult for members to have meaningful relationships and communication. The group may have a designated leader but this is not required. Ideally, the leader should be a group member who is willing to organize the group and facilitate discussion, rather than a health care professional.

Support groups provide social support in a more formal way when individuals are unable to obtain relevant support from their social networks. Members of a social network may not have similar experiences and challenges, which limits their ability to empathize and provide helpful information. An amputee, for example, may not have any other amputees in his or her social network, so attending a support group for amputees offers an opportunity to meet similar people who can relate to the challenges of life as an amputee in more personal and specific ways.

Because support group meetings have a specified time, place, and purpose, participants know they have a set time and place when they can talk about their situation, share concerns, and offer insights. In addition, participants may form relationships that go beyond the group and provide additional support.

Benefits of Support Groups

Some of the benefits of participating in a support group include:

◆ Validation
◆ Normalization of experience
◆ Reduction of isolation
◆ Sense of belonging
◆ Enhanced self-esteem

As mentioned previously, one of the reasons people turn to support groups is that those in their existing social network do not share the same experiences and challenges. One of the benefits of support groups is that during meetings, individuals experience *validation,* or confirmation, of their experiences and feelings when they hear other situations and stories similar to their own.

A support group for individuals with fibromyalgia provides a good example of the importance of validation in support groups. Some of the symptoms of fibromyalgia include widespread pain, especially in the joints, fatigue, and headaches. Some in the medical community question whether fibromyalgia is a physical condition or a psychosomatic/psychological condition. This doubt by some health care providers can be frustrating for those diagnosed with fibromyalgia and can cause them to feel as if others are denying their experience. In a support group for those with fibromyalgia, members recognize the condition and understand other members' pain, which provides validation of their experiences with fibromyalgia (Barker, 2008; van Uden-Kraan et al., 2008).

Another benefit of support groups is the normalization of experience. Similar to validation, support group meetings provide *normalization of experience* by helping reassure members that their experiences are normal and that others are undergoing similar experiences and challenges. For example, children in a support group for those whose mothers were HIV-positive commented that they enjoyed being with other children who "got" what it was like to have a parent with HIV. They also were able to compare experiences and feelings and determine that their reactions and behaviors were normal for kids in their situation (Witte & Ridder, 1999).

A key benefit of support groups is *reduction in isolation,* which is a decrease in the feeling that an individual is the only one with a particular health problem, and others cannot understand what it is like to experience that problem. Living with a disease, health condition, or health-related situation can be very isolating. Imagine, for example, trying to cope with the loss of a parent. Not only might you miss the relationship with your parent, but also you may feel isolated from others who cannot relate to your experience. You may feel uncomfortable talking about your feelings with these other people, leaving you to feel isolated and alone in your grieving. By joining a grief support group, you meet others with similar experiences and feelings and consequently feel less isolated and alone.

A related benefit of participating in support groups stems from a reduction in feelings of isolation by experiencing a sense of belonging. By nature, humans are social creatures, and one of our basic needs is a *sense of belonging* (Schutz, 1958). Associating with and participating in a support group fulfills this need. This is especially important when a disease or health condition prevents one from participating in other groups and activities. For example, individuals struggling with the constant pain and fatigue associated with fibromyalgia know that their abilities and their likelihood of participating in various activities are limited, but they may draw solace from being able to attend a monthly support group meeting where they have an opportunity to interact with others and feel a sense of belonging.

Another noted benefit of participation in support groups is *enhanced self-esteem,* through the sharing of challenges and having the opportunity to listen, give advice, offer suggestions, and be a source of support for group members. Helping others often helps members feel better about themselves. Individuals dealing with health issues require care and support to varying degrees and support groups provide members with a unique context within which to both be cared for by the group and assume the role of caregivers for others in the group.

The benefits of social support groups often are realized through the communication processes of upward comparisons and downward comparisons, which we explain in the next section.

Upward Comparison and Downward Comparison in Support Groups

A primary way that the benefits of social support groups are achieved is through the communication of upward comparisons and downward comparisons. As support group participants listen to other members share their stories, they compare their own situation with the situations of others.

In the *upward comparison* process, support group members serve as positive examples or role models and their stories inspire others or give them something to strive for (Taylor & Lobel, 1989). For example, at a support group for those struggling with eating disorders, a member might share a story of going to a restaurant with her family and ordering and eating an entire meal. Others in the group could interpret this story as a situation to emulate and through the story learn coping techniques from this successful support group member.

In the *downward comparison* process, support group members may hear a story from a member who is having a particularly difficult time and after hearing about the negative situation they may feel that they are doing better than that person, which helps them feel better about their own situation (Taylor & Lobel, 1989; Wills, 1981). In the eating disorder support group example, there could be a member who relates that she has not been able to break her exercise addiction and continues to go to the gym at least twice a day despite always being tired and hungry. Upon hearing this story and comparing it with her own situation, another member of the group may feel as if she is doing a reasonable job resisting the urge to exercise too much because she goes to the gym only four times per week and basically is sticking to a healthy eating plan. When individuals perceive they are doing better than others, this can provide a sense of relief, gratitude for being in a better situation, or a sense of accomplishment in having good coping skills.

In the next section, Alcoholics Anonymous is offered as a quintessential example of the many benefits of social support groups.

Exemplar of Support Group Benefits

Perhaps one of the most widely recognized social support groups is Alcoholics Anonymous (1984; Witmer, 1997), or AA, which was founded in 1935 by Bill Wilson and Bob Smith, two alcoholics who were struggling to overcome their disease. The two met in Ohio to talk about their problems. They realized that talking to a fellow alcoholic was helpful in the recovery process and slowly they began to reach out to other alcoholics. Over time they developed their twelve-step program, which involved many spiritual practices, including surrendering to a higher power, acknowledging one's transgressions, and asking for forgiveness.

Reprinted with permission of AA World Services, Inc.

The principles and strategies of AA spread quickly and within a few years meetings were held throughout the United States and around the world. Today, AA has nearly 2 million members. The basic principles of AA have remained the same since its inception. AA holds open and closed meetings. At open meetings, recovering alcoholics share their experiences of being alcoholics and about being with the program. These meetings are open to anyone, including friends and family members of alcoholics. Closed meetings are only for those who wish to stop drinking. Most open and closed meetings begin with a brief period of socializing, followed by an organized meeting. During meetings, people share their stories as well as participate in discussions of issues relevant to recovering alcoholics.

One of the reasons for the success of AA is that alcoholics help each other through the recovery process because they have an intimate understanding of the trials and tribulations involved in coping with an alcohol addiction. In a cultural analysis of an open AA support group, Witmer (1997) found strong group cohesion despite individual differences in participants' experiences with alcoholism and spirituality. This study also noted that distinct subcultures emerged within the larger support group and that power remained fairly centralized in the group's founder. A fundamental tenet of the Alcoholics Anonymous organization and program is that once individuals are alcoholics, they are always alcoholics, even after they have stopped drinking alcohol. Consequently, individuals sober for a number of years continue to attend and participate in AA support group meetings to provide guidance for those who are newer to the journey toward sobriety. Now that we've considered AA as a prime example of an effective support group, please complete Health Communication Nexus Interlude 6.4.

For this interlude, imagine that a good friend of yours is considering joining Alcoholics Anonymous. Based on your reading about the benefits of social support groups and the example of AA, what three social support benefits of AA open and closed meetings would you mention to your friend? Jot down in your notebook what you would say to your friend to explain what seem to be three benefits of AA support group meetings.

Despite the many benefits of social support groups, there also are some barriers to effective support groups that we review in the next section. In addition to describing the barriers, we offer suggestions for avoiding these barriers while fostering an effective support group.

Barriers to Effective Support Groups

Although support groups can be excellent venues for individuals to go for support and a sense of belonging, sometimes support group participation is not beneficial and does not promote better health and well-being. Barriers to effective support groups include:

◆ Not providing validation or normalization of experience
◆ Expressing too many negative feelings or experiences
◆ Sharing inaccurate or misleading information
◆ Helping others may be a burden

One barrier to effective support groups occurs when members are *not providing validation or normalization of experience*. Some participants may find that their experiences are not akin to those experiences of other members or that their feelings are drastically different. In these cases, the support group meetings may not be helpful and instead may cause a person to feel even more isolated and distressed. For example, members in an amputee support group who have been living for many, many years with the loss of a leg due to complications of diabetes may have difficulty relating to and providing current and helpful information to a new amputee who has recently lost his arm in a workplace accident. This is why it is important to have as much homogeneity of experience as possible represented in the support group.

Another barrier to effective support groups is members' *expressing too many negative feelings or experiences* that could increase other members' level of distress. For some people, talking about negative feelings and experiences can be therapeutic, but sometimes the expression of too many negative feelings and experiences can become emotionally overwhelming and draining for members. Without a certified counselor at meetings, the expression of deeply troubling emotions may become traumatic and distressing for some participants. To avoid this barrier, it is important to plan and follow an agenda for the meeting that mixes in a variety of topics and activities.

A third barrier to effective support groups is the possibility of *sharing inaccurate or misleading information* with support group members. For example, in a support group for people with diabetes, members may share advice about what kinds of foods to eat and avoid. It is possible that someone may unintentionally misrepresent a food as being low in sugar when actually it is not. To avoid acting on false or misleading information, support group members should check with their health care providers if they receive information during a support group that they cannot corroborate as credible and accurate.

A fourth barrier to effective support groups is that *helping others may be a burden* for one or more support group members. Previously in this chapter you learned that helping others by providing social support may build self-esteem. At times, though, helping others can become an overwhelming task, especially when the relationship is not reciprocal. Some members in support groups require an extensive amount of assistance both inside and outside group meetings, and it can be difficult for members who are working through their own struggles to fulfill their needs along with the needs of others. To avoid this barrier, the support group must set realistic expectations and boundaries regarding the types and amounts of support provided. Those expectations and boundaries should be shared with new members at each meeting, which also reminds returning members.

Attention to these potential barriers assists support group members in overcoming them in order to realize the many benefits of social support groups. Because individuals in social support groups realize so many benefits, in addition to in-person support group meetings, computerization and the internet allow for virtual or online support groups, which we discuss in the next section.

Online Support Groups

As we discuss support groups and support group meetings, you may have an image in your mind of a group of people in a room, sitting in a circle of folding chairs, talking and perhaps sipping coffee from Styrofoam cups. Traditionally, this was how support groups were structured. With the advent of the internet, however, some support groups formed and conducted meetings in an entirely new way that was virtual and online.

In *online support groups,* participants connect with one another through the internet to discuss their health issues, problems, concerns, and strategies for better health and well-being (Finfgeld, 2000). Some online support groups offer live chat and others utilize message boards where people can post messages and replies. There are a few distinct advantages of online support groups, which we address in the next section.

Advantages of Online Support Groups

According to Finfgeld (2000), there are three advantages of online support groups:

◆ Loose-tie relationships
◆ Anonymity
◆ Not constrained by space and time

One advantage of online support groups is the tendency to form loose-tie relationships. Because online support group members generally do not communicate in person, their members tend to form *loose-tie relationships* and do not form obligations to each other outside the support group. Loose-tie relationships can alleviate the risk for additional burdens and stress sometimes associated with close-tie relationships that may form during in-person support groups.

Another advantage of online support groups is generally participants maintain *anonymity,* meaning they do not share their full names or where they live. Participants in online support groups often are drawn by the anonymity an online support group offers because they can provide as little or as much information about themselves as they feel comfortable sharing. Because their physical appearance and other aspects of their identities may be kept more private, participants may not need to be as concerned about members discussing their situation with others or about encountering another member outside the support group.

Due to the virtual nature of online support groups, another advantage is participants are *not constrained by space and time,* meaning they do not need to be in the same place at the same time in order to achieve support. Instead, individuals can connect with others from all over the world who share a similar disease, health condition, or health-related issue. This advantage can be especially beneficial in the case of very rare or unique conditions. Those who live in smaller towns or in outlying areas also can benefit from the ability to connect with others through the internet. In addition, online support groups are available whenever it is convenient for the participants. For example, if a member needs support in the middle of the night, he or she just logs on to the computer, accesses the internet and the support group, and posts a message or chats with a fellow member who may be online. Also, participants can be at home and do not have to worry about other challenges, such as weather conditions, child care, or transportation, which may prevent them from participating in an in-person support group.

Now that you're familiar with the advantages of online support groups, let's use an example case to better understand how these advantages are enacted in interaction during online support groups. Researchers considered the types of support exchange in an online support group for individuals with Huntington's disease (Coulson, Buchanan, & Aubeeluck, 2007). Huntington's disease is a rare genetic, neurological condition characterized by the progressive deterioration of movement, cognitive function, and emotional responses. Huntington's disease is fatal and there is no cure. The researchers studied interactions in an online support group for individuals with Huntington's disease, those with family members with Huntington's disease, and individuals considering genetic testing to determine their Huntington's disease status.

Overall, members of this online support group gave and received much emotional and informational support. Examples of messages that were posted included referrals to medical experts, information about treatments, and expressions of care and concern such as "My wife and I wish you all the love in the world" and "I know you can do it." Participants appreciated that they were able to connect with others with similar concerns and often felt validated by the support of others. Expressions such as "We are here for you" also served to strengthen members' sense of belonging. Not surprisingly, tangible support was the least offered form of support. Members rarely met face-to-face and lived all over the world, which limited their abilities to provide tangible assistance. This is just one example that illustrates the advantages of interacting in an online support group. Unfortunately, there also are some disadvantages of online support groups, which we address in the next section.

Disadvantages of Online Support Groups

In addition to the advantages of online support groups, Finfgeld (2000) identified a few disadvantages including:

- ◆ Delayed response
- ◆ Lack of close-tie relationships
- ◆ Lack of tangible support
- ◆ False identity presentation

One disadvantage of online support groups is *delayed response,* or the lack of immediate feedback and support. In online support groups that consist of primarily message boards, participants may have to wait for responses to their postings unless other members happen to be online at the same time. This can be frustrating and problematic for those in need of immediate feedback and support.

Although we discussed that having loose-tie relationships can be an advantage of online support groups, the *lack of close-tie relationships* due to not meeting and communicating in person can limit the amount of support and closeness that members feel from one another. Members may never see each other or hear each other's voices and their relationships may be limited to the online support site, which may cause a decreased sense of feeling supported.

A third disadvantage of online support groups is the *lack of tangible support,* or the inability to provide physical assistance due to lack of physical proximity. At times individuals coping with a health issue may need material support, such as meals or rides to appointments. It is likely that most online support group members are not in physical proximity to one another, so tangible support may not be possible.

A fourth disadvantage of online support groups is the opportunity for *false identity presentation,* meaning that people may represent and present themselves in fictitious ways. In a virtual environment individuals can more easily fake having health conditions or health challenges to receive emotional and tangible support. In some cases support group members have been conned out of money, medications, and other material goods. Responding to these imposters and illegitimate support group members can be emotionally and physically draining for legitimate online support group members.

This problem has become so widespread that Dr. Marc Feldman coined a term for the condition, Munchausen by internet (Feldman, 2000). This term is based on other *factitious disorders* in which individuals feign or self-induce physical or emotional ailments in order to assume the role of a sick person. In Munchausen by proxy, individuals may create or falsify illnesses in others to assume the role of a sick person vicariously. Munchausen's by proxy is a rare condition in which caretakers, usually mothers, cause harm to or make up symptoms for young children in attempts to gain attention from medical staff. Feldman and his colleagues (Feldman, Bibby, & Crites, 1998) applied this same factitious disorder to those who fabricate illnesses or health conditions and join online support groups to gain attention from and/or control others. They also offered several clues to the detection of factitious internet claims, including posts that duplicate content from health-related textbooks or Web sites rather than personal experiences and/or near-fatal bouts with an illness that alternate with miraculous recoveries. If these or other clues emerge about a member, online support group members should question the truthfulness of this members' claims and maintain balance between empathy and caution about this members' intentions.

Now that we have a better understanding of the importance of social support and the advantages and disadvantages of different types of support groups, the following service-learning application provides an idea for how to utilize what you've learned by identifying a need in your area for a social support group, promoting a support group, and organizing the group's first meeting. This application also emphasizes the essential role partnerships play in any service-learning project.

SERVICE-LEARNING APPLICATION

Appreciating Partnerships in Social Support Groups

In this service-learning application, we describe how a social support group gets started by using the example of Amputees in Action. We also place special emphasis on one of the core components of a great service-learning project—*formation and maintenance of partnerships*. This is not just referring to the partnerships within your service-learning project team or among your support group members, but also the partnerships your group makes with outside individuals and organizations. These partnerships should be collaborative, mutually beneficial, and address support group members' needs. Keep in mind that communication with partners needs to be frequent and efficient in order to keep partners informed of the groups' activities, progress, and needs (Corporation for National & Community Service, 2010).

Figure 6.2 ◆ *Amputees In Action Support Group Flyer.*

Call Out!! Amputees in Action

**Meeting
Every First Wednesday
of the Month
at 7 pm at the
Rehabilitation Hospital**

Social Support and More!

Join us at our next meeting to see what's new!

**Phone:
123-456-7890 or
143-642-7788**

Amputees in Action
1st Wed. Every Month
Rehabilitation Hospital
123-456-7890 or 143-642-7788

Amputees in Action
1st Wed. Every Month
Rehabilitation Hospital
123-456-7890 or 143-642-7788

Amputees in Action
1st Wed. Every Month
Rehabilitation Hospital
123-456-7890 or 143-642-7788

Amputees in Action
1st Wed. Every Month
Rehabilitation Hospital
123-456-7890 or 143-642-7788

Amputees in Action
1st Wed. Every Month
Rehabilitation Hospital
123-456-7890 or 143-642-7788

Amputees in Action
1st Wed. Every Month
Rehabilitation Hospital
123-456-7890 or 143-642-7788

Amputees in Action
1st Wed. Every Month
Rehabilitation Hospital
123-456-7890 or 143-642-7788

Amputees in Action
1st Wed. Every Month
Rehabilitation Hospital
123-456-7890 or 143-642-7788

Amputees in Action
1st Wed. Every Month
Rehabilitation Hospital
123-456-7890 or 143-642-7788

The Amputees in Action (AIA) support group was initially conceived by the first author of this book, Professor Mattson, as she lay in the hospital recovering from a motorcycle accident. This is her story of how the support group became reality.

"As I contemplated life without my left leg, I wondered if there were any other amputees I could talk with about the challenges I was facing. I had never met an amputee but thought it was important to my recovery to talk with other amputees who could share their unique experiences. When I inquired, my health care team told me they did not know of another amputee who could visit me in the hospital or of a support group for amputees. When I was released from the hospital and was recovering at home I consulted the internet and discovered the Amputee Coalition of America (ACA). According to this organization's mission statement,

> The ACA is a national, non-profit amputee consumer educational organization representing people who have experienced amputation or are born with limb differences. The ACA includes individual amputees, amputee education and support groups for amputees, professionals, family members and friends of amputees, amputation or limb loss related agencies, and organizations. (Amputee Coalition of America, 2009)

From the ACA's Web site and by calling the ACA's information center I determined there were no support groups available in the city or state where I live. Having studied the benefits of support groups and now realizing a personal need for emotional and information support from others with a similar health issue, I decided to found a support group for amputees as soon as possible.

Approximately one year later, after putting up a few flyers around town, talking with several health care providers and an amputee who previously tried to start a support group, AIA had its first meeting. A few amputees attended and we talked about how we became amputees, our experiences living with amputations, and how we might grow the support group. Later, with the assistance of one of my graduate students, Courtney, who was working on a service-learning project, and a small group of amputees, we more formally organized the support group and created promotional materials, including the flyer in Figure 6.2. As the flyer advertises, the group meets monthly in a location that is accessible and comfortable for members, there is ample handicap parking and the organization that hosts the meeting even serves light refreshments! AIA has a Vice President of Recruitment and Promotion who organizes members of the support group to regularly post our flyer in prosthetic firms, hospitals, physical therapy facilities and anywhere else we think it might be seen by amputees or their friends and family. Members also carry AIA business cards and give them out when we encounter an amputee or when we are approached by people and asked about our prosthetics or about being an amputee.

Each support group meeting features an agenda which typically incorporates time for welcoming newcomers, catching up on each other's lives since the previous meeting, discussion of challenges and tips to overcome those challenges, and either an activity (e.g., designing a support group Web site, light exercises) or a guest speaker (e.g., physical therapist, coordinator of a local sports/recreation program for disabled athletes). The group also participates in events and projects outside the regular meeting time such as an annual picnic, attending baseball games, trainings for peer visitation in hospitals, and advocating for state and federal legislation beneficial to amputees. Usually 6 to 12 people, including amputees and sometimes their caregivers, attend the meetings, events, and projects. Longtime members of the group often comment that they enjoy the group because "it gives them quality time with other amputees who understand their situation and want to encourage them to live a fulfilling life." In addition, the service-learning aspect of this project is meaningful to Courtney and I for several reasons. The issue is personally relevant, the support group helps others cope with a health issues, and we directly experience the results of our service.

Additionally, this project could not be accomplished without key partnerships. What do you think were some of the partnerships that helped launch this support group? A few of the partnerships we formed early on in the process of creating the AIA support group include:

◆ Rehabilitation Hospital to host AIA meetings

◆ Network of prosthetic firms, hospitals, and physical therapy facilities to post AIA flyers and brochures

◆ Amputee Coalition of America

◆ Rehabilitation Hospital Sports Program

As you plan and carry out your own service-learning projects, such as starting a support group, it is important to be thoughtful and purposeful in the ways you select, form, and maintain partnerships. You can form partnerships with other campus departments or services, government organizations, local agencies and businesses, and key individuals. The best partnerships are those in which all of the parties mutually benefit. You may have some great ideas for helping a local agency provide social support, for example, but if those ideas do not fit the agency's mission and goals or benefit its clientele, then likely this will not be an effective and mutually-beneficial partnership.

The Points of Light Institute, an organization dedicated to promoting volunteerism, offers the following tips for establishing effective partnerships (Catania, Coates, & Kegeles, 1994):

◆ Know your objectives. Before contact, build a solid base.

◆ Be able to articulate your goals, your service objectives, and your learning expectations.

◆ Know your volunteers. What types, their range of interests, their limitations, their talents.

◆ Know your resources. Can you provide public relations, transportation, duplication? Remember, simple details loom large to agencies.

Courtesy Points of Light. With permission.

◆ Know agencies and their programs. Understand their structure, their mission, and their activities at least well enough to ask informed questions.

◆ Make a strong effort to involve others in approaching agencies and to use them in an on-going way for program implementation.

As your service-learning project team considers who you may partner with write down a list of what your project team has to offer as well as what your team needs. Then list what the potential partners' needs may be that your team can fulfill and what they may have to offer your team. You can then look for the best match in which all involved parties likely experience satisfaction in meeting their needs while providing support to others. This also helps your team in approaching potential partners if you can clearly explain the mutual benefits to the potential partner in working with your team on the project.

Chapter Summary

In this chapter we covered the important topic of social support and its relationship to health communication. We began by defining social support and then delineated the many types of social support. Next, we explained the health benefits of social support. This was followed by a consideration of supportive communication and the factors that make support messages more or less effective. Then we discussed the role of social networks in providing social support. In the next section we looked at the other side of social support and explored the ways in which people seek social support. We then examined the more formal role of social support in support groups including advantages and disadvantages of both in-person and online support groups. We concluded the chapter with a service-learning application about starting a support group while emphasizing the necessity of creating a network for the support group through partnerships.

References

Albrecht, T. L., & Adelman, M. B. (1987). Communicating social support: A theoretical perspective. In T. L. Albrecht & M. B. Adelman (Eds.), *Communicating social support* (pp. 18–39). Newbury Park, CA: Sage.

Albrecht, T. L., & Goldsmith, D. (2003). Social support, social networks, and health. In T. L. Thompson, A. M. Dorsey, K. I. Miller, & R. Parrott (Eds.), *Handbook of health communication* (pp. 263–284). Mahwah, NJ: Lawrence Erlbaum.

Alcoholics Anonymous (1984). This is A.A.: An introduction to the A.A. Recovery Program. New York: Alcoholics Anonymous World Services, Inc.

Almeida, J., Molnar, B. E., Kawachi, I., & Subramanian, S. V. (2009). Ethnicity and nativity status as determinants of perceived social support: Testing the concept of familism. *Social Science & Medicine, 68,* 1852–1858.

Amputee Coalition of America (2009). About the Amputee Coalition of America. Retrieved August 26, 2009, from http://www.amputee-coalition.org/aca_about.html.

Anderson, E. S., Winett, R. A., & Wojcik, J. R. (2007). Self-regulation, self-efficacy, outcome expectations, and social support: Social cognitive theory and nutrition behavior. *Annals of Behavioral Medicine, 34,* 304–312.

Barbee, A. P., & Cunningham, M. R. (1995). An experimental approach to social support communications: Interactive coping in close relationships. In B. R. Burleson (Ed.), *Communication yearbook 18* (pp. 381–413). Thousand Oaks, CA: Sage.

Barker, G. (2007). *Adolescents, social support and help-seeking behaviour.* Geneva, Switzerland: World Health Organization.

Barker, K. K. (2008). Electronic support groups, patient-consumers, and medicalization: The case of contested illness. *Journal of Health and Social Behavior, 49,* 20–36.

Barrera, M. (1986). Distinctions between social support concepts, measures, and models. *American Journal of Community Psychology, 14,* 413–445.

Brown, P., & Levinson, S. (1978). *Politeness: Some universals in language usage.* Cambridge, MA: Cambridge University Press.

Cassel, J. (1976). The contribution of the social environment to host resistance. *American Journal of Epidemiology, 104,* 107–123.

Catania, J. A., Coates, T. J., & Kegeles, S. (1994). A test of the AIDS risk reduction model: Psychosocial correlates of condom use in the AMEN survey. *Health Psychology, 13,* 548–555.

Choi, J. B., & Thomas, M. (2009). Predictive factors of acculturation attitudes and social support among Asian immigrants in the USA. *International Journal of Social Welfare, 18,* 76–84.

Cobb, S. (1976). Social support as a moderator of life stress. *Psychosomatic Medicine, 38,* 300–314.

Cohen, S., & Willis, T. A. (1985). Stress, social support, and the buffering hypothesis. *Psychological Bulletin, 98,* 310–357.

Corporation for National & Community Service (2010). Learn and Serve America's National Service-Learning Clearinghouse. Retrieved January 12, 2010, from www.servicelearning.org.

Coulson, N. S., Buchanan, H., & Aubeeluck, A. (2007). Social support in cyberspace: A content analysis of communication within a Huntington's disease online support group. *Patient Education & Counseling, 68,* 173–178.

Cutrona, C. E., & Russell, D. W. (1990). Type of social support and specific stress: Toward a theory of optimal matching. In B. R. Sarason, I. G. Sarason, & G. G. Pierce (Eds.), *Social support: An interactional view* (pp. 454–481). New York: John Wiley.

Durkheim, E. (1951). *Suicide: A study in sociology.* London: Routledge.

Egbert, N. (2003). Support provider mood and familiar versus unfamiliar events: An investigation of social support quality. *Communication Quarterly, 51*, 209–224.

Few, A. L. (2005). The voices of Black and White rural battered women in domestic violence shelters. *Family Relations, 54*, 488–500.

Feldman, M. D. (2000). Munchausen by internet: Detecting factitious illness and crisis on the internet. *Southern Medical Journal, 93*, 669–672.

Feldman, M. D., Bibby, M., & Crites, S. D. (1998). "Virtual" factitious disorders and Munchausen by proxy. *Western Journal of Medicine, 168*, 537–539.

Finfgeld, D. L. (2000). Therapeutic groups online: The good, the bad, and the unknown. *Issues in Mental Health Nursing, 21*, 241–255.

Gildea, T. (2010, March 21). Combat vet says gender bias led to untreated PTSD. Retrieved March 30, 2010, from http://www.npr.org/templates/story/story.php?storyId=124500733.

Goffman, E. (1963). *Behavior in public places: Notes on the social organization of gatherings.* New York: Free Press.

Gottlieb, B. (2000). Selecting and planning support interventions. In S. Cohen, L. Underwood, & B. Gotlieb (Eds.), *Social support measurement and intervention* (pp. 195–220). London: Oxford University Press.

Jones, S. (2004). Putting the person into person-centered and immediate emotional support: Emotional change and perceived helper competence as outcomes of comforting in helping situations. *Communication Research, 31*, 338–360.

Levendosky, A. A., Bogat, G. A., Theran, S. A., Trotter, J. L., von Eye, A., & Davidson, W. S. (2004). The social networks of women experiencing domestic violence. *American Journal of Community Psychology, 34*, 95–109.

Lim, J. W., Yi, J., & Zebrack, B. (2008). Acculturation, social support, and quality of life for Korean immigrant breast and gynecological cancer survivors. *Ethnicity & Health, 13*, 243–260.

Lyyra, T. M., & Heikkinen, R. L. (2006). Perceived social support and mortality in older people. *The Journals of Gerontology Series B: Psychological Sciences & Social Sciences, 61B*, S147–S152.

MacGeorge, E. L., Clark, R. A., & Gillihan, S. J. (2002). Sex differences in the provision of skillful emotional support: The mediating role of self-efficacy. *Communication Reports, 15*, 17–28.

MacMillan, D. (2008, December 17). The recession: My Facebook, my therapist. *BusinessWeek.* Retrieved February 10, 2009, from http://www.businessweek.com/technology/content/dec2008/tc20081216_649709.htm.

McDowell, T. L., & Serovich, J. M. (2007). The effect of perceived and actual social support on the mental health of HIV-positive persons. *AIDS Care, 19*, 1223–1229.

Miller, J. E. (1998). *Effective support groups.* Fort Wayne, IN: Willowgreen.

Mortenson, S. T. (2009). Interpersonal trust and social skill in seeking social support among Chinese and Americans. *Communication Research, 36*, 32–53.

Mortimore, E., Haselow, D., Dolan, M., Hawkes, W. G., Langenberg, P., Zimmerman, S., & Magaziner, J. (2008). Amount of social contact and hip fracture mortality. *Journal of the American Geriatrics Society, 56*, 1069–1074.

Motl, R. W., McAuley, E., Snook, E. M., & Gliottoni, R. C. (2009). Physical activity and quality of life in multiple sclerosis: Intermediary roles of disability, fatigue, mood, pain, self-efficacy and social support. *Psychology, Health & Medicine, 14*, 111–124.

Norris, F. H., & Kaniasty, K. (1996). Received and perceived social support in times of stress: A test of the social support deterioration deterrence model. *Journal of Personality and Social Psychology, 71*, 498–511.

Rack, J. J., Burleson, B. R., Bodie, G. D., Holmstrom, A. J., & Servaty-Seib, H. (2008). Bereaved adults' evaluations of grief management messages: Effects of message person centeredness, recipient individual differences, and contextual factors. *Death Studies, 32,* 399–427.

Sarason, B. R., Sarason, I. G., & Pierce, G. G. (1990). *Social support: An interactional view.* New York: John Wiley.

Schaefer, C., Coyne, J. C., & Lazarus, R. S. (1981). The health-related functions of social support. *Journal of Behavioral Medicine, 4,* 381–406.

Schutz, W. (1958). *FIRO: A three-dimensional theory of interpersonal behavior.* New York: Rinehart.

Stohl, C. (1995). *Organizational communication: Connectedness in action.* Thousand Oaks, CA: Sage.

Taylor, S. E., & Lobel, M. (1989). Social comparison activity under threat: Downward evaluation and upward contacts. *Psychological Review, 96,* 569–575.

Taylor, S. E., Sherman, D. K., Kim, H. S., Jarcho, J., Takagi, K., & Dunagan, M. S. (2004). Culture and social support: Who seeks it and why? *Journal of Personality and Social Psychology, 87,* 354–362.

Trotter, J. L., & Allen, N. E. (2009). The good, the bad, and the ugly: Domestic violence survivors' experiences with their informal social networks. *American Journal of Community Psychology, 43,* 221–232.

van Uden-Kraan, C. F., Drossaert, C. H. C., Taal, E., Shaw, B. R., Seydel, E. R., & van de Laar, M. A. F. J. (2008). Empowering processes and outcomes of participation in online support groups for patients with breast cancer, arthritis, or fibromyalgia. *Qualitative Health Research, 18,* 405–417.

Williams, S. L., & Mickelson, K. D. (2008). A paradox of support seeking and rejection among the stigmatized. *Personal Relationships, 15,* 493–509.

Wills, T. A. (1981). Downward comparison principles in social psychology. *Psychological Bulletin, 90,* 245–271.

Witmer, D. F. (1997). Communication and recovery: Structuration as an ontological approach to organizational culture. *Communication Monographs, 64,* 324–349.

Witte, S. S., & Ridder, N. F. (1999). "Positive feelings": Group support for children of HIV-infected mothers. *Child and Adolescent Social Work, 16,* 5–21.

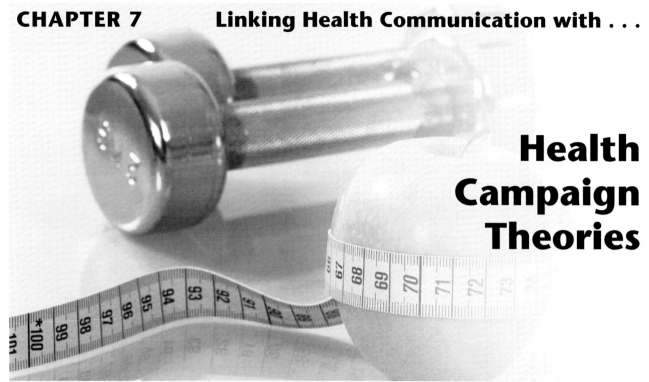

Health Campaign Theories

© 2011, Cindy Hughes, Shutterstock, Inc.

Chapter Learning Objectives

◆ Revisit the definition of theory and discuss the importance of theory in health campaigns
◆ Explain an ecological approach to organizing health campaign theories
◆ List the contexts of influence relevant to health campaigns
◆ Name and describe at least one theory from each context of influence
◆ Provide one example health campaign for each health campaign theory presented

Chapter Preview

Although we already have a chapter devoted to health communication theories and mention other theories throughout this book, in this chapter we focus on six theories or models that typically inform health campaigns. As you read in Chapter 8, "Linking Health Communication with Health Campaign Practice," designing, implementing, and evaluating health campaigns is a complex process that also can demand many resources. In this chapter we argue that if you think about and integrate theory into the health campaign process, the campaign is much more likely to be successful. Several theories already have been developed for health campaigns and much research demonstrates the effectiveness of these theories in guiding decisions throughout the campaign phases of design, implementation, and evaluation. After briefly revisiting our preferred definition of theory presented in Chapter 3, "Linking Health Communication with Theories Informed by Health Communication," we present six health campaign theories or models and provide examples and implications to illustrate how these theories can inform health campaigns.

Revisit Definition of Theory

In Chapter 3, "Linking Health Communication with Theories Informed by Health Communication," we presented our preferred definition of *theory* as a "consciously elaborated, justified, and uncertain understanding" (Babrow & Mattson, 2003, p. 36). According to this definition, a theory needs to be well thought out, specifically communicated, supported by reason and evidence, and tentative in its level of certainty about the phenomenon it is attempting to understand or explain. Theories provide a common language, practical tools, and help those designing, implementing, and evaluating health messages and programs to move beyond their intuition toward established understandings about human interaction and behavior. Theory provides a road map, but also remember that the map is not the territory (Bateson, 1972), meaning that any theory we use for guidance is an incomplete map and only one possible description or explanation of the territory.

Theory needs to be intertwined with practice. As Lewin (1951) contended "there is nothing so practical as a good theory" (p. 169). Theory informs practice and practice informs theory by revising existing theories or creating new theories. In this chapter we focus on how other theories, in addition to those discussed in Chapter 3, "Linking Health Communication with Theories Informed by Health Communication," can inform health campaign practice. Within this chapter we also discuss models used to guide campaign design, implementation, and evaluation. Although most would agree that models technically are not theories, the models included in this chapter are based on research and theoretical concepts.

Ecological Framework of Health Campaign Theories

To organize the health campaign theories we return to the contexts of communication presented in Chapter 1, "Introducing Health as Communication Nexus," and position each theory within the context for which it is best suited. This contextual approach to organizing these theories is consistent with an ecological framework of health campaign theories. An *ecological framework* emphasizes the nature of people's interactions with their environment (Stokols, 1996; Street, 2003). Two interrelated assumptions are key to an ecological perspective. One assumption is that individual behavior is shaped by and shapes the social environment. The second assumption is that human behavior is affected by and affects multiple levels of influence. These levels of influence closely correspond to the contexts of communication, including intrapersonal, interpersonal, small group or team, organizational, and public or mass communication. Because people are situated within and influenced by a variety of social contexts, theories from within the corresponding contexts help inform relevant aspects of the health campaigns that attempt to reach people.

Intrapersonal Context of Influence

The *intrapersonal context of influence* refers to communication with oneself usually involving cognitive analysis or thought about self, others, problems, and situations. Health campaign theories within the *intrapersonal context of influence* encompass individual thought, including self-concept, knowledge, attitudes, beliefs, motivation, past experiences, and individual behavior including skills. This is an important context of influence because the individual is the most fundamental unit of communication and/or behavior that makes up groups, organizations, and communities. So individual-level health behavior also influences these other contexts of communication. Also, health campaign practitioners spend much of their time attempting to change the behavior of individuals. The intrapersonal or individual-level theories covered are:

◆ Health Belief Model
◆ Theory of Reasoned Action and Theory of Planned Behavior
◆ Transtheoretical Model/Stages of Change

Health Belief Model

The Health Belief Model (HBM) fits within the intrapersonal context of influence for health campaigns because it seeks to explain what encourages or discourages individuals to adopt recommended health actions. We only briefly review the HBM here because we discussed the Reconceptualized Health Belief Model (RHBM) in detail in Chapter 3, "Linking Health Communication with Theories Informed by Health Communication." Over the years the original HBM (Rosenstock, 1966, 1974a, 1974b; Rosenstock, Strecher, & Becker, 1988) was expanded to six components (Janz & Becker, 1984) including:

◆ *Perceived susceptibility*—perception of vulnerability to a particular health threat. An individual's perception of susceptibility to a threat influences that individual's behavior to avoid or alleviate the threat. Those who believe they are highly susceptible to a threat are most likely to take actions to prevent against the threat. Conversely, those who feel less susceptible to a threat are less likely to take preventive actions against the threat.

◆ *Perceived severity*—perception of the seriousness of a health threat. The more severe an individual perceives a threat to be the more likely an individual is to take action to avoid that threat.

◆ *Perceived benefits*—perceptions of the advantages of using a recommended health action including perceptions that the behavior will be successful in preventing the threat.

◆ *Perceived barriers*—perceptions of the costs associated with performing the recommended health behavior. Individuals perform a cost/benefit analysis in deciding whether or not to adopt the recommended health action.

◆ *Self-efficacy*—belief in personal ability to adopt a recommended health behavior. If individuals are not confident in their ability to perform certain necessary health actions, they are less likely to try.

◆ *Cues to action*—internal and/or external stimuli that encourage an individual to adopt a recommended health behavior. Cues to action serve to enhance one or more of the other components of the HBM such as perceived severity, perceived susceptibility, and perceived benefits and barriers, which increases the likelihood that the recommended health behavior is adopted.

As Figure 7.1 illustrates, each of these components influences an individual's decision whether to adopt a recommended health behavior. This theory can be used in designing health behavior change campaigns by carefully assessing individual target audience members' perceptions for each of the components within the model. Then the campaign attempts to address any needed changes in the components to motivate target audience members to adopt the recommended health action.

For example, Peng (2009) utilized components of the HBM to design and evaluate a computer game, *RightWay Café*, to promote a healthy diet among young adults. The goal of this computer game was to entertain and educate players about healthy eating options and to change their behavior toward healthier eating. The object of this role-playing computer game was to win a hypothetical reality television show by being the healthiest eater in the campus cafeteria. Players chose an avatar at the beginning of the game and based on the characteristics of the avatar chosen, players received tailored healthy-eating messages. In designing the computer game, components of the HBM, including perceived benefits, perceived

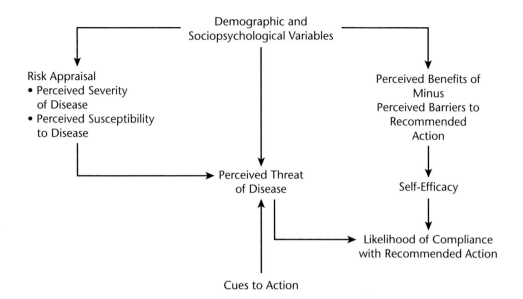

Figure 7.1 ◆ *Health Belief Model (adapted from Janz & Becker, 1984; Becker, 1990)*

barriers, and self-efficacy, were incorporated into the game. Because the game was targeted toward young adults, short-term rather than long-term benefits of healthy eating were emphasized, including better skin, better hair, and stronger muscles. Perceived barriers to healthy eating, such as inconvenient to prepare, cost, and tastiness, were addressed with healthy food options that were easy to make, were reasonably priced, and tasted good. Examples of these healthy options were frozen yogurt and fruit smoothies. Surveys distributed to players before and after playing the game indicated positive effects by increasing knowledge of nutrition, increasing perceived benefits of eating healthy, and increasing perceptions of self-efficacy to eat healthy. Surveys also indicated that game players had increased intentions to maintain a healthy diet.

Theory of Reasoned Action and Theory of Planned Behavior

The Theory of Reasoned Action (TRA) and the Theory of Planned Behavior (TPB) fit within the intrapersonal context of influence for health campaigns because these interrelated theories consider the relationships among an individual's beliefs, attitudes, intentions, and behavior. Over time TRA (Ajzen & Fishbein, 1980; Fishbein & Ajzen, 1975) was expanded by TPB (Ajzen, 1985) to include these components:

◆ *Attitudes*—sum of beliefs about a particular behavior based on an individual's personal evaluation of the behavior.
◆ *Subjective social norms*—influence of people in social environment regarding approval or disapproval of the behavior. Their level of influence is weighted by the importance an individual attributes to others' opinions.

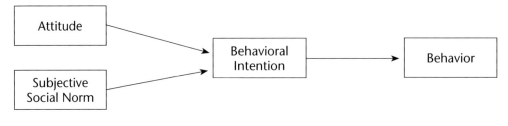

Theory of Reasoned Action

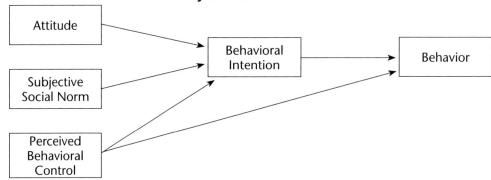

Theory of Planned Behavior

Figure 7.2 ◆ *Theory of Reasoned Action and Theory of Planned Behavior (adapted from Ajzen, 1985)*

◆ *Perceived behavioral control*—"beliefs regarding the possession of requisite resources and opportunities for performing a given behavior" (Madden, Ellen, & Ajzen, 1992, p. 4). Helps to account for situations when an individual intends to carry out a behavior but that intention may be thwarted due to lack of confidence or lack of complete control over the behavior. In other words, the addition of perceived behavioral control to TRA accounts for behaviors outside an individual's control that may affect intention and behavior.

◆ *Behavioral intention*—perceived likelihood of performing a behavior.

Figure 7.2 illustrates how the components of these two theories predict health behavior. According to the model, an individual's attitudes toward a behavior are shaped by beliefs about what is involved in performing the behavior and the outcomes of that behavior. An individual's beliefs about social norms and motivation to comply with those norms influence subjective norms. Circumstances that make it easier or more difficult to perform the behavior affect perceived behavioral control. Consequently, the causal chain of beliefs, attitudes, and intentions drive behavior.

These theories have been widely used to effectively predict behavioral intentions and behavior. Upon comparing the two theories for ten behaviors, including health behaviors such as exercising regularly, getting a good night's sleep, and taking vitamin supplements, Madden, Ellen, and Ajzen (1992) found that the inclusion of perceived behavioral control enhanced the prediction of behavioral intention and performing the behavior. This was especially the case when the behavior presented some problem with respect to the individual's level of personal control over that behavior.

Returning to the example of developing the *RightWay Café* computer game to improve healthy eating behavior among young adults, Peng (2009) also used components of the Theory of Reasoned Action to design the messages that players received as they progressed through the game. Realizing the theory predicts that behavior change is determined by intention to change behavior, which is codetermined by attitudes toward the behavior and the subjective social norm regarding that behavior, messages in the game promoted positive attitudes toward healthy eating. This occurred by providing positive feedback and rewards when players made healthy food choices. Dialogue within the game promoted the norm that eating healthy is socially desirable. Again, results of the evaluation of the computer game indicated that after playing the game, players had an increased intention to maintain a healthy diet compared with a control group of young adults who did not play the computer game.

There are two key implications of TRA and TPB for health campaigns. In assessing the target audience of a health campaign, two sets of beliefs need to be altered prior to behavior change. The first set of beliefs has to do with the consequences of performing the recommended health behaviors. In order to change behavior, an individual must believe that the recommended behavior leads to more positive than negative consequences. The second set of beliefs to be altered concern the opinions of other people whom the individual values and the extent to which the individual is motivated to comply with those referents. Again, ideally an individual's referent others have a positive attitude toward the recommended health behavior and the individual is motivated by those referents to change. The second implication of TRA and TPB for health campaigns is that intervention messages must target an individual's salient or relevant beliefs to influence health behavior intentions and subsequent health behaviors. To determine target audience members' salient beliefs, health campaign planners must ask about these beliefs either in one-on-one interviews or in focus groups or both.

The three theories just covered within the intrapersonal context of influence, the Health Belief Model, the Theory of Reasoned Action, and the Theory of Planned Behavior, are individual decision-making models, whereas the next theory is a process model.

Transtheoretical Model/Stages of Change

Process models of behavior change focus on the individual but instead of assuming that there is one equation to predict whether individuals decide to adopt a healthy behavior, process models assume that individuals go through a series of stages as they transition from unhealthy to healthy behaviors. The two most common process models of health behavior change are the Precaution Adoption Process Model (Weinstein, 1988; Weinstein & Sandman, 1992) and the Transtheoretical

Model (TTM; Prochaska, DiClemente, & Norcross, 1992; Prochaska, Norcross, & DiClemente, 1994). Since the TTM has been around longer and is similar to the Precaution Adoption Process Model, we cover the TTM in detail.

The TTM of behavior change was developed by Prochaska and DiClemente and their colleagues upon identifying common processes of change across several psychotherapy theories. The TTM consists of four major constructs, including stages of change, processes of change, decisional balance, and self-efficacy (Prochaska, Redding, & Evers, 2002). The stages of change is the most prominent construct and the theory often is referred to as the stages of change model. The five *stages of change* are the stages individuals commonly go through in order to successfully change behavior. The *processes of change* are activities that assist individuals in progressing through the stages of change. Upon identifying target audience members' stage of change, health campaigns can promote processes of change to help move individuals toward the next stage of behavior change. *Decisional balance* refers to how individuals weigh the advantages and disadvantages or pros and cons of behavior change. Research indicates that the advantages must increase twice as much as the disadvantages decrease to move an individual from precontemplation to action. So health campaign practitioners should expend more effort increasing benefits for changing behavior than on reducing the costs of and barriers to changing behavior (Prochaska & Velicer, 1997). *Self-efficacy* is individuals' situation-specific confidence in their ability to change to healthier behavior and avoid temptations to return to unhealthy behavior. As also indicated in other theories, health campaign practitioners should work to increase individuals' sense of self-efficacy for performing healthier behaviors.

The underlying premise of the Transtheoretical Model/Stages of Change is that behavior change is a process, not a singular event, and individuals are at varying levels of readiness or motivation to change (Prochaska, DiClemente, & Norcross, 1992; Prochaska, Norcross, & DiClemente, 1994). People at different stages in the change process benefit from different health campaign approaches that are appropriately matched to their stage of change. The six stages of change include:

◆ *Precontemplation*—individual has no intention to take action within the next 6 months.
◆ *Contemplation*—individual intends to take action toward behavior change within the next 6 months.
◆ *Preparation*—individual intends to take action within the next 30 days, has taken some behavioral steps in that direction, and has a plan of action.
◆ *Action*—individual has changed behavior for less than 6 months.
◆ *Maintenance*—individual has changed behavior for more than 6 months and is working on preventing relapse into unhealthy behavior.
◆ *Termination*—individual experiences complete self-efficacy and no longer succumbs to temptation to return to previous unhealthy behavior.

The processes of change are the activities that individuals use to progress through the stages of change. Each process of change provides guidelines for health campaign interventions. The ten processes of change with corresponding guidelines for health campaigns are:

◆ *Consciousness-raising*—involves increased awareness about the causes, consequences, and cures for a particular problem behavior. Campaign interventions that can increase consciousness-raising about a health problem include feedback, confrontation, and media messages.

◆ *Dramatic relief*—involves experiencing the negative emotions, such as fear, anxiety, and worry, that go along with the risks of unhealthy behavior. Campaign interventions can incorporate dramatic relief by producing increased emotional experiences followed by reduced affect if the recommended health behavior change is accomplished. Dramatic relief techniques include role-playing and testimonials.

◆ *Self-reevaluation*—involves realizing that the health behavior change is an important aspect of an individual's personal identity. Campaign interventions can heighten self-reevaluation by combining cognitive and emotional assessments of individuals' self-image with and without the recommended health behavior. Self-reevaluation techniques include comparing an individual with a healthy role model and imagery to help individuals imagine themselves with and without the healthy behavior.

◆ *Environmental reevaluation*—involves realizing either the negative impact of the unhealthy behavior or the positive impact of the healthy behavior on the individual's social and physical environment. Campaign interventions can heighten environmental reevaluation by combining cognitive and emotional assessments of the individual's social environment with and without the recommended health behavior. Environmental reevaluation techniques include motivating target audience members to become role models for others and documentaries.

◆ *Self-liberation*—involves both the belief that an individual can change and personal action on that belief. Campaign interventions can encourage self-liberation by motivating and documenting public commitments to the recommended health behaviors.

◆ *Helping relationships*—involves seeking and utilizing social support to promote health behavior change. Campaign interventions can assist social support activities through techniques such as helplines and buddy systems.

◆ *Counterconditioning*—involves substituting healthy thoughts and behaviors for unhealthy thoughts and behaviors. Campaign interventions can support counterconditioning through techniques such as promoting healthy replacement products and encouraging positive self-talk about healthy alternatives.

◆ *Reinforcement management*—involves increasing rewards for positive change toward healthy behavior and decreasing rewards for the unhealthy behavior. Campaign interventions that can assist in managing behavior reinforcement include behavior contracts and public praise or tangible public rewards.

◆ *Stimulus control*—involves removing reminders or cues to engage in unhealthy behavior and adding reminders or cues to engage in healthy behavior. Campaign interventions that encourage stimulus control include environmental changes and support groups.

◆ *Social liberation*—involves realizing that social norms are changing in favor of the healthy behavior. Campaign interventions that promote social liberation include increasing social opportunities for healthy behaviors.

The TTM emphasizes that relatively few individuals in the target audience of a campaign are ready for action-oriented interventions because they tend to be stuck in earlier stages of change. So campaign practitioners should devote their energies toward moving individuals out of earlier stages of change. Research by Prochaska and Velicer (1997) among others indicated that individuals use specific processes of change during specific stages of change. Matching campaign interventions accordingly is critical to behavior change. So, cognitive, affective, and evaluative processes of change such as consciousness-raising, dramatic relief, self-reevaluation, and environmental reevaluation are most appropriate for individuals in the precontemplation and contemplation stages. Individuals in action and maintenance stages of change are more likely to use behavioral processes of change, including helping relationships, counterconditioning, reinforcement management, and stimulus control. Table 7.1 presents how processes of change should be matched to stages of change.

Stages of Change

	PRECONTEMPLATION	CONTEMPLATION	PREPARATION	ACTION	MAINTENANCE
Processes		Consciousness-raising			
		Dramatic relief			
		Environmental reevaluation			
of			Self-reevaluation		
				Self-liberation	Reinforcement management
Change					Helping relationships
					Counterconditioning
					Stimulus control

Table 7.1 ◆ *Matching Processes of Change to Stages of Change (adapted from Prochaska, DiClemente, & Norcross, 1992)*

Before we continue, please take a few minutes to complete Health Communication Nexus Interlude 7.1, which asks you to practice a stages of change approach to a health issue that's personal for you.

Health Communication Nexus Interlude 7.1

For this interlude, identify and write down in your notebook a health issue that you struggle with or struggled with in the past. Now, address this health issue using a stages of change approach by doing each of the following:

- Based on the definitions presented previously, identify and write down which stage of change you are currently in relative to this health issue.

- Next, determine and write down which process of change most likely would influence you to progress through the stages of change.

- Based on the health campaign intervention guidelines recommended for each process of change, write down at least two ideas of campaign messages/interventions that likely would influence you to progress to the next stage of change regarding the health issue you are facing or faced in the past.

Let's consider an example of how the Transtheoretical Model/Stages of Change was used to develop and evaluate a campaign to promote safe preparation of ground beef. The *160° for Your Family* campaign was implemented in the northwestern United States. The campaign had two target audiences, women in the Women, Infants, and Children (WIC) program, and shoppers at rural grocery stores in the state of Washington. The primary messages of the campaign were that all ground beef needs to be cooked to at least 160 degrees Fahrenheit and the best way to be sure of this is to use a meat thermometer (Erickson, Curry, & Warren, 2010; Erickson & Staszak, 2010; McCurdy & Nalivka, 2010).

Displays were set up at WIC offices and near the meat department in grocery stores. The displays included recipe cards that also contained information about cooking temperature. The displays featured images of families to elicit an emotional response. The grocery store displays had meat thermometers to purchase. The overall goal of the campaign was to move target audience members into the action stage, when they were actively trying to prepare their ground beef in a safe manner.

Evaluation was a key component of the campaign. Survey questions were used to assess the current stage of change of target audience members. Responses to questions regarding ground beef preparation revealed that prior to reading the information on the recipe cards, many audience members owned a meat thermometer but never used it to measure the temperature of ground beef. For the target audience of grocery store shoppers, many of the participants were in the contemplation stage and were thinking about using a meat thermometer but were not actually doing it. Survey results indicated that after reading the information on the recipe cards, participants moved into the action stage, which was indicated by their reported use of a meat thermometer and their knowledge of the correct temperature.

The WIC target audience, which consisted of low-income mothers, moved from the contemplation to the preparation stage. Although the mothers' knowledge of safe meat preparation increased, surveys indicated that the mothers were still planning to use a thermometer but were not actually using it. The survey identified some of the barriers to thermometer use, including that it was not a part of their cooking routine and they did not know anyone who used a thermometer. Go to this book's Web site to learn more about this campaign and see campaign brochures.

Interpersonal and Small Group or Team Contexts of Influence

The *interpersonal and small group or team contexts of influence* refer to communication that takes place one-to-one or among a small collective of individuals. Social Cognitive Theory (SCT) is prominently used by health campaigns that can be categorized within the interpersonal and small group or team contexts of influence. SCT is interpersonal or small group in nature because it describes health behavior as a dynamic process in which individual factors, environmental factors, and human interaction exert influence on each other.

Social Cognitive Theory

Social Cognitive Theory is credited to Bandura (1962, 1977), who proposed that behavioral learning occurs socially through observation and imitation. SCT evolved from Social Learning Theory (SLT), which asserted that individuals learn not only from their own experiences but by observing the actions of others, including the consequences of their actions. SLT was updated to include the concept of self-efficacy, and the title was changed to Social Cognitive Theory. Because the theory draws from cognitive, behavioral, and emotion models, it contains two key assumptions and many core concepts with implications for health campaigns including:

◆ *Reciprocal determinism*—primary assumption of SCT is that behavior, cognitive, and interpersonal factors and environmental events are interactively determined. Health campaign practitioners should consider multiple ways to promote behavior change in the target audience, including influencing personal attitudes but also making adjustments to the environment.

◆ *Observational learning or modeling*—another underlying assumption of SCT is that the environment creates situations in which the behaviors or actions of credible others can be observed along with the consequences of their behaviors or actions. Health campaign practitioners should offer credible role models who perform the desired health behaviors and experience positive consequences from those behaviors. Observational learning is governed by these processes:

❖ Attention—gaining and maintaining attention on the behavior
❖ Motivation—being stimulated to produce the behavior
❖ Reproduction—reproducing the observed behavior
❖ Retention—remembering the behavior

◆ *Behavioral capability*—an individual's knowledge and skill to perform a behavior. Health campaign strategies should promote learning healthy behaviors through skills training.

◆ *Self-efficacy*—confidence in an individual's ability to take action and overcome barriers. Health campaign strategies to address self-efficacy include being specific in how to achieve the desired behavior and approaching behavior change in small steps to build on and grow behavior-change successes.

◆ *Outcome expectations*—anticipated outcomes of a behavior and the value placed on those outcomes. Health campaign strategies to address outcome expectations include modeling positive consequences of healthy behavior.

◆ *Reinforcements*—responses to an individual's behavior that increase or decrease the likelihood of recurrence of that behavior. Health campaign strategies should promote self-initiated incentives and rewards.

To illustrate how SCT is utilized in health campaign interventions, let's return to the *RightWay Café* computer game, which was designed to improve healthy eating behavior among young adults. Peng (2009) also incorporated components of SCT into the game structure and the messages that players received as they progressed through the game. For example, *RightWay Café* players role-play choosing healthy foods in the simulated cafeteria and through trial and error learn which foods are healthy choices. Players who choose healthy foods receive positive feedback in messages from credible characters within the game. If they make unhealthy choices, they are presented encouraging feedback and suggestions for

Ethics Touchstone

Based on what you're learning about health campaign theories, do you think it is unethical to design, implement, and evaluate a health campaign without having a theory or theories to guide the campaign? Jot down your answer to this question in your notebook. Now think about this initial question further by answering these follow-up questions:

◆ Are health campaigns that are not guided by theory unethical? Why or why not?
◆ Does an ethical health campaign need to extend theory?
◆ Did you consider any of the ethical orientations from Chapter 2, "Linking Health Communication with Ethics," when you responded?
◆ Upon considering the ethical orientations, would you change your response to the initial question? Why or why not?

how to make better choices next time. So, if a female avatar who is 15 pounds heavier than her ideal weight follows the suggested daily calorie intake for a week of time in game play, the game simulates a slight weight loss and the player wins points and gets positive feedback about her behavior. If she eats too few calories in a week, the game simulates weight loss but provides warning messages about a possible eating disorder and offers tips for how to achieve healthy weight loss. The evaluation of this computer game indicated that players of the game subsequently increased their intention to maintain a healthy diet compared with a control group of young adults who did not play the game. As this research project demonstrated, theoretical components can be integrated to achieve an effective health campaign intervention.

Organizational Context of Influence

The *organizational context of influence* refers to communication that takes place within the complex, layered systems of organizations, such as companies, schools, and religious groups. Organizational Development Theory can help health campaign practitioners better understand and work within these systems to promote health communication and behavior change.

Organizational Development Theory

There are many theories of organizational change (Burke, 2008) but Organizational Development (OD) Theory can be especially helpful to health campaign efforts. *Organizational Development Theory* recognizes that organizational structures and processes influence employee motivation and behavior, so OD consultants diagnose relevant organizational problems that impede employee functioning, and create action plans that promote strategies for interventions and evaluations that address those problems (Cummings & Worley, 2009). Health campaign practitioners often work as OD change agents with and/or within organizations, as doing so provides opportunities for reaching targeted groups of individuals, as well as through multiple channels such as organizational newsletters and e-mails. Organizations also offer tangible and intangible support for employees enacting behavior changes through strategies such as incentives for working out or support group meetings.

One popular way to promote healthier lifestyles and behaviors in organizations is through workplace wellness programs. *Workplace wellness programs* are defined as programs offered by employers, including a combination of educational, organizational, and environmental activities. These activities are designed to support behavior conducive to the health of employees. Activities often include health fairs, medical screenings, health coaching, onsite fitness programs and/or facilities and educational programs. Companies and organizations are investing more and more resources into wellness programs in an effort to control health care spending. Workplace wellness programs focused on reducing employees' risks for health complications, such as weight loss or smoking cessation, can save on health insurance premiums as well as decrease employee absenteeism and reduce disability claims.

General Mills® has been recognized repeatedly for its workplace wellness programs. At the central headquarters, there is an on-site fitness center where employees can participate in group exercise classes, such as yoga and hip-hop dance. The company also offers healthy cooking classes and same-day appointments at the on-site prevention clinic. General Mills manufacturing sites installed Life Clinic Health Stations, where employees can track their blood pressure, weight, and body mass index (BMI). Each workplace wellness site also identifies local concerns and implements programs and activities, such as weight-loss competitions, to promote healthier behaviors. Additionally, the company created the General Mills Health Numbers screening tool, which is a personalized health risk assessment that assists employees in identifying their health risks and facilitates communication with their physicians. The company estimated that for every dollar they spend on employee wellness programs, they saved $3.50, making it a worthwhile investment (Edelhelt, 2010).

However, research in health communication warns about assuming that workplace wellness programs are positively perceived by employees. In a study of the implementation of a health and recreation center at a manufacturer, Zoller (2003, 2004) found that many employees resented the top-down approach to the development of a corporate recreation center and some employees felt alienated because they had differing perspectives about health than the dominant organizational culture. To address these issues, employees should be involved in developing workplace wellness programs and multiple approaches to health should be respected during planning and implementation.

Public or Mass Communication Context of Influence

The *public or mass communication context of influence* refers to communication that takes place in a large shared space. Often health campaigns within this larger context of influence are working to disseminate information and serve as catalysts for

ETHICAL DILEMMA ◆ What Would You Do?

You were recently hired as a workplace wellness specialist at a large corporation. You are a member of the planning team tasked with designing a workplace wellness health campaign to decrease the company's health insurance claims by 20% over the next two years. During the first meeting of the planning team, you argue that in order to meet this lofty goal the campaign needs to be firmly grounded in campaign theories or you fear it will fail. Some of your colleagues at the meeting respond that the two-year timeframe does not allow the team to take time to consider theories. Others at the meeting wonder if ignoring theories is ethically inappropriate and perhaps even harmful to employees. Everyone at the meeting looks to you and the chairperson of the meeting asks you to respond.

◆ How would you respond?
◆ Would you give in and agree to ignore theories in planning the campaign or would you hold firm to your position?
◆ How could you incorporate an ethical orientation from Chapter 2, "Linking Health Communication with Ethics," into your argument to support your response?

change among many people. Although the public context of influence also includes the media, we thoroughly cover Agenda-Setting Theory and Media Framing Theory, including implications for media campaigns, in Chapter 11, "Linking Health Communication with Media," so we do not reiterate those theories in this chapter. In addition, Diffusion of Innovations Theory is considered a theory of the public or mass communication context of influence, however, we thoroughly cover this theory, including implications for health campaigns and entertainment education, in Chapter 3, "Linking Health Communication with Theories Informed by Health Communication," and Chapter 10, "Linking Health Communication with Entertainment Education." In this section, we focus on the community context of influence and introduce the Community-Organizing Model, which emphasizes how to mobilize community groups and resources to achieve a common health goal.

Community-Organizing Model

Models of community organizing date back to the late 1800s when social workers coined the term community organizing to refer to their efforts to coordinate assistance for new immigrants to the United States (Garvin & Cox, 2001). Since that time other social movements influenced the development of community-organizing strategies. Three other prominent social movements that influenced both the theory and the practice of community organizing include the post-Reconstruction Period, which organized African Americans around freedom rights; the Populist movement, which grew into a political force representing ordinary people; and the Labor movement, which taught the values of forming professional organizations and conflict negotiation and resolution. In the field of health, community organizing took hold in the 1970s when the World Health Organization (WHO) initiated its Healthy Cities movement, which emphasized grassroots community participation and cooperation among government and nongovernment agencies to create sustainable environments and to reduce disparities between groups (Norris & Pittman, 2000).

Community organizing is defined as a process through which community groups are assisted in identifying common problems in their communities, mobilizing resources, and developing and implementing strategies to reach community-determined goals. Key to the process of community organizing is the community self-identifying its problems, which leads to more effective community-organizing projects. Health campaign practitioners often adapt aspects of community organizing to design, implement, and evaluate effective campaigns. A closely aligned approach to community organizing is community building. *Community building* is defined as a process of empowering a community from within, rather than through outside organizers. The Young Women's Christian Association (YWCA) is an example of a community-building organization because the local YWCA employees and community volunteers work from within the city to determine the most pressing problems facing women in that community and develop programs to meet their needs. Now, please take a few minutes to think more about the public context of influence by completing Health Communication Nexus Interlude 7.2.

For this interlude, think of another example, besides the YWCA, of a community-organizing or community-building project in your local community. Write down your example project in your notebook along with your response to these questions:

- Why does this project fit the definitions of communication organizing and/or community building?
- Would you be interested in joining this project? Why or why not?
- How might a health communication specialist lend expertise to this project?

A community-organizing perspective recognizes that health problems are complex and are affected by individual, behavioral, and environmental factors. It also welcomes the integration of a variety of approaches to addressing community health problems. Theories from the other contexts of influence, such as Social Cognitive Theory and the Transtheoretical Model, and concepts from throughout this book, such as social support and entertainment education should be considered and employed if deemed appropriate by the community. Despite the variety of strategies often employed within a community-organizing project, there are several common concepts that are key to achieving and measuring change. These concepts exemplify tenets of a community-organizing perspective and include implications for health campaigns:

◆ *Empowerment*—a process of social action through which people in a community gain mastery over their lives and their communities. Ideally health campaign practitioners are chosen from within the community to increase community power to address health problems and create behavior change.

◆ *Participation*—engagement of community members which leads to community understanding, strong networks, leadership, and access to resources. Health campaign practitioners need to become invested in the community through active partnerships.

◆ *Critical consciousness*—awareness of social, economic, and political forces that contribute to health problems. Health campaigns should offer opportunities to explore root causes of targeted health problems and work with community members to address those problems.

◆ *Community capacity*—aspects of a community that affect its ability to identify, organize around, and create strategies to positively address health problems. Health campaigns should either be part of the community or work alongside active members of the community who understand it, are well networked, and may be among its leaders.

◆ *Issue selection*—identifying health problems and realistic goals for change. Health campaign practitioners include community members in identifying problems and targeting realistic goals for addressing those problems.

The Youth Empowerment Strategies (YES!) project used the concepts of community organizing to address teens' risky health behaviors, such as alcohol and tobacco use, bullying, and school violence. Fifth-grade and sixth-grade students from underachieving schools in West Contra Costa County, California participated in the program. The populations of participating schools ranged from 90% to 98% students of color, of whom 74–92% lived below or near the poverty level. The project was designed to address the environmental issues that often lead students to participate in risky health behaviors.

During the initial phases of the project, health campaign designers recruited and trained local high school and college students to serve as facilitators for an after-school program. Facilitators led small groups of students in different community-building activities such as problem-posing dialogue, risk and asset mapping, interpersonal skill training, and issue selection. Students were encouraged to learn and use techniques to become leaders in enacting positive change.

The teams identified problems in their schools and neighborhoods and then designed and completed a series of social-action projects to address those problems. For example, some of the teams considered low school spirit as a problem that affected health choices and created school spirit T-shirts and started a yearbook as ways to increase school pride. To address risky behaviors such as bullying, students developed skits they performed for their classmates. Students also participated in cleanup projects at their school and in the community to remove graffiti and clean up trash.

Overall, the YES! project was effective in building a sense of community in the participants and students were successful in designing and implementing social-action projects. Because the students took ownership in the program and developed relationships with their peers, they changed the environment to support individual change (Minkler, Wallerstein, & Wilson, 2008; Wilson, Minkler, Dasho, Wallerstein, & Martin, 2008). Go to this book's Web site to read newsletters about example social-action projects from the YES! campaign.

PROFILE

Using Applied Research to Understand Health Communication Theory

Gary Kreps, PhD—Professor, George Mason University

Gary Kreps is involved with numerous initiatives and organizations, including the Center for Health & Risk Communication, the Center for Social Science Research, the Center for Health & Risk Communication, the National Center for Biodefense & Infectious Diseases, and the Center for Health Policy & Ethics. The commonality among all of his work is his focus on health communication and promotion and his dedication to using applied research methods to increase understanding of health communication theory.

Kreps was drawn to study health communication because of his desire to identify the best methods for changing entrenched health behaviors such as smoking, drinking, diet, and exercise in order to promote improved public health. Health campaigns were a natural topic for him to explore, as campaigns offer a way to reach large audiences. Studying campaigns provides an additional challenge, as the process of altering behaviors is difficult, and effective campaigns are complex and require multiple elements.

For this reason Kreps is dedicated to utilizing relevant communication theories and evidence-based practices to design and implement health campaigns. When it comes to theory, Kreps does not have a favorite, but instead feels strongly that campaign designers must select the theories that are most relevant and that best address the problem and its communication needs. Most recently, he is working on projects using Weick's (1979) Model of Organizing, which comes from systems theory. Weick's model asserts that individuals learn how to interact within their organizations through preset rules and communication exchanges. Identifying the existing rules and communication patterns can help campaign designers target what needs to be modified in order to promote healthier behaviors.

For example, one current project Kreps is involved with is a partnership with the National Minority AIDS Council that aims to educate African American and Latino populations about HIV-vaccine research. Many members of these communities are wary of medical research and are concerned about the potential side effects of an HIV vaccine and therefore refuse to participate in programs that involve medical research. A community liaison project was created to dispel commonly held myths and increase support for HIV-vaccine research. Rather than running a large-scale media campaign, the program focused on recruiting community liaisons who were trained to recruit other community members to spread the word about HIV-vaccine research. After culturally-sensitive messages were created, the project adopted an "each-one-teach-one" approach. Individuals who speak with campaign volunteers are encouraged to share the information they learn with at least one other person and then ask that person to do the same. In this way the information spreads at the grassroots level.

Kreps sees health communication as playing a unique role in the design and development of health campaigns. He explains, "The best campaigns are driven by revealing data about audiences, messages, channels, and social structure. Health communication research and theory can provide the evidence base for developing, implementing, refining, and evaluation of health promotion campaigns."

Now that we discussed some of the prominent theories that inform health campaigns, we offer a service-learning application designed to integrate health campaign theory within a health campaign.

Health Campaign Theory
Informing a Health Campaign

As discussed in the service-learning application in Chapter 3, "Linking Health Communication with Theories Informed by Health Communication," one of the reasons to learn theories is to apply them to actual health-related problems and campaigns. Professor Kreps also reiterated this point in his health communication profile presented in this chapter. Service-learning projects provide excellent opportunities to gain experience applying theories. Theoretically-grounded projects also give you a sense of how theories can make health campaign projects more successful.

Service-learning projects also tend to be more effective if the components of service learning are included. In this service-learning application we emphasize a link to curriculum. *Link to curriculum* means that the service-learning project is purposely integrated into the course by the instructor to meet the learning goals of the course and that the course helps students transfer knowledge and skills from one setting to another (Corporation for National & Community Service, 2010). In other words, the service you are engaging in should reflect the material you are learning in class and provide you with ample opportunities to practice and apply the concepts and skills you are learning. As you are working on all phases of your project, you should take time both individually and as a group to reflect upon ways you are using your class readings, assignments, discussions, and lectures in your service-learning project.

So if two of the learning goals of a course are to learn relevant theories and understand how those theories apply to health issues, a service-learning project could be designed in which students partner with a community health organization, together identify a community health issue, and then incorporate theory learned in the course to address that health issue. Let's consider an example of how a health campaign course that had these two learning goals, among others outlined in the syllabus, incorporated a service-learning project to apply theoretical concepts to a real-world health issue. For this example, let's return to the Motorcycle Safety at Purdue (MS@P) campaign and consider how a health campaign theory discussed previously in this chapter was incorporated to guide the development of the MS@P campaign.

Early on, a campaign project team established a partnership with American Bikers Aimed Toward Education (ABATE). Through conversations with the organization about motorcycle riding behavior, the campaign project team realized

that one of the theories they needed to integrate into the campaign was Bandura's (1962, 1977) Social Cognitive Theory (SCT). Two key components of SCT are observational learning or modeling and behavioral capability. As you may remember from earlier in this chapter, *observational learning* or *modeling* refers to situations in which the behaviors or actions of credible others can be observed along with the consequences for their behaviors or actions. *Behavioral capability* refers to an individual's knowledge and skill to perform a behavior. Knowing these concepts, the MS@P campaign team brainstormed ways motorcyclists could observe safe riding behavior including wearing proper safety gear and ways to increase motorcyclists' ability to ride safely. Based on their exposure to SCT, the campaign project team understood that motorcyclists would be more likely to adopt the recommended safety behaviors if they could observe and then had the capability to model the safety behaviors. Some of the ideas generated during the campaign project team's brainstorming session, which was guided by SCT, and later implemented by the campaign included:

◆ Having motorcycle safety gear available at MS@P campaign events that motorcyclists and potential motorcyclists could try on.

◆ Providing information about proper fit for safety gear.

◆ Showing videos of safe motorcycling behaviors at campaign events and on the campaign Web site.

◆ Hosting informational sessions for new motorcyclists where they observe and learn basic information about safe motorcycling and proper motorcycle maintenance.

◆ Promoting motorcycle driver education classes.

By using knowledge of theories from their coursework, students were able to bring theoretical concepts to bear on an actual health campaign. And in the process of applying theory to the MS@P campaign, they were linking what they were learning in the classroom to a real-world health issue, which was an objective of the course curriculum. This same strategy to integrate health campaign theory and health campaign practice can be used and expanded to address other health issues in a service-learning project. For more tips on how to integrate theory and campaign practice, go to the service-learning application section of Chapter 3, "Linking Health Communication with Theories Informed by Health Communication."

Chapter Summary

We began this chapter by revisiting our preferred definition of theory as needing to be well thought out, specifically communicated, supported by reason and evidence, and tentative in its level of certainty about the phenomenon it is attempting to understand or explain. Next, we focused on six theories or models that typically inform health campaigns and were not already thoroughly covered in other chapters of the book. The theories in this chapter were organized using an ecological or context of influence framework and included the Health Belief Model, Theory of Reasoned Action/Theory of Planned Behavior, Transtheoretical Model/Stages of Change, Social Cognitive Theory, Organizational Development Theory, and the Community-Organizing Model. In addition to covering key concepts within each theory or model and implications for how these theories can inform health campaigns, we highlighted example campaigns. We concluded by sharing how the MS@P campaign team integrated theoretical concepts into the campaign while linking their service-learning activities to the course curriculum.

References

Ajzen, I. (1985). From intentions to actions: A theory of planned behavior. In J. Kuhl & J. Beckman (Eds.), *Action-control: From cognition to behavior* (pp. 11–39). Heidelberg, Germany: Springer.

Ajzen, I., & Fishbein, M. (1980). *Understanding attitudes and predicting social behavior.* Englewood Cliffs, NJ: Prentice Hall.

Babrow, A., & Mattson, M. (2003). Theorizing about health communication. In T. L. Thompson, A. M. Dorsey, K. I. Miller, & R. Parrot (Eds.), *Handbook of health communication* (pp. 35–61). Mahwah, NJ: Lawrence Erlbaum.

Bandura, A. (1962). Social learning through imitation. In M. R. Jones (Ed.), *Nebraska symposium on motivation* (Vol. 10). Lincoln: University of Nebraska Press.

Bandura, A. (1977). *Social learning theory.* Englewood Cliffs, NJ: Prentice Hall.

Bateson, G. (1972). *Steps to an ecology of mind.* New York: Ballantine Books.

Becker, M. H., Shumaker, S., Schron, E. B., & Ockene, J. K. (Eds.). (1990). Theoretical models of adherence and strategies for improving adherence. *The handbook of health behavior change.* New York: Springer.

Burke, W. W. (2008). *Organization change: Theory and practice* (2nd ed.). Thousand Oaks, CA: Sage.

Corporation for National & Community Service (2010). Learn and Serve America's National Service-Learning Clearinghouse. Retrieved January 12, 2010, from http://www.servicelearning.org.

Cummings, T. G., & Worley, C. G. (2009). *Organization development & change* (9th ed.). Mason, OH: South-Western Cengage Learning.

Edelhelt, J. (2010, May 3). Interview with Dr. Julia Halberg. *Corporate Wellness Magazine.* Retrieved August 6, 2010, from http://www.corporatewellnessmagazine.com.

Erickson, A., Curry, J., & Warren, K. (2010). *"160° F for Your Family" campaign: Listening to the audience—identifying common consumer cooking methods for thermometer accuracy testing in ground beef patties.* Paper presented at the Food Safety Education Conference, Atlanta, GA.

Erickson, A., & Staszak, C. (2010). *"160° F For Your Family" campaign: Harnessing power of emotion to change consumer food thermometer behaviors.* Paper presented at the Food Safety Education Conference, Atlanta, GA.

Fishbein, M., & Ajzen, I. (1975). *Belief, attitude, intention, and behavior: An introduction to theory and research.* Reading, MA: Addison-Wesley.

Garvin, C. D., & Cox, F. M. (2001). A history of community organizing since the civil war with special reference to oppressed communities. In J. Rothman, J. L. Erlich, & J. E. Tropman (Eds.), *Strategies of community intervention: Macro practice* (6th ed.) Itasca, IL: Peacock/Wadsworth.

Janz, N., & Becker, M. (1984). The health belief model: A decade later. *Health Education Quarterly, 11,* 1–47.

Lewin, K. (1951). *Field theory in social science: Selected theoretical papers.* New York: Harper.

Madden, T. J., Ellen, P. S., & Ajzen, I. (1992). A comparison of the theory of planned behavior and the theory of reasoned action. *Personality and Social Psychology Bulletin, 18,* 3–9.

McCurdy, S., & Nalivka, T. (2010). *"160° F For Your Family" Campaign: Accuracy of dial and digital food thermometers to measure endpoint temperature in ground beef patties.* Paper presented at the Food Safety Education Conference, Atlanta, GA.

Minkler, M., Wallerstein, N. B., & Wilson, N. (2008). Improving health through community organization and community building. In K. Glanz, B. K. Rimer, & K. Viswanath (Eds.), *Health behavior and health education: Theory, research, and practice* (4th ed., pp. 287–312). San Francisco: Jossey-Bass.

Nigg, C. R., Burbank, P. M., Padula, C., Dufresne, R., Rossi, J. S., Velicer, W. F., et al. (1999). Stages of change across ten health risk behaviors for older adults. *Gerontologist, 39,* 473–482.

Norris, T., & Pittman, M. (2000). The health communities movement and the coalition for healthier cities and communities. *Public Health Reports, 115,* 118–124.

Peng, W. (2009). Design and evaluation of a computer game to promote a healthy diet for young adults. *Health Communication, 24,* 115–127.

Prochaska, J. O., DiClemente, C. C., & Norcross, J. C. (1992). In search of how people change. *American Psychologist, 47,* 1102–1114.

Prochaska, J. O., Norcross, J. C., & DiClemente, C. C. (1994). *Changing for good: A revolutionary six-stage program for overcoming bad habits and moving your life positively forward.* New York: Avon Books.

Prochaska, J. O., Redding, C. A., & Evers, K. E. (2002). The transtheoretical model and stages of change. In K. Glanz, B. K. Rimer, & F. M. Lewis (Eds.), *Health behavior and health education: Theory, research, and practice* (3rd ed.). San Francisco: Jossey-Bass.

Prochaska, J. O., & Velicer, W. F. (1997). The transtheoretical model of health behavior change. *American Journal of Health Promotion, 12,* 38–48.

Rosenstock, I. M. (1966). Why people use health services. *Milbank Memorial Fund Quarterly, 3,* 94–127.

Rosenstock, I. M. (1974a). Historical origins of the health belief model. *Health Education Monographs, 2,* 1–8.

Rosenstock, I. M. (1974b). The health belief model: Origins and correlates. *Health Education Monographs, 2,* 336–353.

Rosenstock, I. M., Strecher, V. J., & Becker, M. H. (1988). Social learning theory and the health belief model. *Health Education Quarterly, 15,* 175–183.

Stokols, D. (1996). Translating social ecological theory into guidelines for community health promotion. *American Journal of Health Promotion, 10,* 282–298.

Street, R. L. (2003). Communication in medical encounters: An ecological perspective. In T. L. Thompson, A. M. Dorsey, K. I. Miller, & R. Parrott (Eds.), *Handbook of health communication* (pp. 63–89). Mahwah, NJ: Lawrence Erlbaum.

Weick, K. E. (1979). *The social psychology of organizing* (2nd ed.). Reading, MA: Addison-Wesley.

Weinstein, N. D. (1988). The precaution adoption process. *Health Psychology, 7*, 355–386.

Weinstein, N. D., & Sandman, P. M. (1992). A model of the precaution adoption process: Evidence from home radon testing. *Health Psychology, 11*, 170–180.

Wilson, N., Minkler, M., Dasho, S., Wallerstein, N. B., & Martin, A. C. (2008). Getting to social action: The Youth Empowerment Strategies (YES!) project. *Health Promotion Practice, 9*, 395–403.

Zoller, H. M. (2003). Working out: Managerialism in workplace health promotion. *Management Communication Quarterly, 17*, 171–205.

Zoller, H. M. (2004). Manufacturing health: Employee perspectives on problematic outcomes in a workplace health promotion initiative. *Western Journal of Communication, 68*, 278–301.

Health Campaign Practice

Chapter Learning Objectives

◆ Define public health and the related terms of health education and health promotion
◆ Outline the ten essential public services that public health provides
◆ Understand the links between beliefs, attitudes, and behaviors
◆ Describe the difference between a public health and health communication perspective on health campaigns
◆ Explain the difference between marketing and social marketing
◆ Identify and provide examples of the 4 Ps of social marketing
◆ Describe how the process of audience segmentation generates target audiences
◆ Review the four phases of the Messaging Model for Health Communication Campaigns (MMHCC)
◆ Provide what SWOT analysis stands for and explain how it is used
◆ Distinguish a push strategy from a pull strategy for health campaign message dissemination
◆ Discuss the importance of the three forms of evaluation in the MMHCC
◆ Refer to two health campaign process guides beyond the MMHCC
◆ Illustrate the use of the MMHCC in large-scale and small-scale health campaigns

Chapter Preview

This chapter explores perhaps one of the most public forms of health communication: health campaigns. First, the chapter provides an overview of the public health perspective and then focuses in on a social marketing approach to health campaigns. Next, the chapter introduces the Messaging Model for Health Communication Campaigns (MMHCC), which incorporates components of social marketing but emphasizes the communicative aspects of health campaigns, particularly audience analysis and message design. Third, two campaigns that are based on the MMHCC are described in detail; CDC's DES Update and the Motorcycle Safety at Purdue (MS@P) campaign. Finally, the chapter presents ways to utilize components of the MMHCC while monitoring progress in a small-scale service-learning project.

This image is a promotional piece that is part of the Centers for Disease Control and Prevention's (CDC) "5 A Day" campaign which aims to encourage audience members to consume at least five fruits and vegetables per day. This massive, nationwide campaign promotes the basic message that for a healthy lifestyle it is important to consume an adequate amount of fruits and vegetables. The message is distributed through a variety of communication channels, including flyers, merchandise, educational materials, and posters.

Are you familiar with the 5 A Day campaign and its messages? If so, you participated in a health communication campaign. In this chapter we take a closer look at the link between health communication and health campaign practice by discussing the development, design, implementation, and evaluation of health campaigns.

Public Health Perspective on Health Campaigns

One goal of this chapter is to clearly distinguish how a health communication approach to health campaigns is different from and adds to a public health approach. To accomplish this, we first must define and understand a public health perspective on health campaigns.

Defining Public Health

The American Public Health Association (2007), a professional organization comprising public health scholars and practitioners, offered a three-part definition of *public health*. First, public health is the prevention of disease and illness among groups of people. Second, public health involves the creation of public policy regarding health issues. Third, public health is responsible for community health surveillance, which includes tracking of diseases as well as research to better understand the causes of and cures for diseases and other health issues.

Another integral aspect of the definition of public health is learning the function or *purpose of public health*. The Institute of Medicine (1988) described the mission of public health as undertaking actions that "fulfill society's interest in assuring conditions in which people can be healthy" (p. 7). Although this mission is rather broad, as there are numerous activities that contribute to a healthy society, it does provide a sense of what public health is aiming to accomplish through its various activities.

CDC further details these activities by describing the ten essential public services that public health provides:

1. Monitor health status to identify community health problems.
2. Diagnose and investigate health problems and health hazards in the community.
3. Inform, educate, and empower people about health issues. ✳
4. Mobilize community partnerships to identify and solve health problems.
5. Develop policies and plans that support individual and community health efforts.
6. Enforce laws and regulations that protect health and ensure safety.
7. Link people to needed personal health services and assure the provision of health care when otherwise unavailable.
8. Ensure a competent public health and personal health care workforce.
9. Evaluate effectiveness, accessibility, and quality of personal and population-based health services.
10. Research for new insights and innovative solutions to health problems.

As you can see from this list, public health encompasses a variety of activities, from enforcing laws regarding vaccinations to tracking the incidences of illness and accidents in an area. Public health officials and practitioners are involved in a myriad of health situations, from disease outbreaks to handling the aftermath of natural disasters. In this chapter we focus on the third essential public health service, which is to inform, educate, and empower people about health issues. We focus on this public health service because it is most closely aligned with health campaign activities.

The goal of most health campaigns is to provide information to the public about a health issue and to influence the audience's beliefs, attitudes, and/or behaviors related to that health issue. Before proceeding with our discussion of public health, we need to consider the important role of beliefs, attitudes, and behaviors in shaping an individual's health.

◆ Belief—acceptance of something as true or not true
◆ Attitude—a feeling or opinion about something, either positive or negative
◆ Behavior—actions

In terms of health, an individual's beliefs influence that individual's attitudes. In turn, both beliefs and attitudes influence that individual's behavior. For example, consider the issue of oral health. An individual may believe that daily flossing is essential to oral health. This belief then influences that individual's attitudes about flossing, including the attitude that flossing is good. If the individual believes that flossing is essential to oral health and has the attitude that flossing is good and easy to do, it is likely that the individual's behavior incorporates flossing regularly. Another individual may have the belief that flossing is important for oral health. However, this individual may have the attitude that flossing is negative because it causes pain and bleeding gums. This belief and attitude influences the behavior of this individual, who likely does not floss regularly.

Returning to a public health perspective on health campaigns, the primary goal of some health campaigns is to inform the audience by providing them with necessary information so they can avoid a health risk. For example, a public health campaign designed to raise awareness about West Nile Virus and how to prevent it needs to explain the disease to the audience, including how it is contracted and its symptoms, as well as offer tips on how to prevent contracting the disease, such as removing any standing water from land and using bug repellent when outdoors.

Some campaigns aim to promote healthier behaviors that lead to healthier lives. Examples of these types of campaigns are those that encourage a better diet, such as the 5 A Day campaign that we mentioned at the beginning of this chapter or campaigns that promote more physical activity such as the VERB™ campaign, which prompts children and teens to do something active.

Extending from these two goals, those within the field of public health often refer to their activities as either health education or health promotion. *Health education* is defined as "any combination of planned learning experiences based on sound theories that provide individuals, groups, and communities the opportunity to acquire information and the skills needed to make quality health decisions" (Joint Committee on Terminology, 2001, p. 99). *Health promotion* is defined as "any planned combination of educational, political, environmental, regulatory, or organizational mechanisms that support actions and conditions of living conducive to the health of individuals, groups, and communities" (Joint Committee on Terminology, 2001, p. 101). Although these definitions are similar, the difference is that health promotion is a more comprehensive approach that involves both health information and the environmental support mechanisms or resources required to live a healthier life (Green & Kreuter, 1990).

Health promotion can occur in an interpersonal or small group setting, such as when a physician or nurse makes recommendations to a patient for how to eat healthier to avoid or control diabetes or a health educator conducts a workshop on smoking cessation. Health promotion also can occur on a wider scale or in the public context through mass media, which is what we typically think of in terms of health campaigns. For the remainder of the chapter we focus on the specific efforts involved in health campaigns. A campaign framework known as social marketing provides an outline for the variety of efforts involved in a health campaign.

Social Marketing

One of the most common frameworks used in public health for designing, implementing, and evaluating campaigns is social marketing. *Social marketing* is defined as the application of commercial marketing principles to social issues (Kotler & Lee, 2008). The idea behind social marketing is that just as marketing techniques convince consumers to buy certain brands and certain products, such as Nike tennis shoes, marketing techniques also can convince audience members to adopt healthier attitudes and behaviors, such as eating five fruits and vegetables each day to stay healthy. A social marketing approach is based on the assumption that health attitudes and behaviors are "products" that can be "sold" to audiences. Also keep in mind that health campaigns span the spectrum from small-scale to large-scale and from nonfunded to funded.

The 4 Ps

One of the cornerstones of a social marketing approach to health campaigns is a strategic emphasis on the *4 Ps of social marketing* (Kotler & Lee, 2008), which are:

◆ **P**roduct
◆ **P**lacement
◆ **P**rice
◆ **P**romotion

Next we'll define each of the 4 Ps of social marketing and describe how they relate to the marketing of health attitudes and behaviors. The first P stands for product. A *product* is defined as that which is offered to address or solve a particular health or social issue. When you read the word "product," you may be thinking of a tangible item, such as a running shoe or protein bar, but products also are services, practices, or behaviors, such as flossing every day or getting at least 30 minutes of exercise per day. Products do not have to be something as concrete as a behavior. Products also are intangibles such as beliefs or attitudes. For example, the belief that eating five fruits and vegetables per day is an important component of good nutrition is one of the products marketed by the 5 A Day campaign. Before we discuss products in more detail, please complete Health Communication Nexus Interlude 8.1.

Health Communication Nexus Interlude 8.1

For this interlude, take a few minutes to think about promoting safer sex and preventing sexually transmitted diseases (STDs), such as herpes or HIV/AIDS. Now think of a product that could be marketed for each of the following categories that would aid in solving the health problem of STDs. Jot down your product ideas in your notebook.

◆ Tangible
◆ Behavior
◆ Service
◆ Intangible

Keep your product ideas for each of these categories in mind as we further discuss products and social marketing.

As mentioned previously, tangible products probably first come to mind when you are thinking of a product to market. In the case of safer sex perhaps you listed condoms as a tangible product to protect individuals from STDs. For the behavior category you may have written products, such as using a condom every time an individual engages in sexual activity or being able to use a condom correctly. Keep in mind that behaviors may need to be taught as well as encouraged. Services that could be marketed may include free STD testing or sexual health counseling. In the intangible category you needed to think of an idea or belief to promote. This may be an idea, such as monogamy, which is having only one sexual partner during a period of time, or even the idea of abstinence.

The second P of social marketing stands for placement. *Placement* is defined as how the product gets to the audience. Placement could be a physical location. In our promoting safer sex example, placement of condoms would refer to where individuals get condoms. Are condoms being distributed at the campus health center and/or are condoms available in public restrooms? Placement also refers to the ways that messages about behaviors and intangible products are distributed. So placement also could be a billboard, a pamphlet at the doctor's office, or a national public service announcement promoting safer sex. The challenge is to determine locations or placement where the target audience likely or easily encounters the products of the campaign.

Ideal locations for placement of campaign products often include *life path points* of audience members, meaning the places where audience members typically go or the locations they typically pass through or by during their daily lives. For example, think about the path you take on a typical day in your life. All the places you pass through or by, as you're getting ready in the morning, such as the radio or television; during your commute to and from school or work, such as a billboard you always pass on your way or the convenience store you stop at to grab a cup of coffee; and while you are at school or work, such as the student union, the break room, or the cafeteria. All of these are considered life path points for you. Your life path points also may be good placement points for campaign products if you are a target audience member of a health campaign.

The third P of social marketing stands for price. *Price* is defined as the cost of the product for individuals in the target audience. The cost could be financial. In our example of promoting safer sex, monetary cost could be purchasing a box of condoms or having an STD test. There also may be nonmonetary costs such as time, other resources, or emotional or psychological consequences. In our example, taking time to go to the doctor or clinic to have an STD test is a cost. An example of an emotional cost might be initiating a conversation with a partner about practicing safer sex which could be embarrassing or even lead to rejection by the partner. The challenge in health campaigns regarding price is to convince the target audience that the benefits of the product are greater than the costs.

The fourth P of social marketing stands for promotion. *Promotion* is defined as raising awareness about the products of the campaign through creating and disseminating messages. Often, advertising comes to mind when we think about promotion. A 30-second commercial and a full-page ad in a magazine are two examples of product promotion for a campaign. However, other possibilities include holding events, sponsoring programs, using direct mailings, and promotional items. In general, integrated campaigns that incorporate several promotional techniques work best. In our example of promoting safer sex, possible ways to promote condom use would be distributing condoms at health clinics and bars and placing signs in public buses.

As you learn the 4 Ps of social marketing, be sure to keep in mind that promotion is only one of the 4 Ps. When thinking about health campaigns, it is easy to get caught up in planning for promotional items and advertisements to be distributed to the audience. Although these are essential components of the campaign because they are ways to reach the audience, the campaign is unlikely to succeed unless you are mindful of planning ways to promote the product, to make the price or costs reasonable, and to distribute messages to the audience through the most effective means.

Audience Segmentation

Another key component of social marketing is *audience segmentation,* which is defined as dividing up the larger population into smaller groups of individuals that require unique strategies to be persuaded to change their behaviors. From these smaller groups one or more target audiences is selected for the campaign (Kotler & Lee, 2008). A target audience can be as broad as the entire population of an area, but often is much more specific. For example, a campaign about breast cancer most likely targets women of a certain age or women with a family history who may be more at risk for breast cancer, rather than the entire population of females.

It is important to remember that when trying to confront health issues and promote health products, the audience is rarely homogeneous, meaning that all individuals within that audience rarely are exactly the same. Audience members vary on a variety of factors, including but certainly not limited to gender, age, culture, and needs, which is why audience segmentation is necessary. Returning to our safer-sex campaign example, some ways to segment the audience could be having one target audience of males and one of females, as each of these groups may have different concerns about how to protect themselves from STDs. The target audiences for the safer-sex campaign also could be segmented by age groups such as traditional college students and older adults, who may differ in terms of lifestyle or attitudes, and therefore require unique strategies to encourage them to practice safer sex.

Although the number of ways of segmenting the population into target audiences may seem infinite, keep in mind that the purpose of audience segmentation is to divide the audience into meaningful groups so that the campaign can tailor its efforts and messages for those groups. Also, if the needs of one identified segment or group are not unique from another segment, there is no need to divide the audience into two target audiences, instead maintain the larger segment or one target audience.

Marketing or Social Marketing?

As you may already be sensing, social marketing is a complex tool for health promotion. A health campaign that simply uses marketing techniques such as advertising to promote a prosocial behavior is not necessarily a social marketing campaign and likely is not as effective. If a health campaign does not include all the components or engage all the steps of social marketing, it likely is an advertising campaign rather than a social marketing campaign.

Let's consider an example campaign that transformed from a marketing campaign into a social marketing campaign and because of the transformation became more effective. You are probably familiar with the "Got Milk?" campaign and the trademark milk mustaches celebrities wear in its messages.

The *Got Milk?* campaign began in 1993 when Peter Manning was hired by the California Milk Processor Board to increase milk consumption in the state because milk consumption and milk sales steadily declined over the previous 15 years. Manning hired the advertising agency Goodby, Silverstein & Partners and together they developed the Got Milk? campaign (Holt, 2002).

Prior milk campaigns focused on the nutritional benefits of drinking milk, which led to the campaign slogan "Milk does a body good." Research showed consumers were aware of the health benefits of milk, including its high calcium content and ability to prevent osteoporosis. Therefore, Manning made the decision to switch from promoting milk as a health product to promoting it as a beverage of choice among its major competitors of soft drinks and sports drinks.

In an effort to motivate people to buy more milk, the Got Milk? campaign used the core concept that there are certain foods, such as peanut butter or a cookie, that go best with a cold glass of milk. The advertising tried to create a feeling of need in the audience by depicting situations in which individuals needed a glass of milk. For example, one of the first television ads featured a man with his mouth full of peanut butter sitting in an apartment full of historical memorabilia listening to a quiz show on the radio. The $10,000 quiz question was, "Who shot Alexander Hamilton in that famous duel?" The man dials the quiz show phone number and tries to answer the question correctly but is unable to be understood due to his mouth being full of sticky peanut butter. The commercial ends with the now famous tag line, "Got Milk?" This spot won several advertising awards, and the concept was expanded to other treats, such as Hostess cupcakes, which were pictured without milk.

Courtesy Lowe Worldwide, Inc., as agent for National Fluid Milk Processor Promotion Board.

Figure 8.1 ◆ *Got Milk? advertisement*

The phrase "Got Milk?" soon became a product as the slogan was used in print ads featuring celebrities with milk mustaches, such as the ad in Figure 8.1. Although the ads were wildly popular and the slogan Got Milk? was widely recognized, the campaign did not succeed in persuading the audience to buy more milk. At this point, the advertising agency went to the audience to learn why the campaign was not increasing milk sales and by doing so began to transform the campaign from an advertising campaign into an effective social marketing campaign.

From the audience of potential milk buyers, the campaign team learned that although the ads were fun and popular, they were not motivating a need in the audience to buy milk. To remedy this, point of purchase displays were created to encourage shoppers to buy milk while at the grocery store. The team also determined from interviewing audience members that they wanted more ways to learn about milk and its benefits, especially via the internet. Subsequently, the Got Milk? Web site was revamped to be much more informative and interactive. Target audience members, including milk shoppers and drinkers, could go online and play games and participate in other activities as they learned about milk. Go to this book's Web site to see the Got Milk? campaign's homepage, which serves as a point of entry into several different aspects of the campaign depending on your interest in the topic of milk. Although the core concept of the campaign did not change and it continues to produce ads with milk mustaches, the campaign expanded to meet the unique needs of its target audiences.

Got Milk? and other successful social marketing campaigns, such as "Click It or Ticket," the National Highway Traffic Safety Administration's seat belt enforcement campaign, illustrate that social marketing involves multiple components that need to be carefully planned and implemented throughout the campaign.

Next we turn to a communication perspective on social marketing and provide a four-phase approach for designing, implementing, and evaluating a health communication campaign.

Messaging Model for Health Communication Campaigns

Despite its prevalence in public health, there have been criticisms of the traditional social marketing framework. One of the major criticisms is that social marketing campaigns have failed to bring about or maintain desired behavioral changes (MacStravic, 2000). One proposed reason is a lack of emphasis on the message design process in the social marketing framework. Specifically, critics noted the lack of tailored messages for target audiences. Even when audience segments were identified, messages were not created specifically to meet audience needs (Mattson & Basu, 2010a, 2010b). Consider for example a campaign in Australia that tried to increase the number of women who breastfed their children (Hughes, 1999). In addition to targeting mothers, the campaign also targeted older women and men who were not comfortable with women breastfeeding in public. Despite careful audience segmentation, the same messages were produced for all target audiences, which led to an ineffective campaign.

The Messaging Model for Health Communication Campaigns (MMHCC; Mattson & Basu, 2010a, 2010b) was developed in response to this criticism about messaging in social marketing and provides an extension of the social marketing framework. Grounded in a communication perspective, the MMHCC centralizes the messaging process in campaign planning. By emphasizing message design, the model attempts to ensure that the messages audiences receive are those that meet their needs and are more likely to have the desired impact.

The MMHCC distinguishes four phases in the campaign process:

◆ Phase 1—Establish working group and campaign goal
◆ Phase 2—Strategic planning from formative research including messaging process
◆ Phase 3—Implementation and evaluation
◆ Phase 4—Correction loop based on process evaluation and outcome evaluation

The phases of the MMHCC are depicted in Figure 8.2.

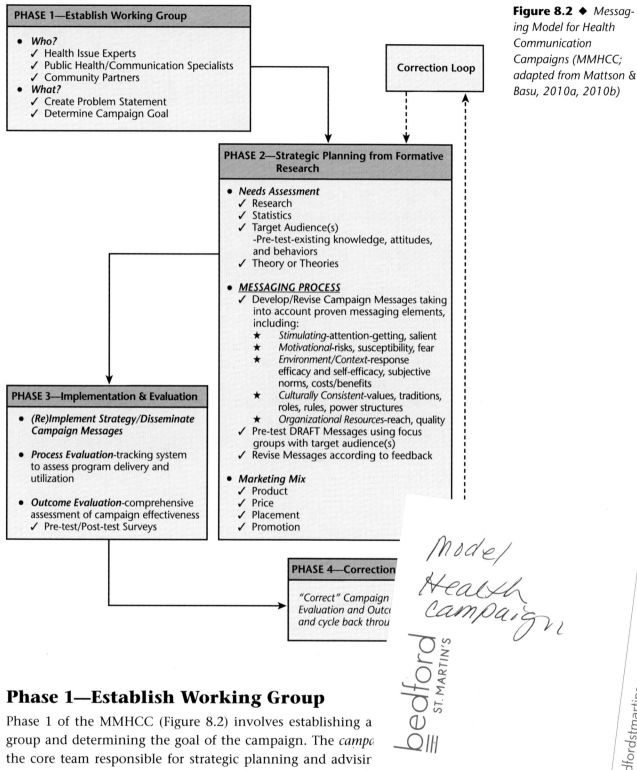

PHASE 1—Establish Working Group

- *Who?*
  - ✓ Health Issue Experts
  - ✓ Public Health/Communication Specialists
  - ✓ Community Partners
- *What?*
  - ✓ Create Problem Statement
  - ✓ Determine Campaign Goal

Correction Loop

PHASE 2—Strategic Planning from Formative Research

- *Needs Assessment*
  - ✓ Research
  - ✓ Statistics
  - ✓ Target Audience(s)
    - -Pre-test-existing knowledge, attitudes, and behaviors
  - ✓ Theory or Theories

- *MESSAGING PROCESS*
  - ✓ Develop/Revise Campaign Messages taking into account proven messaging elements, including:
    - ★ *Stimulating*-attention-getting, salient
    - ★ *Motivational*-risks, susceptibility, fear
    - ★ *Environment/Context*-response efficacy and self-efficacy, subjective norms, costs/benefits
    - ★ *Culturally Consistent*-values, traditions, roles, rules, power structures
    - ★ *Organizational Resources*-reach, quality
  - ✓ Pre-test DRAFT Messages using focus groups with target audience(s)
  - ✓ Revise Messages according to feedback

- *Marketing Mix*
  - ✓ Product
  - ✓ Price
  - ✓ Placement
  - ✓ Promotion

PHASE 3—Implementation & Evaluation

- *(Re)Implement Strategy/Disseminate Campaign Messages*

- *Process Evaluation*-tracking system to assess program delivery and utilization

- *Outcome Evaluation*-comprehensive assessment of campaign effectiveness
  - ✓ Pre-test/Post-test Surveys

PHASE 4—Correction

"Correct" Campaign
Evaluation and Outc
and cycle back throu

Figure 8.2 ◆ *Messaging Model for Health Communication Campaigns (MMHCC; adapted from Mattson & Basu, 2010a, 2010b)*

Phase 1—Establish Working Group

Phase 1 of the MMHCC (Figure 8.2) involves establishing a
group and determining the goal of the campaign. The *campa*
the core team responsible for strategic planning and advisir
The campaign working group should consist of health exp
interest such as health care providers and researchers, con
stakeholders who have a vested interest in the outcomes of

health and health communication specialists to guide campaign process, and representatives from the target audiences for the campaign. Involving multiple perspectives within the campaign working group not only provides voice to those interests but also offers a variety of points of view to consider when attempting to tackle a complex health issue. Ideally, the campaign working group meets periodically, and although it is best for the members of the working group to remain consistent, occasionally working group members may be added or changed as long as changes are in keeping with the goal of the campaign.

Take for example a group of people that wants to establish a campaign on a college campus that raises awareness about depression and the available resources for those suffering from depression. The campaign working group likely would need to include health care providers who specialize in treating depression, an expert on depression research, representatives from community partners who work in the realm of depression, such as the student wellness center and the local chapter of the National Alliance on Mental Illness, public health and communication specialists who have expertise in campaign process, and representatives of the target audiences, such as students and faculty and staff.

Before deciding how to best approach the health issue, the campaign working group must agree on what the health issue is and how it can be solved. To reach agreement the campaign working group delves into research to learn and discuss the facts about the health issue. From these discussions and agreements, the working group creates a problem statement and a goal statement to guide the campaign.

Returning to our example, prior to proceeding with a campus depression campaign, a qualified campaign working group first must agree on what depression is in terms of its definition as a medical condition, the symptoms of depression, the appropriate ways to treat depression, and the resources available on campus. Upon agreement, the working group creates a viable problem statement containing the extent of depression as a health issue and a goal statement for the campaign to address the issue of depression on campus.

At this juncture, most health campaigns also benefit from establishing relevant community partnerships. *Community partners* are organizations and businesses in the community who have an interest in the campaign project or the population the campaign serves. Input and resources from community partners often make health campaigns possible. In addition to input on the campaign working group, resources community partners may contribute include:

◆ Money
◆ Materials
◆ Expertise
◆ Time
◆ In-kind donations

For example, a local pizza place with many student customers may be interested in supporting the campus depression campaign by providing free food for campaign-related meetings and allowing the campaign to place promotional materials in the restaurant. In addition to providing needed resources, community partners lend credibility to the campaign as audience members may have a relationship with the partners and partners enhance community buy-in and support for the campaign. When working with community partners, it is important to keep in mind that there should be benefits to the partners for participating; and when approaching potential community partners, present a list of those benefits.

For example, when CDC planned its *Get Smart* campaign, which addresses the growing problem of antibiotic resistance, a large group of community partners was amassed, including organizations and individuals from:

◆ State and local health departments
◆ Universities
◆ Managed care organizations
◆ Patients
◆ Consumer advocacy groups
◆ Professional organizations
◆ Pharmaceutical companies
◆ Businesses

These community partners were able to provide many valuable resources to the Get Smart campaign such as expertise and in-kind donations, but also there were benefits to the community partners. These benefits included:

◆ Public recognition as a CDC campaign partner
◆ Sharing of information
◆ Use of CDC educational materials and campaign products
◆ Improved health of constituents

Establishing the campaign working group and creating a problem statement and campaign goal provides the foundation for the campaign that is built upon in the next phase, which involves strategic planning. Although strategic planning is based on the goal statement created by the campaign working group, a campaign team performs the day-to-day activities of the campaign, with the campaign working group serving in an advisory capacity for guidance and advice.

Phase 2—Strategic Planning from Formative Research

Phase 2 of the MMHCC (Figure 8.2) involves creating a strategic plan for the campaign based on formative research. A *strategic plan* is based on the campaign goal statement and maps out the plan of action for the campaign.

SWOT Analysis

One of the first major projects a campaign team should accomplish is to evaluate the current situation or environment in which the campaign is being created by conducting a SWOT analysis. SWOT is an acronym that stands for:

◆ **S**trengths
◆ **W**eaknesses
◆ **O**pportunities
◆ **T**hreats

A *SWOT analysis* is a traditional marketing tool that audits the situational factors and forces in the internal and external environment that likely impact the campaign and need to be recognized in campaign planning. SWOT analyses also can be used for social marketing efforts.

The first two categories, *strengths and weaknesses*, are internal assessments of what campaign strengths need to be maximized and what weaknesses need to be minimized. In other words, what are the strengths and weaknesses of the campaign team? Strengths could be anything from having experienced team members to having adequate time for the project to the salience of the health issue. Weaknesses could be lack of expertise in a needed area, such as graphic design skills or a limited budget.

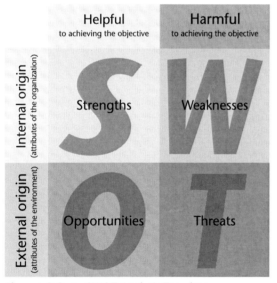

Figure 8.3 ◆ *SWOT Analysis Template*

The next two categories, *opportunities and threats*, refer to external factors that could have an impact on the campaign. Opportunities are outside events or entities that could help the campaign meet its goal. Opportunities could include circumstances such as uniqueness of the campaign, grassroots support, or lots of partnership availabilities. Threats are outside events or entities that may compromise the campaign in meeting its goals. Threats could be circumstances such as competing campaigns and messages, poor policies and laws, or a resistant audience.

One easy way to organize the campaign team's ideas for the SWOT analysis is to fill in a SWOT analysis table such as the SWOT template in Figure 8.3 or the SWOT analysis example in Table 8.1. By filling in a SWOT analysis table, the campaign team is conducting an environmental scan or situational analysis. Entries into the SWOT analysis table should be fairly brief because in-depth analysis is not required at this early stage in the campaign.

For example, Table 8.1 shows how one of the target audience teams from the Motorcycle Safety at Purdue (MS@P) adapted the SWOT analysis template to address strengths, weaknesses, opportunities, and threats of both the campaign team and their target audience. Notice in this example that entries into the SWOT analysis table are brief but identify key strengths and opportunities that the campaign team can build on and weaknesses and threats that the campaign team can work to overcome.

	STRENGTHS	WEAKNESSES	OPPORTUNITIES	THREATS
Target Audience Team	◆ Research and evaluation skills ◆ Knowledge of campaign planning practices ◆ Knowledge of health communication theories ◆ Harm reductionist (i.e., sensitive to ethical issues and personal needs) ◆ Understand importance of message and communication channels	◆ Unfamiliar with motorcycling culture ◆ Lack of motorcycle knowledge ◆ No direct contact with target group ◆ Where will we find them? ◆ Campaign inexperience ◆ Currently lack campaign funding	◆ Access to resources ◆ University affiliation (credibility, network, research) ◆ Funding through public agencies ◆ Ability to partner with interested groups	◆ Hard to penetrate the motorcycling culture as outsiders ◆ Glamorizing message to ride ◆ Will our message have to compete for attention? ◆ Competing health campaigns ◆ Emphasis on personal freedom ◆ Competing laws and policies (i.e., helmet law)
Friends and Family of Motorcyclists	◆ Interpersonal relationships (knowledge of personal history/background) ◆ Love/care ◆ Strong desire to change motorcyclist's behavior ◆ Access to motorcyclists	◆ Interpersonal relationships (unwilling to risk) ◆ Low self-efficacy to have conversation on a difficult topic ◆ Opinions in concordance with motorcyclist's	◆ Currently no forum for this group. Group may desire information and help	◆ Stubborn partner (difficult to converse with/unwilling to listen) ◆ Emphasis on personal freedom ◆ Increasing number of motorcyclists ◆ Competing messages

Table 8.1 ◆ *SWOT Analysis by a Target Audience Team of the Motorcycle Safety at Purdue campaign*

After the campaign team performs a SWOT analysis and anticipates a variety of circumstances, it is ready to conduct formative research.

Formative Research

When planning all aspects of the campaign, especially message design, it is essential to conduct thorough formative research. *Formative research* is defined as "research used to help form strategies, especially to select and understand target audiences and develop draft marketing strategies" (Kotler & Lee, 2008, p. 75). Decisions about how to implement a campaign cannot be made without gaining a deeper understanding of the audience for the campaign. Formative research is the first form of campaign evaluation conducted by the campaign team. A needs assessment can be very helpful in understanding the audience for the campaign.

Needs Assessment

The first step in formative research is conducting a needs assessment. A *needs assessment* answers the basic question "Is a health campaign really necessary to address this health issue?" To answer this question, a needs assessment undertakes a systematic process to determine and document a population's or a community's needs (Gilmore & Campbell, 2005). A needs assessment is a way to discover the health issues that are influencing a community, including the underlying factors that contribute to a community's needs and what needs there are in terms of health campaigns. For example, health officials may know that community members are not eating nutritious foods, but a needs assessment can reveal the reasons this is not happening, such as a lack of easy access to grocery stores or people not knowing how to prepare healthy foods.

Needs assessments are designed to gather information directly from the audience you are trying to reach. This direct contact with the audience can translate into added legitimacy for the campaign, as the community is more likely to perceive the campaign as originating from a genuinely concerned source rather than a source with little understanding of the community. A needs assessment also means that the campaign incorporates audience involvement from early on, a factor that may translate into greater community support for the campaign.

There are four basic techniques for conducting a needs assessment including:

◆ Key informants
◆ Community forum
◆ Survey
◆ Social indicators

These needs assessment techniques can be used alone or in tandem.

In the *key informants* approach to needs assessment, key individuals in the community are identified and interviewed. The idea behind this approach is that key informants have insights into the community and can articulate the community's needs. For example, if you wanted to address the health issue of poor nutrition in a community, you would want to identify and speak with some key informants. These key informants might include individuals who regularly prepare meals for their families, social service workers who meet with families and discuss nutrition, or even managers at local grocery stores. One drawback of this approach is that the informants may not be able to accurately speak for all members of the community. More prominent and vocal members of a community may not share the same characteristics and experiences as more typical community members.

A *community forum* approach to needs assessment involves holding public meetings and inviting interested community members to attend and voice their concerns about the health issue and implementing a campaign to address the issue. This approach allows for multiple voices to be heard and considered. One drawback of this approach is similar to the drawback mentioned for the key informants approach. Again, the campaign team may be receiving input from only the most motivated and concerned members of the community as well as those who have the resources to attend the meeting. Although the information the campaign obtains though this approach is helpful in understanding the community, the campaign team needs to keep in mind that the information may not be representative of all community members.

Another way to gather multiple voices for needs assessment is to administer a survey to a sample of the community. One benefit of surveys is that many people can be reached and asked questions about their and their community's health needs. Another benefit is that surveys are less labor intensive than other needs assessment methods. One limitation of surveys is that the questions may not tap into all the needs of the community because information provided by survey respondents tends to be limited by the questions on the survey. A way to address this limitation is to include open-ended, free-response questions where respondents can expand on their answers and/or write about additional needs and concerns.

A more indirect way of approaching needs assessment is to use *social indicators*. This approach uses statistics from already published reports to determine the needs of a community or population. This method is relatively easy and inexpensive because the data already are gathered. This method is limited, though, because broad social indicators, for example, a low literacy rate or a low vaccination rate, might not indicate the underlying factors causing a health issue or sufficiently pinpoint the health needs of a community.

When the needs assessment is completed and the campaign team, in consultation with the working group, agrees that a health campaign is necessary and what the specific goals and the potential target audience for the campaign are, the campaign team must continue conducting other forms of formative research. Formative research is particularly useful to specifically profile the target audience by learning as much as possible about that audience. It is not enough to simply designate an audience such as men or women. Research needs to investigate what makes an audience different and unique relative to the health issue of interest. Also, from needs assessment through formative research, the campaign team should be thinking about which theoretical approach is most relevant and applicable to the campaign. Is it one of the theories informed directly by health communication research and discussed in Chapter 3, "Linking Health Communication with Theories Informed by Health Communication," or one of the campaign theories presented in Chapter 7, "Linking Health Communication with Health Campaign Theories?" Or perhaps a combination of theories is appropriate? The campaign team needs to consider questions of theory carefully and throughout the campaign to increase chances of campaign success.

Pre-Campaign Survey

The two most common methods of formative research are surveys and focus groups. You most likely have filled out some type of survey before. A survey is an excellent way to reach a large number of people and a survey allows projection of the results onto an entire community. In other words, by questioning a sample of the target audience, the campaign team can make assumptions about the entire audience. Surveys also serve as a baseline against which future campaign results can be measured. Items on a pre-campaign survey should measure the audience's attitudes, beliefs, and behaviors regarding the health issue.

For example, when designing a pre-campaign survey for the campus depression campaign, the campaign team would want to include items that assess the campus's current knowledge about depression, the causes of depression, and the symptoms of depression. The survey may determine that there are many misconceptions about depression that the campaign needs to correct. The pre-campaign survey also should investigate the audience's attitudes and beliefs about depression. Does the audience think that depression is a valid condition that needs treatment or is there a belief that those with depression are just feeling sorry for themselves? In addition, the pre-campaign survey could determine respondents' behaviors regarding depression. Are respondents suffering from symptoms of depression? Do respondents know how to treat depression?

Focus Groups

A focus group is a way to gather in-depth information from a small group of audience members (Krueger, 1998). During a focus group, a facilitator and co-facilitator meet with between 6 and 12 individuals to gather opinions from the group. The size of the group is important, as there needs to be enough people to allow for the exchange of ideas and discussion, but not too many people that not everyone can easily join in the conversation. Focus groups are an important way to gather opinions from the target audience about a health issue. The primary benefit of focus groups is that as participants interact, they synergistically build on each others' ideas and opinions, which often leads to a robust discussion of the topic, resulting in rich data for the campaign team to consider.

Messaging Process

After determining the baseline attitudes, beliefs, and behaviors of the target audience through surveys or focus groups, the campaign team can begin designing and determining ways to distribute messages. Knowledge of communication theory and message design are major insights that health communication specialists offer to enhance the effectiveness of a health campaign. Mattson and Basu (2010a, 2010b) argued that when designing messages, campaign teams must take established message elements into account including:

◆ Stimulating
◆ Motivational
◆ Appraisal of environment/context
◆ Culturally consistent
◆ Organizational resources

Stimulating refers to the inherent capability of the message to encourage the exposed audience to take notice and attend to the message. Creating a salient stimulus involves incorporating message features, such as attractiveness, music, and color that capture the audience's attention. Think about all the commercials you see on television; occasionally a commercial has a catchy jingle or an attractive model. These stimuli might grab your attention enough to compel you to stop and pay attention to the message. Marketers work very hard to incorporate stimuli that produce such a reaction. With so many messages from a wide variety of sources available to an audience, it is important to include stimuli that bring attention to your campaign message.

An important attribute of a stimulating message is saliency, which is different than an attribute that can be seen or heard. If a message is not *salient*, meaning the audience considers it to be timely and relevant, the audience will not attend to the message. For example, if you are thinking about including testimonials or personal stories as a part of a health campaign, it is very important that the audience regard the story as relevant to them and their life situation. For example, a study of anti-drug advertisements showed that when a message about parents was used, teens did not find the message to be personally salient, therefore the message had no effect on the teens (Pechmann & Reibling, 2006). In our designing a campus depression campaign example, a messaging process challenge would be to make depression a relevant health issue for college students.

Motivational refers to features in the message that help the audience decide whether or not to act on the message. In other words, motivational cues are aspects of the message that prompt action. Typical motivational cues include severity, threat, and susceptibility components in the message. Remember these components from Chapter 3, "Linking Health Communication with Theories Informed by Health Communication?" Severity, threat, and susceptibility are included in both the Extended Parallel Process Model and the Reconceptualized Health Belief Model. If a message presents a health condition as severe, the audience may be motivated to take action to prevent that condition. For the campus depression campaign, the campaign team might find they need to motivate the audience to take action to avoid depression by making audience members aware that they are at risk for depression. This might be accomplished by including messages with statistics of college students and faculty who suffer from depression. The severity of depression also could be emphasized with messages about some of the more serious consequences of depression, such as total withdrawal from society or suicidal thoughts.

Appraisal of the environment or context refers to the audience's perceptions that the suggested health actions promoted in a message can be undertaken in their environment given their available resources. Often when individuals are confronted with a health recommendation, they consider their environment and available resources to determine if that recommendation is feasible. The challenge for message designers is to craft messages that assist the audience in coping with their existing environment and resources. One specific way to do this is to incorporate response-efficacy and self-efficacy messages. *Response-efficacy messages* promote a strategy that works and *self-efficacy messages* promote individuals' confidence in their own ability to perform the recommended action. In the campus depression campaign example, messages such as "Medication works in treating over 90% of depression cases" and "You can easily access free resources you need to combat depression by visiting your campus health center" are a response-efficacy and a self-efficacy message respectively. A campaign may have lots of resources available in its environment or context to combat a health problem, but if the audience does not believe that the resources are effective, the audience will not utilize the resources.

Other concerns that an appraisal of the environment and context addresses are subjective norms and normative influence. *Subjective norms* are what individuals believe other people normally think or do. *Normative influence* refers to the powerful impact of norms on behavior because most people prefer to conform with the rules of society in order to fit in. This can be problematic when the prevailing norms encourage unhealthy behaviors. Prevailing norms also may stigmatize behaviors. In the case of depression, seeking help may be seen as a sign of weakness or the prevailing norms may stigmatize the use of medication for depression. Message designers need to be aware of subjective norms and normative influence so messages either reinforce the norms or address norms that need to be changed.

Messages also must be *culturally consistent,* meaning that because cultural influences are very strong, beliefs and values of an audience's culture likely impact the audience's reception of messages and their ability to react to those messages. Culture is much more than one's race, ethnicity, or location. *Culture* is a much broader term and can be used to describe the beliefs, values, and/or way of living of any particular group. This means, for example, that an entire hospital system can have a culture, as can a subset of individuals, such as nurses at one hospital location.

Cultural practices have enormous influence on health-related behaviors and campaign teams need to be aware of these influences. For example, the 2009 season of the television reality show *The Biggest Loser* featured a team of Tongan cousins, Filipe and Sione, who were trying to lose weight. Throughout the show they talked about their Tongan culture and how it influenced their unhealthy eating habits and inactive lifestyle. Any health campaign targeting Tongans needs to account for these cultural influences and try to find ways to include healthier habits into the Tongan lifestyle.

Organizational resources refer to the organization producing the campaign messages and that organization's ability to create and disseminate quality messages. Generally, this aspect of the messaging process relates directly to the message designers rather than the audience. For example, the campaign working group could devise an excellent idea for a message to incorporate into a 20-second public service announcement (PSA). However, if the campaign team does not have adequate skills or equipment to create the PSA or the monetary resources to have the PSA produced, the PSA may be of poor quality or may not be possible. The campaign working group and campaign team members must honestly recognize their abilities and resources when creating the strategic plan. And keep in mind the SWOT analysis provides insight on organizational resources.

Testing and Revising Messages

Once draft messages are developed with consideration of the previous messaging elements, the MMHCC indicates that messages should be pretested with members of the target audience and be revised based on the feedback before being widely disseminated. We cannot overemphasize the importance of pretesting messages to determine if the messages foster the desired responses. This step can vastly improve messages and prevent ineffective messages from being widely disseminated. There is no way of knowing if the features in a message are effective without previewing the messages with target audience members. For a detailed case study of the importance of pretesting messages, read about Kosmoski, Mattson, and Hall's (2007) experience with the Motorcycle Safety at Purdue campaign.

Message Dissemination Strategy

Another strategic decision made during Phase 2 of the MMHCC (Figure 8.2) is the plan for message dissemination. This involves determining what communication channels will be used to distribute the messages to the audience. One of the basic determinations that must be made is whether to use a push or a pull strategy.

A *push strategy* is much like it seems, messages are pushed to the audience. This message dissemination strategy is what you may typically think of when you hear about a health campaign. Messages are pushed out to the audience through various channels such as ads on the radio or on billboards around town. The challenge of a push strategy is finding the strategic locations so the information reaches the audience. As discussed previously in this chapter, this involves finding life path points or daily message intersections for the audience as well as their media use patterns and preferences. If a target audience for the campus depression campaign is college males, you would want to think about places where males likely would be to intercept the campaign messages. The life path points for these males might include the dining halls, the gym, and the student union.

A pull strategy is the opposite of a push strategy. In a *pull strategy*, the audience pulls or seeks information and messages from the campaign. When implementing a pull strategy, the campaign lets audience members know that information is available, but then waits for the audience to request the information. If you ever saw a commercial about a health condition or an advertisement with the phrase, "for more information call," you experienced a pull strategy. The advantage of a pull strategy is that interested and motivated audience members are getting the information so resources are more concentrated on the target audience.

Whether a push or pull strategy is used, the campaign team also needs to consider what communication channels are appropriate for message dissemination. Before we discuss communication channel options, please take a few minutes to complete Health Communication Nexus Interlude 8.2.

For this interlude, imagine you are responsible for disseminating messages for the campus depression campaign. Take a few minutes to jot down in your notebook a list of relevant communication channels you could use to disseminate messages for the campaign. Think about the life path points of your target audience. Now for each message dissemination channel on your list answer these questions:

◆ What are the costs of using this communication channel?

◆ Do the benefits of using this communication channel outweigh the costs?

◆ Are there any ethical concerns associated with using this communication channel?

Keep your message dissemination channel ideas in mind as we further discuss communication channel options.

Hopefully you formed a long list of potential communication channels for the campus depression campaign. Perhaps you started with some basic media channels such as television, radio, or the local newspaper. Other options could include billboards, posters around campus, the internet, or brochures available at the health center. You also may have thought of some interpersonal communication channels such as a counselor at the health center talking with a student or a counselor giving a presentation on depression at one of the dorms. Communication channels also can be more creative such as producing a song, creating a video game, or putting a message on a unique promotional item. A stress ball imprinted with a campaign message, for example, might be an effective message dissemination strategy for a campus depression campaign. It is important to remember that there are a multitude of message channels available and campaign teams should be open to discovering communication channels that reach target audiences in creative but effective ways. Table 8.2 includes a list of potential campaign message channels. Also, asking the target audience during focus groups or informal interviews for their ideas about and reactions to potential message channels likely will reveal some effective message channels.

All decisions made in Phase 2 about how the campaign will be designed and implemented need to be written into a strategic plan. This document should include as much information as possible because it serves as a blueprint for the campaign team.

Phase 3—Implementation and Evaluation

Phase 3 of the MMHCC (Figure 8.2) occurs when the campaign is rolled out and the strategic plan is implemented. Campaign implementation includes the day-to-day operations of the campaign. Implementation is when campaign plans are put

Table 8.2 ◆ *Potential campaign message channels.*

◆ Television

◆ Radio

◆ Newspaper

◆ Billboards

◆ Web sites

◆ E-mail

◆ Text messages

◆ Posters

◆ Social networking sites

◆ Conversations

◆ Promotional items

◆ Brochures

◆ Telephone

Are there any other message channels on your list from Health Communication Nexus Interlude 8.2 that are not included on this list?

into action. In general, the more strategic planning, the more smoothly the campaign runs. That being said, implementing a health campaign is incredibly time consuming, labor intensive, and challenging. Unexpected situations sometimes emerge and roadblocks appear that must be overcome or managed. Major activities during campaign implementation include:

◆ Message production
◆ Message dissemination
◆ Campaign team meetings with
  ❖ Staff
  ❖ Working group
  ❖ Partners
◆ Process evaluation
◆ Outcome evaluation

An important activity to highlight during this phase of the campaign is conducting *process evaluation,* which is the ongoing tracking and evaluation of campaign activities, how and where the campaign is distributing messages, and who the campaign is reaching. Process tracking involves a variety of tasks, such as maintaining an inventory of campaign products and materials, tracking the number of people the campaign team talks with at events, or recording the number of times a commercial airs on radio or television. A spreadsheet can aid in administering the tracking process. Process tracking allows the campaign team to evaluate the reach of the campaign. Careful process tracking also allows for easy reporting of activities to campaign management and/or funding organizations. In the example of the campus depression campaign, the campaign team would track the number of posters placed around campus, including in campus dormitories and student apartment complexes, and the student health center might track the number of students who come in for assistance to combat symptoms of depression.

Phase 4—Correction Loop

Phase 4 of the MMHCC (Figure 8.2) incorporates a correction or feedback loop which stems directly from the evaluation phase. During this phase the campaign team reflects on what the campaign has accomplished, what has been effective, and what has not been effective, and determines what changes need to be made. Like all decisions made during the entire campaign process, changes to the campaign should be based on thorough research. Campaigns should routinely conduct *outcome evaluation* to determine the effectiveness of the campaign. The results of a post-campaign survey determine who is familiar with campaign messages as well as how those messages have changed knowledge, attitudes, and behaviors of the target audience. Keep in mind, in order to have useful post-campaign data, though, the campaign team must conduct a thorough pre-campaign survey. Without this pre-campaign/post-campaign survey design, there is no way to compare the target audience's knowledge, attitudes, and behaviors before, during, and after the campaign to determine any changes. Comments and feedback from audience members and partners also can be used to justify changes to the campaign.

Campaign practitioners must keep in mind that strategic plans and health campaigns are always works in progress. Campaign teams must be open to revising messages, obtaining new partnerships, and going in new directions in order to bring about the desired knowledge, attitude, and behavior changes in target audiences. If outcome evaluation reveals that a target audience is not changing its behavior, the campaign team must work on developing new messages and/or dissemination strategies to persuade the audience to change. Openness to feedback, even if the feedback is negative, is an important quality for campaign teams to possess. It is through adapting to constructive feedback that campaigns are most effective.

Health Campaign Process Guides

Following the MMHCC (Figure 8.2) may seem like a daunting process. However, there are several resources available to assist you in all stages of the planning, development, implementation, and evaluation of a campaign. Two helpful health campaign process guides are:

◆ *Making Health Communication Programs Work*
◆ *CDCynergy*

Making Health Communication Programs Work, also known as the "Pink Book," is a publication by the National Cancer Institute available free via download at the Web site for this book. The Pink Book is a quick reference guide for all stages of a health communication campaign. With a strong communication focus, the Pink Book provides helpful suggestions for pretesting, message development, and evaluation, as well as tips for working effectively with partners and choosing the most effective communication channels.

Another helpful health campaign tool is the *CDCynergy* CD-ROM created by CDC. This practical computer program provides step-by-step guidance for every stage of the campaign process. In addition to answers to frequently asked questions and printable worksheets, the program also contains numerous examples and case studies as well as expert commentary. There also are tailored editions of the program that address specific health issues and populations, including sexually-transmitted diseases, diabetes, the health concerns of Native Americans and Alaskans, as well as many others. The basic *CDCynergy* program and its many editions can be purchased from CDC. To learn more about *CDCynergy,* visit the Web site for this book.

Now that we explained the MMHCC in some detail and provided two useful campaign process resources, we review two campaigns that were designed and implemented using the MMHCC framework with assistance from the Pink Book and *CDCynergy*. First we consider CDC's DES Update campaign, followed by the Motorcycle Safety at Purdue (MS@P) campaign.

CDC's DES Update

Diethylstilbestrol (DES) was a medication that contained synthetic estrogen and was prescribed to pregnant women from 1938 to 1971 to prevent miscarriages and premature births. Some prenatal vitamins even included DES, so many women were unaware that they were taking DES. DES has been associated with many health risks for those prescribed it, as well as their offspring. Some of the side effects experienced by those exposed to DES either while they were pregnant or were in the womb of a pregnant woman are breast cancer, vaginal cancer, and cervical cancer. In addition, the offspring of those prescribed DES are at risk for health issues such as infertility and pregnancy complications in daughters, and cysts in sons.

In 2003, the United States Congress mandated that CDC, in conjunction with the National Cancer Institute, create a comprehensive campaign to provide accurate and current information about DES exposure and its health effects. One of the challenges with DES exposure and its complications is that many people are unaware of their exposure. Women struggling with infertility or facing a difficult pregnancy might not know if their mother was prescribed DES while pregnant, which is information that could help their physicians treat their symptoms.

In Phase 1 of the campaign, CDC's DES Update campaign team convened a working group to understand the problem, establish goals for the campaign, and begin work on a strategic plan. The campaign working group was comprised of CDC staff, women exposed to DES, including both women exposed to DES while pregnant and daughters born of those pregnancies, health care providers, health care associations, and community outreach organizations. An important campaign partner was a grassroots organization, DES Action, which was instrumental in lobbying Congress to create and fund CDC's DES Update. Members of DES Action were women prescribed DES and their children. The group brought their passion and experiences to the campaign, as well as an established network for reaching those affected by DES.

Based on formative research, including focus groups, the campaign team decided to concentrate on two target audiences which were:

- ◆ Consumers
  - ❖ Those who know they were exposed to DES either by prescription or in utero
  - ❖ Those who may have been exposed to DES
- ◆ Health care providers
  - ❖ Physicians
  - ❖ Physicians assistants
  - ❖ Nurses
  - ❖ Midwives

These target audiences had distinctly different informational needs and the campaign team worked closely with members of both audiences to plan and design messages and message dissemination strategies. After an initial series of materials was created, the materials were pretested with the target audiences through a series of focus groups conducted via telephone. These groups provided valuable feedback and the campaign team made needed changes to campaign messages and materials.

One of the central marketing products of the campaign was a binder containing pages of information for the consumer audience. The cover of the binder included photos of different families. Focus group participants informed the campaign team that all the photos were of White families who were smiling, which was not representative of the target audience. Another product the campaign team designed was a DES self-assessment guide. The original design was a square with pages that folded out, much like a map. Focus group participants reported that the piece was awkward, confusing to follow, and difficult to fill out, as it required a large flat surface to unfold and write on it. Participants commented they were unlikely to pass the self-assessment tool on to others because it was inconvenient to use. Even the original title for the campaign, DES Check-up, met with resistance. Focus group participants commented that it sounded too medically oriented and the tone was cold.

 Based on feedback obtained during pretesting, the campaign materials were revised. Pictures of diverse families were added to the binder cover, the folded self-assessment was changed into a small booklet, and the title of the campaign was changed to CDC's DES Update. Go to this book's Web site to see the revised binder cover with more diverse images and the interactive DES self-assessment guide. Without pretesting, the campaign team may have squandered a lot of money and effort producing and distributing ineffective and even offensive materials.

During Phase 2, the campaign team also had to determine a message dissemination strategy. The campaign team learned from talking with health care providers that they did not have a lot of time to read through medical literature and comprehensive reports instead they wanted the information about DES exposure to be easily accessible. This feedback lead to the formation of a Web site targeted toward health care providers. Campaign team members also attended several medical conferences and set up informational booths. One of the challenges the team faced was attracting attention to their booth while other competing and well-funded booths were giving away attractive free items, something that was not in CDC's DES Update campaign budget. One technique the campaign team used was to hang graphic images of malformations caused by DES exposure, which captured physicians' and other health care providers' attention. Continuing education courses for nurses also were offered at these conferences as a way to get the message about DES across to health care professionals.

When it came to addressing the consumer audience or those who may have or had been exposed to DES, the campaign team decided that because the health issue was a highly specific problem, they would use a pull rather than push strategy. Instead of running a mass media campaign that would reach across the entire United States, the campaign team chose to have information available to those who requested it. Partnering with organizations that served women and men who may have or had been exposed to DES, such as DES Action, the DES Cancer Network, the Women's Health Network, and CDC's 1-800 information hotline gave target audience members several outlets for requesting information. Information that could be requested included a DES self-assessment guide and a binder filled with DES-related information. After the strategic plan was finalized through Phase 2, CDC's DES Update campaign was launched with targeted messages for consumers and health care providers.

During Phase 3, implementation of the campaign, careful process tracking was conducted, including a detailed database of all campaign materials that were requested and distributed. CDC partnered with a clearinghouse that was responsible for compiling and shipping requested DES information and presented inventory reports on a regular basis. Hits to CDC's DES Update Web site were counted and a news clipping service was hired to track media mentions of DES and/or the campaign. The campaign team used this process tracking to evaluate the reach and impact of the campaign.

Phase 3 of CDC's DES Update campaign also involved outcome evaluation consisting of a pre-campaign/post-campaign survey design to measure knowledge, attitudes, and behaviors related to DES exposure. Results indicated some positive changes.

Unfortunately CDC's DES Update did not include a comprehensive Phase 4, the correction loop, because funding was exhausted, so no major adjustments or corrections were made to the campaign. The campaign continues primarily through the Web site, which provides extensive information about DES exposure and its health effects for consumers and health care providers. And most recently DES Update Partners was added as a target audience to provide virtual tools for partners to share CDC's DES Update information with their organizations, including promotional materials, a Web site linking kit, fact sheets, and newsletter articles.

CDC's DES Update not only followed the process outlined in the MMHCC, this campaign informed the ongoing development of this campaign model. While on a fellowship at CDC during a sabbatical year, the first author of this book, Professor Mattson, became a member of CDC's DES Update campaign team. In addition to working on the campaign, she pondered how a communication perspective could extend the traditional social marketing approach to health campaigns. Now that you're getting the hang of how health campaigns can use the MMHCC, let's review a smaller-scale example, the Motorcycle Safety at Purdue campaign.

Motorcycle Safety at Purdue Campaign

After highlighting a large-scale national campaign that generally followed the MMHCC, we consider a more recent, local-level, smaller-scale health campaign, Motorcycle Safety at Purdue (MS@P). Although we discuss aspects of this campaign throughout this book, in this section we focus on the development of this campaign using the MMHCC (Figure 8.2).

As you probably know from reading other chapters in this book, the inspiration for creating a motorcycle safety campaign arose after the first author of this book, Professor Mattson, lost her leg in a motorcycle accident. Although she and

ETHICAL DILEMMA ❖ What Would You Do?

You are working as a health communication specialist at Centers for Disease Control and Prevention (CDC) and one of your assignments is to review CDC's DES Update Web page to make sure it remains as current as possible. You receive a phone call from a man who claims that his mother was prescribed DES while she was pregnant with him and he now has a brain tumor that his mother believes was caused by his exposure to DES. He also says he knows of other cases of men with brain tumors whose mothers were prescribed DES. He wants to know why the link between DES exposure and brain tumors is not included in CDC's DES Update campaign materials. You know from reading the materials that there is no scientific evidence of a link between DES exposure and brain tumors in men. However, you feel very bad about the caller's health situation. Based on this situation, answer these questions:

◆ Do you tell the man that CDC is looking into the possibility of a link between DES exposure and brain tumors in men even though you don't know for sure if there are any studies occurring? Why or why not?

◆ Do you explain to the man that CDC has a policy of reporting only health risks that are supported by scientific evidence even though you know this news will be very disappointing? Why or why not?

◆ Do you refer the man to CDC's DES Update Web page for information to answer his question? Why or why not?

◆ Do you take the man's contact information and offer to look into his question further and get back to him? Why or why not?

◆ Which of these health communication strategies about CDC's DES Update campaign is most ethical? Why?

her students conceived the idea for creating a campaign, they knew that their belief that motorcycle safety was important was not enough to justify a health communication campaign. Therefore, they set out to learn more about the need for a motorcycle safety campaign in their community.

Campaign Aims to Spread Safety Message to All Who Use Roadways*

By SOFIA VORAVONG

The Web address for a new motorcycle safety campaign at Purdue University zeroes in on creator Marifran Mattson's intent: All drivers share responsibility on the roadway.

The site breaks down facts and safety tips for motorcycle riders and drivers of semitrailers and other vehicles. It includes a separate educational section for friends and family.

"Oftentimes, motorcyclists feel they are put under pressure to ride safely, but it applies to other drivers too," said Mattson, an associate professor of communications at Purdue who lost part of her left leg in a horrific crash two years ago.

Mattson was riding her motorcycle south of Tippecanoe County when, while navigating a curve, her vehicle and a semitrailer traveling in the opposite direction collided. The driver said he did not see her.

The campaign—designed and developed over the past year after Mattson returned to work—rolled out late last month at the beginning of Purdue's academic year. Mattson, her graduate student assistants and others are holding numerous informative events to spread their message, including a safety session for riders later this month and participation in Purdue's Homecoming activities, as the end of the motorcycle season nears in October.

According to the National Highway Traffic Safety Administration, 4,553 motorcyclists died in crashes nationwide last year—a 13 percent jump from 2004 and continued eight-year trend of increasing motorcycle fatalities. Seven deaths occurred in Tippecanoe County.

Motorcycle Safety at Purdue campaign organizers have placed posters in CityBus routes near campus and partnered with several organizations, including Action Motor Sports in Lafayette and ABATE, or American Bikers Aimed Toward Education.

Local bookstores have donated items to be given away at campus events. Funding is provided by the Motorcycle Safety Foundation. Even the Purdue football team is helping.

"They wear their safety gear on the field, so why don't you on a motorcycle?" Mattson said of campaign ads featuring the football players.

Jay Jackson, executive director of ABATE of Indiana, said Mattson's effort comes as a larger mix of vehicles—semis, cars, SUVs and motorcycles—share the roadways every day.

By design, motorcyclists are most vulnerable to serious injury, he said.

"Everyone needs to be looking out, watching for riders and watching other drivers," Jackson said. "There are more vehicles, more chance for injury."

Part of the Purdue campaign also includes starting a student organization on campus and possibly offering motorcycle licensing in the future. If the campaign is successful, Mattson wants to take it statewide and nationwide.

"We didn't see any other comprehensive campaigning, and we did a very formal needs-analysis," she said of the outreach effort. "We're going to build success here first."

Learn More

Motorcycle riders interested in a safety session being planned for late September at Purdue University can call professor Marifran Mattson at (765) 494-7596.

Campaign Aims to Spread Safety Message to All Who Use Roadways by Sofia Voravong, *Journal & Courier*, September 15, 2006. Reprinted by permission of the *Journal & Courier*.

During Phase 1 of the MMHCC (Figure 8.2), an initial campaign working group was formed including Professor Mattson, graduate students, a representative from a motorcycle advocacy group, and a marketing manager of a motorcycle dealership. The professor and students, who comprised the day-to-day campaign team, researched and agreed upon the basic facts about motorcycle-related accidents. They gathered statistics about the number of motorcyclists in the area as well as the number of accidents, injuries, and fatalities in the area. The team also compared local data with state and national data to get a sense of the scope of the issue. The team knew that nationally motorcycle accidents and corresponding injuries and fatalities were on the rise and wanted to see if that trend held true for the local area. This information was shared with the campaign working group and a goal statement for the campaign was created and later revised to become the mission statement of the campaign. The mission statement of the MS@P campaign is:

◆ The goal of the Motorcycle Safety at Purdue (MS@P) campaign is to make the road safer for everyone. The campaign aims to accomplish this in three ways:
  ❖ Encourage *motorcyclists* to engage in safety practices such as wearing proper safety gear, becoming properly licensed, and obeying traffic laws;
  ❖ Encourage *drivers of cars and trucks* to be aware of motorcycles and to avoid aggressive driving;
  ❖ Encourage *friends and family of motorcyclists* to talk about motorcycle safety.

To further study the local area's need for a motorcycle safety campaign, during Phase 2 of the MMHCC, the campaign team conducted a needs assessment to determine what information the community needed and wanted about motorcycle safety. This involved talking with community members and conducting focus groups initially with motorcyclists and later drivers of cars and trucks and friends and family of motorcyclists. From the results of the needs assessment, the campaign working group determined that a motorcycle safety campaign was necessary but it should start with an emphasis on the campus community's unique needs, with the objective of eventually growing the campaign to the larger local area and beyond. In addition, based on the results of the needs assessment, the campaign working group decided to target three distinct audiences:

◆ Motorcyclists
◆ Friends and family of motorcyclists
◆ Drivers of cars and trucks

When talking with motorcyclists in focus groups, the campaign team learned motorcyclists had a lot of fear and frustration regarding the behaviors of drivers of cars and trucks toward motorcyclists. The motorcyclists described feeling as if they were a target on the road and also feeling as if other drivers could not see them or chose to ignore them, putting their safety at risk. This led the campaign team to talk with drivers of cars and trucks, during which the campaign team learned that many drivers of cars and trucks were unsure about how to safely share the road with motorcyclists and that driving near motorcycles made some drivers of cars and trucks very anxious. Talking with both of these groups and visiting online chat rooms also revealed that friends and family of motorcyclists are a strong influence on motorcyclists, but friends and family of motorcyclists were unsure how to broach the topic of safety with the motorcyclists in their lives.

Following the needs assessment, the campaign team confirmed and decided to expand the campaign working group to include additional representatives of key community partners. A major concern of the campaign team was gaining legitimacy with the motorcycle riding community because none of the campaign team members were current riders. Consequently, one of the key partnerships the team formed was with American Bikers Aimed Toward Education (ABATE) of Indiana. ABATE is a nonprofit motorcycle advocacy group responsible for motorcycle rider education and training courses in the state. Partnering with ABATE had multiple advantages. First and foremost it gave the campaign credibility with the motorcycling community, as ABATE is a highly recognized and respected organization among many motorcyclists. Also, ABATE had access to needed resources such as literature, motorcycles for display at campaign events, and safety courses and safety instructors. Additional partnerships included a local motorcycle dealership, the campus football team, and the city bus company, which provided mass transportation on campus.

The next step in Phase 2 of the campaign process was to develop messages for the campaign. For each target audience, including motorcyclists, drivers of cars and trucks, and friends and family of motorcyclists, the campaign team developed a list of information they wanted that audience to know. For example, the information for drivers of cars and trucks included:

◆ Importance of watching for motorcycles on roads
◆ Motorcycles should be treated like any other vehicle on the road
◆ Need to give motorcycles appropriate spacing on the road
◆ Risks of being involved in an accident with a motorcycle

From this list of information and other data gathered during the needs assessment, the campaign team drafted a variety of messages in a variety of formats. This process included developing a logo and slogan for the campaign, developing content for a Web site, creating signs, and other informational materials. The campaign team created multiple versions of each message using different approaches, layouts, and designs. The campaign team then conducted focus groups with members of each target audience to gain feedback on the draft messages as well as gather information regarding potential channels for message dissemination.

Based on the results of the focus groups, the campaign team consulted the campaign working group and made final decisions regarding campaign messages. Orders were placed to produce signage and other promotional items, and campaign literature such as brochures. You can see some examples of messages and promotional items the team produced at the Web site for this book.

The next step of the campaign, also part of Phase 3 of the MMHCC, was campaign implementation. The MS@P campaign roll-out was timed for late August which coincided with the start of the school year and the later part of motorcycling season. Because Indiana is a state with cold winters, the motorcycling season generally occurs between early spring and late fall. To roll out the MS@P campaign, the campaign team participated in an Activities Bonanza and Health and Safety Day on campus unveiled the Web site (www.ItInvolvesYou.com), and posted signs on campus, in campus busses, and in local businesses. Both the campus newspaper and the local community newspaper ran stories about the campaign and the campus radio station interviewed Professor Mattson.

Also during Phase 3 of the campaign, the MS@P campaign team engaged in *process evaluation* to carefully track the activities and messages of the campaign including using a spreadsheet to keep an updated inventory of all promotional products and campaign literature distributed. In addition, during campaign events, a campaign team member was assigned to count the number of people who interacted with the campaign team. Another process evaluation technique was a counter on the campaign Web site to track the number of unique hits before and after campaign events. Process tracking not only helped the campaign team gauge the reach of the campaign, but also helped the campaign team determine which promotional products were most popular and which items were not having the intended reach.

During Phase 3 of the MMHCC (Figure 8.2), the MS@P campaign team conducted *outcome evaluation* to determine the effectiveness of the campaign. The strategic plan for the MS@P campaign included outcome evaluation using a pre-campaign baseline survey and an annual follow-up campaign survey distributed on campus. The pre-campaign survey measured the target audiences' knowledge, attitudes, and behaviors regarding motorcycle safety prior to implementation of the campaign. The data from this pre-campaign survey served as the outcome evaluation baseline survey against which annual campaign survey data is compared. These comparisons allowed the campaign team to measure the ongoing effectiveness of the MS@P campaign and aspects of the campaign in need of improvement.

The results of the two forms of campaign evaluation in Phase 3 feed back into this ongoing campaign through the correction loop in Phase 4 of the MMHCC (Figure 8.2). Results from outcome evaluation and process evaluation provide essential feedback for the *correction loop,* which guides the campaign team in making changes to messages and campaign products. Campaign evaluation feedback loops back into Phase 2, where research with target audiences again informs campaign changes and future campaign process.

For example, MS@P survey results indicated that the current campaign messages were not changing the audience's perceptions about the severity of motorcycle crashes. Based on these results, the campaign team, working with an undergraduate class, created two new campaign messages to highlight the severity of motorcycle crashes. One strategy the team used in these messages was to be more blatant in illustrating and stating what motorcycle crash outcomes could be. Go to the Web site for this book to see the two new messages on the MS@P campaign Web site which illustrate this strategy and the process of campaign correction. By

PROFILE

Experiencing Small-Scale and Large-Scale Health Campaigns

*Carin Kosmoski, PhD—Research Scientist,
Centers for Disease Control and Prevention*

Throughout this book you've been reading about the Motorcycle Safety at Purdue (MS@P) campaign. Now let's learn more about one of the campaign team members who was involved in every aspect of the campaign from its initial conception through three annual follow-up campaign surveys.

Carin Kosmoski became involved in MS@P while a doctoral student at Purdue University studying health communication. Her interest in studying health communication arose out of two of her primary interests, communication and medicine. Despite a strong interest in the medical field, she did not feel she had the stomach to handle the blood and grime involved in performing medical procedures. In studying communication, she was especially interested in media and its influence, making the study of a health campaigns a natural fit. The motorcycle safety campaign then presented itself as an excellent opportunity to gain real-world campaign skills and observe firsthand how communication theory is applied at all phases of the campaign process.

Kosmoski played multiple roles in the MS@P campaign. One of her primary roles was assisting in the development, distribution, and data analysis of the pre-campaign baseline survey and annual follow-up campaign surveys. This was a huge task that involved developing the survey questions, pretesting those questions with the target audiences, having the surveys printed and distributed, entering data, converting the survey to an online format, and performing statistical tests on the data that was collected.

For Kosmoski, one of the most rewarding aspects of her involvement in the MS@P campaign was talking with audience members at various campaign events. Face-to-face interaction allowed her to have conversations with both motorcyclists and nonmotorcyclists during which she could share with them some helpful information. There were even times when audience members would return to the MS@P booth at another event and talk about changes they made or how they talked about the campaign with a friend. These positive interactions allowed Kosmoski to actively experience effective campaign messages which was exciting and kept her motivated.

On the flip side, one of the most challenging aspects of her campaign work was trying to convince drivers of cars and trucks that the motorcycle safety campaign pertained to them. A main goal of the campaign was educating drivers of cars and trucks how to safely share the road with motorcycles. Upon hearing the term "motorcycle safety," though, many of these drivers of other vehicles would tune out or walk away, thinking that only motorcyclists should be concerned. Working with a resistant audience required a lot of planning and thinking about counter arguments and how to make the issue of motorcycle safety more salient for nonmotorcyclists.

Upon graduation, Kosmoski was offered the position of Research Scientist with Centers for Disease Control and Prevention (CDC) working on safety campaigns for mine workers. She feels that her hands-on campaign experience with MS@P and especially her experience with uninterested and resistant audiences was invaluable in preparing her to work on even larger-scale campaigns. Her solid foundation in theory and research methods also gave her the tools she needs to approach the research questions and dilemmas she currently faces in her health communication career.

incorporating a correction loop, the campaign remains fluid and can constantly evolve to meet the dynamic needs of the target audiences.

Through explication and these two example campaigns, you now have a strong working knowledge of the Messaging Model for Health Communication Campaigns (MMHCC) process and are able to embark on developing a campaign to address a health issue. The service-learning application in the next section is designed to give you a positive start toward accomplishing a health campaign.

SERVICE-LEARNING APPLICATION

Monitoring Progress in Large-Scale and Small-Scale Health Campaigns

In this service-learning application, we reiterate that health campaigns can be either large scale or small scale. It is not so much the size or scope of the campaign that matters, rather it's the effectiveness of the campaign that makes a difference to the health of an audience. The effectiveness of a health campaign and the effectiveness of a service-learning project can be measured, in part, through monitoring progress. *Progress monitoring* refers to engaging both academic and community participants in an ongoing process to assess the quality of implementation and progress toward meeting specified goals, and uses results for improvement and sustainability (Corporation for National & Community Service, 2010). In addition to being a core component of evaluating a health campaign, progress monitoring is a core component of evaluating service-learning projects.

As you read through this chapter and considered the two campaign case studies presented, you may have considered the prospect of developing and implementing a full-fledged health campaign overwhelming. Health campaigns can take lots of time and resources, assets you might not have if you are working on a class or other small project. With the time and resources you do have, however, you could complete a small-scale health campaign or some aspect of a campaign, and you certainly can apply the principles of audience analysis and message design to any health communication projects you are working on.

For example, imagine that your project team would like to help the campus counseling center promote some of the support groups they offer. Following the principles of the MMHCC (Figure 8.2) you learned about previously in this chapter, you would first want to conduct a needs assessment. You could begin this process by meeting with representatives from the counseling center to determine what the problem is as well as to fully understand what support groups are offered. It also would be important to determine what ways the counseling center is promoting its support groups. This type of information is essential to your project. With whatever health campaign project you take on, you must understand, through needs assessment, what the problem is and what resources are available to your audience. Understanding what is currently done or has been done also prevents you from duplicating existing efforts or replicating failed efforts. Your campaign team also must know what resources they are promoting, as it would not be wise for a team to promote support groups that do not exist.

The next step in the needs assessment process is to conduct a thorough audience analysis to understand to whom you are promoting the support groups. This could involve conducting a random survey of students or talking with a focus group of students. Through audience analysis you gather data and make decisions about audience segmentation. Will you design messages to reach all students or do you want to focus on more targeted audiences such as males or females, or students who live on campus and/or those who live off campus? In talking with relevant audience members, you need to gather some of the following information:

♦ Current awareness of available support groups

♦ Audience's perceptions of support groups

♦ Audience's knowledge of the benefits of support groups

♦ Audience's reasons for avoiding support groups

♦ Audience's preferred media sources

After your project team determines what it is promoting and to whom it is promoting, you can begin to develop promotional messages. In this case you develop draft messages to promote support groups to your target audiences. In addition, think about possible communication channels for distribution of these messages. Once the initial design work on your draft messages is complete, you again must turn to members of the target audience to pre-test your messages and gather feedback. Although this may not seem like an essential step because your team already conducted a needs assessment, you can never be sure how your audience will react to your draft messages. Even minor features such as the images you choose or the color of the ad could influence whether or not your target audience attends to and reacts to the message. Conducting thorough audience analysis at the beginning of any campaign results in more effective campaign messages and promotional products and saves wasting time and other valuable resources on ineffective initiatives.

Based on the results of pretesting your project team's draft messages, you can finalize the messages and channels of distribution. At this point it is always a good idea to check with the organization you are developing your project for to be sure that your ideas fit with the organization's mission and standards before dissemination.

Each phase in the process of developing, implementing, and evaluating either a large-scale or small-scale health campaign serves a progress monitoring function and can also help you evaluate your service-learning experience. For example, when you check back with the community organization for whom you are developing support group promotional materials to show your revised messages which grew out of pretesting draft messages, you are performing progress monitoring not only of your progress on the campaign goals but also of your experience conducting a service-learning project. Because you are consistently monitoring progress, you can make adjustments to ensure both the campaign and the service-learning project are effective and rewarding.

Certainly each project you engage in will be unique in its needs and challenges. However, for projects that involve aspects of health campaigns, consulting the MMHCC guides you by keeping the importance of audience analysis and theoretically-grounded message design in the forefront of your activities. In addition, attention to progress monitoring throughout the process encourages ongoing improvement and sustainability of the project.

Chapter Summary

This chapter explored health campaigns, an often-practiced aspect of health communication. In an effort to differentiate but encourage engagement between a public health and a communication perspective on health campaigns, first the chapter provided an overview of the public health perspective and a social marketing approach to health campaigns. Next, the chapter introduced the Messaging Model for Health Communication Campaigns (MMHCC), which incorporates components of social marketing but emphasizes the communicative aspects of health campaigns, particularly audience analysis and message design. Third, two campaign case studies that are based on the MMHCC were reviewed, CDC's DES Update and the Motorcycle Safety at Purdue (MS@P) campaign. Finally, the chapter presented ways to utilize components of the MMHCC while monitoring progress in a small-scale service-learning project.

References

American Public Health Association (2007). *What is public health? Our commitment to safe, healthy communities.* Washington, DC: Author.

Corporation for National & Community Service (2010). Learn and Serve America's National Service-Learning Clearinghouse. Retrieved January 12, 2010, from www.servicelearning.org.

Gilmore, G. D., & Campbell, M. D. (2005). *Needs and capacity assessment strategies for health education and health promotion* (3rd ed.). Sudbury, MA: Jones and Bartlett.

Green, L. W., & Kreuter, M. W. (1990). Health promotion as a public health strategy for the 1990s. *Annual Review of Public Health, 11*, 319–334.

Holt, D. B. (2002). Got milk? Retrieved August 6, 2010, from http://www.aef.com/on_campus/classroom/case_histories/3000.

Hughes, R. (1999). Use of social marketing strategy to promote community acceptance of breastfeeding in public. *Australian Journal of Nutrition & Dietetics, 56*, 108–110.

Institute of Medicine (1988). *The future of public health.* Washington, DC: National Academy Press.

Joint Committee on Terminology (2001). Report of the 2000 Joint Committee on Health Education and Promotion Terminology. *American Journal of Health Education, 32*, 89–103.

Kosmoski, C. L., Mattson, M., & Hall, J. (2007). Reconsidering motorcycle safety at Purdue: A case study integrating campaign theory and practice. *Cases in Public Health Communication & Marketing, 1.* Available at http://www.gwumc.edu/sphhs/departments/pch/phcm/casesjournal/volume1/peer-reviewed/cases_1_07.cfm.

Kotler, P., & Lee, N. R. (2008). *Social marketing: Influencing behaviors for good* (3rd ed.). Thousand Oaks, CA: Sage.

Krueger, R. A. (1998). *Focus group kit.* Thousand Oaks, CA: Sage.

MacStravic, S. (2000). The missing links in social marketing. *Journal of Health Communication, 5*, 255–263.

Mattson, M., & Basu, A. (2010a). Centers for Disease Control's DES Update: A case for effective operationlization of messaging in social marketing practice. *Health Promotion Practice, 11*, 580-588.

Mattson, M., & Basu, A. (2010b). The message development tool: A case for effective operationalization of messaging in social marketing practice. *Health Marketing Quarterly, 27*, 275–290.

Pechmann, C., & Reibling, E. T. (2006). Antismoking advertisements for youths: An independent evaluation of health, counter-industry, and industry approaches. *American Journal of Public Health, 96*, 906–913.

© 2011, Margaret M Stewart, Shutterstock, Inc.

CHAPTER 9   Linking Health Communication with . . .

Risk Communication and Crisis Communication

Chapter Learning Objectives

◆ Define and distinguish risk and crisis communication
◆ Understand relationship between perceptions of hazard and outrage
◆ Acknowledge the goals of risk communication
◆ Identify necessary information components of risk communication
◆ Review process of developing effective risk messages
◆ List challenges to risk communication and ways to overcome these challenges
◆ Outline messaging components for consideration during a crisis
◆ Review guidelines for effective crisis communication
◆ Suggest communication strategies to manage various emotions during crises
◆ Provide best practices for risk communication and crisis communication
◆ Explain importance of integrating students' voices into service-learning projects

Chapter Preview

In this chapter, we compare and contrast risk communication and crisis communication. To avoid misunderstanding and misuse, we begin by pointing out some key distinguishing features of risk communication and crisis communication. Then throughout the chapter, we thoroughly define each of these concepts and offer several examples to further illustrate and highlight the distinguishing features. We also provide strategies and best practices for engaging in either risk communication or crisis communication. We conclude the chapter with a service-learning application that emphasizes the importance of integrating students' voices while designing risk messages for a community health campaign.

The Motorcycle Safety at Purdue campaign Web site opens with one of five images and facts associated with motorcycle safety. In addition to providing an attention-getter for visitors to the Web site, these are examples of risk communication because the images and statistics convey the risks associated with riding a motorcycle.

Distinguishing Risk Communication and Crisis Communication

One of the key roles the media and health campaigns play in imparting health-related information is communicating risk and crisis information to the public. Generally, "Risk communication contains rather static, persuasively-oriented messages regarding known probabilities of negative consequences and how those consequences may be reduced. . . . Crisis communication contains more dynamic primarily informative messages about the current state of a particular event (or set of events) including the cause, duration, magnitude, and immediacy of that event" (Dutta-Bergman & Mattson, 2006). The distinction between risk communication and crisis communication often is misunderstood and either crisis events are treated from a measured risk communication perspective or ongoing risks are addressed using more immediate strategies appropriate for crises.

Risk Communication

According to the National Research Council (1989), *risk communication* is the "interactive process of the exchange of information and opinion among individuals, groups, and institutions that involves multiple messages about the nature of risk and other messages not strictly about risk, that express concerns, opinions, or reaction to risk messages or to legal and institutional arrangements for risk management" (p. 5).

At first glance, this definition of risk communication may be somewhat confusing but the essential idea in this definition is that risk communication is any exchange of information about risk. So the question is, what is a risk? A risk is anything that can be considered potentially harmful. Therefore, risk communication can be about the risk, reactions to the risk, or measures in place to reduce or prepare for the risk. An example of risk communication is a warning label on a package of cigarettes cautioning users that smoking can lead to lung cancer or an article in a women's magazine about the risks of having unprotected sex.

Perceptions of Hazard and Outrage

As you can see from the previous examples, there are many kinds and levels of risk, which lead to different types of risk communication. One way to classify a risk is to compare the level of hazard with the level of outrage. The *level of hazard* is equivalent to the amount of damage a risk may potentially cause. A high-hazard risk is a risk that could potentially cause a lot of harm, such as serious injury or death. For example, riding a motorcycle is considered a high-hazard risk because compared with being a passenger in a car, a motorcyclist is approximately 39 times more likely to die in a traffic accident (National Highway Transportation Safety Administration, 2010). A low-hazard risk is a risk that most likely would cause minimal damage, such as mild pain. For example, riding a bicycle on a designated bike trail while wearing a helmet is a low-hazard risk since the trail is designed and maintained for safe riding. If you crash, you're likely to sustain only mild discomfort. Risks vary along a continuum from low-hazard to high-hazard (Figure 9.1).

Figure 9.1 ◆ *Hazard of risk continuum*

The *level of outrage* is the amount of concern the public has about a risk. When there is a high level of outrage the public is greatly concerned about the risk. For example, in the spring of 2009 the public became very concerned about the risk of contracting the H1N1 virus, also known as swine flu. This concern occurred after there were 100 reported deaths in Mexico and many more reported illnesses due to the virus in several countries across the world. The high level of outrage prompted travel restrictions for nonessential travel to Mexico by citizens from countries such as the United States, Canada, and Spain (National Public Radio, 2009). When there is a low level of outrage the public is not very concerned about the risk. Risks also vary along a continuum from low-outrage to high-outrage.

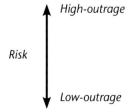

Figure 9.2 ◆ *Outrage toward risk continuum*

Taken together, we can create a graph to plot a risk.

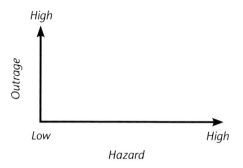

The level of outrage does not always correspond to the level of hazard. In other words, there may be a very high level of outrage about a relatively minor risk or there may be minimal outrage over a very relevant and high risk. Consider, for example, the risk of dying in an airplane crash. The odds of dying in a plane crash are roughly 8 million to 1, which is a very low risk. Despite the low risk, there are many who have a high level of outrage about flying, including extreme fear. Now consider the risk of dying in a car crash, which is 1 in 83 (National Safety Council, 2005). These are much greater odds than those of dying in a plane crash, but there are few who express any outrage over driving or riding in a car. To practice using this graph, please complete Health Communication Nexus Interlude 9.1.

Factors that Influence Outrage

There are several factors that influence the public's sense of outrage including:

◆ Coercive versus voluntary nature of risk
◆ Fairness
◆ Dread
◆ Organization imposing the risk
◆ Catastrophic versus chronic nature of risk

Individuals tend to feel more outrage when a risk is imposed on them or they are *coerced* into accepting a risk than when they *voluntarily* choose to accept a risk. For example, those who opt to use tanning beds rarely feel outrage about the stated risk of developing skin cancer. Other risks, however, are not undertaken voluntarily and instead are imposed upon people by the government or other organizations. For example, the risk of contracting food poisoning from eating tainted food is not a voluntary risk and instead people may unknowingly ingest food products containing salmonella or Escherichia coli bacteria that entered the food at a packaging plant. Therefore, a high level of public outrage often accompanies outbreaks of food contamination.

A second factor that determines level of outrage about a risk is *fairness*. In other words, people want to know whether a risk equally affects everyone or a certain population is at greater risk. For example, when a chemical factory is built in a low-income neighborhood within a town, those residents near the chemical factory are more at risk for harmful effects due to chemical exposure than those living

To make perceptions of risk more relevant to you, take a few minutes to plot the two examples of risks discussed, dying in an airplane crash versus dying in a car crash. Using the information and statistics provided and your own feelings about the risks, first plot the risk of dying in an airplane crash along both the hazard and outrage continuums.

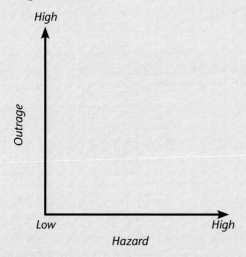

Now plot the risk of dying in a car crash along both the hazard and outrage continuums.

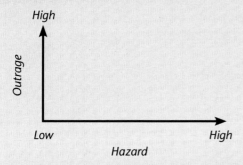

Where your points from each continuum meet within the graph represents your perception of the risk.

Compare your perceptions of your risk of dying in an airplane crash with your perceptions of your risk of dying in a car crash. Based on your comparison, answer these questions:

◆ What does the difference between these perceptions tell you about yourself and your perceptions of risk? Perhaps, for example, you realize risks exist but you do not consider yourself very susceptible to them.

◆ Do you think your perceptions of risk may change over time? Why or why not?

in more high-income areas of town. This suggests an unfair distribution of risk among residents in the low-income area.

Another factor that determines level of outrage about a risk is dread. *Dread* refers to how much people fear or want to avoid encountering a risk and its consequences. The higher the level of dread, the more outrage the public generally has about a risk. For example, the idea of contracting Ebola, a flesh eating virus, most likely evokes a lot of dread in the public and therefore elicits a high level of outrage.

A fourth factor that determines level of outrage about a risk is the *organization imposing the risk*. Some people inherently mistrust certain organizations, such as the government or big corporations, and therefore experience a high level of outrage when one of these entities is responsible for creating a risk. In 2007, for example, it was discovered that many toys imported from China contained lead. In addition to concern about the threat to millions of children who might ingest lead, the public was highly outraged by the lack of regulations the Chinese government imposed on its toy industry (Centers for Disease Control and Prevention, 2007; World Net Daily, 2007).

A fifth factor in determining level of outrage about a risk is whether the risk leads to a *catastrophic or a chronic problem*. This is why people become very outraged over relatively low probability risks such as dying in an airplane crash or developing a brain tumor. Although the occurrence of these health threats is very rare, the outcomes are catastrophic and often result in death. On the other hand, people regularly expose themselves to the much greater risk of heart disease by consuming trans fats, which are known to clog arteries. However, the consequences of exposure to trans fats develop over time, creating a chronic health risk which because of its slow progression tends to instill less outrage.

Goals of Risk Communication

Risk communication and its goals vary depending on the level of risk and the level of outrage perceived by the target audience. Often, risk communication efforts are geared toward informing the public about a risk or trying to get individuals to be concerned about a risk. Think about some of the health campaigns that you encounter on television or the internet or that may be occurring on your campus. For example, if you saw an advertisement promoting condom usage or if you ever were in a physician's waiting room and read a pamphlet about decreasing your risk for heart disease or the dangers of drinking and driving, you were involved in risk communication. In cases such as these, often the goal of risk communication is to increase the outrage people feel about a risk. For example, an expressed goal of Mothers Against Drunk Driving (MADD) is to increase the outrage people feel about drinking and driving. Attempts to increase outrage sometimes employ drastic measures. For example, those promoting the use of sober drivers may stage a mock car crash at a high school or college to illustrate just how deadly drinking and driving can be.

Sometimes, the goal of risk communication is to pacify the audience or lower the audience's sense of outrage. This is especially likely in times of panic or when the public is highly outraged about a fairly low or controllable risk. In the 1980s, for example, HIV/AIDS was a relatively new and misunderstood disease. Often people had false information about how the disease was spread and believed that having any sort of contact with an infected individual, such as shaking hands, could lead to transmission of the disease. Consequently, one of the goals of risk communication efforts regarding HIV/AIDS was to correct the misconceptions so that the public would understand the actual risk behaviors they needed to avoid, in this case bodily fluids, and to ease fears about interacting with those who were infected.

Information Components of Risk Communication

No matter what the goal of risk communication, there is basic information that all risk communication should include. The National Research Council (1989) advises that complete risk communication should contain these components:

◆ The nature of the risk
◆ Benefits of the hazard
◆ Available alternatives
◆ Uncertainty about risks or benefits
◆ How to manage risk

One component of the list that might initially strike you as odd is including information on the benefits of the hazard. A health issue or related behavior may be risky, but also might include benefits. Risk communication should inform you about both the benefits and risks of that health issue or related behavior. For example, think of any medication you take or have taken. In addition to the benefits for which you are taking or have taken the medication there is an accompanying list of risks. To make an informed decision about taking the medication you need to be aware of both the benefits and risks and any alternatives that may allow you to avoid those risks. Risk communication also should acknowledge any uncertainty or unknowns about the risks or benefits. Additionally, the audience needs information about how to manage the risk meaning both how to avoid the risk and how to handle the risk once it is encountered.

Steps to Developing Effective Risk Messages

Witte, Meyer, and Martell (2001) offered a three-step guide to developing effective health risk messages, which is based on the Extended Parallel Process Model (EPPM) presented in Chapter 3, "Linking Health Communication with Theories Informed by Health Communication." The three steps to developing effective health risk messages are:

◆ Step 1: Determine goals and objectives of the health risk message
  ❖ Questions for message designers

- What is the threat you are trying to prevent?
- What is the specific recommended response to avert the threat?
- Who is the specific target audience?

♦ Step 2: Ask target audience members questions to determine:
  ❖ Salient beliefs
  ❖ Recommended responses
  ❖ Salient referents meaning relevant individuals/groups who have influence
  ❖ Communication source/channel preferences
  ❖ Stage of readiness to change behavior (from the Stages of Change Model presented in Chapter 7, "Linking Health Communication with Health Campaign Theories")

♦ Step 3: Develop health risk message(s)
  ❖ Develop prototypical characters of target audience
  ❖ List preferred source(s), channel(s), and message type(s)
  ❖ Identify stage of change of target audience
  ❖ Chart beliefs and referents, from Step 2, to decide if need to reinforce, refute, or introduce new beliefs
  ❖ Develop message(s) using prototypical audience member and other factors determined in Steps 1–3

As you may notice, this step-by-step process to develop effective risk messages is consistent with the messaging process described in the Messaging Model for Health Communication Campaigns (MMHCC) presented in Chapter 8, "Linking Health Communication with Health Campaign Practice." Although this approach to developing risk messages is based on theory and target audience analysis, you may still encounter communication challenges to effective risk messages. However, there are ways to overcome the challenges.

PROFILE

Applying Theory to Balance Risk and Efficacy Messages

Kim Witte, PhD—Professor, Michigan State University

Have you ever wondered why people continue to smoke after being shown graphic pictures of blackened and diseased lungs or why people continue to use tanning beds despite dire warnings about the risk of skin cancer and death? Kim Witte has spent the majority of her career studying how individuals react to fear appeals. Her theory, the Extended Parallel Process Model (EPPM), explains the different processing routes individuals use when they encounter fear-inducing messages. The EPPM is widely applied in the development of health messages as message designers work to balance the arousal of fear with the encouragement of efficacy.

Witte's interest in studying health communication came from a strong desire to help others. She shares a story of being a Brownie when she was a young girl and attending a meeting during which the troupe leader read a story about how elves cleaned the house to help the poor overworked mother and father. So the next day she got up around 4 AM, picked up everything, washed the dishes, and then went back to bed. Witte's career allows her to continue helping others as she works on health campaigns in countries including Kenya, Ethiopia, and the United States. Two of the health issues she addresses are HIV/AIDS and occupational hearing loss.

Witte explains that she did not begin her career out in the field working on large-scale campaigns, but instead began her career systematically testing her ideas in tightly controlled experiments in a lab. As she began to see consistent results she started doing some fieldwork and survey research to confirm her ideas. Through this comprehensive approach she was able to demonstrate the efficacy of her ideas and was offered the opportunity to work on the national level with large-scale campaigns. One of the projects she really enjoyed was utilizing the EPPM to guide entertainment education programs at Johns Hopkins Center for Communication Programs. One of the programs she worked on was a radio drama in Ethiopia titled *Journey of Life*. She and a team of researchers conducted a formative evaluation which the creative team used to develop the script. The research team then conducted a process evaluation and an outcome evaluation. All of the research was guided by theory.

For Witte, health communication focuses more holistically on communication issues including channel, message, feedback, etc., than psychologically-based behavior change campaigns. Also, health communication campaigns can be conducted across different levels of society such as individual, interpersonal, group, and mass media which can lead to more real and sustainable change because all elements of a system are simultaneously addressed.

Communication Challenges to Effective Risk Communication

Communicating risk to the public in an effective way can be very challenging. Some common communication challenges that need to be recognized and addressed when trying to help an audience understand a risk include:

- ◆ Using technical language
- ◆ Unequal comparison of risks
- ◆ Expressing risks in unfamiliar magnitudes
- ◆ Contradictory messages from variety of sources

When experts or those who are familiar with a risk talk about that risk, it may be second nature to use *technical language* or jargon to describe the risk. However, when technical language is unfamiliar to an audience, it can alienate the audience and prevent them from understanding the message and the risk. To illustrate the limitations of technical language, please complete Health Communication Nexus Interlude 9.2.

To complete this Interlude read the following statement describing a health risk to an organization's employees.

*"Employees who fit into the following categories should be aware of an increased susceptibility to contracting methicillin-resistant **Staphylococcus aureus:***

◆ Use invasive devices

◆ Have been treated with fluoroquinolones (ciprofloxacin, ofloxacin or levofloxacin) or cephalosporin

◆ Weakened immune system

◆ Have been a resident at a health-related facility for a duration of fourteen or more days"

As you read the statement again, jot down in your notebook what you think this message means and answer these questions:

◆ Was this message difficult to interpret?

◆ Do you have any questions about what terms or phrases in the statement mean?

◆ Given the meaning of the message that you jotted down, do you think it was an informative and helpful message?

Keep this risk communication example and your reactions to it in mind as we continue to discuss effective risk communication.

You probably had some difficulty understanding the risk message in Health Communication Nexus Interlude 9.2 unless you have an extensive background in medicine and pharmacology. Perhaps you didn't even understand what risk the message was addressing. Now let's consider the same risk communication message that uses common rather than technical language:

"Employees who fit into the following categories should be aware that they are more likely to contract MRSA, a drug-resistant staph infection:

◆ Individuals who are on dialysis or have a catheter or a feeding tube

◆ Individuals who have recently been on an antibiotic

◆ Individuals who have a weakened immune system due to HIV/AIDS or other immune-compromising conditions

◆ Individuals who have had a recent hospital stay over two weeks long"

Was this revised message more understandable? Incorporating more familiar language and fewer technical terms makes the message more accessible to the audience and easier to understand and act upon.

Another common problem in risk communication is making an *unequal comparison of risks*. This occurs when a serious risk is compared to a more common, less serious risk. For example, one might compare the risk of contracting avian influenza virus, also known as bird flu, to that of catching a bad cold. Although both are illnesses, bird flu has more severe consequences, including the possibility of death. In making an unequal comparison of risks, the seriousness of a risk often is diminished or even trivialized.

When discussing risk, people often want to know what their chances are of encountering the risk or what their chances are of being harmed by the risk. The most common way to express a risk is to use percentages such as a .5% chance or numbers such as a 1 in 80,000 chance. However, avoid *expressing risks in unfamiliar magnitudes* that may be too large or too abstract for the audience to comprehend. When communicating risk, the challenge is to present the numbers in a way the audience can easily understand. Instead of stating that there is a 1 in 80,000 chance of contracting a rare cancer, you could ask the audience to picture a college football stadium with the seats full with fans and then explain that one individual in those stadium seats would have this rare form of cancer.

When communicating risk, we must always be aware that individuals live in a media-rich and message-rich society that may result in *contradictory messages from a variety of sources*. This means that individuals rarely use one source for information and the different information sources they use may be communicating different and conflicting messages. For example, consider the issue of vaccines and autism. Government and medical sources, including Centers for Disease Control and Prevention (CDC) and the American Pediatric Association, argue there is no link between vaccines and autism. However, there are several other sources that dispute this claim and believe there is a link between vaccines and autism. Many parents of children with autism, for instance, insist that their children were developing normally prior to receiving their vaccinations.

When physicians and public health officials are trying to ensure that all children are vaccinated properly to protect the children and others against severe illnesses such as rubella or measles, they must try to allay parents' fears that the vaccines harm rather than protect their children. It can be difficult to convince parents that vaccines present minor health risks to children when other sources are informing parents that there are serious health risks associated with vaccinations. Parents are then faced with the task of sifting through the contradictory information to make decisions.

To address the challenge of contradictory information in risk communication, it is important for the source of the information to have high credibility with the audience in order to establish trust. Incorporating comprehensible evidence such as facts and examples to support claims about the magnitude and likelihood of a risk also strengthen the message and increase its acceptability.

ETHICAL DILEMMA ◆ What Would You Do?

Beginning in the late 1990s parents became concerned over a potential link between childhood vaccines and the development of autism. Despite repeated government studies and reports denying a link, parents continue to worry about the risk. The American Academy of Pediatricians takes a firm stance on the issue and clearly recommends vaccinations for all children to prevent the reoccurrence of disease, such as measles and mumps. Some parents decide not to vaccinate their children, believing that the risk for autism outweighs the risk for illness. Some pediatricians refuse to see patients who do not vaccinate, as they consider these children potential risks to other children seen within their medical practice. Based on this information, answer these questions:

◆ Do parents have the right to not vaccinate their children?

◆ Do pediatricians have the right to refuse to see children who are not vaccinated?

◆ If you were a pediatrician, would you refuse to see children who were not vaccinated?

◆ On which ethical orientation presented in Chapter 2, "Linking Health Communication with Ethics," do you base your answers to these questions?

Now that you have a better understanding of risk communication, let's discuss crisis communication and explain how it is different yet related to the concept of risk communication.

Crisis Communication

Crisis communication is a special case of risk communication that occurs when both the hazard and the outrage regarding that hazard are high. When this situation happens, information needs to be presented to the public to both calm fears and provide information on how to minimize the threat of the risk. Examples of a crisis include a disease outbreak, a national disaster, such as a flood or hurricane, or a product recall.

Components of Crisis Communication

When dealing with a crisis, several components of crisis communication need to be taken into account including:

◆ Information content
◆ Media logistics
◆ Audience assessment
◆ Audience involvement
◆ Meta-messages
◆ Organizational issues

As you can surmise from this list, crisis communication involves much more than simply providing information to the public. Accurate *information content* that the public can understand is a vital component of any crisis communication effort. In addition, designers of crisis messages must take into account several other factors as they plan and deliver crisis messages.

A key concern for effective crisis communication is *media logistics*, which refers to how the messages are disseminated through the media. Crisis communication planners must select relevant media outlets such as television, the internet, and radio and determine how to get the message to those outlets. There are a variety of options for message delivery to media outlets, such as issuing a statement or press release, scheduling a press conference, and buying media time. In times of crisis, media outlets must be selected that deliver the messages to the intended audiences as quickly as possible.

When planning crisis messages, an *audience assessment* must be conducted. This analysis involves determining what the audience knows and thinks about the health issue. The messages need to address the audience's needs. Imagine that a city is faced with an outbreak of the measles, for example, and the audience assessment determines that the public is unsure about the specifics of who is susceptible to contracting measles and how measles are spread. Based on this audience assessment, crisis messages must contain basic explanations of the disease, how it is spread, and what precautions the public should take. Additionally, message planners must determine how they receive feedback from the audience once the initial crisis messages are sent to determine *audience involvement*. This feedback is essential to gauge if messages are effective and to determine how subsequent messages need to be adapted to meet the audience's changing needs.

In addition to audience assessment, selecting the content of the messages, and attending to media logistics, crisis communication specialists must be aware of and manage meta-messages. *Meta-messages* refer to the nonverbal elements of the message, such as posture, tone, and facial expressions as well as the location of the message and how many people are available to deliver the message. For example, imagine that an employee at a local fast-food restaurant tested positive for hepatitis A, a very contagious disease. The public needs to be alerted about the situation and assured that the situation is under control. Specific instructions need to be given to those who ate at the restaurant within the past 48 hours. In addition to providing health information, public health officials want to reassure the public that it is now safe to eat at this restaurant. To reinforce this message, the restaurant's communications director could address the media from the restaurant parking lot with a large soda from the restaurant in her hand. These actions by an organization representative add credibility and emphasis to her message that it is safe to eat at the restaurant.

A related concern is to address any internal *organizational issues*. Depending on the situation, an organization may simultaneously be dealing with major internal issues that could hamper crisis communication efforts. Organizations need to recognize these internal issues and conflicts in order to present the most positive and cohesive message about the crisis. Returning to our hepatitis A example, in addition to the public health department and the restaurant releasing pertinent information to the public, the restaurant would need to engage in internal crisis communication as well. In this case, the restaurant examines its procedures and policies for maintaining employee cleanliness as well as the culpability of the organization in the outbreak. There also may be privacy and/or legal issues to protect the infected employee and the organization that need careful consideration.

Waiting until a crisis strikes to determine a crisis communication plan is too late. Because there is much that can be considered in planning for a crisis and in determining how to balance crisis communication and communication about reasonable risks, a set of guidelines for effective risk and crisis communication is presented in the next section.

Guidelines for Effective Crisis Communication

Each crisis situation is unique and calls for distinct communication, but there are some basic guidelines or tips for providing effective crisis communication. These guidelines include:

- Legitimate the public's fears
- Acknowledge any uncertainty
- Establish spokesperson's humanity
- Offer specific actions

First, the public health agency and/or the organization involved in the crisis should *legitimate the public's fears*, even if those fears appear to be unfounded or overreactions. For example, if individuals fear they may develop brain cancer from using a cell phone, this fear should be acknowledged, but then evidence can be used to explain why this fear may be unrealistic. However, it is important not to overly reassure the audience if there is at least some risk involved. Many aspects of life are associated with some reasonable level of risk, even if the risk is minor, and individuals and the public have the right to know about these risks in order to make informed decisions.

Similarly, it is important to *acknowledge any uncertainty* about the crisis. In a crisis situation, there may be many unknowns, which should not be hidden from the public but instead be openly acknowledged. For example, in 2001, shortly after the September 11 attacks on the World Trade Center in New York, the Pentagon in Washington, DC, and Flight 93 in Pennsylvania, letters containing anthrax were mailed to a few television stations and government offices. Anthrax is a deadly bacterium. At least 22 people became seriously ill from exposure to anthrax and five were killed. Early on it was unknown who or what organization was mailing the letters and where the letters were coming from. Although initially hesitant to do so, federal public health and law enforcement officials had to admit there were many unknowns surrounding the case. This was a very scary situation for the public across the United States and many began to fear opening their mail. Eventually, the tainted letters stopped arriving in mailrooms and mailboxes, the fear subsided, and the crisis was averted.

World Trade Center Towers after attack by airplanes on September 11, 2001

© Hubert Boesl/dpa/Corbis

Letter that contained anthrax

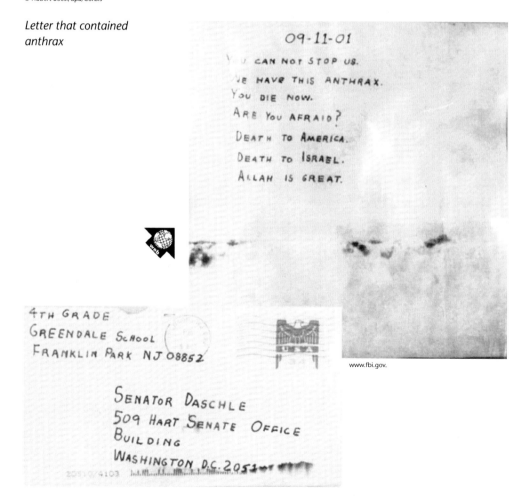

www.fbi.gov.

In communicating during a crisis situation, it is important to establish the spokesperson's humanity. If you are designated as the official spokesperson for the department of health or for your company in a crisis, the public looks to you not only as a source of information but possibly a source of comfort. *Establishing the spokesperson's humanity* means showing compassion and concern for the situation and those affected by it. At times it is appropriate to be emotional and show sadness, although you must always maintain your composure in order to maintain the audience's trust in your abilities to handle the situation. On the other hand, a lack of human emotion in a crisis event could come across as cold and unfeeling. For example, when giving an update on the status of raging wildfires, a fire chief should show sympathy and regret when reporting how many homes were engulfed by the flames. As another example, Mayor of New York City Rudolph Giuliani was praised in the aftermath of 9/11 for his ability to show strength as well as grief and sadness as he addressed the public.

Because people are looking to a spokesperson as a source of information, it is important to *offer specific actions* that people should take. Simply telling people not to worry or to be on alert is not effective in keeping people calm or helping them cope with the crisis. In the anthrax crisis, for example, government officials gave the public specific steps to protect themselves against potential anthrax exposure. This included giving a precise description of anthrax and a list of steps to take if someone encountered a potentially threatening package or letter. These steps included covering the suspicious powder found in the letter or package to avoid stirring it, leaving the area immediately, and contacting the police.

Health risks and health crises are some of the most difficult and frightening issues and events people encounter during their lives. Dealing with people's emotions associated with these health issues and events can be very challenging, however, preparation is essential. In the next section we discuss emotion management in risk communication and crisis communication.

Emotion Management in Risk Communication and Crisis Communication

One of the challenges in both risk communication and crisis communication is contending with the wide variety of emotions that risk or crisis can arouse. Sometimes the goal of communication is to arouse a desired emotion, whereas other times the goal is to minimize an unwanted emotion. Before we further discuss emotion management, please complete Health Communication Nexus Interlude 9.3.

Begin this interlude by taking a few minutes to read the following scenario.

Over the past month there have been an increasing number of reports of attacks and break-ins both on and around the college campus in your community. Two males wearing dark ski masks have been breaking into dorm rooms as well as off-campus residences. Several females reportedly have been sexually assaulted during these break-ins and valuables and cash have been taken. University officials were aware of the reports but did not issue a public statement or warning until recently, citing that public safety officials were unsure if the attacks were related and there was a desire to protect the privacy of those involved. It is believed that the men are still in the area of the campus, and police are searching for any clues as to their identity and whereabouts.

Now take a few more minutes to jot down in your notebook any emotions you would feel if this situation was currently occurring at your school or in your community. Keep these emotions in mind as we discuss the link between the public's emotions and risk and crisis communication.

Following is a list of some of the most common emotions that may need to be addressed and managed by public health and safety officials during risk communication and crisis communication:

◆ Apathy
◆ Fear
◆ Anger
◆ Panic
◆ Misery
◆ Depression

These emotions also may apply to the scenario in Health Communication Nexus Interlude 9.3. Did you include any of these emotions on your list in response to the scenario?

Apathy can be very frustrating to those who are trying to warn members of the public about a potential risk or an impending danger. Members of the public who are *apathetic* do not care or are indifferent about the risk, and therefore are unmotivated to take protective actions. For example, those who try to communicate risk messages regarding potential natural disasters such as hurricanes often encounter citizens who are apathetic to the potential risks. These people may have experienced many false alarms of serious hurricanes that were predicted but never hit land. Others might believe that nature takes its course so they might as well stay put and wait. When officials are trying to evacuate a town, it is difficult to convince apathetic audience members to leave. Apathy also can be seen in those who do not feel as if the risk is personally relevant or who believe they are immune to the risk. In the scenario provided in Health Communication Nexus Interlude 9.3, some may feel they are immune to the risk of being attacked by thieves because they do not fit the profile of those previously attacked.

When confronting an apathetic audience, a risk or crisis communication specialist's goal is to arouse feelings of concern in the audience. To do this, messages must show why a threat is relevant and how ignoring the threat could bring personal harm to an individual or harm to those an individual knows. In the case of the threat of a natural disaster, for example, audience members could be graphically reminded of past disasters during which residents, like themselves, did not evacuate and were seriously endangered or harmed. More specifically, near where the authors of this textbook live in Lafayette, Indiana, the Tippecanoe River flooded twice in 2008, causing serious threat to residents' safety and serious damage to property including the complete loss of many homes. Several residents' safety was compromised when they decided to wait out the floods rather than follow official emergency management agency evacuation orders to leave and stay with relatives or friends or check into a Red Cross shelter. When water rose to a dangerous level after a dam was breached, many residents had to be rescued because they could not escape the flood. In 2009, heavy rains over several days again caused flooding in the same area of the Tippecanoe River but admittedly local officials were better prepared given their crisis experience from the previous year. In addition, media outlets including the local newspaper, the *Journal & Courier,* warned residents about the eminent threat and used recent history to support their warnings to evacuate (Malik, 2009; Scott, 2009a, 2009b). As the newspaper headlines and corresponding stories illustrate (Figure 9.3), the media explained why the threat of flooding was relevant and reminded residents about the unnecessary risk and harm that was caused the previous year when residents ignored warnings and stayed with their homes. This time almost all the residents affected heeded the warnings and left their homes before the situation turned serious and remained away until officials deemed it was safe to return. The newspaper articles in Figure 9.3 reported the floods.

Figure 9.3 ◆ *Local newspaper articles that reported on Tippecanoe River floods.*

In Search of Higher Ground*

Memories of 2008 Floods Still Fresh for Many

DELPHI—After the Tippecanoe River flooded twice in 2008—in January and again in February—Nancy Mesaros' home on Tecumseh Bend Road was so damaged she demolished it.

To prevent the situation from repeating itself, she's in the process of building a new home with cement walls and only a garage on the first floor.

So when the Tippecanoe River started to rise Monday after heavy rains Sunday afternoon and the prediction of more rain coming today, Mesaros went to work.

She wasn't alone. People were being evacuated from their homes near the Oakdale Dam in Carroll County Monday in advance of significant flooding expected in the area today.

*In Search of Higher Ground by Michael Malik, *Journal & Courier,* March 10, 2009. Reprinted by permission of the *Journal & Courier.*

Dave McDowell, director of the Carroll County Emergency Management Agency, said there could be some similarities between this flood and the floods in 2008, which caused widespread damage.

"At least we can get the word out a little bit," McDowell said. "Last year, a lot of us didn't have the experience of a big flood."

John Kwiatkowski, a science officer with the National Weather Service, said the Tippecanoe River Basin, which includes Kosciusko, Marshall, Fulton, Pulaski, White and Tippecanoe counties, would receive as much as two inches of rain by tonight. Rain that falls in that basin flows into the Tippecanoe River.

"Considering the basin is pretty waterlogged, I would think that would jack us up to at least moderate flooding, possibly more," Kwiatkowski said.

Mark Kirby, director of the Tippecanoe County Emergency Management Agency, said the situation was less serious along the Wabash River in Tippecanoe County on Monday.

By Monday night, floodwaters had forced the closure of Indiana 225, which Kirby said will likely remained closed for a week. Indiana 43, north of West Lafayette, also was closed, Indiana State Police said.

"I am cautiously optimistic that the Tippecanoe (River) has pretty much seen its crest," Kirby said. "The Wabash (River) will continue to go up the next couple of days. I think it will crest under 20 feet."

The Wabash River's flood stage is 11 feet. Kirby said more roads will likely be closed if the rain comes as predicted. However, he said, residents will not likely have to be evacuated.

The Wabash River was at slightly more than 18 feet Monday evening, according to the weather service. The service was predicting the river would crest at 21.4 feet Thursday morning, which means Lafayette's Shamrock Park and other low-lying areas would flood.

In Carroll County, efforts to move things to higher ground continued much of Monday along County Road 1225 West and Tecumseh Bend Road.

Water from the Tippecanoe River was flowing through the Oakdale Dam, which is just north of the homes that were being evacuated, at a rate greater than the flood flow rate of 13,000 cubic feet per second. Monday night, the flow was 14,350 cubic feet per second.

By comparison, in February 2008, the highest rate flowing through the Oakdale Dam was nearly 26,000 cubic feet per second.

Mesaros said Monday that she didn't know whether she'd evacuate.

But Mesaros and her neighbor, Jeanne Tucker, were working Monday to move building materials and possessions to the second floor of the home that's still under construction.

"From the 2008 flood, we don't have much left," Mesaros said. "What we do have left we're holding on to—to not lose it, too."

Tucker's home also was hit hard by the 2008 floods, too. Tucker said she and her husband lost everything that was in their house.

Tucker said she worries about flooding every day.

"It scares me," Tucker said. "It really scares me."

'We Are as Prepared as We Can Be'*

DELPHI—People who live along the Tippecanoe River apparently were paying attention, emergency management officials said Tuesday, and had evacuated their homes ahead of a possible flood.

A drive Tuesday afternoon through the Tippecanoe River neighborhoods at Tecumseh Bend, Horseshoe Bend and the area just south of the Oakdale Dam found many empty homes.

More rain was predicted for early today across an already waterlogged Lafayette region and points farther up the river in northern Indiana.

Today could be tough day for the river folks.

Dave McDowell of the Carroll Emergency Management Agency said "people are paying attention now," especially after last year's disastrous flooding. The Tippecanoe River flooded twice during the winter of 2008. McDowell started calling for voluntary evacuations on Monday.

"Pretty much everybody is aware of possible flooding," he said. "Everybody who was going to leave has left.

"For the rest of them, good luck. I don't know what more we can do."

Mark Kirby of the Tippecanoe Management Agency said the Wabash River would likely crest at about 21 feet late tonight or early Thursday.

"I think we are as prepared as we can be' he said late Tuesday afternoon. "If there is a lot of rain north of us, it will affect the Tippecanoe and Wabash."

Residents Read the Signs*

DELPHI—Gloria Clark was taking no chances when the Tippecanoe River started lapping at her home's deck steps just south of Oakdale Dam.

She and her boyfriend evacuated their Carroll County house Monday afternoon to live in an American Red Cross shelter at Assembly of God Church just west of Delphi on U.S. 421.

"It got us by surprise last year," she said of floodwaters that hit in January 2008. "Water was up to my chest, and the sheriff's department rescued us by boat.

"I sat in my sofa Monday and watched the river rise up toward my porch. I decided to take action."

She said some of her neighbors also got out Monday and others were expected to leave Tuesday.

Chris Brady of the Tippecanoe County chapter of the American Red Cross said she and other volunteers are ready for more evacuees. She said parents with four children also checked into the shelter Monday.

"This is a good location for a shelter because we are in the vicinity of the river and we are close to Delphi," she said.

Clark said she has lived at her river home for 20 years and never experienced flooding like she did last year. The river flooded in January and again

*'We Are as Prepared as We Can Be' and, Residents Read the Signs, by Bob Scott, *Journal & Courier*, March 11, 2009. Reprinted by permission of the *Journal & Courier*.

in February 2008. The couple rebuilt with the help of federal money and short-term housing from the Red Cross.

"We got new carpeting, cabinets, drywall and blinds," she said.

She said she has flood insurance this year, but it may not matter if the house is flooded badly.

"I'm negative now," she said. "If it happens two years in a row and does more damage, I will sell the house and never live on a river again."

On the other side of the river from Clark, members of the Ford family calmly fished Tuesday afternoon. Herbert Ford and his brother, Gordon Ford, fished with Gordon's son, Douglas Ford, near riverfront property that's been in the family since the early 1960s.

Four fishing trailers are on the property year-round. Last year, one was damaged severely and has not been repaired.

"If we get two or three inches of rain, we'll be in trouble," said Herbert Ford of Walton.

Gordon Ford of Brookston said, "We came Monday and started putting things up on tables."

The Fords said they monitor the water release rate from the nearby Oakdale Dam. It was about 12,500 cubic feet per second in the afternoon. The flood rate is 13,000 cubic feet per second.

"If it gets to 19,000 cubic feet a second, we'll get water into the trailers," Herbert Ford said.

"Nobody will have to get us. We'll be gone before that."

Red Cross Shelter

The Tippecanoe County chapter of the American Red Cross has set up an emergency shelter in the Assembly of God Church, 9835 U.S. 421, between Delphi and Brookston. For more information, call (555) 182-4466.

Heavy Rains, Evacuations

Heavy rains north of Tippecanoe County late Tuesday led to flash flood warnings in Benton, Jasper and White counties, along with evacuation orders.
The White County Sheriff's Department said evacuations had begun by 11 p.m. in the Diamond Point and Bluewater areas. Lake Arthur Mobile Home Park on the south side of Remington also was evacuated, with residents of the 55 homes transported to the First Christian Church in Remington.

While the forecast calls for mostly sunny skies today and Thursday, flooding along the Wabash and Tippecanoe rivers will continue for several days, the National Weather Service reported. As of late Tuesday, the Tippecanoe River flow at Oakdale Dam exceeded 19,100 cubic feet per second, surpassing Sunday's level and far above 13,000 flood stage.

Road Closings

In Tippecanoe County, Indiana 225 between Indiana 25 and Battle Ground is closed, as is Indiana 43 by Wabash Valley Hospital, north of West Lafayette.

In Carroll County, County Road 1200 is closed and County Road 1225 is expected to be closed.

Ethics Touchstone

Please tease out the three foundational concepts of values, morals, and ethics that we used to define ethics in Chapter 2, "Linking Health Communication with Ethics," after answering these questions:

◆ Do you think choosing to stay in your home is an ethical response to crisis messages in the media, such as flood evacuation warnings, hurricane evacuation orders, and wildfire evacuation orders? Why or why not?

◆ Would you stay or leave your home if there were an evacuation warning or order? Why?

◆ What would it take to change your mind in either direction?

Jot down your responses to the questions in your notebook. Next, think about and write in your notebook how your responses to the questions are based on the following three concepts:

◆ Your values
◆ Your morals
◆ Your ethics

At the opposite end of the continuum from apathy are emotions such as fear. *Fear* is an emotion of distress aroused by the perception or actual threat of impending danger. From the perspective of those developing and delivering risk or crisis messages, fear can be either a desirable or undesirable reaction by an individual or the public. In some cases fear of a risk is desirable because being afraid can motivate individuals to take action. Consider, for example, the risk of skin cancer. Those who fear skin cancer and skin damage caused by overexposure to the sun are more likely to take protective actions, such as wearing sunscreen and a hat to protect their skin from exposure to the sun. However, when an audience is apathetic about skin cancer, the goal of communication efforts may be to raise fear levels to promote action.

There are times, though, when too much fear can have a negative influence. Instead of motivating individuals to address the risk, fear can be paralyzing. For example, in response to fear-inducing messages about skin cancer, individuals experiencing too much fear about the issue may stop leaving the house during daylight hours or obsessively check their skin for signs of irregular moles. As another example, shortly after the terrorist attacks on 9/11, many Americans were paralyzed with fear about experiencing another terrorist attack and avoided traveling and being in large crowded places. In response, several government officials including the then Mayor of New York City Rudolf Giuliani encouraged members of the public through press conferences and interviews with the media to rise above their fears and continue leading their normal lives. One of his central messages was that giving in to the fear was allowing the terrorists to win. Increased security at airports and public places also helped alleviate some of the fear and allowed the country to move forward.

Sometimes a crisis invokes anger in the audience. *Anger* refers to strong feelings of displeasure or hostility that are generated by a real or supposed wrongdoing. Oftentimes this anger is directed toward the source of the crisis or at agencies that are handling the crisis. Anger can be useful in motivating an audience to try and bring about change in a situation, such as demanding more regulation of food products to reduce contamination. However, too much anger or fear resulting from that anger also can distract an audience from dealing with the risk or crisis in a timely manner.

For example, in the aftermath of Hurricane Katrina in 2006, people were very angry at the government's response and handling of relief efforts. Although this anger may have influenced the government to reconsider aspects of the response, it also consumed time and energy and may have caused mistrust of those trying to aid hurricane victims. In particular, displaced residents, as well as those around the country who saw the situation being mishandled, became angry with the Federal Emergency Management Agency (FEMA) and its director Michael Brown. News coverage was dominated by criticisms of the agency and attention was focused on what was being done wrong rather than developing a plan to address the situation. Displaced residents angry with the way they were being treated, including their difficulties accessing social services, were impatient and often unwilling to work cooperatively with local FEMA agents.

When emotions such as anger and fear become too overwhelming, feelings of panic can ensue. *Panic* occurs when an individual or group is faced with an overwhelming fear that leads to hysterical or irrational behavior. Panic tends to spread quickly. Mass panic over a crisis can lead to major unrest and cause people to take actions that may be ineffective. Previously in this chapter we discussed that much was unknown during the anthrax crisis of 2001. The many unknowns led to a high level of fear within the public and in some cases caused panic. Early

Bioterrorism

The deliberate release of viruses, bacteria, germs, or other agents used to cause illness or death in people, animals, or plants. These agents typically are found in nature, but it is possible they could be changed to increase their ability to cause disease, make them resistant to current medicines, or increase their ability to be spread into the environment. Biological agents can be spread through the air, through water, or in food. Terrorists use biological agents because they can be extremely difficult to detect and do not cause illness for several hours to several days. Examples of agents used for bioterrorism are anthrax and smallpox (adapted from Centers for Disease Control and Prevention, www.cdc.gov).

Figure 9.4

on in the crisis, some members of the public rushed to purchase gas masks and people were encouraged to seal windows and vents with duct tape to protect against being exposed to anthrax spores. Eventually, these strategies proved unnecessary and ineffective.

Two other related emotions that communication specialists in risk and crisis situations may need to address are misery and depression. *Misery* refers to a sense of distress or suffering caused by need. Misery can lead to depression. *Depression* is a feeling of prolonged sadness and withdrawal. When a risk or crisis is overwhelming or especially terrible, members of the audience may consider the situation very depressing. Even those not directly involved in the tragedy may experience a sense of misery or become depressed as they watch or hear coverage of the tragedy. Further, those who are depressed may fall into despair and, like those who are apathetic, may have trouble feeling the needed motivation to respond to the crisis.

Now that we discussed many of the possible emotions that can be aroused in crisis situations, return to Health Communication Nexus Interlude 9.3. What were some of the emotions you listed? Would you be fearful of a possible assault on your campus or in your community? Would you be angry with how officials handled the situation? Given the variety of emotions that risk and crisis communication can arouse, it is important to monitor the audience for counterproductive emotions and adapt messages based on the audience's emotional needs. Consequently, a good risk communication or crisis communication plan should contain an audience feedback system.

Now that you understand the intricacies involved with risk communication and crisis communication, we present a list of best practices to apply to crisis situations (Covello, 2003):

◆ Accept and inolve stakeholders as legitimate partners
  ❖ Identify who is affected by the risk or crisis
  ❖ Include them in the decision-making process
◆ Listen
  ❖ Find out audience members' concerns
  ❖ Empathize with their concerns
◆ Be truthful, honest, frank, and open
  ❖ Share all information you have
  ❖ Acknowledge what you do not know
◆ Coordinate, collaborate, and partner with other credible sources
  ❖ Identify sources that have quality information
  ❖ Identify sources trusted by the audience
◆ Meet the needs of the media
  ❖ Be available
  ❖ Keep interviews and statements short and to the point

So far this chapter defined and distinguished between risk and crisis communication. After presenting an exemplar crisis case study, we provide an example of how to apply risk concepts within a service-learning project.

A Crisis Communication Case Study

Tylenol Poisoning

To further illustrate crisis communication, we offer an exemplar case of how crisis communication was effectively used to protect the public and protect an organization's reputation with consumers. In 1982, seven people in the Chicago area died after ingesting Extra-Strength Tylenol capsules that were laced with potassium cyanide. Investigators quickly determined that the poisoning occurred after the production process and it was believed that an individual tampered with packages in stores and added the poison to the capsules.

The knowledge that likely there were additional tainted capsules sold caused many people in the Chicago area, as well as around the United States, to panic. Johnson & Johnson, the manufacturer of Tylenol, immediately issued a nationwide recall of the capsules. In addition, to protect those who already purchased tainted capsules, police cars drove through Chicago streets blasting warnings over loudspeakers. Although this alerted people to the situation, it also caused a near panic in the area. Across the country, many people threw away any Tylenol capsules in their possession. Fortunately, the crisis was contained and no other cases of poisoning were reported.

Even though the poisonings were not the fault of Johnson & Johnson, the company took full responsibility for the situation and immediately took decisive action to prevent further illness and to restore the public's faith in their products. In addition to the massive recall of Tylenol, Johnson & Johnson opened a crisis hotline which provided information about the poisonings, symptoms of cyanide poisoning, and safety measures. Johnson & Johnson's swift and positive reaction not only prevented further harm but also allowed the company to maintain the prominence of its Tylenol brand.

One key to the success of this crisis communication effort was the immediate reaction by both Johnson & Johnson and public officials. The public was updated on the situation and all possible steps were taken to prevent anyone from

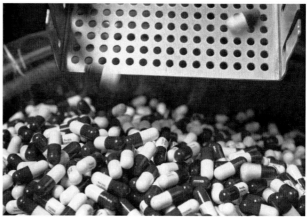

© Leif Skoogfors/CORBIS

consuming tainted capsules. Following the unfortunate tragedy, Johnson & Johnson also made changes to its packaging, creating plastic safety seals to prevent tampering. Eventually, Johnson & Johnson stopped the production of capsules, as it was determined that capsules were too easy to tamper (Benoit & Lindsey, 1987; Snyder, 1983). This Tylenol tampering case is credited with aggressive development of tamper-proof seals on medications.

So given what you know about the Tylenol tampering case and risk and crisis communication, what do you consider the best measure of the effectiveness of the crisis communication employed in this case? Perhaps it's that no additional people were killed after the initial tainting was discovered. Or the fact that Extra-Strength Tylenol remains a successful product for sale on store shelves today. Or that as a result of this case, manufacturers began to more aggressively develop safety-seal packages so that tampering could be determined before the tainted product was ingested. Or that we have an excellent example to illustrate the importance of effective crisis communication to the public's health.

SERVICE-LEARNING APPLICATION

Integrating Multiple Voices in a Campaign Project

In this service-learning application, we describe how the Motorcycle Safety at Purdue (MS@P) campaign developed risk messages about motorcycling for its community audience. While developing risk messages for this campaign, it was important to be mindful of the voices of our target audiences, including motorcyclists, drivers of cars and trucks, and friends and family of motorcyclists, but also the voices of our campaign team members, that is, the service-learning students working on the campaign. Another of the core components of service learning is the inclusion of youth voices in service-learning activities. *Inclusion of youth voices* means that although you may be guided by your instructor and your community partner, your team's ideas and opinions should play a central role in the service-learning activities you engage in from planning, implementing, and evaluating your service-learning experiences (Corporation for National & Community Service, 2010). In other words, service learning is not just going to a community agency and doing a job they ask you to do, such as painting a room or doing some data entry. In authentic service-learning, your input is essential to all aspects of the project.

As a case in point, let's consider how members of the MS@P campaign team worked to design and disseminate risk messages to their target population. Initial needs assessment research prior to launching the MS@P campaign suggested that many preexisting campaign efforts regarding motorcycle safety existed. Those efforts centered around informing those who ride motorcycles or those thinking about riding motorcycles about potential safety risks involved in riding. And even though a primary finding of the needs assessment was that there are other target audiences that need to pay attention to motorcycle safety, including drivers of cars and trucks and friends and family of motorcyclists, motorcyclists still needed to be addressed. The risks of riding a motorcycle include:

◆ Being involved in a crash

◆ Minor injuries (e.g., most road rash)

◆ Serious injury

◆ Death

Upon performing the needs assessment, the MS@P campaign team determined one of their greatest challenges was trying to raise the level of concern about the risks of motorcycling in the target audience of motorcyclists. Early interviews revealed that some motorcyclists were unaware of some of the risks, but many others knew of the risks and had become at least somewhat apathetic about the risks. Motorcyclists' beliefs that either they were immune to the risks or that if they were in a crash it was fate made them an especially challenging audience to approach and persuade about motorcycle safety behaviors.

The needs assessment revealed that the campaign team needed to make several important decisions regarding motorcycle safety messaging for the target audience of motorcyclists including:

◆ Message content

◆ Message design

◆ Channels for dissemination

With respect to *message content*, the campaign team had to determine what risks they wanted to present to the target audience of motorcyclists and what tone and word choices the messages would incorporate. Additionally, the campaign team had to determine what the message designs would look like. *Message design* included decisions about aspects from font style and size on written materials to the color scheme of graphics. Finally, the team needed to determine what *message channels* were most effective for transmitting their risk messages to the target audience of motorcyclists. Each of these messaging decisions involved not only input from the needs assessment, which interviewed target audience members, but also the input or voices of the project teams working on the campaign.

Based on the needs assessment research and their own input, the campaign team created several draft versions of risk messages to appeal to motorcycle riders using different text, tag lines, and with different graphics and color schemes. For three examples of draft messages go to the Web site for this book.

As you can see from these draft messages, the service-learning project team tried to practice the principles of effective risk communication while integrating their unique voices and understanding of the bigger picture of motorcycle safety. Some of the draft messages incorporated a humorous approach and others kept a serious tone. Can you identify which draft messages were meant to be humorous or serious in tone? Also, in order to increase the emotional reaction of this audience, some draft messages included statistics about the number of accidents and deaths each year as well as personalized examples and stories. The campaign team tested these draft messages with a sample of the target audience of motorcyclists by conducting a series of focus groups within their university community. During the focus groups, motorcyclists were asked to express their opinions about the messages and make suggestions for how the messages could be improved. Participants also were asked their opinions on what the best communication channels were for reaching them with these messages.

Based on feedback the campaign team received, coupled with the team's knowledge of risk communication and their own experiences as members of the university community, the campaign team made decisions about what messages to use, how to present those messages, and which channels to use for message dissemination. One of the primary media channels for dissemination of the campaign messages is the campaign MS@P Web site (www.ItInvolvesYou.com). Go to this Web site now to see if you can determine which messages from those draft messages were chosen for further development and which messages were not chosen for further development. Why do you think the messages that do not appear on the Web site were discontinued? To learn more about how the MS@P service-learning campaign team designed the initial messages for the campaign and to see more draft message examples, go to the Web site for this book to read an article about the campaign (Kosmoski, Mattson, & Hall, 2007). In addition to the Web site, the MS@P campaign messages appear through a variety of media outlets around campus, including city buses, the university's cable TV station, digital signs in campus buildings, banner signs around campus, and ads during movies sponsored by the university's student union.

Now that you read about how the campaign team members were involved in all aspects of creating risk messages, think about ways to ensure that your youth voice is being heard as you engage in your own service-learning projects. This is not to say, however, that other voices should not be involved, as the ideas and opinions of your service-learning partners are invaluable. Here are some questions to guide you as you integrate your unique voice and ideas:

◆ What ideas does our service-learning project team have?

◆ What ideas do our service-learning partners have?

◆ Why do we like our service-learning project team's ideas?

◆ What are the benefits of our ideas?

◆ Are there ways to combine our project team's ideas with our service-learning partners' ideas?

◆ Who can we designate as a spokesperson for presenting our ideas to our partners?

In thinking about the various ideas for projects, be sure of what ideas are yours and what ideas come from your partners. It is great to use the ideas of your partners but also be sure to bring your team's ideas to the project. Articulating the benefits and logistics of your ideas goes a long way toward encouraging others to accept your ideas.

Chapter Summary

In this chapter we compared and contrasted risk communication and crisis communication and incorporated several examples. First, we defined and discussed risk communication and the factors that influence individuals' perceptions of risk. Next, we identified the information components to consider when determining effective ways to convey risk. We then considered challenges to risk communication and ways to overcome these challenges. In the second half of the chapter we defined and discussed crisis communication. We outlined messaging components to consider during a crisis along with effective strategies for crisis communication. In addition we covered several emotions aroused during crises and through a case study and a list of best practices offered practical ways to address tensions during crises. We concluded the chapter by emphasizing the role youth voice should play in service-learning projects and we illustrated how students' voices were incorporated into the designs of risk messages for the MS@P campaign.

References

Benoit, W. L., & Lindsey, J. J. (1987). Argument strategies: Antidote to Tylenol's poisoned image. *Journal of the American Forensic Association, 23*, 136–146.

Centers for Disease Control and Prevention (2007). Childhood lead exposure. Retrieved February 21, 2009, from http://www.cdc.gov/Features/ChildhoodLead/.

Corporation for National & Community Service (2010). Learn and Serve America's National Service-Learning Clearinghouse. Retrieved January 12, 2010, from http://www.servicelearning.org.

Covello, V. T. (2003). Best practices in public health risk and crisis communication. *Journal of Health Communication, 8* (Supplement), 5–8.

Dutta-Bergman, M., & Mattson, M. (2006). Decomplexifying communication strategies in response to bioterrorism: Toward a synergistic crisis communication model. In S. Amass, F. A. Bhunia, A. R. Chaturvedi, D. R. Dolk, S. Peeta, & M. J. Atallah (Eds.), *The science of homeland security* (vol. 1, pp. 11–36). West Lafayette, IN: Purdue University Press.

Kosmoski, C. L., Mattson, M., & Hall, J. (2007). Reconsidering motorcycle safety at Purdue: A case study integrating campaign theory and practice. *Cases in Public Health Communication & Marketing, 1*. Available at http://www.gwumc.edu/sphhs/departments/pch/phcm/casesjournal/volume1/peer-reviewed/cases_1_07.cfm.

Malik, M. (2009, March 10). In search of higher ground: Memories of 2008 floods still fresh for many. *Journal & Courier,* pp. B1, B4.

National Highway Transportation Safety Administration (2010). Traffic safety facts 2008: Motorcycles. Retrieved August 9, 2010, from http://www-nrd.nhtsa.dot.gov/pubs/811159.pdf.

National Public Radio (2009). Travel restrictions tighten amid swine flu concerns. Retrieved April 27, 2009, from http://www.npr.org/templates/story/story.php?storyId=103517402.

National Research Council (1989). *Improving risk communication.* Washington, DC: National Academy Press.

National Safety Council (2005). Injury facts. Retrieved March 28, 2009, from www.nsc.org.

Scott, B. (2009a, March 11). Residents read the signs. *Journal & Courier,* p. A6.

Scott, B. (2009b, March 11). "We are as prepared as we can be." *Journal & Courier,* p. A1.

Snyder, L. (1983). An anniversary review and critique: The Tylenol crisis. *Public Relations Review, 9,* 24–34.

Witte, K., Meyer, G., & Martell, D. (2001). *Effective health risk messages: A step-by-step guide.* Thousand Oaks, CA: Sage.

World Net Daily (2007, June 7). China exports lead poisoning: From eye shadow to glazed pottery, products pose danger to U.S. kids. Retrieved August 9, 2010, from http://www.wnd.com/?pageId=41959.

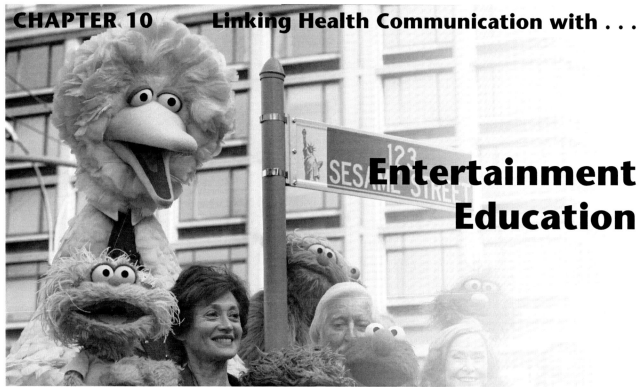

Entertainment Education

© SHANNON STAPLETON/Reuters/CORBIS

Chapter Learning Objectives

◆ Define entertainment education
◆ Review the history of entertainment education
◆ Provide examples of entertainment education
◆ Reiterate the three-step process of creating entertainment education programming
◆ Understand the advantages of entertainment education
◆ Recognize the various formats of entertainment education
◆ Identify opportunities for working in entertainment education
◆ Incorporate reflection questions into service-learning experiences

Chapter Preview

In this chapter we consider the use of entertainment education as a way to educate mass audiences about health issues. We begin by defining entertainment education and reviewing the history of entertainment education within the field of health communication, including examples from around the world. Within the history, we emphasize the important role Miguel Sabido played in creating a formula for entertainment education interventions as well as spreading entertainment education as a communication strategy. Next, the advantages of an entertainment education approach are discussed. This is followed by an overview of the different formats of entertainment education within the United States, including some of the unique challenges faced by entertainment education. We then explore the possibilities of working as a health communication specialist within the entertainment education process. We conclude the chapter with a service-learning application that highlights developing a video game and the role of student reflection.

In the image that begins this chapter, do you recognize some of the characters from the cast of one of the longest running and most popular children's television shows? In November 2009, *Sesame Street* celebrated its 40th birthday. For 40 years this television program has been teaching children numbers, letters, shapes, and colors, as well as tackling important life skills, such as basic hygiene, safety, and sharing. *Sesame Street* is unique in that it was the first children's program specifically designed to educate and entertain. In fact, many credit *Sesame Street* with starting the edutainment movement, as people quickly realized that children could learn from watching television programs. In this chapter we consider how the ideas of edutainment are used to promote health.

Entertainment Education Defined

Entertainment education (EE) is defined as "the process of purposely designing and implementing a media message both to entertain and to educate, in order to increase audience members' knowledge about an education issue, create favorable attitudes, and change overt behavior" (Singhal & Rogers, 1999, p. 9). In other words, entertainment education is the insertion of health-related storylines into entertainment programs. For example, you may recall watching a favorite television show in which a character dealt with an illness such as cancer or a stroke. Although these storylines add an element of drama to a program and provide entertainment, they also can contain important medical, disease-prevention, and health-promotion information.

History of Entertainment Education

One of the first examples of entertainment education programming was a Peruvian soap opera, *Simplemente Maria,* which first aired in 1969. The main character in the soap opera was Maria, who used her skills with a Singer sewing machine to rise above her humble beginnings and become rich and famous. Although it was not purposeful, the messages in the show regarding sewing and adult literacy led numerous women in Spanish-speaking countries to enroll in sewing and adult literacy classes. Additionally, sales of Singer sewing machines rose dramatically. Female viewers were so enthralled with Maria and her story that they were inspired to emulate her and copy her actions to better their lives.

The idea of purposely embedding health or socially-conscious messages into entertainment programs then took root in the early 1970s (Singhal & Rogers, 1999). Inspired by the success of *Simplemente Maria*, Mexican director Miguel Sabido began creating telenovelas. *Telenovelas* are serial dramas similar to soap operas designed to promote prosocial ideas such as family planning and improved literacy in Latin American countries. These programs were very successful in promoting these prosocial behaviors. For example, Mexico experienced a 34% decline in the birth rate during the years that a telenovela focused on family planning methods aired. As Sabido worked on his telenovelas, he developed a basic three-step process for creating programs that would be entertaining and educational.

Three-Step Process for Creating Entertainment Education

The first step in the process of creating entertainment education is to decide on a central value to promote, such as family planning, preventing domestic violence, or gender equality. Plotlines for the show are written to emphasize examples of people accepting or rejecting the central value and the outcomes of their attitudes and behaviors regarding that central value.

The second step is to create a cast of characters. Sabido was very specific regarding the types of and numbers of characters. All of his dramas contained three types of characters including:

◆ Positive role models
◆ Transitional characters
◆ Negative role models

His formula also specifies how many of each character there needs to be in the program. In every program there needs to be at least four positive characters, four corresponding negative characters, and three transitional characters. Figure 10.1 illustrates the character roles and their relationships in the three-step process to EE.

Positive role models in EE are the characters who already accept and live by the central value. These characters are shown engaging in behaviors that embrace the central value and are immediately rewarded for their actions. These characters are happy, find love, and are successful. The *negative role models* in EE are the characters who reject the central value and act and think in ways directly against the central value. Whenever the characters go against the central value, they are immediately punished. These characters are unhappy, unhealthy, unloved, and needy.

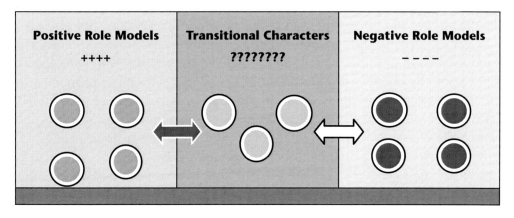

Figure 10.1 ◆ *Character roles and relationships in three-step process of entertainment education*

Perhaps the most interesting characters in Sabido's formula are the transitional characters. The *transitional characters* are those in the middle who are considering changing and adopting the central value. As the formula indicates, there are three transitional characters. One of the transitional characters adopts the central value about one-third of the way through the program and is immediately rewarded. The second transitional character takes longer to decide and adopts the central value about two-thirds of the way through the program and then is rewarded. The third character decides to reject the central value at the end of the program and is severely punished, often through death. The audience is most likely to identify with the transitional characters. The goal is to have the audience model the characters who accept the central value of the program.

The third step in Sabido's process involves establishing an efficient production system for creating the telenovelas in order to keep the initiative cost-effective. The telenovelas Sabido created ran from one to two years. This was a long enough timeframe to develop the storyline and have the audience become invested in the characters and stories. It also was a short enough timeframe to wrap up the stories so the audience could see how each character's situation ended.

Hum Log

Due to the success of telenovelas, the concept of using entertainment media to improve health and promote health-related behaviors quickly spread. In 1984, India premiered its first television soap opera, *Hum Log*, based on the ideas and concepts of Sabido and EE. *Hum Log* portrayed a middle-class Indian family and their daily interactions and struggles. Presented as an entertainment program, the episodes also included prosocial and pro-health messages and themes about issues such as family planning, gender equality, and national integration. One of the unique features of *Hum Log* occurred at the end of each episode, when a famous Indian actor, Ashok Kumar, came on and discussed the episode and provided some general questions for the audience to think about. This prologue served as a catalyst for viewers to connect the program with their lives. The show was widely successful, and on average 50 million viewers tuned in for each episode. In some villages, nearly 50% of the residents watched the program each week.

Diffusion of Innovations

Another influential person in entertainment education was Everett Rogers. In Chapter 3, "Linking Health Communication with Theories Informed by Health Communication," we considered this scholar and his research with Diffusion of Innovations theory. Rogers realized that EE initiatives were a novel phenomenon within which he could apply the concepts of his theory. Together with Arvind Singhal, he wrote *Entertainment-Education: A Communication Strategy for Social Change* (1999), which contains many examples and ideas for implementing EE initiatives. Because entertainment education was a relatively new approach to health communication, Rogers studied how this approach diffused information about various health issues through various relevant audiences.

EE programs still are used frequently in developing countries with limited media resources. In countries such as India and Peru, access to media is quite limited and oftentimes the government controls the media. In situations like these, health educators can create new or adapt existing programs to promote health or social issues. And because few competing media options are available, those conducting EE efforts can be relatively certain that their messages are reaching the target audiences.

EE programming continues throughout the world. Researchers and practitioners are learning more about the theory behind EE and its success in order to create better and more effective programs. Advances in technology are introducing new avenues for EE, such as internet and computer applications.

Now that you understand the history of EE and how it developed as an area of health communication research and practice, we highlight some other examples of international EE initiatives.

International Entertainment Education Examples

One very successful entertainment education intervention took place in rural India. From 1996 to 1998, All Indian Radio (AIR) aired episodes of the serial radio drama *Tinka Tinka Sukh*, meaning "little steps to a better life" (Papa, Singhal, & Papa, 2006; Sood, 2002). The series followed the lives of three families in a northern Indian village. One family with a son portrayed the ideal, progressive family, while another family with a son was depicted as troubled and still practicing traditional customs of the village. A third family, comprising a widow with three daughters, was the transitional family and was used to illustrate many issues facing women in a patriarchal society, including their roles and pressures to be married. Health issues addressed in the program included HIV, women's health, dowry practices, and natural resource conservation.

The show was very popular in Hindi-speaking areas of India. Each episode ended with a song composed and sung by a popular Bollywood singer to reinforce the message of the episode. In addition, famous singers and musicians frequently contributed other songs to the program. The characters were so popular with the audience that the local broadcasting offices were flooded with letters from listeners that commented on the issues raised by the show and complimented the show creators for openly addressing those issues. Nearly 40 million listeners tuned in to the bimonthly program. Follow-up studies of the audience found that 81% of those listeners identified with the characters and thought about the issues raised after listening to the program (Sood, 2002).

Another example of a successful EE program was *Makgabaneng*, meaning "a rocky place." This radio serial aired in Botswana and was designed to promote HIV/AIDS prevention. Botswana is an African country hit hard by the HIV/AIDS epidemic. In 2004, it was estimated that nearly 25% of the population was HIV-positive, although many of those infected were unaware of their HIV-positive status. *Makgabaneng* was developed in conjunction with other outreach programs to encourage Botswanans to protect themselves and others against the spread of HIV. Some of the specific HIV issues the program addressed were getting tested for HIV, reducing mother-to-child-transmission of the disease, and reducing the stigma associated with having HIV.

Two episodes of the program aired each week and audiences listened and learned how various characters dealt with HIV-related issues. For example, one storyline featured a man and woman who went together to get tested for HIV prior to getting married. Another storyline focused on a man who had an affair and contracted HIV. His wife, who tested negative for HIV, remained with him after his diagnosis, as he promised to remain faithful. Post-viewing assessments found positive reactions and changes in audience members' intentions to get tested and enroll in mother-to-child-transmission programs, willingness to talk to partners about HIV tests and status, and an overall reduction in the stigma attached to an HIV-positive status (Kuhlmann et al., 2008; Pappas-DeLuca et al., 2008).

From this discussion of EE, you probably surmised that EE is a popular way of disseminating health information and health messages to mass audiences. However, some have critiqued EE interventions for their top-down approach. Generally it is the government and health-related agencies that determine the health issues addressed and then they design the programs with very little input from the target population (Dutta, 2006). Despite criticisms, however, the use of EE continues to grow. The question then is, why is EE so popular? In the next section we consider some of the advantages of EE, which may explain its wide use.

Advantages of Entertainment Education

Johns Hopkins School of Public Health developed the following list of advantages of entertainment education, called the "Nine Ps" (de Fossard & Lande, 2008).

- Pervasive—forms of entertainment are everywhere
- Popular—audiences enjoy and keep tuning in to good programs
- Personal—individuals identify with characters and storylines
- Participatory—audiences play a role in development of EE by responding to programs
- Passionate—storylines appeal to emotions
- Persuasive—individuals learn from role models
- Practical—infrastructure for production is in place
- Profitable—attractive to potential producers and sponsors
- Proven effective—evidence that EE leads to behavior change

As this list suggests, there are several noted advantages to embedding health messages into entertainment programs rather than relying on typical health education and promotion efforts such as running a public service announcement or distributing pamphlets at physicians' offices. One of the greatest advantages of EE is that the *persuasion is not explicit,* meaning that the audience may not be aware that they are being persuaded. Green and Brock (2000) described how viewers become absorbed in reading a book or watching a television show and are transported into the fictional world of the story. In this transported state individuals are more likely to be influenced by the happenings in the narrative partly because the logical side of their brain that develops counter-arguments is not as active.

EE is effective in that it helps to overcome the initial resistance individuals have to persuasive efforts. Many people inherently bristle at being told what to do. So, for example, a public service announcement from the National Drug Council encouraging teenagers to avoid using drugs may be perceived as controlling and may not be very effective. However, a storyline integrated into a popular TV show, such as *Beverly Hills 90210,* about a character sent to a drug rehabilitation center is not considered a direct attempt to tell the viewer what to do, and might be more palatable and acceptable to the audience. When persuasive efforts are subtle, innate resistance to persuasion might not be activated (Moyer-Gusé & Nabi, 2010).

Another advantage of entertainment education is that *audience members may develop vicarious relationships with the characters* in a show. If viewers develop sympathy or a liking for certain characters in an entertainment program, they may be more likely to follow these characters' actions. Sometimes the liking goes even further and audience members develop parasocial relationships with characters. A *parasocial relationship* is a one-sided relationship between an audience member and a character or celebrity (Giles, 2002). Audience members may feel as if they are friends with celebrities or characters despite never meeting or interacting with them. Those who develop parasocial relationships with program characters are more likely to be influenced by those characters, similar to the way individuals are more easily influenced by their friends. Before we further explore the impact of parasocial relationships, please take a few minutes to complete Health Communication Nexus Interlude 10.1.

One of the key factors that influences the development of parasocial relationships is identification with the characters. Identification is the process of seeing similarities between oneself and others. In the context of entertainment education, *identification* is defined as "an emotional and cognitive process whereby a viewer takes on the role of a character in a narrative" (Moyer-Gusé, 2008). When audience members identify with characters, they envision aspects of themselves in the characters and therefore can imagine themselves taking similar actions and behaving in similar ways. Think about the character you selected for Health Communication Nexus Interlude 10.1. In what ways do you identify with the character you selected?

EE programs also tend to *engage the audience emotionally*. When audiences feel emotional about an issue, they tend to be more involved with the issue and more likely to take action regarding the issue. When health issues are placed within a drama, audiences can get caught up in the emotions of the characters. For example, a fictional portrayal of a young child struggling with autism may evoke feelings of sympathy and frustration much more readily than a brochure listing symptoms of autism.

Consider, as another example, a research project that studied an audience's emotional responses to an EE television program designed to promote cornea donation. Prior to the show, most of the audience was unaware of the issue. Those who became the most emotionally involved with the storyline and the characters also were most involved with the issue of cornea donation after viewing the program (Hyuhn-Suhck & Kang, 2008).

Audiences also *model the behavior of the characters* in EE programs. According to Bandura's (1977) Social Cognitive Theory, individuals learn by observing the actions of others and the consequences of those actions. Additionally, observing others increases perceptions of self-efficacy, as seeing behaviors enacted by others gives individuals a more concrete idea of what needs to be done and how to do it. Therefore, characters in EE programs can serve as excellent role models of desired health behaviors. For example, audience members may have the opportunity to watch a character on an EE program turn down an offer to use illicit drugs or accept an opportunity to go to a clinic for an HIV test. Consequently, those audience members may feel better prepared and able to perform those actions themselves.

EE also provides *reach and access to desired populations*. When messages are intended for mass audiences such as entire countries, a popular entertainment program can easily access much of that audience. In countries where media options are limited, an entertaining radio or television program attracts a lot of attention. Even in countries where media options are not so limited, entertainment programming has a broad reach. Studies show that nearly 88% of Americans garner health-related information from television (Henry J. Kaiser Family Foundation, 2004), making television an efficient medium for providing accurate and useful health information to many. In addition, entertainment media is an effective way to make contact with hard-to-reach audiences, such as adolescents who may not be interested in attending a seminar or listening to a speaker but welcome the opportunity to watch a television program.

This approach to reaching target audience members also is *cost-effective*. If health messages are embedded into an existing program, the cost may be little more than the time spent consulting with the media producers and writers. Messages airing on entertainment programs essentially are free or very low cost. Even when a radio or television program is created and produced for the purpose of health education, because it has such wide reach it can be less expensive than distributing literature or disseminating on-site health interventions in communities. In some cases EE is more cost-effective than incorporating media in more traditional ways during a health campaign because the reach of EE interventions tends to be wider and these programs tend to have more positive results. So even though

PROFILE

Developing an Appreciation for Entertainment Education

Arvind Singhal, PhD—
Samuel Shirley and Edna Holt Marston Endowed Professor,
University of Texas, El Paso

Arvind Singhal's interest in studying communication and entertainment education took root in his early childhood. Each day his grandfather would offer him a reward for writing and reading a page in English, a page in Hindi, and completing ten math problems. These early exercises developed into a love of writing and orating. After completing his Bachelor's degree in Engineering in India, Singhal came to the United States to achieve a graduate degree in radio, television, video, and film production. The more he studied production the more he developed an interest in what meanings audience members derived from media content and the ways content influences audiences. Entertainment education provided an excellent avenue for bringing his interests in media and communication together.

After earning his doctoral degree in the Annenberg School of Communication at the University of Southern California, Singhal has spent his career working on a variety of entertainment education projects in the United States and some two dozen countries in Asia, Africa, and Latin America. These projects focused on health issues such as HIV/AIDS, child sex-trafficking, female genital mutilation, and reproductive health and population control. Singhal published ten books including *Entertainment-Education: A Communication Strategy for Social Change* which he co-authored with Everett Rogers. His research program provides additional understanding of key theories and frameworks such as Diffusion of Innovations, Social Cognitive Theory, Social Marketing, and Communication and Social Change.

More recently, Singhal has been studying the concept of positive deviance and its contribution to social change. *Positive deviance* (PD) is the idea that in all communities there are individuals who are able to find unique and creative ways to overcome common obstacles and challenges. These individuals are deviants because they are not the norm and they are positive as they are able to thrive despite facing overwhelming odds. Singhal and his collaborators identify positive deviance in community settings and then facilitate processes to amplify these strategies within the community. For example, in a PD project in Vietnam dealing with childhood malnutrition, there were some poor and under-resourced parents who engaged in certain practices that kept their children healthy. For example, some parents added tiny shrimps and crabs from rice paddies and others added greens of sweet potato plants. Such practices were uncommon but helped keep their children healthy. Once these positively-deviant practices were identified, they could be amplified to other community members.

When thinking about health and improving health issues, Singhal considers communication an essential factor that can play a unique role in improving health at micro-levels and macro-levels. Singhal prefers to define health broadly as a combination of biomedical, psychological, and socio-cultural factors. Entertainment education initiatives provide ways to improve the health and wellbeing of individuals by transforming the health of larger units such as families, villages, and communities. Specifically, entertainment programs can expose communities to new ideas and help reduce some of the stigma and discrimination often associated with serious health conditions, such as HIV/AIDS. By improving the social ethic of care even sick individuals can experience better lives.

the overall cost of creating an EE program initially may be higher, the cost per person reached by an EE intervention actually is lower (Sood & Nambiar, 2006).

Entertainment Education in the United States

Entertainment Education on Television

In the United States, entertainment education interventions developed and are used somewhat differently. This is the case in part because most media is owned by private industry, so programming is not as easily and consistently controlled by a central source, such as the government. The majority of television stations are privately owned and are for-profit entities. Two notable exceptions are the Public Broadcasting Service (PBS), which has aired *Sesame Street* for the past 40 years, and the Cable-Satellite Public Affairs Network (C-SPAN) which airs continuous coverage of government proceedings and public affairs programs. Consequently, rather than developing programs specifically to promote prosocial or health behaviors, prosocial and health messages and storylines are embedded into existing programs.

One of the first examples of EE in the United States was on the popular television show *Happy Days*. An episode featured one of the lead characters, Fonzie, going to the library to get a library card. Afterwards, libraries reported a dramatic increase in library card applications as American youth tried to emulate one of their beloved characters.

One of the earliest coordinated EE efforts was the Harvard Alcohol Project, which was spearheaded by the Harvard School of Public Health's Center for Health Communication (Harvard School of Public Health, 2009). From 1988 to 1992, more than 160 prime-time television programs included storylines and messages promoting the use of a designated driver. At the time, "designated driver" was not part of common language, so the term was diffused through popular media to educate the public about what a designated driver is and to encourage those who were out drinking alcohol to appoint a designated driver.

Popular television shows at the time, including *Cheers*, *L.A. Law*, and *The Cosby Show*, devoted entire programs to the issue. Shows focused on what the responsibilities of a designated driver are, why designated drivers are needed, and the potential consequences of drinking and driving. The Harvard Alcohol Project was considered to be quite successful, and the term *designated driver* was added to the *Random House Webster's College Dictionary* in 1991 and is defined as selecting an individual to remain sober in order to drive companions. Ninety percent of Americans reported being familiar with the campaign and gave it an 81% favorability rating. The campaign also was successful in changing behaviors as 52% of Americans under age 30 reported taking on the role of designated driver (Harvard School of Public Health, 2009).

Since this initial EE effort in the United States, more and more health issues are addressed in television programs. Perhaps one of the most noted examples from the past ten years is the medical drama *ER*. *ER* is set in the emergency room of a county hospital in Chicago and follows the complex relationships of the physicians and nurses who work there. Each episode highlights the cases of a wide variety of patients

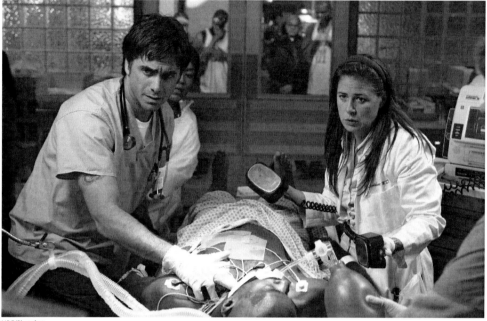

Physicians on the medical drama ER *tend to a patient. During its run,* ER *provided information about a variety of health issues, from sexual assault to drug abuse.*

NBC/Photofest

while providing an extensive amount of information to the public regarding medical conditions and treatments.

A specific example of *ER*'s impact as a source of education is a 1997 episode in which a female college student came into the emergency room explaining that she had been drugged and date-raped. During the course of this episode, viewers saw how a rape kit was used to collect evidence and saw the woman being offered an emergency contraceptive in the form of taking several birth control pills to reduce her chance of becoming pregnant as a result of the attack. At the time this episode aired, emergency contraceptive pills, sometimes referred to as morning-after pills, were not familiar to the public. Consequently, awareness of the use of birth control pills as a form of emergency contraception increased 17% among viewers (Piotrow, Kincaid, Rimon, Rinehart, & Samson, 1997).

Another example from *ER* is a minor storyline that involved an African American teenager who was being treated for burns he received while working. Testing done in the emergency room revealed that the teen, who was overweight, had high blood pressure. His treating physicians recommended that he eat more fruits and vegetables and get more exercise. The recommendation to eat more fruits and vegetables was intended to promote and reinforce the message of the national 5 A Day campaign. Follow-up research reported positive changes in the viewing audience's behaviors related to diet and exercise (Valente et al., 2007). It is important to note that these positive changes occurred from just one minor storyline on the program. Due to these encouraging possible outcomes for influencing viewers, a wide variety of health issues from autism to measles are incorporated into popular entertainment programs.

However, one of the challenges of EE efforts in the United States is *media saturation,* meaning the plethora of media options available to target audiences.

Between cable, broadcast programs, and the internet, the public has multiple options for how to spend viewing time, which can limit the reach of a program. To think more about some of the challenges of conducting EE interventions in the United States, please complete Health Communication Nexus Interlude 10.2.

Health Communication Nexus Interlude 10.2

For this interlude, imagine that you are working on a campaign in the United States to raise awareness among teens about the potential dangers of the "choking game." The choking game, also referred to as the fainting game, involves teens intentionally choking themselves or each other with hands, belts, or other types of ropes to temporarily cut off oxygen supply to the brain. Teens try to stop the choking right before they pass out so that the blocked blood rushes to the brain, which leads to the sensation of being high. Each episode of the choking game kills brain cells that have been deprived of oxygen for too long. Teens who choke themselves run the risk of passing out before removing the belt or rope and then hanging themselves, which can lead to permanent brain damage or death. Teens who engage in the choking game often do so because it is a way to get high without using drugs or alcohol.

You decided to use an EE strategy for your health campaign about the dangers of the choking game. Based on what you know about the target audience, teens ages 13–16, and the current media environment in the United States, jot down in your notebook the television shows you would recommend for potentially embedding campaign messages and storylines and then answer these questions:

◆ Why did you choose these shows?

◆ How would the storylines fit into the shows?

◆ What limitations do you anticipate with your EE strategy?

One strategy for overcoming the challenge of media saturation is to place similar messages on multiple programs. This allows for wider reach and reinforces the message when programs have overlapping audiences (Hether, Huang, Beck, Murphy, & Valente, 2008). In 2005, the medical dramas *ER* and *Grey's Anatomy* both featured a storyline regarding breast cancer and genetic testing for the BRCA1 gene mutation. Having the BRCA1 gene mutation drastically increases a woman's risk for developing breast cancer, as up to 85% of those with the mutation develop breast cancer. Both programs addressed the issue of inherited risk for breast cancer, the importance of mammograms, and the use of prophylactic mastectomies to prevent the development of cancer. Analysis of the outcomes associated with viewing the programs revealed that viewers who saw both programs changed in more behavioral and attitude outcomes than those who saw only one program

(Hether, Huang, Beck, Murphy, & Valente, 2008). During Health Communication Nexus Interlude 10.2, as you were thinking about potential television programs to include storylines about the health concerns of the choking game, did you suggest multiple programs? If you did, it was a good strategy, as different programs could reach a wider variety of teens and reinforce your message.

Media scholar John Sherry (2002) studied the difficulties media saturation presents to EE efforts in the United States. He proposed suggestions for overcoming those challenges based on some leading media effects theories. He too recommends placing similar messages on a variety of programs in order to create a cultivation effect. *Cultivation theory* posits that media effects come from repeated exposure to messages over time (Gerbner, Gross, Morgan, & Signorielli, 1986; Signorielli & Morgan, 1990). A message on a single episode of one program most likely does not bring about sustained changes in behaviors and attitudes. However, the same message on multiple programs over time may work its way into the minds of audience members and influence their attitudes and behaviors. Sherry also pointed to the need to appreciate individual differences in audience members and target messages accordingly. It is highly unlikely that one theme on one program reaches all of an intended audience. Therefore, audiences need to be properly segmented, so that EE initiatives and messages are targeted toward the smaller audience segments.

So far, the EE examples we reviewed from the United States were on television programs. Television is a popular choice for EE efforts because television is so popular in the United States and the format allows for narratives that engage both the visual and auditory senses. With so many media options, though, EE initiatives expanded to other media, including popular magazines and video games.

Entertainment Education in Magazines

Another entertainment education venue for health-related messages is popular magazines. Take, for example, women's and teen's magazines such as *Cosmopolitan*, *Ladies' Home Journal*, *Marie Claire*, and *Seventeen*. Women and teens read these magazines for fun but also consider them important sources of information for topics and issues from fashion to health (Hust & Andsager, 2003; Park, 2005). For example, while reading a magazine for fun as they are waiting for an appointment to start or during a break at work, women can learn about the newest hair products as well as tips for eating a healthier diet or fitting exercise into their daily routine. Some men's magazines, such as *Men's Health,* also mix entertainment articles with important health information on topics such as nutrition, exercise, and sexual health.

Because health messages are couched beside and/or within entertainment articles, readers might be more likely to read this information than they would other health promotion literature, such as brochures and posters. The articles are written in an attention-getting or entertaining way and often contain personal stories. In addition, these articles usually are presented in an easy-to-follow format, such as a bulleted list or a series of tips, making the information more palatable.

Research on the coverage of health issues in popular magazines provides mixed reviews. On the positive side, research found that important health issues, including breast cancer, menopause, skin cancer, and safer sex, are being covered, which at a minimum raises awareness about these health issues. On the negative side, though, researchers discovered that often health-related messages are presented among many unhealthy messages. For example, an analysis of magazine coverage of skin cancer found that although many magazines recommended actions to reduce the risk for skin cancer, these messages often were accompanied by pictures of women in swimsuits lounging by the pool in direct sunlight. Magazines also highlighted the benefits of appearing tanned, such as looking thinner and healthier (Cho, Hall, Kosmoski, Fox, & Mastin, 2010). These conflicting messages could minimize the pro-health messages audiences are reading.

Entertainment Education in Gaming

Games provide another opportunity for entertainment education. Gaming in all its forms, from paper-and-pencil games to board games to video and computer games, is growing in popularity. In particular, video and computer games really took off over the past few years. The Federation of American Scientists (2005) reported these statistics about video and computer gaming in the United States:

◆ 50% of Americans play video and/or computer games
◆ 75% of heads of households game
◆ Children ages 8 to 18 play video and/or computer games 50 minutes per day
◆ Adult females play video and/or computer games 7.4 hours per week
◆ Adult males play video and/or computer games 7.6 hours per week

Given the number of people gaming and the amount of time they spend gaming, some communication specialists have turned to video and computer games to spread health messages. Research across studies demonstrated mostly positive health-related behavior changes as a result of playing video games (Baranowski, Buday, Thompson, & Baranowski, 2008; Peng, 2009).

The development of games for educational purposes is known as serious gaming. The term *serious games* was defined, even before the widespread use of computers, as games that have an explicit and carefully thought out educational purpose and are not intended to be played primarily for amusement (Abt, 1970). More recently, Zyda (2005) defined a serious game as "a mental contest, played with a computer in accordance with specific rules, that uses entertainment to further government or corporate training, education, health, public policy, and strategic communication objectives" (p. 26).

One of the basic concepts underlying serious gaming is that although players are learning, they are entertained while they learn. Serious games assume that play is an important aspect of human development, maturation, and learning. Based on this assumption, serious games are designed with the intention of improving some specific aspect of learning (Derryberry, 2007). Consider, for example, Nintendo Wii's popular game series Wii Fit. Users are playing a game while performing various aerobic, strengthening, and stretching exercises, including boxing, yoga, and step aerobics. Along the way, the game offers tips and suggestions for adopting a healthier lifestyle, such as drinking enough water each day and incorporating physical activity into a daily routine. The idea behind the game is that because users have fun doing it, they are more likely to exercise and learn healthier strategies.

As alluded to in Zyda's (2005) definition of a serious game, the growing field of serious gaming creates games for various industry sectors, including education, health, corporate training, and the military. The Serious Games Initiative was formed to coordinate efforts and encourage the expansion of the serious gaming industry. The Games for Health sector of the Serious Games Initiative specifically focuses on how gaming can improve the quality of health care as well as promote the health of the public. To learn more about the Serious Games Initiative and its activities, visit the Web site for this book. 🎮

One avenue for serious game distribution is the internet and, in particular, social networking sites. This is an emerging area of the gaming industry as more and more individuals, including those who are not in the typical gamer demographic, such as women and older adults, enjoy playing internet-based games. An example of this type of serious game is the *Fantastic Food Challenge* developed at Michigan State University in partnership with the U.S. Food and Drug Administration (FDA). The various games in the challenge include information about nutrition, food safety, food preparation, and comparison pricing. One of the games requires players to sort foods into the correct food group, such as grains or fats, by dropping food into the correct container, while another game challenges players to find the cheapest product (Silk et al., 2008). Wii Fit also is an example of a serious game that incorporates the internet to encourage and expand use of its fitness system. As these examples illustrate, distributing serious games through the internet and social networking sites allows an ever-expanding opportunity for health communication.

Entertainment Education and Decision Aids

Another new avenue for entertainment education is the development of entertainment-based decision aids. *Decision aids* are tools to help patients make health-related decisions. Decision aids contain information on different options available and the outcomes associated with those options. *Edutainment decision aids* combine the entertaining aspects of soap operas and dramas with interactive elements on computers to assist users in making health-related decisions. Users can watch video clips, answer questions, and work through the decision aid to learn more about the decisions they need to make. These decision aids are unique, not because they are interactive, but because they include entertaining storylines to engage the user and present essential health information.

Jibaja-Weiss and Volk (2007) developed the *Edutainment Decision Aid Model* (EDAM) to guide the process of creating entertaining, computer-based, health-related decision aids. Specifically, these aids are designed to assist populations with lower levels of health literacy. For a more detailed discussion of health literacy, refer to Chapter 4, "Linking Health Communication with Patient Interaction."

An example of an edutainment decision aid is a tool that was created to assist women in making breast cancer treatment decisions. One focus of the decision aid was to help women in clarifying their values and seeing how those values related to their decisions. As women worked through the model, different issues related to surgical treatment for breast cancer were represented as pieces of jewelry. Women were able to collect or flag the issues they found most relevant by placing them in the jewelry box. Initial testing of the model found positive results, as women with lower health literacy found the tool useful and were able to identify the key concerns that would inform their decisions (Jibaja-Weiss et al., 2006).

Another example is a decision aid created to assist men in making decisions about prostate cancer screening (Jibaja-Weiss et al., 2006). The decision aid featured clips of a drama in which a male character, who matched the user's ethnicity, went through the process of deciding to have prostate cancer screening. Between clips, men participated in interactive segments. Testing of the aid found that those with higher levels of health literacy thought the tool was too lengthy and preferred a list of facts. Those with lower levels of health literacy, however, enjoyed the aid and requested more information after they completed it. These examples suggest that EE decision aids offer an opportunity for assisting those with health literacy challenges to process and understand relevant health information.

Careers in Entertainment Education

As you read about entertainment education, you may be wondering how those who work in health communication are involved in creating and producing EE programs, or more specifically how you become involved in this health communication career path. One way is to work for an international agency or non-governmental organization (NGO) that develops EE programs. For example, the NGO Minga Perú produces participatory health education programming in the Peruvian Amazon. A health communication specialist working for this NGO might be involved in producing *Bienvenida Salud*, a radio program designed to increase audience members' knowledge about reproductive health, sexual rights, and gender equality.

If you prefer to work in the United States, the situation is somewhat different. In the United States, it is more challenging to influence what the entertainment industry produces because the media is not controlled by the government. Rarely you find an entire program for adolescents or adults that is explicitly designed for educational purposes. Instead, health messages are embedded into programs being created. One way to become involved in the process is to become a health communication specialist and work toward getting accurate and relevant health messages into currently available entertainment programming.

One key role of a health communication specialist is to *advocate* for health issues, which means persuading entertainment producers to include health-related storylines in their programs. This could involve projects such as recommending storylines to program writers, pitching ideas to television producers, or suggesting feature stories on health conditions or health issues to popular magazines or trade journals. For example, a health communication specialist may pitch an idea for a feature story on men battling testicular cancer to the popular *Men's Health* magazine. One of the main challenges to effectively pitching ideas and storylines to the media is having the appropriate contacts within media organizations.

Health-related storylines are popular in many types of media programs, from soap operas to prime-time dramas, due to the dramatic nature of health and illness. Medical dramas such as *ER* and *Grey's Anatomy* are popular formats and provide an immeasurable amount of information about health issues, so health communication specialists work to ensure that the health messages presented during these programs are accurate and helpful to audiences.

Because many viewers use entertainment media as a primary source for health information, health communication specialists often advocate for accuracy in the portrayal of health issues by serving as consultants to the entertainment industry.

Media consultants with expertise on relevant health issues read over scripts and provide on-site advice to actors in an effort to make the portrayal of physicians and patients as realistic as possible. For example, the Fox medical drama *House* has a team of technical consultants on its staff to help ensure that the show portrays its baffling medical mysteries as accurately as possible. Initially Dr. David Foster worked as a part-time consultant for the show until he accepted a full-time position on the writing staff. His extensive experience at Harvard's Beth Israel Deaconess Medical Center and his work with the Harvard School of Public Health as well as his previous consultation for the programs *Gideon's Crossing* and *Law and Order* made him an excellent fit for the show's writing team.

Another way that accurate information is provided to the media is through fact sheets created by Centers for Disease Control and Prevention (CDC). Health communication specialists are involved in creating and disseminating these fact sheets. These reference sheets are downloadable from CDC's Web site. The fact sheets provide basic information about various health issues, including, causes, treatments, and ways of prevention. These fact sheets also may include sample storylines to inspire media writers, producers, and directors. For example, a media release from the National Institute of Occupational Health and Safety (NIOSH) illustrates how this CDC-affiliated agency partnered with Telemundo, a United States television network that broadcasts in Spanish, to include workplace safety messages in its prime-time telenovela, *Pecados Ajenos*. The media release also serves as a fact sheet about workplace safety in the construction industry.

Hollywood, Health & Society (HH&S), a program of the University of Southern California's Annenberg Norman Lear Center, serves Hollywood's writers and producers as a single access point to medical experts, information, and script ideas. Writers and producers contact HH&S to request an answer to a specific health question or a more extensive consultation. HH&S also partners with the entertainment industry to provide additional services and programs, such as hotlines, Web sites, Facebook, and Twitter, so viewers of media programming can have health-related questions answered and find credible sources of health information during and after a program airs. The organization also publishes a quarterly newsletter, *Real to Reel,* which updates producers and writers about current health issues around the country. Another important activity of HH&S is conducting ongoing research projects to learn more about how television and film influence audiences and change the knowledge, attitudes, and behaviors of viewers.

Hollywood & Health Society logo. For more information, visit their Web site.

Since 2000, in conjunction with CDC, Hollywood, Health & Society has hosted the Sentinel for Health Awards to recognize exemplary TV health storylines. These annual awards are given to writers who excel in writing scripts that motivate and inform the public about serious health issues. In 2010, finalists for the awards included episodes of *Law & Order: Special Victims Unit* concerning the global issue of violence against women, *Army Wives* for a diabetes storyline, and *Grey's Anatomy* for an episode highlighting the obesity epidemic. Hollywood, Health & Society Director Sandra de Castro Buffington said, "The Sentinel for Health Awards give us a chance to shine a spotlight on the world's master storytellers who use their power not only to write compelling shows, but also to educate viewers about lifesaving health topics."

Another agency instrumental in providing accurate health information to Hollywood is Advocates for Youth (for a link to their Web site with more information, visit the Web site for this book), which has run The Media Project since 1980. The primary goal of The Media Project is to have accurate, health-promoting sexual messages for teenagers included in popular television programs. The Media Project offers a free helpline which assists Hollywood producers and writers by providing them with research and up-to-date information about sexual and reproductive health issues. Each year, the helpline gets more than 100 requests for assistance. Shows that used the helpline to create education storylines include *Felicity, Dawson's Creek, Strong Medicine, ER,* and *Moesha.* For example, in an episode of *Felicity,* a television drama about the main character Felicity's journey through college, she visited the campus health center during her freshman year to learn about her birth control options. During the episode, Felicity also watched a demonstration of how to properly put on a condom.

In addition to its helpline, The Media Project also hosts periodic information briefings for the entertainment industry during which panelists provide insight into some of the most pressing sexual health issues facing teens and the concerns involved with addressing those issues on television. Past briefings have addressed the controversy over abstinence-only versus comprehensive sexual education in schools, and the challenges of being a gay teenager. Transcripts of the briefings and panel discussions are available on The Media Project Web site.

The Media Project branched out into advocacy as it fights for open and honest portrayals of sexual and reproductive health issues on television. With strict regulations from the Federal Communications Commission (FCC) regarding appropriate content on television, some networks, producers, and shows are concerned about showing information and storylines that could be considered too graphic or inappropriate for television audiences. Other shows may worry about being offensive and losing commercial sponsors. The Media Project Web site provides links for the public to easily write to and commend television programs that are willing to show honest portrayals of teenage sexuality. They also work on

ETHICAL DILEMMA ◆ What Would You Do?

Imagine you are the producer of a popular television program with a target audience of teens ages 13–18. You are approached by The Media Project about the possibility of running a storyline about the morning-after pill and its availability over the counter for those older than 17. Now answer these questions:

◆ Do you have any concerns about portraying this storyline on your show?

◆ Do you think teens should have direct access to this information?

◆ Would you have any concerns that this storyline might promote risky sexual behaviors or encourage abortions?

◆ After wrestling with these questions, would you agree to produce the storyline? Why or why not?

circulating petitions and lobbying lawmakers to maintain the discussion of sexuality and health on television.

Now that we covered the basics of entertainment education and included several international and domestic examples of EE along with ways to work in the entertainment industry to promote EE, we present a service-learning application about how a health communication campaign is branching out into EE. This application emphasizes the important role of reflection in service-learning projects.

SERVICE-LEARNING APPLICATION:

Integrating Gaming with Reflection

In this service-learning application, we describe a project associated with the Motorcycle Safety at Purdue (MS@P) campaign that integrates entertainment education and gaming. As we describe this project, we emphasize one of the key components of any service-learning project—critical reflection. *Critical reflection* is defined as a continual interweaving of thinking and doing (Schön, 1983). In other words, critical reflection is the process of considering and deriving meaning from your activities. It is through reflection that you and your project team both individually and as a team consider links between what you're learning from books and in class and your service-learning project. During the reflection process you also consider what you did well as well as what you could improve or change. Reflection is not simply a recounting of what was done, but instead involves serious thought about why the service was done and what the service means (Corporation for National & Community Service, 2010). Next we present an EE example that developed from the MS@P campaign and illustrate how reflection was incorporated into this project.

As we mentioned previously in this chapter, gaming and social networks are very popular and can be incorporated into health communication initiatives. The service-learning class described in this example is developing a prototype game for Facebook users while also teaching students about interdisciplinary aspects of game development and health advocacy in a virtual community. The project was initiated through a small seed grant. After reading the abstract from the grant proposal, you are asked to brainstorm ways that you could gather with other students to develop a serious game to address a health issue in your community. In addition you are encouraged to incorporate reflection into your serious game project ideas by considering several reflection questions.

Serious Game

◆ A game that has an explicit and carefully thought out educational purpose and is not intended to be played primarily for amusement (Abt, 1970).

◆ "[A] mental contest, played with a computer in accordance with specific rules, that uses entertainment to further government or corporate training, education, health, public policy, and strategic communication objectives" (Zyda, 2005, p. 26).

Project Abstract: Interdisciplinary Game Design for Advocacy Course

This project brings together faculty and students from Liberal Arts and Computer Technology to forward both the storyline and the technological design of a serious game to promote motorcycle safety in a university community. The course addresses a community need to improve traffic safety so is service-learning oriented and engages students beyond the classroom. Such an undertaking requires the participation of experts and partners in several complementary areas. Three faculty members with expertise in this and other public health campaigns, game narrative, and computer technology will design and team-teach this innovative course. Because the course product is the design of a prototype Facebook game, relevant community partners, such as law enforcement and a nonprofit motorcycle driver training program, will participate in each phase of the process from testing game story concepts to beta testing the prototype game.

The topic of motorcycle safety was chosen for the prototype game because prior needs assessment research suggested that given the thrill-seeking nature of its target audiences in a university community, a local motorcycle safety campaign would benefit from the popularity of video gaming technology. However, a serious game distributed via a social network site would be most appropriate because this approach to gaming goes beyond current video games that simply race motorcycles for entertainment value toward a game that promotes learning strategies for motorcycle safety while appealing to players' sense of adventure and participation in social networks. Currently no such serious game exists. This course format could be adapted to meet other community needs.

Students should expect the following outcomes from the course:

◆ Learn about and become comfortable with the underlying assumptions of other disciplines and learn to work with people from other disciplinary perspectives to accomplish a goal.

◆ Understand the role of cutting-edge serious gaming technology in educating relevant publics about motorcycle safety (and other community) issues.

◆ Learn to identify community needs and build interdisciplinary project teams to meet those needs.

◆ Complete a serious gaming project that can be highlighted in a professional portfolio.

In addition to a series of quizzes that measure student comprehension of course material, an integral part of course assessment is individual and project team reflection. Within biweekly team progress reports and workshopping of game story ideas, students respond to four reflection questions linking course content to students' service-learning experiences. Example reflection prompts (Ash & Clayton, 2009) include:

◆ Since our last progress report, I/we have learned that . . .

◆ I/we learned this when . . .

◆ This learning experience matters because . . .

◆ In light of this learning experience I/we will . . .

Brainstorming Serious Game Project Ideas

Now that you reviewed the abstract from the example proposal, brainstorm a list of serious game ideas that you'd like to develop with friends, fellow students, and community partners. Remember that each game idea needs to engage a physical and/or virtual community while addressing a health issue.

Reflection Questions to Consider

As you work on your service-learning project ideas, it is important to periodically reflect on what you are doing and why you are doing it. Reflection should not take place only when your project is completed but should occur throughout all phases from idea formation to conclusion. Here are some questions to guide your reflection process:

◆ What impact do you think your project will have?

◆ What needs does your project meet?

◆ Why do those needs exist?

◆ What factors contribute to the problem you addressed?

◆ What surprises you about your project?

◆ How do your thoughts about the project relate to what you're learning in class?

◆ How does your experience differ from what you're learning in class?

◆ What was the best part about your project? Why?

◆ What was the worst part about your project? Why?

This list is just to get you started. Any questions that lead you and your project team to think more deeply about your service and the larger world, as well as the course content, are great questions to use.

Chapter Summary

In this chapter we considered utilizing entertainment education as a mass communication avenue for communication about health issues. We began by defining EE and reviewing the history of EE, including the important role Miguel Sabido played in creating a formula for EE interventions. We provided both international and domestic examples of EE to point out both advantages of EE and challenges to EE efforts. The chapter also highlighted other media formats that feature EE, including magazines and video games. The chapter then described some opportunities for health communication specialists within the field of EE. Finally, we emphasized the role of reflection in service learning and read how reflection questions were incorporated into a serious game project for the MS@P campaign.

References

Abt, C. C. (1970). *Serious games*. New York: Viking.

Ash, S. L., & Clayton, P. H. (2009). Generating, deepening, and documenting learning: The power of critical reflection in applied learning. *Journal of Applied Learning in Higher Education, 1*, 25–48.

Bandura, A. (1977). *Social learning theory*. Englewood Cliffs, NJ: Prentice Hall.

Baranowski, T., Buday, R., Thompson, D. I., & Baranowski, J. (2008). Playing for real: Video games and stories for health-related behavior change. *American Journal of Preventive Medicine, 34*, 74–82.

Cho, H., Hall, J. G., Kosmoski, C., Fox, R. L., & Mastin, T. (2010). Tanning, skin cancer risk, and prevention: A content analysis of eight popular magazines that target female readers, 1997–2006. *Health Communication, 25*, 1–10.

Corporation for National & Community Service (2010). Learn and Serve America's National Service-Learning Clearinghouse. Retrieved January 12, 2010, from http://www.servicelearning.org.

de Fossard, E., & Lande, R. (2008). *Entertainment-education for better health*. Baltimore, MD: Johns Hopkins Bloomberg School of Public Health.

Derryberry, A. (2007). *Serious games: Online games for learning*. Unpublished manuscript.

Dutta, M. J. (2006). Theoretical approaches to entertainment education campaigns: A subaltern critique. *Health Communication, 20*, 221–231.

Federation of American Scientists (2005, October 25). *Summit on educational games: Harnessing the power of video games for learning*. Paper presented at the The Summit on Educational Games, Washington, DC.

Gerbner, G., Gross, L., Morgan, M., & Signorielli, N. (1986). Living with television: The dynamics of the cultivation process. In J. Byant & D. Zillmann (Eds.), *Perspectives on media effects* (pp. 17–40). Mahwah, NJ: Erlbaum.

Giles, D. C. (2002). Parasocial interaction: A review of the literature and a model for future research. *Media Psychology, 4*, 279–305.

Green, M. C., & Brock, T. C. (2000). The role of transportation in the persuasiveness of public narratives. *Journal of Personality and Social Psychology, 79*, 701–721.

Harvard School of Public Health (2009). Center for Health Communication: Harvard Alcohol Project. Retrieved May 18, 2009, from http://www.hsph.harvard.edu/research/chc/harvard–alcohol–project/.

Henry J. Kaiser Family Foundation (2004). Entertainment education and health in the United States. Retrieved May 20, 2009, from http://www.kff.org/entmedia/loader.cfm?url=/commonspot/security/getfile.cfm&PageID=34381.

Hether, H. J., Huang, G. C., Beck, V., Murphy, S. T., & Valente, T. W. (2008). Entertainment-education in a media-saturated environment: Examining the impact of single and multiple exposures to breast cancer storylines on two popular medical dramas. *Journal of Health Communication, 13*, 808–823.

Hust, S. J. T., & Andsager, J. L. (2003). Medicalization vs. adaptive models?: Sense-making in magazine framing of menopause. *Women & Health, 38*, 101–122.

Hyuhn-Suhck, B., & Kang, S. (2008). The influence of viewing an entertainment-education program on cornea donation intention: A test of the theory of planned behavior. *Health Communication, 23*, 87–95.

Jibaja-Weiss, M. L., & Volk, R. J. (2007). Utilizing computerized entertainment education in the development of decision aids for lower literate and naive computer users. *Journal of Health Communication, 12*, 681–697.

Jibaja-Weiss, M. L., Volk, R. J., Friedman, L. C., Granchi, T. S., Neff, N. E., Spann, S. J., et al. (2006). Preliminary testing of a just-in-time, user-defined values clarification exercise to aid lower literate women in making informed breast cancer treatment decisions. *Health Expectations, 9*, 218–231.

Kuhlmann, A. K. S., Kraft, J. M., Galavotti, C., Creek, T. L., Mooki, M., & Ntumy, R. (2008). Radio role models for the prevention of mother-to-child transmission of HIV and HIV testing among pregnant women in Botswana. *Health Promotion International, 23*, 260–268.

Moyer-Gusé, E. (2008). Toward a theory of entertainment persuasion: Explaining the persuasive effects of entertainment-education messages. *Communication Theory, 18*, 407–425.

Moyer-Gusé, E., & Nabi, R. L. (2010). Explaining the effects of narrative in an entertainment television program: Overcoming resistance to persuasion. *Human Communication Research, 36*, 26–52.

Papa, M. J., Singhal, A., & Papa, W. H. (2006). *Organizing for social change: A dialectic journey of theory and praxis*. Thousand Oaks, CA: Sage.

Pappas-DeLuca, K. A., Kraft, J. M., Galavotti, C., Warner, L., Mooki, M., Hastings, P., et al. (2008). Entertainment-eduction radio scrial drama and outcomes related to HIV testing in Botswana. *AIDS Education & Prevention, 20*, 486–503.

Park, S. (2005). The influence of presumed media influence on women's desire to be thin. *Communication Research, 32*, 594–614.

Peng, W. (2009). Design and evaluation of a computer game to promote a healthy diet for young adults. *Health Communication, 24*, 115–127.

Piotrow, P. T., Kincaid, D. L., Rimon, J. G., Rinehart, W., & Samson, K. (1997). *Health communication: Lessons from family planning and reproductive health*. Westport, CT: Praeger.

Rubin, A. M., & Perse, E. M. (1987). Audience activity and soap opera involvement: A uses and effects investigation. *Human Communication Research, 14*, 246–268.

Schön, D. A. (1983). *The reflective practitioner: How professionals think in action*. New York: Basic Books.

Sherry, J. L. (2002). Media saturation and entertainment-education. *Communication Theory, 12*, 206–224.

Signorielli, N., & Morgan, M. (Eds.). (1990). *Cultivation analysis: New directions in media effects research*. Thousand Oaks, CA: Sage.

Silk, K. J., Sherry, J., Winn, B., Keesecker, N., Horodyński, M., & Sayir, A. (2008). Increasing nutrition literacy: Testing the effectiveness of print, Web site, and game modalities. *Journal of Nutrition Education & Behavior, 40*, 3–10.

Singhal, A., & Rogers, E. M. (1999). *Entertainment-education: A communication strategy for social change.* Mahwah, NJ: Lawrence Erlbaum.

Sood, S. (2002). Audience involvement and entertainment-education. *Communication Theory, 12,* 153–172.

Sood, S., & Nambiar, D. (2006). Comparative cost-effectiveness of the components of a behavior change communication campaign on HIV/AIDS in North India. *Journal of Health Communication, 11,* 143–162.

Valente, T. W., Murphy, S., Huang, G., Gusek, J., Greene, J., & Beck, V. (2007). Evaluating a minor storyline on *ER* about teen obesity, hypertension, and 5 A Day. *Journal of Health Communication, 12,* 551–566.

Zyda, M. (2005). From visual simulation to virtual reality to games. *Computer, 38*(9), 25–32.

© Bettmann/CORBIS

Chapter Learning Objectives

◆ Define media within the context of health communication
◆ Discuss the role of media in contemporary society
◆ Explain the notion that media messages are social constructions
◆ Compare and contrast Agenda-Setting Theory and Media Framing Theory
◆ Elucidate the link between media literacy and media advocacy
◆ List the four steps of media advocacy planning
◆ Match the appropriate media with the media advocacy situation
◆ Provide an example of a media advocacy initiative

Chapter Preview

This chapter focuses on issues surrounding the intersection of health communication and media. We first present a definition of media followed by a discussion of the role media play in contemporary society. Next, we explain that media messages are social constructions meaning they are created by people and often are economically and/or politically motivated. After these initial sections, the theoretical foundations of health communication and the media in Agenda-Setting Theory and Media Framing Theory are covered including assumptions associated with each theory and research stemming from these theories. We then turn to a discussion of the active role consumers can play in accessing, processing, analyzing and influencing the ways in which health information is presented in the media through media literacy and media advocacy. Finally, in the service-learning application we consider an example of media advocacy by illustrating how a series of project teams is funding, creating, producing, evaluating, and reflecting upon a public service announcement for a health communication campaign.

Do you ever watch *The Dr. Oz Show?* If not, go to this book's Web site to view the show's Web page. Do you think this television show or its Web site are examples of health communication in the media? Why or why not? Television shows and Web sites are two forms of media that distribute health information in a public or mass communication context. What other forms of media shape our meanings of health and/or illness and disease? To spark your thinking about health communication and media, please complete Health Communication Nexus Interlude 11.1.

Health Communication Nexus Interlude 11.1

In your notebook make a list of all forms of media you can think of that may contain health messages. Next to each form of media you thought of, jot down a specific example of that form of media. Keep your list nearby because we return to it throughout this chapter.

Defining Media

For our purposes, *media* is defined within health as a medium or channel of communication that reaches many people and has the potential to broadly influence people about health. Media has many goals from entertaining to educating. Media not only conveys but also shapes public opinion. Those working in the media sift through and interpret information for the public. As we learned in Chapter 1, "Introducing Health as Communication Nexus," the media is part of the public or mass communication context.

We live in a media-rich society. The list of media you created in Health Communication Nexus Interlude 11.1 illustrates the wide variety of media available. In your list of media examples, you likely included media such as television, the internet, smart phones, PDAs, magazines, and advertisements. Our media-rich society means that media is an omnipresent and a constant source for all kinds of health-related images and information. For example, *The Dr. Oz Show* and Web site provide a plethora of health information and many persuasive health messages. This television show and Web site represent just two ways that media are used in health communication and health promotion. If you click and scroll through *The Dr. Oz Show* Web site you are exposed to many health messages about a wide variety of current topics. At the same time, other forms of media also are rife with health information and persuasive messages about healthy and unhealthy options. All of these forms of media about health issues make for an interesting, challenging, and/or sometimes overwhelming communication environment.

Role of Media in Contemporary Society

As we already mentioned, media plays an omnipresent role in society. Media is everywhere. In other words, the influence of media is all around us and influences many aspects of our lives including our health. You probably noticed the ubiquitous nature of media when you were completing Health Communication Nexus Interlude 11.1. From your textbook about health communication, to the music you may be listening to as you read and take notes, to the internet where you may have purchased your textbook or even found the music you're listening to, media is involved. Media connects individuals with the world around them and assists in the formation and development of communities. Although word of mouth is still among the most powerful forms of communication, media assists in making exchange of information instantaneous.

Individuals working in the media, including writers, journalists, producers, directors, and even actors, interpret information for audiences. They sort through information about issues, organize information, and communicate information either allowing audience members to form their own opinions or persuading audience members of a certain point of view. For example, a National Public Radio (2010) story told of a woman faced with the knowledge that she is a carrier of a rare genetic disease she could pass to her sons. She and her husband decided to pursue having biological children despite knowing she is a carrier. Upon learning that their unborn baby inherited the disorder, she and her husband decided to abort the child. The journalist who interviewed this woman simply described their story, leaving the audience to decide what they thought about the couple's decisions in this case.

Now that we defined the term media, you thought about the forms of media that convey health messages, and we considered the role of media in contemporary society, the question is: Does media help or hinder health communication? According to prominent scholars of health communication and the media, the answer to this question creates a paradox. Although the media represents a viable

ETHICAL DILEMMA ◆ What Would You Do?

Go to the National Public Radio (NPR) story at their Web site, which is linked from the Web site for this book, and after listening to the story answer these questions:

◆ Do you agree with the couple's decision to have biological children despite their knowledge that she is a carrier of a rare genetic disease? Why or why not?

◆ Do you agree with the couple's decision to abort their baby because he likely would have the genetic disease?

◆ On which ethical orientation from Chapter 2, "Linking Health Communication with Ethics," do you base your answers to the previous two questions?

◆ Do you think NPR was neutral or biased in presenting this story?

◆ Did NPR's coverage of this story influence your reaction to the story and your responses to these questions?

opportunity to disseminate health information and influence health behavior, it also is part of the problem with miscommunication of health issues (Schwitzer, 2009; Wallack, Dorfman, Jernigan, & Themba, 1993). Throughout this chapter we further consider this question about whether media helps or hinders effective health communication. And in doing so, hopefully you formulate your own unique response to the question including strategies for how to access and evaluate health messages.

Media Messages Are Social Constructions

As we continue to ponder the links between health communication and media, it is important to keep in mind that media messages are social constructions and often the construction of media messages is an economic and political process (Share, 2009). This means that health messages presented by media really are not neutral because media are not transparent conveyers of information. Instead, the meanings associated with messages we experience through media outlets are negotiated between senders and receivers of those messages. Although creators of media messages are representing a point of view which contains biases, receivers of media messages also are involved in the process by assigning meaning to what is seen and/or heard.

Theoretical Foundations of Health Communication and Media

Media can be an effective way to raise awareness and stimulate interest about health issues and health risks (Freimuth, Linnan, & Potter, 2000). However, in addition to raising awareness, media sources may unduly influence not only what health issues we think about but how we think about and behave relative to those health issues (Kline, 2003). Two theories address this link between media and health communication and are described in the next sections.

Agenda-Setting Theory

The first theory, Agenda-Setting Theory, was proposed by McCombs and Shaw (1972) to explain the influence media have on setting the public agenda. According to *Agenda-Setting Theory*, through coverage of certain topics and issues, media essentially tell the public what topics and issues to think about, but not necessarily how to think about those topics and issues. Research shows that issues discussed in the media are the most prominently thought about issues by the public (Feeley & Vincent, 2007; Groshek, 2008; Miller & Wanta, 1996; Roberts, Wanta, & Dzwo, 2002). Perhaps the earliest research that attempted to establish the agenda-setting role of the media regarding health behaviors was conducted by Pierce, Dwyer, Chamberlain, Aldrich, and Shelley (1987) who noted the "possible importance of an agenda-setting role for the mass media in promoting change" (p. 816) among smokers targeted in an anti-smoking campaign. In this study smokers were more likely to report intentions to change their smoking status if they perceived smoking as a community health problem based on media messages in addition to having personal health beliefs about the negative effects of smoking. This was among the first studies to report an interaction between health beliefs and social influence imposed by media.

Media Framing Theory

The second theory, Media Framing Theory, stems from the concept of agenda setting but extends even further in its explanation of the influence media has in shaping our ideas and opinions about health issues. This extended explanation emerged when researchers discovered that focusing only on media's transfer of an issue's salience or importance to the public was limited. Instead, these researchers argued that media not only influences what topics people think about and discuss but also how people think about those topics, thus "framing" issues for the public (Iyengar, Peters, & Kinder, 1982). *Media Framing Theory* considers how issues are portrayed in popular media and posits that media not only sets the public agenda, but also dictates how the public should think about issues based on the ways media frame issues. Media framing literature largely explains the role of the news media not just in amplifying issues, but also in defining issues for the public, thereby expanding agenda setting from merely drawing attention to a topic to actually articulating and influencing points of view regarding that topic (Weaver, 2007).

The frames around an issue influence the extent of attention received by the issue, the ways in which the public discuss the issue, the perceptions of risk, the attitudes toward the issue, and the ways in which the public behaves at the individual, interpersonal, and collective levels. Frames are critical in influencing the climate of perceived risk around an issue and in drawing attention to possible courses of action in response to an issue. In their project about how women's magazines framed breast cancer, Andsager and Powers (1999) defined *framing* as the "selection and emphasis of certain aspects of issues" (p. 531). The media performs a gatekeeping or monitoring function by framing issues using reporting priorities, such as taking a particular angle on an issue because it garners the most impact or attention for the media outlet, rather than necessarily providing the most clear and accurate information for the public. So, for example, by continually showing underwater video of gushing oil caused by the 2010 British Petroleum (BP) oil rig explosion and oil spill in the Gulf Coast, some wondered if the media was hyping aspects of the spill for economic and political attention. If so, this approach may have provided inaccurate and harmful information about the region associated with the spill (Goldberg, 2010; Mayo, 2010).

Research on the gatekeeping function of media reveals that reporters and editors institute a set of shared news values when determining priorities for newsworthiness. These news values, or priorities, typically include prominence, human interest, conflict, novelty, timeliness, and proximity or local appeal (Gans, 1979). For example, Wallington, Blake, Taylor-Clark, and Viswanath (2010) found that in the realm of health communication, health reporters and editors working for small media organizations were significantly less likely to use government scientists and officials or university-based scientists or researchers as sources of information compared with reporters and editors working for larger organizations. Respondents from small media organizations also were significantly less likely than those from large organizations to believe that disseminating new and accurate information is important. In addition, small organization respondents were 40% less likely to say that controversial news is an important angle to pursue. Journalists who focus only on one subject are found mostly in larger media organizations that can afford larger staffs and resources for reporting, whereas reporters in smaller media organizations often cover multiple subject areas or beats and may be less able to specialize in any particular subject. This may in turn influence their perceptions about the importance of providing new and accurate health information.

Research on Agenda Setting and Media Framing

Evidence of agenda setting and media framing was discovered through research projects about a variety of health issues. Several of these media studies focused on women's health issues. For example, systematic analyses of newspaper and television news stories about human papilloma virus (HPV) in the United States found that information provided about HPV not always was accurate and often failed to include basic facts that women want to know, such as information about transmission (Anhang, Stryker, Wright, & Goldie, 2004; Calloway, Jorgensen, Saraiya, & Tsui, 2006). In an analysis of HPV messages presented in the British national press, Forster, Wardle, Stephenson, and Waller (2010) indicated that newspapers provide parents with broadly positive descriptive norms about vaccination, however, the concern that adolescents engage in risky sexual behaviors following HPV vaccination is regularly discussed in the national press and has the potential to increase parents' apprehension about vaccination.

In a study about breast cancer, Nekhlyudov, Ross-Degnan, and Fletcher (2003) found that although women preferred breast cancer screening information be supplied by a primary care provider, their health care providers actually played a limited role in information provision. Instead most information came from mass media sources. However, information from mass media was found to lead to distorted perceptions of breast cancer. Media observers such as Paulos (1995) also discussed how anecdotes and reporting practices lead media consumers to make false inferences of cancer risk. On the positive side, findings from a study by Andsager and Powers (1999) suggested that women's magazines framed breast cancer through personal stories and in terms of risk factors and ways of coping with the disease. The researchers concluded that these frames may offer readers viable ways to make sense of the issue of breast cancer. Relatedly, Kline (1999) argued that media coverage of women's health issues, particularly breast cancer, has the ability to empower or disempower women in the decisions they make about treatment options. In her rhetorical analysis of over 300 popular media accounts about the practice of breast self-examination (BSE) to prevent breast cancer, women were sometimes blamed and chastised for not doing their part to reduce the incidence of breast cancer by performing BSE. So by covering and framing health messages in certain ways, media can have both a positive and negative influence on what we think about, and how we think about and respond to breast cancer and related issues.

With respect to another women's health issue, Shoebridge and Steed (1999) found that magazine coverage of menopause used the themes of disease and dysfunction. These themes reinforced menopause as a negative health condition rather than a natural aspect of the aging process (for other example studies, read Carlson & Holm, 1997; Lyons & Griffin, 2003; MacDonald, 2005).

Several other researchers examine how various health issues are covered by media and the impact that coverage has on the public's feelings about their health and health care decisions. Regarding the controversial topic of organ donation, through analysis of newspaper articles in high-circulation newspapers over a two-year period, Feeley and Vincent (2007) found there were significantly more positive than negative or neutral stories about organ and tissue donation. Further, the researchers determined that there seemed to be a link between media coverage of organ and tissue donation and the public's positive attitude toward organ and tissue donation. In particular, Agenda-Setting Theory seemed to explain why some minority groups who have a lower level of newspaper readership also were less likely to favor organ and tissue donation.

Another study of the framing of organ donation in media went the next step to answer the question, if so many people have a positive attitude toward organ donation, why when asked to make a decision about donating the organ of a loved one did only 30% to 50% agree? The researchers (Morgan, Harrison, Chewning, Davis, & DiCorcia, 2007) examined entertainment shows on network television over two years. These shows occurred during both prime-time and daytime hours. Prime-time shows included *ER*, *Law & Order*, and *Seinfeld*. Daytime shows included soap operas such as *One Life to Live*. Analysis revealed that shows tended to frame organ donors as good people but the organ donation system as corrupt. Corruption frames in the shows included the depiction of physicians as vultures waiting for patients to die or prematurely killing patients to harvest their organs, physicians determining who they wanted to receive donated organs, a black market for organs, "bad" people receiving organs such as prisoners, abusers, and alcoholics, rich people who could buy donated organs, and donors as sites of spare parts for those awaiting a transplant. These findings suggested that entertainment television was exploiting negative myths about organ donation, which may have influenced people not to agree to donate. To combat this, the researchers recommended that the organ donation procurement community and government agencies that support organ donation work more closely with the entertainment industry to promote positive organ donation plotlines. Also, they stressed that organ donation advocates need to speak out against the inaccurate portrayal of organ donation in the media.

Another example of media framing research is offered by Kim and Willis (2007) about the coverage of obesity in newspaper articles and television news.

These researchers wondered how these media were covering the causes and solutions for obesity. The results of the study indicated that over a 10-year period, from 1995 to 2004, mentions of personal causes for obesity, such as overeating and not exercising enough, and personal solutions to overcome obesity, such as healthy eating and physical activity, significantly outnumbered mentions of societal causes for obesity, such as fast food industry marketing and lack of physical education in schools. However, these researchers noted that in the more recent years they studied, mentions of societal causes and solutions for obesity increased considerably. Nonetheless, their finding that media presents an unbalanced emphasis on personal responsibility over societal responsibility for public health is consistent with previous studies regarding a variety of health issues (Guttman & Ressler, 2001; Wallack, et al., 1993). This study also supported Media Framing Theory by determining that particularly in television news, the focus tends to be on "individual behaviors and motives, rather than on broader socioeconomic or political conditions, in presenting who is responsible for causing and solving a social problem" (p. 373) such as obesity.

Coverage of natural disasters also exhibited evidence of agenda setting and media framing. In examining local, state, and national newspapers related to the Hurricane Katrina disaster, Barnes et al. (2008) found that the media framed most Hurricane Katrina stories by emphasizing government response and less often addressing individuals' and communities' levels of preparedness or responsibility. Hence, more articles covered response and recovery than mitigation and preparation. By having the power to select certain issues for social attention and providing a certain lens or perspective through which to consider those issues, media plays an important role in shaping public and personal opinions about these and many other health issues (Entman, 1993; Hertog & McLeod, 2001; Kline, 2003; McCombs & Ghanem, 2001).

Now that you have a sense of the role media plays in society, including theoretical explanations for this role and sample research on Agenda-Setting Theory and Media Framing Theory, let's briefly return to the topic of health literacy and expand it into other media forms through media literacy.

Media Literacy

Those in the field of health communication often are faced with the daunting task of trying to disseminate accurate and useful health information to the public, as well as ensuring that the information is accessible and easily understood by a variety of audiences. In Chapter 4, "Linking Health Communication with Patient Interaction," we discussed health literacy as an important macro-level influence on patient/health care provider interaction. *Health literacy* is defined as "the degree to which individuals have the capacity to obtain, process, and understand basic health information and services needed to make appropriate health decisions" (U.S. Department of Health and Human Services, 2009, p. 2.1). In Chapter 5, "Linking Health Communication with Health Care Provider Interaction," we presented several techniques for improving health literacy that also apply to health communication specialists focusing on mass media rather than individual patients. However, as we also discussed when defining communication in Chapter 1, "Introducing Health as Communication Nexus," and in discussing communication as a transactional process, consumers of health communication through media have a mutual responsibility for understanding health communication. This means that although health care providers and health communication specialists have a responsibility to provide accurate and useful health information, health consumers have a duty to critique the relevancy and accuracy of information they receive from media before applying that information to their own and/or others' health needs. In the next sections, we turn to the active role consumers need to play in accessing and processing health information by discussing media literacy and media advocacy.

Defining Media Literacy

After reading the first few sections of this chapter, you now realize that media coverage of health issues shapes what health issues we think about and even how we think about those issues. However, you are not rendered powerless by this realization. As consumers of health communication in the media, we need to carefully and thoughtfully critique the media we are exposed to as we attempt to gain understanding. Potter (2008) defined *media literacy* as awareness and skills that allow an individual to evaluate media content in terms of what is realistic and useful. Put another way, media literacy is the ability of consumers to access, analyze, and/or produce health information that is clear and useful. According to these definitions, media literacy is an active process that involves not only being exposed to media messages but also consciously thinking about the influence that media is having on our understanding, thoughts, and actions regarding health issues. Or Thoman (1999) even more straightforwardly explained that media literacy involves:

> the ability to create personal meaning from the verbal and visual symbols we take in every day through television, radio, computers, newspapers and magazines, and, of course, advertising. It's the ability to choose and select, the ability to challenge and question, the ability to *be conscious* about what's going on around us—and not be passive and vulnerable. (p. 50)

Media Literacy Education

Media literacy education takes the concept of literacy a step further to include all forms of media. The goal of *media literacy education* is to help people become literate, competent, and critical in all media forms so they control the interpretation of what they see or hear rather than letting the media's interpretation of ideas and events control them. The first step in media education is to understand five core concepts about any media message (Bergsma et al., 2007; Thoman, 2003). These five core concepts include:

- ◆ Media messages are socially constructed
- ◆ Media messages use rule-governed, creative language
- ◆ Media messages are embedded with values and points of view
- ◆ Different people experience the same media messages differently
- ◆ Most media messages are produced to gain profit and/or power

As explained previously in this chapter, all *media messages are socially constructed.* In addition, *media messages use rule-governed, creative language,* meaning that every media message is crafted by an individual or a group of individuals who follow a set of rules based on the media format. Once this construction of an idea or event by an individual or group of people is presented over mass media, it essentially becomes the way it is for the rest of us. However, we do not get to see or hear what was left out or rejected when the media message was produced; we see and/or hear only what was accepted for inclusion in the message. Realizing this helps us understand how media shapes what we know, enjoy, or dislike. For example, Facebook posts that contain health-related content are media messages that some people enjoy reading or viewing and find helpful, while others avoid this media outlet altogether because they may be concerned about the credibility of posts or question the level of privacy associated with interacting on this social media site.

A third core concept is that *every media message is embedded with values and points of view,* meaning that because media messages are constructed, they carry a subtext about what is important to the individual or individuals who constructed the messages. Media messages tell stories containing characters, plots, and context. The choices made about each of these elements of the story are biased by the points of view of those creating the stories. Choices about gender, age, race, lifestyles, settings, and actions, for example, all contain embedded values that influence audience members' experiences as they encounter the messages. Understanding what these story choices within health messages may reveal about the creators' point of view is important to judging for ourselves whether we accept or reject the messages.

A fourth core concept is that *different people experience the same media messages differently,* meaning that because each of us was brought up and experience the world around us differently, we also experience the same visuals and verbals within media messages differently. And we do not passively experience media because from early on we are trying to make sense of what we see, read, and hear. Just think about how many media images you took in already today. Although you probably didn't attempt to understand every media image or message, much of your cognitive energy was taken up wondering what those images or messages were trying to communicate. If you listened to the local news on the radio as you got ready this morning, you constantly attempted to understand what the newscasters were trying to convey whether it was the weather forecast which helped you decide what to wear or the latest update on local reaction to the federal health care reform legislation.

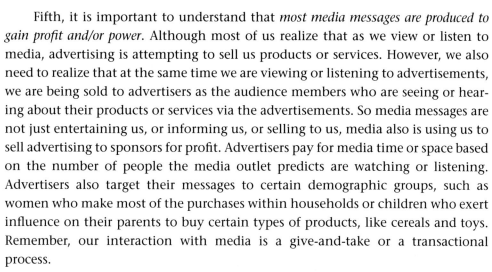

Media Literacy Questions: Key Questions to Ask about Any Health Message

◆ Who is the intended audience?

◆ Whose point of view is being expressed?

◆ What is the goal of the health message, report, or advertisement?

◆ Is the creator of the health message, report, or advertisement credible?

◆ Is the health message, report, or advertisement based on facts or opinions—or a mix of both?

◆ Is there evidence to support each claim?

◆ Can you confirm the source of the evidence?

◆ Is the information valid and current?

◆ What is not being told? Why?

◆ How would you present the health message, report, or advertisement differently?

◆ What conclusions can you come to about this health message, report, or advertisement?

(adapted from Quesada & Summers, 1998; Share, 2009)

Fifth, it is important to understand that *most media messages are produced to gain profit and/or power.* Although most of us realize that as we view or listen to media, advertising is attempting to sell us products or services. However, we also need to realize that at the same time we are viewing or listening to advertisements, we are being sold to advertisers as the audience members who are seeing or hearing about their products or services via the advertisements. So media messages are not just entertaining us, or informing us, or selling to us, media also is using us to sell advertising to sponsors for profit. Advertisers pay for media time or space based on the number of people the media outlet predicts are watching or listening. Advertisers also target their messages to certain demographic groups, such as women who make most of the purchases within households or children who exert influence on their parents to buy certain types of products, like cereals and toys. Remember, our interaction with media is a give-and-take or a transactional process.

Based on these core concepts fundamental to media literacy education, Share, Jolls, and Thoman (2007) forwarded five questions to ask yourself when encountering a media message:

◆ Who created this message and why are they sending it?
◆ What techniques are being used to attract my attention?
◆ What lifestyles, values, and points of view are represented in the message?
◆ How might different people understand this message differently than me?
◆ What is omitted from this message?

Before we proceed to discuss research on media literacy in health communication, Health Communication Nexus Interlude 11.2 challenges you to apply an expanded version of these five questions to a health-related advertisement.

Health Communication Nexus Interlude 11.2

For this interlude, choose an example of a health-related advertisement in a magazine, newspaper, or on the internet. With a copy of the advertisement in front of you, write down in your notebook your response to each of the following media literacy questions. These questions are designed to help you assess the quality, credibility, accuracy, and impact of this advertisement on yourself and others.

- Who is the intended audience?
- Whose point of view is being expressed?
- What is the goal of the advertisement?
- Is the creator of the advertisement credible?
- Is the advertisement based on facts or opinions—or a mix of both?
- Is there evidence to support each claim?
- Can you confirm the source of the evidence?
- Is the information valid and current?
- What is not being told? Why?
- How would you present the advertisement differently?
- What conclusions did you come to about this advertisement?

Keep in mind that these questions can be applied to any health message, health report, or health-related advertisement to aid you in actively critiquing the coverage of health issues in any media. By asking yourself these questions, you will not unconsciously accept the health message but instead determine the value of the message for you.

Now based on your response to the questions, summarize your critique of this health-related advertisement.

Health Communication Research on Media Literacy

In this section, we highlight two research projects that considered aspects of media literacy. The first study evaluated physical activity Web sites. The second study assessed the effectiveness of a media literacy education intervention designed to teach children about violence in the media.

Bonner-Kidd and her colleagues (2009) used a media literacy approach to evaluate the quality and accuracy of physical activity information on the internet.

They analyzed a sample of 41 Web sites that featured physical activity information. To determine quality, the researchers used the American Medical Association's (AMA) benchmarks of quality information on the internet (Silberg, Lundberg, & Musacchio, 1997). The AMA's benchmarks include:

◆ Author of and contributors to Web site identified
◆ Disclosure of Web site ownership and sponsorship
◆ Dates content posted and updated
◆ References for content provided
◆ Health on the Net seal visible
◆ Contact information and/or e-mail address provided

Health on the Net Seal awarded to health-based Web sites that have met quality standards. For an example of a Web site that displays this seal, go to www.cancer.org and identify the seal.

Each Web site was closely reviewed for evidence of the AMA benchmarks. For each Web site, each AMA benchmark was scored as either 1, meaning that benchmark was included on the Web site, or 2, meaning that benchmark was not included on the Web site. A quality score was then obtained for each Web site by summing the score for each benchmark. A composite quality score of 3 or less indicated low quality and a composite quality score of 4 or more indicated high quality.

To rate the accuracy of the physical activity information on these Web sites, the researchers used the American College of Sports Medicine (ACSM) and Centers for Disease Control and Prevention (CDC; Table 11.1) recommendations for physical activity. The ACSM recommends structured exercise that targets different components of fitness including cardiovascular fitness, muscular fitness, and flexibility. Within each of these areas there are specific recommendations for frequency, intensity, and time spent doing the activity. In addition to vigorous physical activity promoted by the ACSM, CDC promotes moderate physical activity such as brisk walking, climbing stairs, swimming, or gardening for at least 30 minutes five days per week. The ACSM Web site (use the link at the Web site for this book) and Table 11.1 provide the specific physical activity recommendations from each of these organizations. For each Web site in the study, each of the physical activity recommendations was scored as either 1, meaning it was included on the Web site, or 2, meaning it was not included on the Web site. An accuracy score was obtained for each Web site by summing the score for each physical activity recommendation. A composite accuracy score of 3 or less indicated low accuracy, 4 to 8 was considered moderate accuracy, and 9 to 13 indicated high accuracy.

The researchers found that only 22% of Web sites in the study had high-quality physical activity information and none of the Web sites were rated as having highly accurate physical activity information. Overall, educational institution Web sites, ending in the suffix .edu, and Web sites ending in the suffix .net were rated as significantly higher in quality and accuracy. Based on the results of this media literacy study, the researchers concluded that given the generally poor ratings for quality and accuracy, physical activity information seekers may be at risk for injury and disease if they depend on physical activity Web sites for information. Given this, the researchers emphasized the need for more education about content quality guidelines for health information seekers and Web site developers.

For Important Health Benefits

Adults need at least:

- ◆ 2 hours and 30 minutes (150 minutes) of moderate-intensity aerobic activity (e.g., brisk walking) every week **and** muscle-strengthening activities on 2 or more days a week that work all major muscle groups (i.e., legs, hips, back, abdomen, chest, shoulders, and arms).

Or

- ◆ 1 hour and 15 minutes (75 minutes) of vigorous-intensity aerobic activity (e.g., jogging or running) every week **and** muscle-strengthening activities on 2 or more days a week that work all major muscle groups (i.e., legs, hips, back, abdomen, chest, shoulders, and arms).

Or

- ◆ An equivalent mix of moderate- and vigorous-intensity aerobic activity **and** muscle-strengthening activities on 2 or more days a week that work all major muscle groups (i.e., legs, hips, back, abdomen, chest, shoulders, and arms).

Table 11.1 ◆ *Centers for Disease Control and Prevention's Physical Activity Guidelines*

In a study by Byrne (1996), primary school children were taught media literacy skills in an effort to reduce the negative effects of viewing media violence on television. Children were taught media literacy skills by learning about violence in the media and in the real world, the effects of media violence, ways to avoid these effects, and ways to evaluate media characters that use violence. In addition some of the children participated in a cognitive activity that involved writing a paragraph about what they learned and they were videotaped reading their paragraph aloud. Results indicated that children who participated in the cognitive activity after receiving the media literacy training experienced an immediate reduction in their willingness to use aggression after exposure to violent media. If they received the media literacy training without the cognitive activity afterward, they tended to experience an increase in their willingness to use aggression after exposure to violent media. Follow-up results indicated that this effect of media violence remained over time.

Now that you have a better understanding of how media constructs health messages and a set of media literacy questions to encourage taking a more active role in critiquing health messages in the media, let's consider another form of active participation in media messaging called media advocacy.

Media Advocacy

The American Public Health Association (APHA; 2002) explained that *advocacy* is "used to promote an issue in order to influence policy-makers and encourage social change . . . and plays a role in educating the public, swaying public opinion or influencing policymakers" (p. 2). *Media advocacy* is using the media to gain the attention of the public, spur communities to action, and/or influence decision-makers to instigate or change health policies (Wallack, et al., 1993).

PROFILE

Searching for Health Information

Marcia Zorn, MA, MLS—Reference Librarian,
National Library of Medicine, National Institutes of Health

For individuals to practice and utilize their health literacy skills they must first have access to health information. Health information is found in a plethora of locations, including physicians' offices, the internet, and pharmacies. Another location that people may overlook for health information is medical libraries. *Medical libraries* are libraries that specialize in collecting and cataloging medical publications such as journal articles and books. Medical libraries are found in many hospitals and at many universities. The federal government also funds four national libraries, including the National Library of Medicine (NLM), which is part of the National Institutes of Health. The mission of the NLM is to acquire, organize, archive and disseminate health-related information by providing access to health information resources. The NLM provides MEDLINE, a bibliographic database that contains references to over 18 million journal articles to help do this. The NLM also coordinates the National Network of Libraries of Medicine (NN/LM), a nationwide network of health science libraries and information centers that serves the biomedical information needs of the nation. Established in the Medical Library Assistance Act of 1965, member libraries and information centers in the NN/LM provide health professionals and the general public health information resources and services.

One unique career in health communication is being a medical librarian. Marcia Zorn has worked as a librarian at the NLM since 1991, and was previously a hospital librarian for twelve years. As a *reference librarian* her primary responsibility is to assist library patrons in locating and accessing materials. Although the NLM is housed in a large building, a small percentage of patrons access the library and its services at the physical location. Most patrons make inquiries via telephone or e-mail. This is a strong indication of how technology has drastically altered how individuals seek information and interact with others.

Each day Zorn responds to e-mail inquiries from patrons interested in finding medical information. If patrons ask for medical advice or opinions though, she is only qualified to direct patrons to health information. In other words, she can help a patron find studies about a new medical treatment such as stem cell therapy, but cannot advise whether or not stem cell therapy is a viable treatment for the patron's condition.

Zorn says one of the greatest challenges for medical librarians and those that assist the public in finding and processing health information is understanding how the public uses the internet and interprets information they find via the internet. In her experience, many individuals perform a quick Google search on a medical condition or treatment and click on the first few links the search returns. She explained that often the National Library of Medicine pops up toward the top of the returned search list and individuals might quickly contact the NLM with a mistaken understanding of what services the library provides. Zorn often encourages patrons to start more locally in their quest for medical information by contacting local libraries and local medical schools to ask about resources.

Framing Media Advocacy

Consistent with our discussion of Agenda-Setting Theory and Media Framing Theory, a media advocacy perspective respects that the media frames issues but emphasizes that individuals and communities can play a strategic role in determining the ways in which media cover health issues. There are three broad aspects of framing media advocacy (Wallack et al., 1993):

◆ Framing for access
◆ Framing for content
◆ Framing to advance policy

Framing for access involves making sure your story is considered newsworthy so media covers it. As Daniel Schorr, a longtime journalist and respected commentator on National Public Radio said, "If you don't exist in the media, for all practical purposes, you don't exist" (Communications Consortium Media Center, 1991, p. 7). With this in mind, you need to frame your health issue so it gains the attention of media outlets.

Attention getting is a key aspect of effective communication (Morgan, 2008) and there are several techniques that can be used to gain attention. One technique is to *frame the health issue as a controversy or injustice*. For example, if you're concerned about the lack of flu vaccinations available for college students in your community, you could draft a press release for local media that questions why some groups of people are given preference over others in the distribution of flu vaccines. To *piggyback on another current news story* that already is receiving media attention is another effective attention-getting technique. In Lafayette, Indiana, for example, advocates for the prevention of child abuse used the murder of a 4-year-old girl, Aiyana Gauvin, by her stepmother to raise awareness about the prevalence of child abuse in the community and to push for policy changes to address the issue (Wilson, 2006). A third media attention-getting technique is to *highlight a new discovery, reaching a milestone, or an anniversary*. For example, environmental advocacy groups such as the Sierra Club likely will use the anniversary of the 2010 BP oil spill in the Gulf Coast to raise awareness about the United States' dependence on oil and to question off-shore oil drilling policies while gaining media attention. A fourth technique is to *include strong images,* because media stories need good visuals. These visuals can be images or vivid word descriptions that create visuals for people in their mind's eye. For example, images of oil-soaked wildlife in the Gulf Coast drew much media attention about the environmental disaster associated with the BP oil spill. Figure 11.1 illustrates the impact of the oil spill on wildlife and other aspects of the environment in the Gulf Coast region.

The second aspect of framing media advocacy is *framing for content,* which involves shaping the way a health issue is covered in the media or shaping the health issue debate. Defining a health problem and its solution can be very difficult because usually there are a variety of perspectives on any given health issue. And as Wallack and his colleagues (1993) contended, in the United States we tend to frame health issues at the individual level rather than at more complex levels

Figure 11.1 ◆ *Oil-covered stork*

© 2011, Zoran Mijatov, Shutterstock, Inc.

such as families, industries, communities, and societies. The challenge is to shift media's attention from the individual or micro level to include the complex macro levels that influence behavior. For example, in her book *Moral Threats and Dangerous Desires: AIDS in the News Media,* Lupton (1994) argued that AIDS news reports focused on micro-level issues such as anxieties about contracting AIDS, deviant behaviors, bodily control, and medical solutions. Instead, AIDS advocates should attempt to shift media attention to include societal issues such as prejudice and funding inequities in the ongoing fight against HIV/AIDS.

The third aspect of framing media advocacy is *framing to advance policy*, which involves influencing policymakers to pay attention and act upon a health issue or story through well-conceived and well-positioned media coverage. The tragic case of Aiyana Gauvin again serves as an example. Even after Aiyana died from injuries inflicted by her stepmother, the community urged media to continue covering the case. Ongoing in-depth coverage included the trials of her stepmother for murder and her father for fatal neglect of a dependent. Media also picked up on a related story of the sheriff's deputy who initially lied about performing a thorough wellness check of Aiyana in the days before her death. The deputy later admitted he did not insist on seeing the child when he went to her home after reports of abuse. He eventually resigned his position with the sheriff's department. Decision makers and policymakers took notice and they along with many in the community credit media coverage of the case for serving as the impetus for substantially changing the way child abuse is handled in this community (Wilson, 2006).

Planning for Media Advocacy

Much like we learned in Chapter 8, "Linking Health Communication with Health Campaign Practice," an effective media advocacy communication strategy, which is a type of health campaign, must have a clear goal, target audience, message, and evaluation. These must-haves form the four steps of media advocacy planning which are:

- ◆ Goal
- ◆ Target audience
- ◆ Message
- ◆ Evaluation

The first step answers the question, "What is your goal?" In most cases, the ultimate *goal of a media advocacy* effort is a new policy or policy change but many other goals can be accomplished while striving for the ultimate goal. Are you trying to motivate the community to take action on a health issue such as exercising? Or are you trying to raise awareness about the issue? In establishing your goal, be sure to clearly define the health problem or issue you are drawing attention to. Once you define the problem or issue, if there is a solution to solve the health problem or issue, amplify the solution. Another important part of goal setting is identifying who can make the solution possible and whose support you need to accomplish the solution. Once these important players are identified, be sure you also know how to get their attention. In other words, determine which media works best to gain their attention. Both long-term goals, or ultimate goals, and short-term, or near-future goals, should be considered when goal setting.

For example, when the first author of this book, Professor Mattson, was involved in an advocacy campaign promoting equal coverage of prosthetics by all health insurance plans, the ultimate goal of this prosthetic parity initiative was to pass a state law that provides equal coverage of prosthetics across health insurance plans (Mattson, 2010). The advocacy group, Indiana Amputee Insurance Protection Coalition (IAIPC), realized that most people are not amputees or have limb differences. Therefore, they may not be aware of the issues associated with coverage of prosthetics by health insurance companies. Consequently, the media advocacy component of this prosthetic parity campaign had a short-term goal of raising public awareness by consistently alerting the media that members of their advocacy group were available for media interviews before and after testimony was provided to legislators.

The second step in media advocacy planning answers the question, "Who is your target audience?" The *target audience* is the specific audience or audiences you are trying to influence about a health issue. Target audiences to address when involved in media advocacy are policymakers or legislators, the segment of the population you are trying to get to support your health-policy initiative, opinion leaders within the community, and people in the community who vote. Once you identify your target audiences, every aspect of your media advocacy campaign needs to be tailored to those target audiences' needs regarding the policy initiative. Aspects of the advocacy campaign that must consider the target audiences include how the campaign frames itself for the audiences, the campaign messages, and the channels or media through which the messages are sent to the target audiences.

For example, the target audiences of the prosthetic parity policy initiative were state legislators, the state amputee and limb difference community and their caregivers, health care providers who specialize in amputees such as prosthetists and physical therapists, and prosthetic manufacturers. Media messages focused on these target audiences and were sent through media channels via special interest stories on television and radio and letters to the editor in newspapers. After the media stories aired more amputees became involved in the policy initiative and more prosthetic manufacturers and health care providers donated money to the initiative.

The third step of media advocacy planning involves answering the question, "What is your message?" A *message* contains the content you want to communicate about the health issue to your target audiences. All members involved in the health policy initiative need to present consistent messages about the initiative. These messages should stem directly from the goals of the advocacy campaign. Once the group decides on its messages, all materials going to media need to support the message. Creating and practicing *media bites*, which are 7-second to 15-second encapsulations of the goals of the policy initiative, are a good way to ensure the messages of the initiative are consistent and in a format that media can easily work from to create and present a story.

Returning to the example from the prosthetic parity policy initiative, to create messages for the initiative, the IAIPC worked with information from the Amputee Coalition of America (ACA), including a fact sheet provided at this book's Web site. To remain consistent in its message, the IAIPC provided the ACA fact sheet in a handout to every legislator and created media bites to use when talking with the media. An example media bite from the campaign was:

> Do you assume that your health insurance plan covers a prosthetic if you lose a limb in an accident or because of disease? Well the facts indicate that more and more insurance companies are excluding or severely limiting coverage for prosthetics. Our Prosthetic Parity initiative seeks to remedy this situation. We speak for the thousands of amputees in Indiana and those who may become amputees in the future. There are 185,000 new amputations in the United States every year. If we don't have health insurance coverage for our prosthetics, we probably won't be able to afford to buy these devices ourselves and will have to go without prosthetic arms or legs. This will severely limit our ability to be independent and may even mean we can't work. If we can't work, we won't be paying income taxes and we may become burdens on the state health care system. By passing a Prosthetic Parity law in Indiana we can have health insurance coverage for our prosthetics and remain productive members of our society.

Members of the IAIPC reviewed and practiced this media bite so if the media approached them for a story, they were prepared with a consistent message.

The fourth step in the media advocacy planning process involves answering the question, "How will you measure success?" Measuring success means *evaluation* of your media advocacy efforts for effectiveness. There are several measures of effectiveness including:

- ◆ Policy change
- ◆ Amount of media coverage
- ◆ Snowballing across media

To determine the effectiveness of your media advocacy campaign, return to the goals of your initiative. If one of the goals is *policy change,* this simply is measured by whether or not a policy is created or revised as a result of your campaign. You also can track the *amount of media coverage,* or media hits, by counting the number of times your advocacy initiative is covered by media. Another important measure of success is how much your health issue *snowballs across media* or how much your initiative gets coverage across media channels. This snowballing effect indicates that your health issue is becoming part of the public agenda and creates awareness in the public for your issue.

The prosthetic parity initiative was deemed successful based on several measures of effectiveness. Most importantly, prosthetic parity became a law in Indiana in 2008. This occurred in part because the story snowballed across state media. The media was especially interested in the effect that lack of health insurance coverage for prosthetics had on children, so many media stories featured children. Stories and testimony about the positive effect of prosthetic parity legislation for children with amputations or limb differences seemed to most influence legislators.

Now that you understand the steps in the media advocacy planning process, you may wonder how to go about obtaining media coverage. In the next section, we discuss several communication strategies for media advocacy.

Communication Strategies for Media Advocacy

There are a variety of communication strategies to obtain media coverage. However, before determining which strategy to use, return to the goals of your media advocacy campaign to make sure there is a fit between the advocacy initiative and the media strategies. Potential strategies for attracting media attention include:

- ◆ Newspapers and magazines
    - ❖ Op-eds
    - ❖ Letters to the editor
- ◆ Television
- ◆ Internet
- ◆ Call-in radio
- ◆ Alternative media
- ◆ Social media

Newspapers and *magazines* may publish an article about a health issue that you write for their opinion section or in the letters to the editor section. Generating several letters and communicating with the editorial staff increases the likelihood that your health issue is considered newsworthy and appropriate for publication. Elected policymakers pay attention to these sections of newspapers and magazines within their districts because they realize that these are media-provided spaces for community members to present their perspectives on current issues.

Television contains news programming and entertainment programming that may cover your health issue. Much like newspapers and magazines, for television or cable stations to cover a health issue it must be newsworthy and/or entertaining for their audiences. Policymakers and the general public watch a lot of television so having your story air on television provides excellent exposure. For example, if a health issue such as childhood obesity gets coverage on *The Dr. Oz Show* and/or *Oprah*, it is likely to be considered an important health issue by the public and policymakers alike. Upon seeing these programs, advocates for healthy children could piggyback on these national programs and encourage their local media to run news stories about preventing childhood obesity in the local community.

The *internet* provides a low-cost outlet for self-publishing or posting audiovideos and opinion statements about health issues. These postings are easily shared or people may discover them while searching the internet. For example, Amnesty International's Web site includes position statements, visual aids, and policy action steps for a variety of health issues, including conflict diamonds. *Conflict diamonds* are diamonds that are mined and sold to fund wars which endanger the well-being of many innocent people, who are placed at risk and may die. This human rights' organization is involved in promoting the Kimberley Process Certification Scheme, which imposes requirements on participant companies to certify that shipments of rough diamonds are conflict free.

The movie *Blood Diamond* is based on the issue of conflict diamonds. Amnesty International's Web site includes a companion curriculum guide to this movie which provides activities and lessons to engage learners in discussions about the complex and challenging issues associated with conflict diamonds, such as the connection between natural resource exploitation and regional conflict. Visit the Web site for this book to view the front cover of Amnesty International's *Blood Diamond* curriculum guide. To support the curriculum guide, the Web site contains additional advocacy resources, including interactive maps, fact sheets, and links for ways to take action about the issue.

Talk radio provides a unique communication strategy for media advocacy because it provides listeners an opportunity to call in and discuss their opinion. You can utilize these opportunities to talk about a health issue and encourage others to take action too. So, for example, if the topic of *The Diane Rehm Show* on National Public Radio is "Understanding the New Health Care Law," you could call in to discuss your opposition to the new federal law passed in March 2010 and encourage other people to support efforts to legally challenge the law.

Social media is defined as sites on the internet that are driven by user-generated content (Tredinnick, 2006). Additionally users virtually network with organizations and each other using these sites. Examples of social media sites include Facebook, YouTube, Twitter, and Flickr. Millions of people access these sites daily, so social media can be a great way to raise awareness and build interest in, interaction about, and involvement with a health issue. By interacting with people through social media, health care organizations and health campaigns can build relationships with relevant audiences.

To effectively cultivate virtual relationships with target audiences, research consistently indicates the importance of incorporating three features into an organization or campaign's social media profile. These critical features of a social media site are disclosure, usefullness, and interactivity (Waters, Burnett, Lamm, & Lucas, 2009). Similar to the AMA benchmarks for determining a quality Web site discussed previously in this chapter, inclusion of these features indicates a quality social media profile. *Disclosure* refers to the organization or campaign being transparent by providing a profile that includes a detailed description and history of the organization, its mission, logo, and a list of individuals responsible for maintaining the organization's profile. Second, the organization or campaign's social media profile should be *useful* to its target audiences. Social media site components that accomplish this include links to video or audio files from the organization or its supporters and press releases or other summaries of current happenings within the organization. Also, the message board or discussion wall can be used to post announcements and answer questions. Third, the organization or campaign's social network profile should be *interactive*. Encouraging supporters to become involved by sharing their stories, providing them with tools such as action kits to become involved, or an option to donate money or volunteer time are three ways to be interactive while communicating with target audiences via a social media Web site. To further encourage their social networking presence, health organizations and campaign Web sites also should provide links to their social media sites on their own Web sites. For example, visit this book's Web site or the American

Diabetes Association Web site and see if you can identify the links to their social media pages.

Some research addresses the use of social media in health communication and political campaigns and this area of study is likely to grow along with the steady increase in social media networking. In a content analysis of Facebook profiles for 275 nonprofit organizations, Waters, Burnett, Lamm, and Lucas (2009) found that although these organizations used some aspects of Facebook, they were not incorporating all of the resources available. These organizations seemed to understand the importance of disclosure but underestimated the influence of making their social media profile useful and interactive. To distribute organization messages, they most often used a discussion board and photos but did not tend to distribute organization news. Of particular concern, these organizations did not provide many ways for advocates to become involved in the organization, except by posting an e-mail address if someone wanted to contact the organization for more information. In light of these findings and the dominance of social media, the researchers recommended that nonprofit organizations more fully utilize social networking sites to provide a variety of public relations including, for example, more multimedia files and more press releases to document what is happening within the organization. If financial and other resources to accomplish this are limited, nonprofits may be able utilize the services of college interns or volunteers to maintain their social media presence and enlist software programs for social media to aid them in fundraising efforts online.

After considering how Barack Obama's successful presidential campaign in 2008 used new media to reach, engage, and inspire supporters and obtain votes, Abroms and Lefebvre (2009) discussed the implications of new media for health campaigns. They defined *new media* as "media that are based on the use of digital technologies such as the Internet, digital video, and mobile devices" (p. 415). New media applications include Web sites, social network sites such as Facebook and MySpace, YouTube channels, Twitter, targeted text messaging for mobile phones, and unofficial campaign materials designed and disseminated by supporters. The Obama campaign utilized all of these new media applications very effectively. The results of that effective political campaign offered these implications for health campaigns:

◆ *Reach out to people in multiple ways* using a variety of media, including social media.
◆ *People are more likely to connect to, learn from, and trust network peers.* This is consistent with another study that found that people most often use social networking Web sites to interact with people they already know rather than meet new people. Those who spent the most time online said they would be open to receiving health information via social networking Web sites (Uhrig, Bann, Williams, & Evans, 2010).
◆ There is a *change in power occurring from people simply being supporters of campaigns to becoming creators of message content.* Although this may pose challenges for health campaigns, namely it may be difficult to keep

messages consistent if a variety of individuals are creating messages, it also expands the capabilities and reach of the campaign by getting more people involved on their own terms.

◆ *Acts of engagement ripple through social networks* and people get other people involved. So use social media to encourage grassroots campaign activities.

Please take a break from reading to complete Health Communication Nexus Interlude 11.3, which asks you to create a health message for social media.

Health Communication Nexus Interlude 11.3

For this interlude, make a list in your notebook of all the social media or new media you utilize to interact with others. From your list choose one form of social media or new media you use. Write an example health message you'd be open to receiving via this form of social media or new media. Now, answer these questions about your example message:

◆ Do you think your health message would be effective with most of the other users of this social media? Why or why not?

◆ Do you think your message would be effective with the network of friends you have through this same social media? Why or why not?

Alternative media outlets are outside mainstream media. Often these media are targeted toward niche audiences and have broad reach. For example, ethnic radio and television stations often broadcast in a language other than English and are preferred by individuals for whom English is not their first, primary, or preferred language. If you deem that the audiences of alternative media are relevant to your health advocacy effort, consider these media but be sure to tailor stories to the audiences. For example, the advertising campaign "Which One Deserves to Die?," by the advocacy organization San Francisco Hep B Free, targeted the Asian American population. They chose this target audience because Asian Americans are at high risk for contracting hepatitis B. The campaign produced ads in English and several Asian languages and used a variety of mainstream and alternative media. Go to the Web site for this book to see the juxtaposition of two of the ads from this campaign.

Three recent studies emphasized that media campaigns targeted toward minority populations need to use more empowering media advocacy efforts to effectively frame health issues. In a study of the tobacco control movement in the 1990s, Malone, Wenger, and Bero (2002) found that although messages targeted to youth were part of the movement, these messages often were negatively challenging to youth and inconsistently presented. To combat this, the researchers suggested that media advocacy about tobacco control should focus on framing messages for youth that are easily communicated, consistently used, and compatible with the developmental tasks of youth such as the desire to model older youth.

To make this possible, they suggested youth journalists be included in media advocacy planning to create youth-driven messages that emphasize tobacco industry manipulation rather than messages that frame smoking as an adult activity.

In another study about media and tobacco use, Smith, Offen, and Malone (2006) considered the normalization of tobacco use in newspapers and magazines targeting the lesbian, gay, and bisexual (LGB) community. They found that messages about tobacco use in these media were predominantly positive or neutral and more often were provided through imagery rather than text. Based on these findings, the researchers suggested that advocates for LGB health lobby for LGB media to establish policies that refuse noncommercial tobacco promotion in much the same way these media refuse tobacco advertising.

In a third study, magazine advertisements and editorial content targeting Black women were examined by Mastin and Campo (2006). Content was analyzed in a sample of 500 food and nonalcoholic beverage ads and 31 articles about weight and obesity in the magazines *Ebony*, *Essence*, and *Jet* over a 20-year period. Results indicated that the ads promoted foods that were high in empty calories and had low nutritional value. Editorial content of the articles contradicted these ads by discussing balanced diet, fewer calories, and physical activity as solutions to being overweight or obese. However, advertisements outnumbered articles by 16 to 1. Similar to the previous two studies, these researchers suggested media advocacy efforts to promote the communication of clear and consistent messages about health issues. In addition, this research project emphasized the need to include both individual and environmental and community solutions in media content (for a related study, read Campo & Mastin, 2007).

Now that you understand the process and role of media advocacy in health communication, let's turn to a service-learning application that illustrates how to apply this knowledge to fund, design, produce, and disseminate a public service announcement.

SERVICE-LEARNING APPLICATION

Creating a Public Service Announcement for Media Advocacy

In this service-learning application, we describe an in-progress media advocacy project associated with the Motorcycle Safety at Purdue (MS@P) campaign and again emphasize one of the key components of any service-learning project— *critical reflection*. This media advocacy project is funding, designing, producing, and promoting a public service announcement (PSA) featuring the campaign spokesperson. The MS@P campaign spokesperson is Mayor of West Lafayette, John Dennis. West Lafayette is the city where Purdue

University is located. Mayor Dennis is an avid motorcyclist and has been in several motorcycle crashes resulting in a variety of injuries. This project spans over two semesters and one summer session and involves three different project teams. The first project team secured funding for expenses associated with the project. This team wrote a proposal that was funded by a service-learning project grant offered by the university's Office of Engagement. The project description and budget from the grant proposal follow.

APPLICATION
2009/2010 (2ND SEMESTER)
PURDUE UNIVERSITY
STUDENT GRANT PROGRAM
FOR
COMMUNITY SERVICE/SERVICE LEARNING PROJECTS

Please Type or Print Clearly ~ Complete All Sections

Name of Student Contact   Zachary Colvin

Phone ▮▮▮▮▮▮▮▮   **E-mail** ▮▮▮▮▮▮▮▮

Class # or Title   COM 320: Small Group Communication

TITLE OF PROJECT   Partnering with the Mayor to Promote Motorcycle Safety in the West Lafayette/Greater Purdue University Community

Approximate Number of Purdue students involved in organizing this project   25

Proposed Starting and Ending Dates of Project   3/1/10 – 4/30/10

2. **Community Organization Partner**   City of West Lafayette

Name of Contact   John Dennis, Mayor

Address   City of West Lafayette, 609 Navajo Street, West Lafayette, IN 47906

Phone   555-555-5500   **Email**   jdennis@westlafayette.in.gov

3. **Purdue University Sponsor**   Marifran Mattson, PhD, Associate Professor

Campus Mailing Address of Department   COM, BRNG 2114

Department Business Office where funds will be distributed   Lucy Orozco, Business Office, Dept. of COM

Phone ▮▮▮▮▮▮▮▮   **E mail** ▮▮▮▮▮▮▮▮

Description of Project
Partnering with the Mayor to Promote Motorcycle Safety

The number of deaths and injuries caused by motorcycle crashes is on the rise across the country and in Indiana. Nationally, in 2008 almost 5,300 motorcyclists died in motorcycle crashes and 96,000 were injured (National Highway Traffic Safety Administration, 2010). Statewide, 130 motorcyclists were killed in 2008 which is an increase of 22 deaths from 2006 (Indiana Criminal Justice Institute, 2010). Locally, a Purdue student was killed in Fall 2008 while riding a motorcycle, the mayor of West Lafayette was involved in a motorcycle crash in summer 2009, and several students, faculty, and staff report being involved in a motorcycle crash (www.ItInvolvesYou.com). Consequently, it is imperative to raise awareness about motorcycle safety and inform all drivers on our community roads about the risks and strategies to reduce their risks of being involved in a motorcycle crash. An excellent way to raise awareness is through a high-profile spokesperson. Because of his interest in riding and motorcycle safety, West Lafayette Mayor John Dennis has agreed to serve as a spokesperson for the Motorcycle Safety at Purdue campaign.

To effectively utilize our spokesperson's visibility as a community leader, the goal of this semester's Small Group Communication's class team project is to design, test, and pitch an effective public service messages proposal for motorcycle safety to our community partner, Mayor Dennis. The proposal will seek to engage the greater West Lafayette/Purdue University community about the importance of practicing motorcycle safety with messages that will have both awareness and behavioral impact. The target audiences for our safety messages include motorcyclists but also drivers of cars and trucks and friends and family of motorcyclists. Upon Mayor Dennis' approval of the proposal we will work toward implementing the proposal with the Mayor as our spokesperson.

Proposed Budget

Income   List expected revenue for the project (if any) including sources and amounts. Community organizations or agencies receiving the service might choose to participate in the cost of the project or service.

None

Expenses   <u>Provide an itemized list of the expected expenses by expenditure type that will be charged to this grant</u>. The following items are included as approvable expenditures: publicity, printing, postage, transportation, supplies and materials necessary to complete the project, and <u>minimal</u> refreshment costs where justified as necessary for the service or project.

Testing of Spokesperson Message Ideas: Focus Groups

Refreshments $150
Incentive for Participation ($10 gas cards X 30) $300

.... $450

Spokesperson Message Production

Audio-Video Production of Public Service Announcement $200
Printing of Approved Messages in Color (60 posters) $245
Production of 1 Tail of Greater Lafayette CityBus Sign $140

.... $585

Spokesperson Message Distribution

1 Tail of Bus Sign for 3 Months

.... $450

TOTAL AMOUNT REQUESTED   **$1485.00**

Another project team developed concept ideas for the PSA and contacted local media to determine if they would air the PSA. An example of the e-mail sent to local media follows.

Dear WBAA,

My name is Andrew De Lucio and I am a senior at Purdue University working with Professor Marifran Mattson on the Motorcycle Safety at Purdue campaign. The goal of the campaign is simply to make the road safer for everyone. More information including campaign history, campaign involvement, and contacts can be found on the campaign's website at http://itinvolvesyou.com.

My project team, consisting of other Purdue seniors, is currently working on creating script concepts for a Public Service Announcement (PSA) to be aired on local radio. We would like to know if you would consider airing this PSA upon completion. The completion of this thirty (30) second PSA is expected to be the end of the fall semester of the 2010 academic year.

At this time, we are just touching base with you to get confirmation as to whether or not you would be interested and / or willing to air this motorcycle safety PSA upon completion. We kindly ask that you please reply to this email or contact either me or Professor Marifran Mattson with a simple yes or no or to ask any questions that you may have. We furthermore invite you to our class presentation of the extent of the work performed this past semester with which our project team was part of. Here, you may be able to, first-hand, gain a better understanding of what is is that we are proposing. The presentation will be held at 9:00 AM on the morning of June 11th in room 2290 of Purdue's Beering (BRNG) Hall located on University St. If interested, upon completion of the PSA, you will be contacted again and the PSA will be turned over to you. In addition, we would like to air a televised PSA through the Boiler TV network. If either of you have contacts that may be able to help us with this situation, they would greatly be appreciated. Thank you for your time.

Dr. Marifran Mattson, the campaign's main influence, can be reached via telephone at 765-494-7596 or via email at mmattson@purdue.edu.

Respectfully
Andrew De Lucio

Response to this e-mail was very positive. Most of the media stations contacted agreed to air the PSA.

The concept ideas for the PSA are being shared with the mayor for his approval. In addition, the approved concept ideas will be discussed during focus groups of target audience members of the MS@P campaign to determine if additional changes need to be made before production. Next semester, a project team will produce the concept ideas into an audiovisual PSA that will be broadcast on local media and posted on MS@P's Web site and its YouTube channel. To evaluate the effectiveness of the PSA, the campaign will track the number of times the PSA airs and the number hits on the Web site and on the YouTube channel.

In addition to working on the PSA, this project emphasizes one of the key components of any service-learning project—critical reflection. Remember, it is through reflection that you and your project team consider links between what you're learning from readings and class discussions and your service-learning project along with what you're doing well and what you could improve or change (Ash & Clayton, 2009; Corporation for National & Community Service, 2010). In biweekly team progress reports, students respond, both individually and as a team, to four reflection questions linking course content with their service-learning experiences. Abbreviated examples of an individual response and a team response from a project team working on the MS@P PSA follow:

Individual Response

- Since our last progress report, I have learned that . . . *Purdue can have a greater impact on the community than just the school and issues regarding the school. The students that attend here can also be used as a community involvement program. Instead of spending all day in lecture and doing group projects to fill a grade the project can be world related.*

- I learned this when . . . *I thought about the idea that a motorcycle alert sign could be placed on an interstate at the entering and exiting of both Lafayette and West Lafayette. There could be four signs on one road that convey a message across to everyone at a key point in their life, i.e., every time they leave or enter town it's a little reminder to pay attention.*

- This learning experience matters because . . . *it could be used as an eye opener of how easy it is to get a message out to the public as long as you have an effective team of people who are motivated to make the connections, do the work, and apply the knowledge they have to complete the task.*

- In light of this learning experience I will . . . *probably talk to the mayor face-to-face.*

Team Response

- Since our last progress report, we have learned that . . . *it's rather difficult to come together as a team, but we did realize that the forming of a group does happen in stages.*

- We learned this when . . . *we had to come up with the PSA concepts. Completing the group cohesion process was difficult enough and it was hard to come up with ideas that everyone was OK with. While going through the process, we realized that what each of us was good at and used these personalities to dictate roles when coming up with PSA concepts.*

- This learning experience matters because . . . *it has taught us as individuals how to communicate better when coming up with ideas and concepts while also teaching us how to develop better as a group and team. If each person understands team development, the steps within team formation come quicker and easier.*

- In light of this learning experience we will . . . *plan to better communicate personalities/ideals when we are challenged with this type of situation in the future. It is with better communication that better ideas come into existence.*

Developing a Media Advocacy Plan

Now that you've been exposed to a service-learning project example that incorporates aspects of media advocacy planning and execution, how would you or your project team develop a media advocacy project for a health issue of concern to you? Start with the primary steps in media advocacy planning and build your project from the results of taking these steps:

- Goal
- Target audience
- Message
- Evaluation

Don't forget to consider along each step in the process what media outlets you'll use to communicate your advocacy message, such as newspapers and magazines, television, internet, call-in radio, alternative media.

For a media advocacy planning template, visit the Web site for this book.

Chapter Summary

This chapter focused on issues surrounding the intersection of health communication and media. We first presented a definition of media followed by a discussion of the role media plays in contemporary society. Next, we explained that media messages are social constructions and often politically motivated. This was followed by coverage of the theoretical foundations of health communication and the media including Agenda-Setting Theory and Media Framing Theory. We then turned to a discussion of the active role consumers can play in accessing, processing, and influencing the ways in which health information is presented in the media through media literacy skills and media advocacy initiatives. Finally, in the service-learning application we considered an example of media advocacy by illustrating how a series of project teams funded, created, produced, evaluated, and reflected upon a public service announcement for a health communication campaign.

References

Abroms, L. C., & Lefebvre, R. C. (2009). Obama's wired campaign: Lessons for public health communication. *Journal of Health Communication, 14*, 415–423.

American Public Health Association (2002). *APHA media advocacy manual*. Unpublished manuscript, Washington, DC.

Andsager, J., & Powers, A. (1999). Social or economic concerns: How news and women's magazines framed breast cancer in the 1990s. *Journalism and Mass Communication Quarterly, 76*, 531–550.

Anhang, R., Stryker, J. E., Wright, T. C., & Goldie, S. J. (2004). News media coverage of human papilloma virus. *Cancer, 100*, 308–314.

Ash, S. L., & Clayton, P., H. (2009). Generating, deepening, and documenting learning: The power of critical reflection in applied learning. *Journal of Applied Learning in Higher Education, 1*, 25–48.

Barnes, M. D., Hanson, C. L., Novilla, L. M., Meachum, A. T., McIntyre, E., & Erickson, B. B. (2008). Analysis of media agenda setting during and after Hurricane Katrina: Implications for emergency preparedness, disaster response, and disaster policy. *Government, Politics, and Law, 98*, 604–610.

Bergsma, L., Considine, D., Culver, S. H., Hobbs, R., Jensen, A., Rogow, F., et al. (2007). *Core principles of media literacy education in the United States*. Unpublished manuscript, Denver, CO.

Bonner-Kidd, K. K., Black, D. R., Mattson, M., & Coster, D. (2009). Online physical activity information: Will typical users find quality information? *Health Communication, 24*, 165–175.

Byrne, A. (1996). Harm minimization approaches to drug misuse: Current challenges in evaluation. *Substance Use & Misuse, 31*, 2017–2028.

Calloway, C., Jorgensen, C. M., Saraiya, M., & Tsui, J. (2006). A content analysis of the news coverage of the HPV vaccine by U.S. newspapers, January 2002–June 2005. *Journal of Women's Health, 15*, 803–809.

Campo, S., & Mastin, T. (2007). Placing the burden on the individual: Overweight and obesity in African American and mainstream women's magazines. *Health Communication, 22*, 229–240.

Carlson, E. S., & Holm, K. (1997). An analysis of menopause in the popular press. *Health Care for Women International, 18,* 557–564.

Communications Consortium Media Center (1991). *Strategic communications for nonprofits: Strategic media—Designing a public interest campaign.* Washington, DC: Benton Foundation, Center for Strategic Communications.

Corporation for National & Community Service (2010). Learn and Serve America's National Service-Learning Clearinghouse. Retrieved January 12, 2010, from www.servicelearning.org.

Entman, R. (1993). Framing: Toward a clarification of a fractured paradigm. *Journal of Communication, 43,* 51–58.

Feeley, T. H., & Vincent, D. I. (2007). How organ donation is represented in newspaper articles in the United States. *Health Communication, 21,* 125–131.

Forster, A., Wardle, J., Stephenson, J., & Waller, J. (2010). Passport to promiscuity or lifesaver: Press coverage of HPV vaccination and risky sexual behavior. *Journal of Health Communication, 15,* 205–217.

Freimuth, V. S., Linnan, H., & Potter, P. (2000). Communicating the threat of emerging infections to the public. *Emerging Infectious Diseases, 6,* 337–347.

Gans, H. (1979). *Deciding what's news.* New York: Patheon.

Goldberg, J. (2010, May 3). Let's keep oil spill in perspective. *USA Today.* Retrieved August 10, 2010, from http://www.usatoday.com/news/opinion/forum/2010-05-04-column 04_ST_N.htm.

Groshek, J. (2008). Homogenous agendas, disparate frames: CNN and CNN international coverage online. *Journal of Broadcasting and Electronic Media, 52,* 52–68.

Guttman, N., & Ressler, W. H. (2001). On being responsible: Ethical issues in appeals to personal responsibility in health campaigns. *Journal of Health Communication, 6,* 117–136.

Hertog, J., & McLeod, D. (2001). A multiperspectival approach to framing analysis: A field guide. In S. D. Reese, J. O. H. Gandy, & A. E. Grant (Eds.), *Framing public life: Perspectives on media and our understanding of the social world* (pp. 139–162). Mahwah, NJ: Lawrence Erlbaum.

Indiana Criminal Justice Institute. (2010). Indiana Crash Facts: 2008. Retrieved January 27, 2009, from http://www.in.gov/cji/files/FactBook_2008.pdf.

Iyengar, S., Peters, M. D., & Kinder, D. R. (1982). Experimental demonstrations of the "not-so-minimal" consequences of television news programs. *The American Political Science Review, 76,* 848–858.

Jensen, J. V. (1997). *Ethical issues in the communication process.* Mahwah, NJ: Lawrence Erlbaum Associates.

Kim, S. H., & Willis, L. A. (2007). Talking about obesity: News framing of who is responsible for causing and fixing the problem. *Journal of Health Communication, 12,* 359–376.

Kline, K. I. (1999). Reading and reforming breast self-examination discourse: Claiming missed opportunities for empowerment. *Journal of Health Communication, 4,* 119–141.

Kline, K. I. (2003). Popular media and health: Images, effects, and institutions. In T. L. Thompson, A. M. Dorsey, K. I. Miller, & R. Parrott (Eds.), *Handbook of health communication* (pp. 557–581). Mahwah, NJ: Lawrence Erlbaum.

Lupton, D. (1994). *Moral threats and dangerous desires: AIDS in the news media.* London and Bristol, PA: Taylor & Francis.

Lyons, A. C., & Griffin, C. (2003). Managing menopause: A qualitative analysis of self-help literature for women at midlife. *Social Science & Medicine, 56,* 1629–1642.

MacDonald, S. P. (2005). The language of journalism in treatments of hormone replacement news. *Written Communication, 22,* 275–297.

Malone, R. E., Wenger, L. D., & Bero, L. A. (2002). High school journalists' perspectives on tobacco. *Journal of Health Communication, 7*, 139–156.

Mastin, T., & Campo, S. (2006). Conflicting messages: Overweight and obesity advertisements and articles in Black magazines. *Howard Journal of Communication, 17*, 265–285.

Mattson, M. (2010). Health advocacy by accident and discipline. *Health Communication, 25*, 622–624.

Mayo, M. (2010, May 15). For South Florida, will oil spill bring harm-or just hype? Slow-motion disaster feels like hurricane-but dirtier. *Sun Sentinel*. Retrieved August 10, 2010, from http://articles.sun-sentinel.com/2010-05-15/news/fl-oil-spill-mayocol-b051510-20100515_1_spill-environmental-disaster-south-florida.

McCombs, M., & Ghanem, S. (2001). The convergence of agenda setting and framing. In S. D. Reese, J. O. H. Gandy, & A. E. Grant (Eds.), *Framing public life: Perspectives on media and our understanding of the social world* (pp. 67–82). Mahwah, NJ: Lawrence Erlbaum.

McCombs, M., & Shaw, D. (1972). The agenda setting function of mass media. *Public Opinion Quarterly, 36*, 176–187.

Miller, R., & Wanta, W. (1996). Race as a variable in agenda setting. *Journalism and Mass Communication Quarterly, 73*, 913–925.

Morgan, M. (2008). *Presentational speaking: Theory and practice* (6th ed.). Indianapolis: McGraw Hill.

Morgan, S. E., Harrison, T. R., Chewning, L., Davis, L., & DiCorcia, M. (2007). Entertainment (mis)education: The framing of organ donation in entertainment television. *Health Communication, 22*, 143–151.

National Highway Transportation Safety Administration. (2010). Traffic safety facts 2008: Motorcycles. Retrieved January 27, 2010, from http://www.nhtsa.gov.

National Public Radio (2010, May 23). Genetic disorder brings mother to hardest decision. Retrieved May 25, 2010, from http://www.npr.org/templates/story/story.php?storyId=127069417.

Nekhlyudov, L., Ross-Degnan, D., & Fletcher, S. W. (2003). Beliefs and expectations of women under 50 years old regarding screening mammography. *Journal of General Internal Medicine, 18*, 182–189.

Paulos, J. A. (1995). *A mathematician reads the newspaper*. New York: Anchor.

Pierce, J. P., Dwyer, T., Chamberlain, A., Aldrich, R. N., & Shelley, J. M. (1987). Targeting the smoker in an anti-smoking campaign. *Preventive Medicine, 16*, 816–824.

Potter, W. J. (2008). *Media literacy*. Los Angeles: Sage.

Quesada, A., & Summers, S. L. (1998). Literacy in the cyberage: Teaching kids to be media savvy. *Technology & Learning, 18*, 30–36.

Roberts, M., Wanta, W., & Dzwo, T. (2002). Agenda setting and issue salience online. *Communication Research, 29*, 452–464.

Schwitzer, G. (2009). *The state of health journalism in the U.S.* Menlo Park, CA: Henry J. Kaiser Family Foundation.

Share, J. (2009). *Media literacy is elementary: Teaching youth to critically read and create media*. New York: Peter Lang.

Share, J., Jolls, T., & Thoman, E. (2007). *Five key questions that can change the world: Lesson plans for media literacy*. Retrieved August 10, 2010 from http://www.medialit.org/reading-room/five-key-questions-can-change-world.

Shoebridge, A., & Steed, L. (1999). Discourse about menopause in selected print media. *Australian and New Zealand Journal of Public Health, 23*, 475–481.

Silberg, W. M., Lundberg, G. D., & Musacchio, R. A. (1997). Assessing, controlling, and assuring the quality of medical information on the internet: Caveant lector et viewor—Let the reader and viewer beware. *Journal of the American Medical Association, 277*, 1244–1245.

Smith, E., Offen, N., & Malone, R. E. (2006). Pictures worth a thousand words: Noncommercial tobacco content in the lesbian, gay, and bisexual press. *Journal of Health Communication, 11*, 635–649.

Thoman, E. (1999). Skills and strategies for media education. *Educational Leadership, 56*, 50–54.

Thoman, E. (2003). *MediaLit kit: A framework for learning and teaching in a media age.* Santa Monica, CA: Center for Media Literacy. Retrieved May 20, 2010, from http://www.medialit.org/sites/default/files/mlk_orientationguide.pdf.

Tredinnick, L. (2006). Web 2.0 and business: A pointer to the intranets of the future? *Business Information Review, 23*, 228–234.

Uhrig, J., Bann, C., Williams, P., & Evans, W. D. (2010). Social networking Web sites as a platform for disseminating social marketing interventions: An exploratory pilot study. *Social Marketing Quarterly, 16*, 2–20.

U.S. Department of Health and Human Services (2009). Quick guide to health literacy: Fact sheet. Retrieved February 15, 2009, from http://www.health.gov/communication/literacy/quickguide.

Wallack, L., Dorfman, L., Jernigan, D., & Themba, M. (1993). *Media advocacy and public health.* Newbury Park, CA: Sage.

Wallington, S. F., Blake, K. D., Taylor-Clark, K., & Viswanath, K. (2010). Antecedents to agenda setting and framing in health news: An examination of priority, angle, source, and resource usage from a national survey of US health reporters and editors. *Journal of Health Communication, 15*, 76–94.

Waters, R. D., Burnett, E., Lamm, A., & Lucas, J. (2009). Engaging stakeholders through social networking: How nonprofit organizations are using Facebook. *Public Relations Review, 35*, 102–106.

Weaver, D. H. (2007). Thoughts on agenda setting, framing, and priming. *Journal of Communication, 57*, 142–147.

Wilson, S. R. (2006). First and second-order changes in a community's response to a child abuse fatality. *Communication Monographs, 73*, 481–487.

CHAPTER 12   Linking Health Communication with . . .

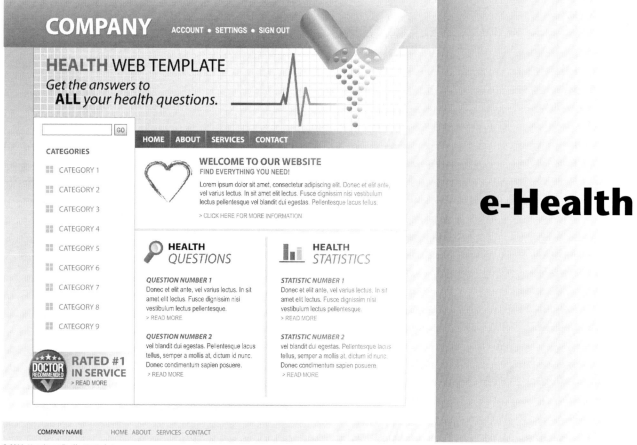

e-Health

© 2011, Haywiremedia, Shutterstock, Inc.

Chapter Learning Objectives

- ◆ Identify role of technology in health tourism
- ◆ Review major milestones in history of health and technology
- ◆ Define and provide examples for key terms at intersection of health and technology
- ◆ Provide rationale for adopting the term e-Health to describe intersection of health and technology
- ◆ List communication barriers to and benefits of e-Health
- ◆ Explain the process of tailoring health communication
- ◆ Describe the five technology-based approaches to health communication
- ◆ Understand three theoretical explanations for using technology in health care
- ◆ Discuss the implications of e-Health on health communication
- ◆ Consider ways to present health communication initiatives in an e-Health environment

Chapter Preview

In this chapter we focus on the intersection of health communication and technology. We begin with a brief history of when and how this intersection occurred. Next, we define and offer examples of the many terms and concepts in the literature and in the marketplace that are associated with health and technology and decide to adopt the term e-Health. Afterwards we shift our focus more directly toward communication by offering communication barriers and benefits of e-Health followed by a discussion of the importance of tailoring health messages. We then review the different types of technology-based approaches to health communication, including ways that tailored messages become incorporated within those technologies. To facilitate understanding of e-Health uptake and e-Health processes, we touch on three theories that inform health communication practices and research in the e-Health environment. This is followed by consideration of the implications of e-Health on interpersonal and organizational health communication. We conclude the chapter with a service-learning application that highlights project presentation through developing a Web site.

According to the Medical Tourism Association (www.medicaltourism.com), *medical tourism* is defined as occurring when "people who live in one country travel to another country to receive medical, dental and surgical care."

People decide to travel for medical care for a variety of reasons, including increased access to care and affordability. For example, the documentary *Farrah's Story* (Stewart, 2009) chronicles actress Farrah Fawcett's fight against cancer. Part of her story involves her search for alternative methods of treatment. To experience some of these unique treatments, she traveled to other countries and upon her return to the United States utilized telehealth to continue this medical care. Fawcett eventually died but her story introduced many people to alternative treatments for cancer and the notion of medical tourism.

Medical tourism is a somewhat controversial issue. And controversial issues often are ethical issues. Explore your reactions to the idea of people traveling to other countries to receive medical treatments in the Ethics Touchstone.

Ethics Touchstone

Do you consider medical tourism an ethical approach to health care? Why or why not?

Jot down your response to this question in your notebook. Now return to Jensen's (1997) Criteria for an Ethical Dilemma presented in Chapter 2, "Linking Health Communication with Ethics," and determine on which of the following three criteria you based your response:

◆ Significant impact on others

◆ Conscious choice between means and ends

◆ Communication can be judged by standards of right and wrong

Write down on which criteria you based your response to the ethical dilemma and your reasoning for choosing this criteria.

You may be wondering why we began this chapter by discussing medical tourism. We did so primarily for two reasons. One reason is that often medical tourism integrates cutting-edge technology and telehealth practices to interact with and treat patients. A second reason is that considering the role of medical tourism within the realm of health communication and technology provides a unique way to bridge Chapter 11, "Linking Health Communication with Media," to this chapter, which focuses on the influence of technology in health care. However, medical tourism is not the only approach to health communication through technology. As we learn in this chapter, health care and technology are intertwined. In the next section we provide a brief history of when and how the intertwining of health care and communication technology occurred.

Milestones in History of Health and Technology

By most accounts of Western history, the intersection of health and technology dates back over the past century when electronic devices were first introduced into society (Bashshur & Shannon, 2009). The introduction of telegraphy, telephony, radio, television, and wireless communication all served as innovative and important ways for health care providers and patients to interact across space and time.

According to Wootton (2001), some of the first instances of telecommunication used for health care were ship-to-shore radio calls by captains of sea vessels seeking medical advice. In the field of health research, the first study to apply telemedicine was in the discipline of psychiatry when in 1959 a two-way closed-circuit microwave television provided successful telemedicine communication between specialists at the Nebraska Psychiatric Institute and general practitioners at the Norfolk State Hospital in Nebraska (Perednia & Allen, 1995). This study seemed to spur the growth of telemedicine research as studies about the influence of telemedicine burgeoned from the early 1970s.

In the 1960s, land-to-space communication was designed such that technology was built into early spacecrafts and spacesuits by the National Aeronautics and Space Administration (NASA) to monitor the physiological condition of astronauts (Allan, 2006). From lessons learned in space travel, NASA developed a telemedicine program called the Space Technology Applied to Rural Papago Advanced Health Care (STARPAHC) to assist Native American patients whose reservations in rural areas of Arizona were miles from the nearest hospital. Using two-way microwave transmissions paramedical personnel in remote locations were connected with medical experts at hospitals in Tucson and Phoenix.

In the 1970s, sites in the rural reaches of Alaska confirmed the reliability of telemedicine via satellite communication through a National Library of Medicine project using a NASA satellite. This type of work continued to extend into other isolated areas and across developing countries (Allan, 2006). Since the 1980s, the costs associated with technologies applied to health decreased substantially paving the way for more widespread consideration and use.

Review the timeline in Table 12.1 for the milestones at the intersections of health communication and technology. Keeping in mind these historical milestones, let's turn our attention to the influence of technology on health communication. To better understand the influence of technology on health communication, it is important first to define the terms and concepts associated with health communication technologies.

Table 12.1 ◆ *Milestones in health communication and technology*

Early 1900s	Ship-to-shore calls for medical advice
1959	First research study to apply telemedicine occurs in Nebraska
1960s	Land-to-space communication incorporated into spacesuits to monitor physiological conditions of astronauts
	NASA develops telemedicine program for Native Americans called Space Technology Applied to Rural Papago Advanced Health Care (STARPAHC)
1970s	National Library of Medicine project uses NASA satellite to reach remote Alaskans
1980s	Costs associated with telemedicine decline, which corresponds with increasing use

(adapted from Allan, 2006; Bashshur & Shannon, 2009; Wootton, 2001)

Terms and Concepts at Intersection of Health Communication and Technology

There are a plethora of terms and concepts at the intersection of health communication and technology. In this section we offer a list of these terms and concepts with definitions and examples.

◆ *Health IT* is health information technology. This term is used to describe the comprehensive management of medical information and its secure exchange between patients or health care consumers and health care providers (www.Healthcare.gov).

For example, a department at a health maintenance organization (HMO) may be called the Health IT Department because this department is responsible for electronically gathering, storing, and distributing all the health information generated by the HMO while maintaining a safe environment for sharing and storing the information. A specific example is the Columbia Basin Health Association located in Othello, Washington, which uses Health IT to allow 25,000 patients access to a variety of medical, dental, and prescription medicine services. In addition, these were among the first health centers in the United States to transition from paper-based charts to an electronic health records system. They used this system to track their diabetic patients in rural communities and substantially increased their access to care for foot and eye exams (Herzer & Seshamani, 2009).

Health IT offers several benefits by allowing for comprehensive management of medical information and its secure exchange between patients and health care providers. Some of the benefits of Health IT for patients and health care providers include:

❖ Complete, accurate, and searchable health information, available at the point of diagnosis and care, allowing for more informed decision making to enhance the quality and reliability of health care delivery.

❖ More efficient and convenient delivery of care, without waiting for the exchange of records or paperwork and without requiring unnecessary or repetitive tests or procedures.

❖ Earlier diagnosis and characterization of disease, with the potential to improve outcomes and reduce costs.

❖ Reductions in adverse events through an improved understanding of each patient's particular medical history, potential for drug-drug interactions, or (eventually) enhanced understanding of a patient's metabolism or even genetic profile and likelihood of a positive or potentially harmful response to a course of treatment.

❖ Increased efficiencies related to administrative tasks, allowing for more interaction with and transfer of information to patients, caregivers, and clinical care coordinators, and monitoring of patient care.

◆ *E-Patient*—describes adults who look online for health information (Fox & Jones, 2009). For example, the first author of this book, Professor Mattson, would be considered an e-Patient because when she went to the dentist recently she asked the hygienist if their dental practice used an autoclave with pressure steam to disinfect the instruments hygienists use to clean teeth. When asked by the hygienist how she knew about the instrument disinfecting process, Professor Mattson answered that she learned via the internet that it is important that dental instruments are not only cleaned but also disinfected using this type of mechanical process. The hygienist responded, "I had a feeling you were going to say you'd read about it on the internet, and yes, we do use that type of system."

To learn more about e-Patients, go to the Web site for this book to read about and listen to a National Public Radio story, "Patients Turn to Online Community for Help Healing." This story features an interview with Susannah Fox of the Pew Internet and American Life Project.

◆ *e-Health*—"health services and information delivered or enhanced through the Internet and related technologies. . . . The term characterizes not only a technical development, but also a state-of-mind, a way of thinking, an attitude, and a commitment for networked, global thinking, to improve health care locally, regionally, and worldwide by using information and communication technology" (Eysenbach, 2001, p. 2). More simply put, e-Health is the use of information technology in the delivery of health care (Oh, Rizo, Enkin, & Jadad, 2005). For example, the Comprehensive Health Enhancement Support System (CHESS) that we cover later in this chapter is considered an e-Health system that integrates information, support, and decision and analysis tools for breast cancer patients.

◆ *Telehealth*—use of telecommunication technologies to provide health care services and access to medical and surgical information for training and educating health care providers and patients, to increase awareness and educate the public about health-related issues, and to facilitate medical research across distances (Mosby, 2009). For example, medical tourism patients often benefit from telehealth for preoperative and postoperative care. A patient who elects to have a colonoscopy in Bangkok, Thailand, because it is less expensive given the constraints of his health insurance coverage in the United States, can accomplish both preprocedure and postprocedure information sharing from home with his health care provider in Thailand via a secure Web server and encrypted e-mail.

◆ *Telemedicine*—use of advanced communication technologies, within the context of clinical health, that deliver care to patients across distance (Matusitz & Breen, 2007; Turner, 2003; Wootton, 2001). Telemedicine is the ability to provide interactive health care utilizing modern technology and telecommunications. Basically, there are two types of telemedicine practice.

❖ *Active telemedicine* allows patients to visit with physicians or other health care providers live over video for immediate care.

❖ *Store-and-forward telemedicine* captures video and/or still images and patients' data, which are stored and sent to physicians or other health care providers for diagnosis and/or follow-up treatment at a later time.

So, whether you live in the center of New York City or deep in the Brazilian Amazon, telemedicine is a health care tool for diagnosis and follow-up care. For example, in the poor and remote Solomon Islands, located northeast of Australia, there is very limited access to medical specialists who diagnose and treat diseases. Thus, a telemedicine project was designed to capture digital photos of tissue samples and send those photos via e-mail for diagnosis to a group of seven pathologists in Switzerland, Germany, and South Africa. This project decreased the amount of time for patient presentation to diagnosis from 60 days to 3 days (Brauchli, 2006). Is this an example of active telemedicine or store-and-forward telemedicine? Why?

◆ *Digital divide*—gap between people who have access to electronic and information technologies and those who do not. van Dijk (2005) challenged this simplistic definition by suggesting that the digital divide is a much more complex problem and that actually there are multiple divides. He described four distinct types of digital access or four distinct types of digital divides.

❖ Motivational access—ambition to use new communication technologies.

❖ Material access—possession of a computer and an internet connection. This is the divide most often considered when discussing the digital divide.

❖ Skills access—ability and confidence to effectively use digital technologies.

❖ Usage access—structural differences in the uses of digital technologies, including usage time, usage diversity, broadband use, and creative use. Usage gaps are bigger than material access gaps and skills gaps. In other words, those rich in access to digital technologies are getting richer. Meaning those already with the most resources and best positions in society also take the most advantage of every new resource.

In a study about the digital divide, Rains (2008) analyzed responses from a survey conducted by the National Cancer Institute and found that those who were younger, more educated, and lived in urban areas were more likely to have a broadband internet connection in their home. So those with a broadband connection were more likely to use the internet for health-related information seeking and communication than those with a dial-up connection. These results support the argument that a digital divide exists and influences access to health information and health communication. One of the concerns with the increase in e-Health initiatives is the populations who lack access to technology and, therefore, cannot take advantage of these initiatives. Are you a victim of the digital divide? Why or why not?

◆ *Electronic medical record (EMR)*—a legal electronic clinical record for a patient that is created in and owned by a health care facility, such as a clinic or hospital, and is used by health care providers within that health care facility to document, monitor, and manage health care delivery. In other words, it is a record of what happened to the patient during encounters at a particular health care facility (Garets & Davis, 2005). For example, when Professor Mattson was in the hospital for a month following the amputation of her leg in a motorcycle accident, an EMR was created by the hospital staff. This record included all the services she received at that hospital until her discharge, including surgical services, nursing care, and physical therapy. Each time Professor Mattson returns to this hospital for a check-up with her surgeon, he and his team access her EMR to review the case and document changes.

◆ *Electronic health record (EHR)*—a longitudinal electronic record of patient health information, including patient input and access, spanning episodes of health care which may include multiple health care organizations within a community, state, or region. For example, Marilyn K. Render (2009) of the American Health Information Management Association (AHIMA) maintains an EHR including "lab reports, weight, vitals, etc.," and she credited this type of record keeping with saving her life when she almost was given the wrong medication by a health care provider. Based on her experience, she contends that having a personal health record allows her to be an educated consumer and patient who can communicate knowledgeably with health care providers and gives her a sense of responsibility for the quality of her health information and health care. If you are interested in creating an EHR, refer to Table 12.2.

The issue of electronic medical records and electronic health records has been an ongoing point of contention and debate in the United States. Many, including those in President Obama's administration, argue that establishing a consistent system of EHRs has the potential to improve health care quality, prevent medical errors, increase the efficiency of care provision and reduce unnecessary health care costs, increase administrative efficiencies, decrease paperwork, expand access to affordable care, and improve population health (www.healthcare.gov). Studies suggest that EHRs could save the United States health care system $81 billion annually in health care efficiency and safety benefits (Hillestad et al., 2005). However, there is widespread concern about the potential of these electronic records to compromise privacy (Healy, 2009).

Although there are a variety of closely related terms and concepts that refer to the intersection of health communication and technology, we adopt the term *e-Health*. The next section explains our rationale for this choice from the terms available.

Rationale for Adopting Term "e-Health"

As you may realize from the definitions presented, the terms telehealth and e-Health are closely intertwined, and many experts may argue that these terms be used interchangeably or as synonyms. However, we prefer the term e-Health and use it in the remainder of this chapter and throughout the book. We prefer e-Health because, as Eysenbach (2001) suggested, e-Health is broadly defined and applicable to the constantly changing electronic environment. Also, we consider the term e-Health more consistent with our Health as Communication Nexus perspective, because e-Health not only focuses attention on the role of communication technologies in health care, it also addresses more directly the impact of these

Questions to Ask When Making Decisions about an Electronic Health Record

There are several ways to develop an electronic health record (EHR). You can do it yourself using resources from the internet or your local library or you can purchase an EHR from a supplier. Regardless of how you develop your EHR, consider this list of questions to guide you during the process.

◆ Content
  ❖ Will the EHR provide all the information I need for a complete health history?
  ❖ Will information be automatically added to the EHR from any other records (e.g., insurance, employment, care)? If so, what information will be added, and how will it be added? Is the information transfer audited?
  ❖ Do I have the opportunity to delete, correct, or add information? How will I do this?

◆ Ownership and use
  ❖ Does the supplier and/or sponsor of my EHR have any ownership rights to the collected information?
  ❖ Can the supplier and/or sponsor of my EHR sell my information to anyone or for any reason? If so, how can I protect my privacy? Can I specify that my information not be sold?
  ❖ Will my information be used for employment or insurance coverage decisions (e.g., to determine insurance eligibility)?

◆ Access and security
  ❖ Who has access to the information in my EHR?
  ❖ Can I choose to give my physician, dentist, and other health care providers access to my EHR? How do I control the sharing of my information?
  ❖ How will my information be protected from unauthorized use?

◆ Portability
  ❖ How can I transfer my information to another EHR sponsor (e.g., a new insurer or new supplier)?

◆ Cost
  ❖ Will there be any cost for me to have an EHR? For example, are there fees if I give my physician, dentist, and other health care providers access to my EHR?

Learn more about EHRs and personal health records (PHRs) and create your own EHR or PHR by visiting the Web site for this book.

(adapted from AHIMA Personal Health Record Practice Council, 2009)

Table 12.2 ◆ *Questions to ask about EHRs*

technologies on health communication and other health care processes and outcomes.

In answering the question "What is e-Health?," Eysenbach (2001) offered "the ten E's in e-Health," which constitute e-Health's essential characteristics. In addition, there are three practical goals or desirable characteristics that e-Health should strive for to increase opportunities to utilize e-Health and realize its benefits. The ten E's in e-Health are presented next, followed by the three desirable characteristics of e-Health.

10 Es in e-Health

◆ *Enabling*—sharing of health information and interaction about health.

◆ *Extending*—broadening the scope of health care and health communication both geographically and conceptually, meaning that consumers can readily obtain health information and interact about health issues with others nearby and far away.

◆ *Empowerment*—allowing access to health information, such as health records and quality comparisons, by patients and consumers who have an increasing sense of personal agency and choice in health care.

◆ *Equity*—promising more equality in health care because more equal access to health information by health care providers, patients, and consumers. Ironically, equal access to technology, known as the digital divide, remains a threat to this promise of equality in health care for those who do not have the resources, such as money, transportation, and skills to access computers and/or the internet.

◆ *Encouragement*—enhancing patients' partnership role in health care decision making.

◆ *Efficiency*—streamlining services or avoiding duplicate services to decrease costs and add value and satisfaction.

◆ *Enhancing quality*—increasing excellence of services by comparing services across units or individuals.

◆ *Evidence based*—measuring efficiency and quality based on systematic evaluation.

◆ *Education*—teaching health care providers, patients, and consumers through electronic sources.

◆ *Ethics*—posing new challenges and threats to moral codes and appropriate conduct surrounding issues such as informed consent, privacy, professional conduct, and relationship equality.

In summary, the ten E's of e-Health constitute the essential or necessary characteristics of e-Health to achieve maximum effectiveness. Ideally, these essential characteristics should be coupled with the three desirable characteristics of e-Health presented in the next section.

3 Desirable Characteristics of e-Health

To offer the benefits within the ten essential characteristics of e-Health listed previously, e-Health systems also must possess three desirable characteristics:

◆ Easy to use
◆ Entertaining
◆ Exciting

Taken together, the essential and desirable characteristics of e-Health help us better understand the potential advantages of e-Health along with the potential impact of e-Health on health communication. However, there are related communication barriers and benefits to e-Health, which are discussed in the next sections.

Communication Barriers to e-Health

Adapted from Turner's (2003) discussion of telemedicine, there are four communication-oriented barriers to realizing the benefits of e-Health including:

◆ Patient privacy
◆ Costs
◆ Organizational concerns
◆ Interpersonal concerns

Let's consider each of these barriers.

Patient Privacy

Patient privacy, or protecting patients' confidential health information, is one of the major barriers to expanding and extending e-Health because concerns about privacy erode patient trust in health care systems and integrating mechanisms that protect patient privacy are costly and not always fail-safe. Because the hallmark of e-Health is the allowance of health communication across the boundaries of space and time, it demands patients' medical records be digitized and potentially widely transmitted, thereby opening the possibility of privacy breaches.

In Chapter 4, "Linking Health Communication with Patient Interaction," we learned about a case study involving release of the details surrounding a patient's personal health problems during an open court hearing even though the patient was not involved in the lawsuit and did not realize permission had been granted to release his medical records. In that same study, Mattson and Brann (2002) reported that in managed care environments, "instead of just the primary physician and immediate staff having access to a patient's information, as many as 17 people now have authorized access to a patient's record" (p. 338). The taken-for-granted use of computers in health care and e-Health systems must be coupled with an explicit understanding that because of computerization, the patient/

ETHICAL DILEMMA ◆ What Would You Do?

You are working at the hospital in your hometown. As part of your data entry job in the patient records department, you have computer access to patients' electronic medical records. Today one of the patient charts you are tasked with entering into an electronic medical record is that of your mom's best friend. Your mom's best friend's chart indicates that she had a positive biopsy for breast cancer. You are tempted to pick up your cell phone and call your mom because you don't think she knows about her friend's health condition and you are confident your mom would want you to tell her.

◆ Do you follow through by dialing your mom's phone number? Why or why not?
◆ Do any of the theories or concepts you learned about in Chapter 2, "Linking Health Communication with Ethics," assist you in deciding whether to call or not call your mom to tell her about her friend's health condition?
◆ Under what circumstances would you be justified in telling your mom what you learned about her friend's health condition?
◆ Could communicating this information with your mom be harmful to her friend? If so, how?

health care provider relationship is extended to those who operate and maintain the computer systems. Also, systematic policies and procedures to maintain privacy must be revisited often and revised when necessary, which can create resource barriers to extending e-Health systems (Turner, 2003).

Costs

Another barrier to e-Health are the *costs* of e-Health, which refer to the expenses associated with the equipment and personnel needed to design, implement, and maintain an e-Health system. Ideally, e-Health has the potential to reduce health care costs due to savings in time and money. Although it is difficult to determine current estimates of the financial and other resource costs of e-Health because estimates vary and often compare relatively discrete aspects of an e-Health system. Generally e-Health promises to decrease health care costs over time. The more immediate costs of designing, implementing, and supporting e-Health systems are high and can be prohibitive for health care organizations.

For example, a Harvard study (Himmelstein, Wright, & Woolhandler, 2010) determined that EMRs did not dramatically reduce administrative costs in the 4,000 United States hospitals analyzed between 2003 and 2007. However, EMRs may have contributed to modest improvements in health care quality for heart attack patients. These researchers also found that Veterans Administration hospitals used EMRs to improve quality and reduce diagnostic test duplication, which equated to cost savings.

Organizational Concerns

The third barrier to e-Health is *organizational concerns,* which involve unique workflow and communication issues that may arise because e-Health systems essentially create a new organizational form that exists mostly if not entirely in a virtual reality. Although the primary health care goal of assisting patients may remain the same, the tasks and communication processes associated with reaching the goal within this virtual organizational form are different so the strategies and work practices must be considered and often adapted to avoid this being a barrier to e-Health implementation.

For example, Page (2003) studied how health care organizations responded to pressures by the health insurance industry to decrease costs through technological innovations that increase efficiency of caregiving. Initially, insurers targeted in-patient hospital care, closely scrutinizing providers' use of various seemingly unnecessary health services and discounting payments to health care providers. Health care providers responded to these challenges by creating loosely coupled contracting networks and partnerships of health care providers and hospitals which were primarily virtual organizational forms. To maintain quality communication with patients and improve patient care in light of these virtual organizational arrangements, this research looked to other human service industries to provide examples. These other industries suggested that creative leadership and strong organizational cultures must be developed and maintained through individual incentives to health care providers and quality improvement processes that self-perpetuate inter-organizational growth and advancement.

Interpersonal Concerns

The fourth barrier to e-Health is *interpersonal concerns,* which involve unique relationship and interaction issues that may arise because e-Health creates a virtual health care environment. The relationships and interactions between patients and health care providers and among health care providers dramatically change and must be fostered via technology. If health care providers adopt e-Health systems, patients likely follow, but attention needs to be paid to the unique aspects of these virtual relationships. As examples, if patients more often are communicating with their health care providers via e-mail rather than face-to-face or by telephone, much contextual information is lost and there is more possibility for misunderstandings because nonverbal cues are minimized in the virtual environment. Also, to conduct an examination using telemedicine, physicians must trust another health care provider to follow their directions and perform the examinations effectively for them. If time and attention is not given to these unique relationships, the success of the e-Health system may be in jeopardy.

Although the barriers to e-Health may pose considerable challenges to effective health communication, there are major communication benefits of e-Health that likely make it worthwhile to overcome the challenges. The communication benefits of e-Health are presented in the next section.

Communication Benefits of e-Health

Adapted from Matusitz and Breen's (2007) discussion of telemedicine, there are four key benefits of e-Health:

- ◆ Transcendence of geographical boundaries
- ◆ Transcendence of temporal boundaries
- ◆ Patient satisfaction
- ◆ Wide distribution of health information

Let's consider each of these benefits.

Transcendence of Geographical Boundaries

Upon reading the milestones in the history of health communication and technology previously presented in this chapter, it becomes apparent that a major advantage of e-Health is its ability to *transcend geographical boundaries,* meaning that because of its virtual properties and use of technological systems health care can occur between patients and health care providers who are located in different places. This benefit increases access to health care and alleviates imbalances in geographic allocation of health care resources, such as physical facilities and personnel.

For example, when 16-year old Kim was brought to Ashley Medical Center, a Critical Access Hospital and skilled nursing facility in rural North Dakota, doctors believed she would never walk or talk again. A serious head injury sustained in a car accident left the teenager in a semi-conscious state, unable to sit up, communicate or even make eye contact with people. However, after intensive physical and occupational therapy at the hospital, Kim is walking with the help of a cane, reading, and doing math problems. Through the St. Alexius Telecare Network, Kim is able to receive speech therapy services as part of her ongoing treatment. Speech therapist Carrie S. notes, "Kim has made remarkable improvement in her cognitive and speech skill. She has progressed from a level of not being able to verbalize, to currently being able to use her voice for basic needs and wants. With gains in her cognitive abilities, Kim has begun to return to her high school classwork. Her motivation and positive attitude are second to none; with hard work, determination and this unique opportunity for intensive speech therapy, she has already far surpassed the cognitive and communication prognosis she was given by medical professionals in the first several months after the accident." Telemedicine was the difference, allowing Kim to receive treatment from a hospital more than 120 miles away. Her parents, who are farmers, simply would not have the time or the resources to travel that distance and Kim would not have made the progress that has given her the quality of life she has today (St. Alexius Medical Center, 2009).

Transcendence of Temporal Boundaries

In addition to reducing restrictions imposed by geographical boundaries, another benefit of e-Health is that it *transcends temporal boundaries,* meaning that because of its virtual properties and use of technological systems, patients and health care providers do not need to be simultaneously present in the same location for health care to be accomplished. This savings in time can result in resource savings for patients, such as savings in time and money traveling to the health care facilities and decreases in anxiety often experienced by patients as they wait long periods of time to see their health care providers.

Patient Satisfaction

Another communication benefit of e-Health is increased *patient satisfaction,* which means that many patients feel more comfortable, confident, and pleased with their health care when they participate in e-Health. Research suggests that this may be due to the focused attention patients experience when health care providers exclusively interface about their case (Turner, 2003). Also, as alluded to in the previous section, one of the reasons patients report satisfaction with e-Health is because they do not have to spend time traveling or waiting for their health care providers.

For example, to illustrate the benefits of telemedicine, including patient satisfaction indicators, REM Health, Inc., a home-Health care services company serving Minnesota, Wisconsin, and Iowa highlights the case of Mrs. Jones (REM Health, Inc., 2009). Mrs. Jones lived alone in a rural area, many miles from the nearest hospital, clinic, or neighbor. With no family members close by, she was extremely anxious, which was aggravating her chronic obstructive pulmonary disease (COPD) and leading to increased respiratory difficulties. She was hospitalized frequently and she called and visited her physician numerous times. Mrs. Jones received one skilled nursing visit and three home health aide visits each week. But

PROFILE

e-Health Blogging for Social Support

Nathan Lawrensen—Husband and Father

The ever-growing popularity of blogging provides expanded opportunities for individuals to give and receive social support. Nathan Lawrensen and his immediate family of three have opened up and shared their story with anyone interested in reading Nathan's blog, cfhusband.blogspot.com. Nathan's story begins when he met and fell in love with Tricia who has cystic fibrosis. Cystic fibrosis is a genetic disease that affects the lungs and in some cases the intestinal tract. After their marriage, Tricia's condition worsened to the extent that she was put on the transplant list to receive a set of lungs. Nathan started his blog to keep family and friends who did not live in the area updated about Tricia's condition and treatments.

Shortly after being placed on the organ donation list, Tricia learned that she was pregnant. Thrilled, the Lawrensens vowed to face whatever the future brought. Being pregnant took Tricia off of the transplant list and placed additional strain on her already failing lungs. At 24 weeks, the Lawrensen's daughter, Gwyneth, was born via emergency c-section weighing just 1 pound 6 ounces and she barely was 12 inches long. Already on a ventilator, Tricia was placed in a medically-induced coma for a week. Amazingly, just seven weeks later Tricia was placed back on the transplant list and just two months after that received her new lungs. Meanwhile, Gwyneth continued to defy the odds and 18 weeks after she was born she was released from the hospital.

Throughout the health challenges his wife and child were facing Nathan kept up his blog, both as a way to keep family and friends informed and as a way for him to process his family's experiences. Friends began to tell friends about the blog and within a few weeks the popularity of the blog had spread and it was receiving over 10,000 hits per day. People across the country and the world were checking in, leaving comments, and offering prayers for and support to the Lawrensen family. Although this was never the purpose of the blog, the widespread network potential of this e-Health medium and the support it provides offers a positive boost to the Lawrensen family.

Nathan considers his blog a tremendous opportunity for social support, but he does recognize the differences between the support from his blog readers and the support from close friends and family. Although his blog readers provide a lot of support and encouragement, he says his family would not have survived without their extended family as well as their close-knit church community. He realizes that by including so much about his life on his blog he has opened up to many strangers who feel as if they know the family and therefore provide both negative and positive comments. Some individuals who visit the blog routinely leave critical and disheartening comments, something Nathan has learned with time to overlook.

As Nathan continues his blog by letting readers know about the progress of his wife and daughter, his primary goals are to raise awareness about cystic fibrosis and premature birth, and to raise money to fund cystic fibrosis research. This e-Health blog allows the Lawrensen family to connect and feel supported by people they otherwise would not have met and, in return, their story serves to inspire and challenge their readers.

it was difficult for the agency to consistently provide a home health aide and nursing visits because of the remote location of Mrs. Jones' home, especially during the winter. Besides that, Mrs. Jones' anxiety made her difficult to work with making it challenging to find staff to visit her. After consultation, Mrs. Jones' physician authorized use of the telemedicine program as a means of providing more home support. The skilled nurse visits were changed to three times per week with one in-home visit and two telemedicine visits.

A very anxious, impatient woman met the staff when they arrived with the telemedicine unit, which was quickly and easily installed by plugging it into a phone jack and an electrical outlet. They showed Mrs. Jones and her home health aide, who would be present at each telemedicine visit, how to use it. At this point, Mrs. Jones still was skeptical that telemedicine was going to benefit her. During the first telemedicine visit the next day, Mrs. Jones appeared anxious and irritated. But, by the second visit, she was calmer and according to her home health aide, Mrs. Jones was sitting at the unit waiting for the telemedicine call before the scheduled time. On subsequent visits Mrs. Jones easily engaged in conversation, displaying a surprisingly witty sense of humor. Over the next three months, her COPD was not exacerbated. During that time, Mrs. Jones made no clinic visits, and she called her physician only once. Mrs. Jones began to trust that help was only a phone call away. And she appreciated that if she wasn't feeling well, her condition could be assessed during an instantaneous telemedicine visit.

Wide Distribution of Health Information

Another benefit of e-Health is due to the growing array and sophistication of technologies, such as the internet and telemedicine, which generated the *wide distribution of health information*. People not only gather information about almost any health issue or product via the internet, in some cases they even participate in consultations with their health care providers via internet portals, e-mail, or other forms of telemedicine. The increase in distribution channels means that more people have access to health information. For example, assuming you have access to a computer and the internet, you can easily look up what dementia is, including symptoms and treatments, after your mother calls to tell you that one of your relatives is suffering from dementia. In fact, one of the main reasons most adults use the internet is to look up health information for themselves or loved ones (Fox & Jones, 2009). Consequently, more and more health-oriented organizations, including hospitals, clinics, pharmaceutical companies, and health products companies, are establishing a strong presence on the internet.

An example of a popular e-Health information tool is WebMD (www.WebMD.com). The goal of this Web site is to provide valuable, timely, and credible health information, tools for managing individuals' health, and support to those who seek health information. It spans the gamut from providing information about various health conditions including symptoms to telemedicine services such as linking consumers with health care providers to perform diagnostics and provide access to treatments. One of the features on this Web site is a symptom checker where users can enter their symptoms and learn potential diagnoses. WebMD also partners with major news organizations to serve as their outlets for expanded coverage of current health issues. For example, when the CBS Evening News covered the H1N1 virus in 2009, it routinely stated at the end of stories to "log on to our partner in health WebMD.com for more coverage of the H1N1 virus."

Now that we've countered the communication barriers to e-Health with the communication benefits of e-Health, we turn to the topic of tailoring health communication. However, before we continue by discussing the importance of tailoring health communication messages, please take a few minutes to complete Health Communication Nexus Interlude 12.1.

Health Communication Nexus Interlude 12.1

Begin this interlude by thinking about a health issue, disease, or condition that you always wanted more information about but just didn't have time to research. Perhaps you'd like to know more about an illness you, a family member, or friend had or maybe you're wondering more generally about your chances of becoming ill with a certain disease. After you think of a health issue you'd like to know more about, go to this book's Web site and browse around the WebMD site or type the health issue into the search engine that is part of the WebMD site. After you review the information provided about the health issue you're interested in, respond to these questions in your notebook:

◆ What is the most interesting piece of information you learned about the health issue, disease, or condition using this Web site?

◆ Do you feel more informed about this health issue, disease, or condition based on the information you learned on WebMD?

◆ Do you think the information you found about this health issue, disease, or condition is credible? Why or why not?

◆ Did you use any of the interactive aspects of WebMD, such as requesting an appointment with a doctor or sharing health information with someone else through the Web site?

  ❖ If yes, which interactive aspects did you use and how was your experience using those interactive aspects of WebMD?

◆ In your opinion, what is one advantage and one disadvantage of this health information Web site?

◆ Would you recommend WebMD to others for gathering health information? Why or why not?

Let's build on our learning of the terminology and the communication barriers and benefits associated with e-Health by turning our attention to the concept of tailoring health communication to effectively intersect with technology.

Tailoring Health Communication

The notion of tailoring health communication developed because health campaign practitioners and researchers increasingly realized that the mass audiences they were attempting to reach were very heterogeneous and there were ways to address the unique needs of audience members via persuasive messages. Hence, the generic health messages produced for mass, undifferentiated audiences and distributed via brochures, pamphlets, and booklets became more tailored and included different versions for different audience segments. Later, using computer technology, tailored versions of health messages could be more individually specific.

Audience Segmentation and Message Tailoring

As we discussed in Chapter 8, "Linking Health Communication with Health Campaign Practice," audience segmentation involves dividing the larger population into smaller groups or target audiences. In describing the process of using computers to narrowcast health messages, Rimal and Adkins (2003) defined *audience segmentation* as the process of "dividing audience members according to some meaningful criterion" (p. 500), which may be determined from a health risk assessment. Next *targeting* occurs, which is defined as the strategic selection and use of communication channels to reach the audience segments. Finally, tailoring refers to "crafting health messages to reflect audience characteristics" (p. 500). More specifically *tailoring* is defined as "any combination of information or change strategies intended to reach one specific person, based on characteristics that are unique to that person, related to the outcome of interest, and have been derived from an individual assessment" (Kreuter, Lukwago, Bucholtz, Clark, & Sanders-Thompson, 2002, p. 137).

Message tailoring is different from segmentation and targeting in two primary ways. One difference is that tailoring is directed toward individuals rather than groups. The second difference is that tailoring is based on known or measured differences that exist between individuals.

Phases and Steps of Message Tailoring

With the assistance of computers, the message tailoring process involves three broad phases. The first phase uses a health assessment instrument filled out by individuals within a population. From the results of the health assessment instruments, a computer program *creates and stores profiles* for individuals and/or communities. During the second phase of message tailoring, a *source file* is created which contains message segments to interface with the individual and/or community profiles. The third phase culminates in the *interface of the profiles and the source file* via an expert system or algorithm which is a sort of decision-tree of if/then statements that places message segments in order according to the individual's profile. These message segments are then available for use as they have been tailored to the individual's unique health characteristics and needs.

Tailored health communication is used to enhance the relevance and salience of information, which leads to increased motivation by the individual to process that information and change health behavior. According to Rimer and Kreuter (2006), tailored health communication increased motivation to process health information in four ways. These four ways also constitute the steps involved in effectively tailoring health information. The *steps to tailoring health communication* are:

◆ Match message content to individual's health information needs and interests
◆ Frame health information in a context that is meaningful to the individual
◆ Use design and production elements that capture the individual's attention
◆ Provide health information in the amount, type, and through channels preferred by the individual

Compared with using generic information, computer-based tailored health communication is more likely to be read, remembered, and considered personally relevant. Also, tailored health communication enables individualized feedback, commands greater attention, is processed more intensively, contains less redundant information, and is perceived more positively by health consumers.

To illustrate the message tailoring process, consider the example offered by Rimer and Kreuter (2006) of colorectal cancer screening (CRCS). This example, depicted in Figure 12.1, shows how health campaign practitioners might tailor messages for individuals at different stages of readiness to change. We learned about the Transtheoretical Model/Stages of Change (Prochaska, DiClemente, &

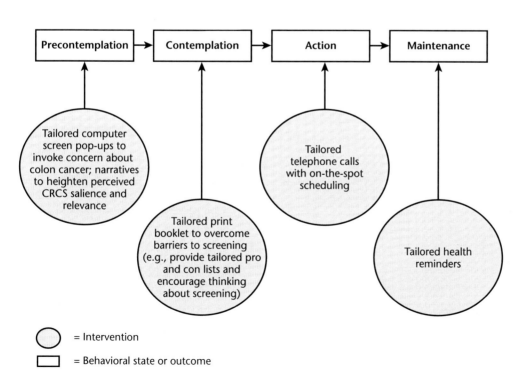

Figure 12.1 ◆ *Example of Message Tailoring (adapted from Rimer & Kreuter, 2006)*

Norcross, 1992) in Chapter 7, "Linking Health Communication with Health Campaign Theories." This example integrates the stages of change with the process of message tailoring. So, referring to Figure 12.1, how is the message to an individual at the contemplation stage different than the message tailored to an individual at the maintenance stage? Can you think of another example of how messages about a certain health issue might be tailored to different individuals?

Now that you understand how the process of message tailoring occurs, let's discuss the variety of technology-based approaches that can be used to tailor health communication.

Technology-Based Approaches to Health Communication

Since the late 1980s, computer technology fostered the growth in use and research of tailoring strategies for health communication. As Suggs (2006) argued in her "10-Year Retrospective of Research in New Technologies for Health Communication," the use of technology-based approaches to health communication has grown substantially within recent years. And the application of these technologies continues to develop into more tailored, cost-effective communications that meet the information and health needs of individuals while maintaining the dynamic connection between patients and health care providers.

We borrow Suggs' (2006) category scheme and provide definitions of the variety of new technologies used in health care settings to enhance health communication. The category scheme includes these categories:

◆ Telephone-based health communication
◆ Stand-alone computer-based health communication
◆ Computer-based tailoring technology
◆ Web-based health interventions
◆ Robotics

Telephone-Based Health Communication

Although some may consider the telephone a low-technology tool and question its usefulness in health communication, it is still an effective way to provide access to health communication for those who may not have ready access to a computer. According to the United States Census conducted in 2000, more than 90% of households in every state except New Mexico had a telephone (National Telecommunications and Information Administration, 2000). Automated telephone technology ranges from voice-interactive health assessments such as those provided by many organizations as part of their workplace wellness programs to automated counseling systems like those used for home HIV testing kits (U. S. Food and Drug Administration, 2009; www.homehealthtesting.com). Most often in telephone-based health communication the telephone serves as the communication medium to push computer-generated health messages to the telephone users.

For example, to answer the question of how to make health information accessible to low-income groups who do not have the resources to comfortably access the internet, Mosavel (2005) determined that telephone-based health information and support may be effective because most people in the United States have access to a telephone including those who are homeless. In this study, individuals from a low-income neighborhood who had been referred to substance-abuse outpatient treatment used a telephone-based information system called Connect to access substance-abuse information and peer support. *Connect* is a telephone system with disease-specific content created by registered users and health care providers. Connect is accessed by a toll-free number and users navigate through a menu by pressing numbers on a touch-tone telephone.

The menu includes various modules such as CareMail, TalkNet, and Community Health Rap. In CareMail, the user receives private messages from health care providers or friends. The messages from health care providers are variations on the theme of coping with substance-abuse addiction. In Community Health Rap, users ask recovery-related questions that are answered by a health expert. In TalkNet users engage in discussion support groups any time of day. Results indicated that those in the outpatient substance-abuse program used the automated, voice interactive telephone-based information system to access substance abuse information and peer support more than they used face-to-face services. More specifically, 47% of the sample did not attend face-to-face outpatient treatment services, but 88% of the sample attempted to use Connect, with 50% of the users accessing Connect between 27 and 4,627 minutes. Even more important is that homeless individuals in this study used Connect significantly more than those who were not homeless. This study suggests that there still is a role for low-technology tools in health communication interventions.

Stand-Alone Computer-Based Health Communication

Health technologies within the category of stand-alone computer-based systems include health communication efforts using public or home computers with software loaded on to the computer hard drive or on CD-ROM, as well as kiosk stations in public spaces, such as shopping malls, drug stores, classrooms, and worksites, and personal digital assistants (PDA) to deliver health information and health messages. These computer-based systems do not use an internet connection but instead the health content is installed on the computer. The health literature includes several examples of stand-alone computer-based communication interventions, such as nutrition (Anderson, Winnett, Wojcik, Winnett, & Bowden, 2001), injury prevention (Eakin, Brady, & Lusk, 2001), and risk reduction (Hornung et al., 2000).

The University of Michigan's Comprehensive Cancer Center launched an example of a stand-alone computer-based communication system. The Michigan Interactive Health Kiosk Project, also referred to as Health-O-Vision, was an award-winning statewide network of multimedia, touch-screen, interactive computer kiosks that linked residents with current health information and motivating messages on a variety of health topics. These kiosks were located in highly accessible public areas frequented by underserved individuals, such as libraries, shopping malls, and health clinics in rural and urban settings. Using interactive communication strategies and individually tailored messages to motivate preventive health behaviors, these kiosks addressed several pressing health issues including, breast and prostate cancer prevention, smoking prevention and cessation, adolescent alcohol intervention, sexually-transmitted disease prevention, bicycle helmet safety, childhood immunization, cardiovascular disease prevention, and Alzheimer's disease. The goal of these kiosks was to reach people in a way they relate to and enjoy, so the kiosks were designed like interactive televisions rather than computers and they allowed people to co-create their experience through touching the screen as they progressed through the program to obtain personally relevant information. Go to the Web site for this book to view an image of Health-O-Vision.

One of the more recently created modules or channels on Health-O-Vision was the Alzheimer's Disease Channel. Connell and her colleagues' (2003) description of the development of this channel coincides with our discussion of how to design, implement, and evaluate a health campaign presented in Chapter 8, "Linking Health Communication with Health Campaign Practice." The goal of the Alzheimer's Disease Channel was to increase knowledge and awareness of Alzheimer's Disease among the general public in Michigan.

Based on what you learned in Chapter 8 about the practice of health campaigns, would these Health-O-Vision kiosks about Alzheimer's Disease be an example of a push or pull strategy? If you said a pull strategy, you are correct, because these kiosks gain information from individuals and then provide health information based on each individual's unique characteristics or questions. So what do you consider the advantages and disadvantages of these kiosk systems?

Another, very different, example of a stand-alone computer-based communication system is the use of PDAs by health care providers in critical care units of some hospitals. As Lapinsky (2007) discovered, these handheld devices offered a convenient mobile platform for efficient and timely point-of-care access to information which may be beneficial to patients. However, these devices are not used widely because many health care providers do not accept or adopt them and there are concerns about the transmission of viruses by these portable devices.

Generally, the outcomes associated with stand-alone computer-based communications demonstrated that these approaches to health communication were effective and overall users were satisfied using these systems (Revere & Dunbar, 2001; Wantland, Portillo, Holzemer, Slaughter, & McGhee, 2004).

Computer-Based Tailoring Technology

Unlike the previous types of technology described, computer-based tailoring technology does not refer to the unique aspects of the physical hardware that is used to advance health communication, instead it refers to an application that uses different forms of hardware. As discussed in a previous section on tailoring health communication, *computer-based tailoring technology* uses sophisticated and proprietary computer software that matches individual responses to health assessment questions with massive message libraries to create tailored health communication, including text, audio, and video messages that address aspects of an individual's health status including health beliefs and attitudes, family health history, stage of change, barriers to change, and self-efficacy. Although we know many of the benefits of tailored health communication, including that tailored communication is more likely to be attended to, processed, and remembered, understanding of computer-tailored health interventions delivered via the internet is still developing.

In their review of computer-tailored health interventions delivered via the internet, Lustria and colleagues (Lustria, Cortese, Noar, & Glueckauf, 2009) concluded that because of the diversity of features and formats used, ranging from simple to complex, it was impossible to fairly compare the programs. To optimize the use and comparison of computer-assisted tailoring of health communication, they suggested developing guidelines for tailoring health communication across populations, health topics, health behaviors, and situations. They also called for more research into the health outcomes of tailored communication to better understand the conditions that lead to effective online interventions.

Web-Based Health Interventions

To address the major limitation associated with the more static aspects of stand-alone computer-based communication, namely keeping information current, Web-based health interventions burst on the scene in recent years and their use is growing. In part, this growth is based on more people having access to the internet and using it to search for health information. Fox and Jones (2009) reported that in 2000, 46% of American adults had access to the internet, 5% of households in the United States had broadband connections, and 25% of American adults looked online for health information. Currently, 74% of American adults have access to the internet, 57% of American households have broadband connections, and 61% of adults look online for health information. Although internet use is neither universal nor equally accessible, its widespread utilization makes it a valuable medium for the dissemination of minimal-intervention health information.

Initially, the first generation of health-related Web sites simply posted print-based information online. For example, Centers for Disease Control and Prevention (CDC) initiated its Web presence by posting fact sheets with static information on various health issues. The fact sheets posted to the www.cdc.gov Web site were identical to those CDC provided in print to its target audiences, including the public and health care providers. CDC's DES Update Web pages still contain many of these types of fact sheets. To experience the difference between early Web postings and current interactive Web sites, please complete Health Communication Nexus Interlude 12.2.

To experience the difference between early and more current health Web site postings and communications, go to the Web site for this book. Take a few minutes to familiarize yourself with CDC's DES Update Web site by navigating around the site and clicking on various links. Then, based on your tour around the site coupled with what you're learning in this chapter, find and identify two fact sheets about DES and jot down in your notebook the title of each fact sheet and where you found the fact sheet on the Web site.

◆ Fact Sheet #1:

◆ Fact Sheet #2:

Next, find an interactive communication tool within CDC's DES Update Web pages and jot down in your notebook the title of the interactive tool and where you found the interactive tool on the Web site.

◆ Interactive Tool:

Which of these two CDC's DES Update resources, the fact sheets or the interactive tool, did you find more helpful and why? Which resource captivated your interest more and why? Write your responses in your notebook and keep your reactions in mind as you progress through this chapter.

Today, second generation health-related Web sites, such as CDC's Web site (www.cdc.gov), are much more interactive and provide immediate feedback, allowing individuals to search for specific information, take quizzes, and interact with others who share their interests in certain health topics. Some health care organizations even use their Web sites to foster interaction between patients and health care providers. Some physicians offer communication with patients through a Web site link to e-mail service or create spaces on their Web site where patients can access and review their charts. Positive outcomes of these more sophisticated channels of communication were reported, including enhancements in attention, active cognitive processing, motivation to learn, self-efficacy, self-management, and social support (Fox & Jones, 2009).

Despite the positive outcomes of Web-based health interventions, there are a few limitations, some of which already were mentioned but bear repeating. These limitations include:

◆ Costs
◆ Access
◆ Information overload
◆ Information quality

The first and second limitations associated with Web-based health interventions are interrelated. Often there are several *costs* an individual, family, or organization incur before gaining access to Web-based health interventions. Accessing the internet involves computer hardware, software, and training, which require resources, such as time and money. If these resources are not attainable or available, *access* to Web-based interventions is not possible. This inability to access Web-based interventions is known as the digital divide. As discussed previously in this chapter, the *digital divide* is defined as the gap between those who have computers with internet access and those who do not, as well as the gap between those who effectively use a computer or are computer literate and those who are not.

The third and fourth limitations associated with Web-based health interventions also are interrelated. *Information overload* refers to the excessive amount of health-related information on the internet and the overwhelming feeling that occurs when realizing the sheer amount of information that is available and likely cannot be processed. According to *Information Processing Theory* (Miller, 1956), humans can attend to and adequately process and remember only so much information. When the amount of information taken in exceeds the upper limit of information processing ability, information overload occurs.

Also related to the excessive amount of information on the internet is the questionable quality of much of the health information available on the internet. *Information quality* refers to the value and usefulness of information content. The questionable quality of information on the internet is due in part to the lack of editorial oversight of internet content. Anyone can post almost anything on the internet. By extension, anyone can offer health information and advice on the internet without possessing any medical or health-related credentials.

For example, during the 2009–2010 H1N1 virus outbreak in the United States, health officials at CDC warned the public to be careful of flu remedies sold on the internet because there are no controls over who can advertise and sell products that claim to cure the flu. These limitations in Web-based health interventions may cause uncertainty about all health information, including legitimate health information, posted on the internet and through other computer-based sources.

Internet users require a certain level of health literacy to discern credible information and effectively use information they find on the internet. Simple strategies such as checking multiple sources and/or verifying information with medical professionals are ways to check the credibility of Web sites and the information they provide. The National Cancer Institute (2009) suggested answering these questions when evaluating health information on the internet:

- ◆ Who owns the Web site?
- ◆ Who funds the Web site?
- ◆ What is the purpose of the Web site?
- ◆ Is information on the site documented?
- ◆ How current is the information?

If answers to these questions raise suspicions about the credibility or reliability of the information on the Web site, either ignore that Web site or crosscheck the information it provides with credible sources.

Robotics

One of the newest forms of technology in the health arena is the use of robots to perform medical procedures. Currently, the most common use of robots is during surgical procedures with a physician controlling the robotic equipment. For example, the da Vinci surgical system, the first approved in the United States, is a robot used to perform laparoscopic procedures, which decreases the size of incisions and allows for faster recovery. During surgery, the surgeon uses hand controls to direct the robotic surgical instruments and the internal cameras and lens and is able to perform the surgery with more precision (Tabor, 2007; Figure 12.2). Other surgical systems are being developed to allow surgeons to be in remote locations while directing robotics to perform surgery independently.

As technology continues to improve and more research is conducted in the area of robotics, many predict that robots will take on an increased role in all aspects of health care delivery. In Japan engineers worked with medical professionals to design and create robots that help care for the aging Japanese population. Robots are being designed to take vital statistics, remind patients to take medication, and even dispense medication. The hope is that with the development of

Figure 12.2 ◆ *da Vinci surgical system*

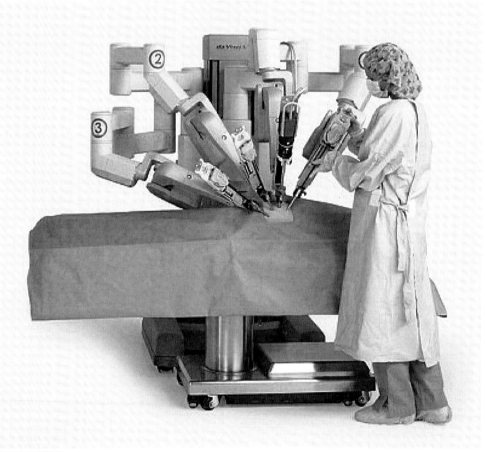

© HO/Reuters/CORBIS

smart robots, robots may be able to take on the role of home health care providers (Wilson, Coledan, Erwin, & Gourley, 2004).

Because the use of robotics is so new, little research considers the influences robotics may have on health communication, including communication among the health care team. To date, most research on robotics in health care emphasizes efficiency and cost savings (Giulianotti, et al., 2003; Krebs, et al., 1999). How do you think including a robot in the health care mix will impact interaction? Will communication be better or worse? Would you want a robot involved in your health care? Why or why not?

Now that we've clarified terminology, considered the communication barriers and benefits of e-Health technologies, and reviewed the types of technologies found at the intersection of health communication and technology, we present a few theories to shed some additional light on the subject of health communication and e-Health.

Theoretical Explanations for Using Technology in Health Care

Three theories are particularly germane to understanding the ever-increasing role technology is playing in our lives generally and in our health care specifically. The theories presented are:

◆ Theory of Reasoned Action
◆ Technology Acceptance Model
◆ Diffusion of Innovations

Theory of Reasoned Action

The Theory of Reasoned Action (TRA) was explained in Chapter 7, "Linking Health Communication with Health Campaign Theories." However, it is worth reviewing TRA again, specifically relative to e-Health. The *Theory of Reasoned Action* asserts that an individual's performance of a behavior is determined by that individual's intention to perform the behavior, which is jointly determined by the individual's attitude and subjective norm concerning the behavior (Ajzen & Fishbein, 1980; Fishbein & Ajzen, 1975). Attitudes are determined by beliefs about outcomes or attributes of the behavior weighted by the evaluations of those outcomes or attributes. So an individual who holds strong beliefs that positively valued outcomes result from performing the behavior have a positive attitude toward the behavior. Similarly, an individual's subjective norm is determined by that individual's normative beliefs about whether important referent others approve or disapprove of performing the behavior, weighted by the individual's motivation to comply with those referents. Thus an individual who believes that certain referents think he or she should perform a behavior, and is motivated to meet the expectations of those referents, has a positive subjective norm. TRA assumes a causal chain that links

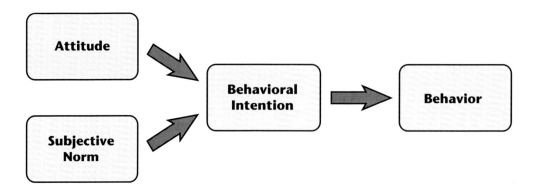

Figure 12.3 ◆ *Theory of Reasoned Action.*

behavioral beliefs and normative beliefs to behavioral intention and behavior, via attitude and subjective norms (Figure 12.3).

For example, TRA could predict whether a person is inclined to use WebMD or not. So, using Figure 12.3 as a guide, how would you apply this theory to predict whether your best friend would use WebMD for health information on a certain topic?

Technology Acceptance Model

The Technology Acceptance Model (TAM; Davis, 1989) is closely related to TRA, however, TRA is a more general theory of human behavior, whereas the TAM is a more specific theory about human behavior and technology use.

The *Technology Acceptance Model* seeks to identify general determinants of computer or information technology acceptance by individual end-users. This theory proposes that two beliefs, perceived usefulness and perceived ease of use, are key to developing positive attitudes about a technology and eventually adopting a technology. *Perceived usefulness* is defined as the prospective user's subjective probability that using a specific technology increases task performance. *Perceived ease of use* is defined as the degree to which a prospective user expects using the technology is effortless. These two beliefs are influenced by *external factors* associated with the technology including characteristics of the technological system, such as icons, menus, touch screens and training in how to use the technology. External factors influence the prospective user's perceptions of usefulness and ease of use. In turn, the prospective user's *attitude toward using the technology* is based on beliefs about usefulness and ease of use. Behavioral intention to use the technology is predicted by attitudes toward that behavior with individuals being more inclined to perform a behavior for which their attitude is positive. *Behavioral intention* is defined as an individual's intent or inclination to perform a behavior.

Unlike TRA, the TAM also predicts a direct effect of the usefulness belief on behavioral intention. That is, if an individual has a positive perception of the usefulness of a technology, this directly effects their intention to adopt the technology

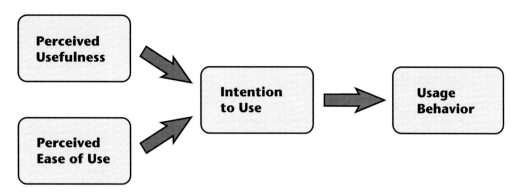

Figure 12.4 ◆ *Technology Acceptance Model*

without that intention being mediated by attitude toward using the technology. Behavioral intention, then, influences actual technology use, meaning that a positive behavior intention leads to technology use, whereas a negative behavioral intention does not lead to technology use. Figure 12.4 illustrates the TAM.

As you may have noticed, another rather blatant difference between TRA and the TAM is that in the TAM *subjective norm*, defined as the influence of an individual's social network on that individual's behavioral intention, is not included as a determinant of behavioral intention. This deletion occurred because research did not consistently show the direct effects of subjective norms on behavioral intentions and the indirect effect via attitudes.

Given what you know about TRA and the TAM, could you describe the model in Figure 12.4 to someone else? What does each box or variable in this model mean and how do the arrows connect each variable? How would you use the model to predict your own or someone else's likelihood to use telemedicine or some other e-Health technology?

Concepts from the TAM predicted both physician and patient attitudes toward telemedicine (Gammon, Johannessen, Wynn, & Whitten, 2008). For example, Werner (2004) and Werner and Karnieli (2003) found that in different clinical settings, including routine and specialized care, patients' acceptance of telemedicine was positively correlated with their relationships with their physicians and negatively correlated with their anxieties toward technology. And, in general, patients were more willing to use telemedicine in routine rather than specialized care, such as psychiatric care. Chau and Hu (2002) determined that physicians were primarily pragmatic in their acceptance of telemedicine and they tended to focus on usefulness rather than ease of use or their colleagues' opinions about using the technology.

We also touch on a third theory, Diffusion of Innovations (DOI). Although we discuss DOI at some length in Chapter 3, "Linking Health Communication with Theories Informed by Health Communication," in this chapter we apply the theory specifically to e-Health.

Diffusion of Innovations

One of the theories we discussed in Chapter 3 was the Diffusion of Innovations. To summarize, this model attempts to explain how ideas and behaviors spread among people. More specifically, *diffusion of innovations* is the process by which new ideas or technologies spread via communication channels over time among the members of a social system (Rogers, 2001).

DOI is a viable framework for understanding the adoption of communication technologies for health care. Although patients and health care providers have used some communication technologies for decades, such as telephones, to communicate about health, more recently a greater variety of technologies were introduced to support a wider array of health care services. Examples of more current communication technologies and/or processes that are enhanced by the use of e-Health technologies include smartphones to track patients and scheduling, tele-consulting between primary care physicians and specialists, and social network Web sites such as Facebook to spread health campaign messages. DOI helps us understand why some members of health care systems are more likely to utilize these new technologies while others are more resistant to utilizing new communication technologies.

In their DOI meta-analysis of telemedicine research in health care systems, Menachemi, Burke, and Ayers (2004) discovered several factors that affect the adoption of telemedicine by physicians, hospital administrators, and health care bill payers (e.g., insurance companies, Medicare, Medicaid). Primarily, there were high levels of uncertainty about the communication technologies used in telemedicine among physicians, patients, health care administrators, and payers. Physicians were uncertain about the impact of telemedicine on the quality of care, quality of services provided, and added complexity to an already strained system. Physicians also were concerned about the ease of using telemedicine systems. If telemedicine systems were not user friendly, they were not adopted even if those systems had many benefits (see also, Falas, Papadopoulos, & Stafylopatis, 2003).

Although patients often were not aware that telemedicine existed, once they knew about these systems they tended to use telemedicine if their health care providers recommended it. For some patients, the learning curve was steep if they did not already used a computer at home. For more tech-savvy patients, because telemedicine systems often used existing telecommunication infrastructures, such as telephone and cable lines and home computers, these patients adapted to and used telemedicine processes fairly quickly and rather effortlessly. Upon using telemedicine, however, patients had concerns about security, confidentiality, privacy, and how the technologies changed their interactions with their health care providers. The biggest advantage that patients realized with telemedicine was considerable savings in travel and wait times which influenced many first-time users to report high satisfaction ratings. However, patients needed adequate time to adjust to this new form of treatment.

For hospital administrators, their concerns were mostly about financial issues, so they tended to be in favor of telemedicine initiatives that saved health care systems money. For example, new telehealth equipment that interfaced seamlessly with existing information technology was more likely to be adopted because implementation and maintenance costs were more reasonable. Also, if telehealth systems were relatively easy for end-users to learn and use, training costs were lower.

For the entities that pay health care bills on behalf of patients and employers, both economic and quality of care arguments affected their endorsement of and reimbursement for telemedicine systems.

An even more specific application of DOI was undertaken by Simon and colleagues (2007). They considered the organizational correlates and barriers to adopting electronic medical records (EMR). Even though in other countries EMRs are used extensively by health care providers, in the United States only about 18% of physicians use this technology (Burt & Sisk, 2005). The findings of their survey suggested that larger, more financially strong, and more technologically advanced medical practices were more likely to use EMRs because these medical practices were more equipped to handle the financial and technological challenges of converting from paper records to electronic records. Not surprisingly, the greatest barrier to adopting EMRs were financial costs. Although this study assessed the use of electronic medical records in one state, Massachusetts, it was consistent with a national survey conducted by Gans, Kralewski, Hammons, and Dowd (2005), which found that lack of support by physicians and inadequate resources were the most substantial barriers to adoption of EMRs.

So what are the implications of e-Health for health communication? In the next section, we take up this question and offer recommendations for integrating e-Health approaches into health care.

Implications of e-Health for Health Communication

In this chapter, we introduce you to concepts and examples at the intersection of health communication and e-Health. You may be wondering, what are the implications of e-Health for health communication? Further, what recommendations can be gleaned from the literature on health communication and e-Health? The implications and recommendations span interpersonal interactions and organizational considerations.

After carefully studying online communication in health settings, Moyer and Katz (2007) offered the recommendations in Table 12.3 for matching communication channel with goals in interpersonal health care interactions:

Table 12.3 ◆ *Recommendations for matching communication channel with heath care interaction goals (adapted from Moyer & Katz, 2007)*

CHANNEL OF COMMUNICATION	RECOMMENDED FOR:
Online communication	Simple issues of low sensitivity
	Service-related issues, such as making appointments or clarifying billing questions
	Simple status reports or test results with little influence on diagnosis, prognosis, or treatment
	Ongoing relationship building with established patients
	Health promotion and disease prevention campaign/programs
Telephone calls	Issues that are too complex for asynchronous communication but simple enough to be handled in one conversation
	Relationship building with patients who have been seen before
Face-to-face visits	Complex or sensitive issues
	Issues related to new diagnosis, prognosis, treatment, surveillance, or important follow-up
	Relationship building, especially with new patients

From an organizational perspective, Whitten, Steinfield, and Hellmich (2001) presented case studies of two e-Health businesses, ePharmacy, an online-only pharmacy, and eDoctor, an online physician's consultation service. Each of these businesses experienced some success but also faced many challenges. Based on what they learned from these cases, the authors determined, from a business perspective, that a "click and mortar model" may be the best strategy for e-Health communication. The researchers explained their determination and defined a *click and mortar model* in this way:

> The best chance for success in the delivery of online health services may exist through the combination of a traditional business with a physical site and a convenient Web presence. The physical location permits easier compliance with extant legal and regulatory requirements. The Web site enables providers to tap into additional value-added services that customers may demand as the health care market grows increasingly competitive. Indeed, we may find that health care organizations wishing to thrive will be required to provide care through a new click and mortar paradigm of care. (p. e12)

We wonder if this click and mortar model also would be best from a communication perspective because it offers patients and health care providers convenience but with the option to interact about health concerns in a face-to-face setting. As those who study virtual teams suggested, ideally the first meeting should be held in person for three reasons (Nemiro, Beyerlein, Bradley, & Beyerlein, 2008). First, so the parties get to know each other and develop a sense of who they are working with. Second, to establish the purpose and action steps for the task at hand but also for the relationship. Third, to set norms for the relationship and the task and to determine the process by which tasks are accomplished. Although these three reasons were developed for virtual teams, they are relevant and applicable to online or other forms of virtual or e-Health communication between health care providers and patients.

Now that we discussed many concepts, issues, and research projects associated with health communication and technology and selected the term e-Health to capture the link between health communication and technology, we turn to a service-learning application that emphasizes the role of e-Health in health campaigns. This application focuses on the demonstration component of service-learning projects.

SERVICE-LEARNING APPLICATION

Demonstrating Project Accomplishment

In this service-learning application we illustrate an e-Health outcome of the Motorcycle Safety at Purdue (MS@P) campaign. Throughout this book we discussed the core components of successful service-learning projects. The final component—*duration and intensity*—involves demonstrating learning and impacts and celebrating successes of the service-learning project (Corporation for National & Community Service, 2010). In other words, demonstration represents the culmination and influence of your service-learning project. Upon completing your service-learning project, it is important to demonstrate or present your project so that others can see what you accomplished, but even more importantly, so others can learn from your project. Demonstrating or presenting your project also provides an opportunity to celebrate and reflect on what you accomplished. In this section we look at an example of how the MS@P campaign demonstrates their project for the public through an e-Health application, that is the MS@P campaign Web site.

As you learned in this chapter, there are a multitude of ways to engage the community in health communication issues using e-Health. This service-learning application highlights one of the primary ways the MS@P campaign team uses its Web site to demonstrate health and safety information it has researched and gathered into messages for one of its target audiences, motorcyclists.

On the MS@P Web site there is a specific section for motorcyclists that contains important information regarding all aspects of safety including proper gear, motorcycle maintenance, and safe riding behaviors. The site offers quizzes to take, reference cards to print out, and video clips to watch, so site visitors can engage in an interactive learning experience. All the materials on the Web site were designed and produced based on careful research and interaction with the target audience. Go to the Web site for this book to view the MS@P's Web page for motorcyclists.

The internet provides a medium for the MS@P campaign team to demonstrate all the work they accomplish in creating educational materials for motorcyclists. These materials are available for the target audience of motorcyclists as well as anyone interested in reviewing the Web site. The Web site also allows campaign partners and funders to observe the campaign team's accomplishments.

As your service-learning team plans and works toward the completion of its project consider the various ways you can present your project to your colleagues and the community. A list of possible ways to demonstrate, reflect on, and celebrate your project outcome includes:

◆ Give an oral presentation and invite community partners
◆ Host a reception
◆ Create a handout or guidebook to distribute
◆ Send letters to community partners describing your work
◆ Construct a Web site or Web page

Chapter Summary

In this chapter we focused on the intersection of health communication and technology. We began with a brief history of when and how this intersection occurred. Next, we defined and offered examples of the many terms and concepts in the literature and in the marketplace that are associated with health and technology and settled on the term e-Health. We then shifted our emphasis more directly toward communication by offering the communication barriers and benefits of e-Health followed by a discussion of the importance of tailoring health messages. We then reviewed different technology-based approaches to health communication including ways that tailored messages become incorporated within those technologies. Three theories relevant to our understanding of e-Health adoption and use were presented. We tied the chapter together by considering the implications of e-Health on interpersonal and organizational health communication. We ended the chapter with a service-learning application that highlighted project presentation through a Web site.

References

AHIMA [American Health Information Management Association] Personal Health Record Practice Council (2009). Helping consumers select PHRs: Questions and considerations for navigating an emerging market. Retrieved August 10, 2010, from http://library.ahima.org/xpedio/groups/public/documents/ahima/bok1_032260.hcsp?dDocName=bok1_032260.

Ajzen, I., & Fishbein, M. (1980). *Understanding attitudes and predicting social behavior.* Englewood Cliffs, NJ: Prentice Hall.

Allan, R. (2006, June 29). A brief history of telemedicine. *Electronic Design.* Retrieved November 3, 2009, from http://electronicdesign.com/Articles/ArticleID/12859/12859.html.

Anderson, E., Winnett, R., Wojcik, J., Winnett, S., & Bowden, T. (2001). A computerized social cognitive intervention for nutrition behavior: Direct and mediated effects on fat, fiber, fruits, and vegetables, self-efficacy, and outcomes expectations among food shoppers. *Annals of Behavioral Medicine, 23,* 88–100.

Bashshur, R. L., & Shannon, G. W. (2009). *History of telemedicine: Evolution, context, and transformation.* New Rochelle, NY: Mary Ann Liebert.

Brauchli, K. (2006). *Telemedicine for improving access to health care in resource-constrained areas: From individual diagnosis to strengthening health systems.* University of Basel, Switzerland.

Burt, C. W., & Sisk, J. E. (2005). Which physicians and practices are using electronic medical records? *Health Affairs, 24,* 1334–1343.

Chau, P. Y. K., & Hu, P. J. (2002). Examining a model of information technology acceptance by individual professionals: An exploratory study. *Journal of Management Information Systems, 18,* 191–229.

Connell, C. M., Shaw, B. A., Holmes, S. B., Hudson, M. L., Derry, H. A., & Strecher, V. J. (2003). The development of an Alzheimer's disease channel for the Michigan Interactive Health Kiosk Project. *Journal of Health Communication, 8,* 11–22.

Corporation for National & Community Service (2010). Learn and Serve America's National Service-Learning Clearinghouse. Retrieved January 12, 2010, from http://www.servicelearning.org.

Davis, F. D. (1989). Perceived usefulness, perceived ease of use, and user acceptance of information technology. *MIS Quarterly, 13,* 319–339.

Eakin, B., Brady, J., & Lusk, S. (2001). Creating a tailored, multimedia, computer-based intervention. *Computers in Nursing, 19,* 152–160.

Eysenbach, G. (2001). What is e-Health? *Journal of Medical Internet Research, 3.* Retrieved August 10, 2010, from http://www.jmir.org/2001/2/e20/.

Falas, T., Papadopoulos, G., & Stafylopatis, A. (2003). A review of decision support systems in telecare. *Journal of Medical Systems, 27,* 347–356.

Fishbein, M., & Ajzen, I. (1975). *Belief, attitude, intention, and behavior: An introduction to theory and research.* Reading, MA: Addison-Wesley.

Fox, S., & Jones, S. (2009). *The social life of health information: Americans' pursuit of health takes place within a widening network of both online and offline sources.* Pew Internet and American Life Project. Retrieved November 2, 2009, from http://www.pewinternet.org/~/media//Files/Reports/2009/PIP_Health_2009.pdf.

Gammon, D., Johannessen, L. K., Wynn, R., & Whitten, P. (2008). An overview and analysis of theories employed in telemedicine studies. *Methods of Information in Medicine, 47*, 260–269.

Gans, D., Kralewski, J., Hammons, T., & Dowd, B. (2005). Medical groups' adoption of electronic health records and information systems. *Health Affairs, 24*, 1323–1333.

Garets, D., & Davis, M. (2005, October). Electronic patient records, EMRs and EHRs: Concepts as different as apples and oranges at least deserve separate names. *Healthcare Informatics Online*, pp. 1–4. Retrieved August 10, 2010, from http://www.provider-sedge.com/ehdocs/ehr_articles/Electronic_Patient_Records-EMRs_and_EHRs.pdf.

Giulianotti, C., Coratti, A., Angelini, M., Sbrana, F., Cecconi, S., Balestracci, T., et al. (2003). Robotics in general surgery. *Archives of Surgery, 138*, 777–784.

Healy, B. (2009). Electronic medical records: Will your privacy be safe? *U.S. News & World Report*. Retrieved August 10, 2010, from http://www.usnews.com/health/blogs/heart-to-heart/2009/02/17/electronic-medical-records-will-your-privacy-be-safe.html.

Herzer, K., & Seshamani, M. (2009). *A success story in American health care: Using health information technology to improve patient care in a community health center in Washington*. Retrieved November 9, 2009, from www.Healthreform.gov/reports.

Hillestad, R., Bigelow, J., Bower, A., Girosi, R. M., Scoville, R., & Taylor, R. (2005). Can electronic medical record systems transform health care?: Potential health benefits, savings, and costs. *Health Affairs, 24*, 1103–1117.

Himmelstein, D. U., Wright, A., & Woolhandler, S. (2010). Hospital computing and the costs and quality of care: A national study. *The American Journal of Medicine, 123*, 40–46.

Hornung, R. L., Lennon, P. A., Garrett, J. M., DeVellis, R. F., Weinberg, P. D., & Strecher, V. J. (2000). Interactive computer technology for skin cancer prevention targeting children. *American Journal of Preventive Medicine, 18*, 69–76.

Jensen, J. V. (1997). *Ethical issues in the communication process*. Mahwah, NJ: Lawrence Erlbaum Associates.

Krebs, H. I., Hogan, N., Volpe, B. T., Aisen, M. L., Edelstein, L., & Diels, C. (1999). Overview of clinical trials with MIT-MANUS: A robot-aided neuro-rehabilitation facility. *Technology and Health Care, 7*, 419–423.

Kreuter, M. W., Lukwago, S. N., Bucholtz, D. C., Clark, E. M., & Sanders-Thompson, V. (2002). Achieving cultural appropriateness in health promotion programs: Targeted and tailored approaches. *Health Education & Behavior, 30*, 133–146.

Lapinsky, S. E. (2007). Mobile computing in critical care. *Journal of Critical Care, 22*, 41–44.

Lustria, M. L., Cortese, J., Noar, S. M., & Glueckauf, R. L. (2009). Computer-tailored health interventions delivered over the Web: Review and analysis of key components. *Patient Education & Counseling, 74*, 156–173.

Mattson, M., & Brann, M. (2002). Managed care and the paradox of patient confidentiality: A case study analysis from a communication boundary management perspective. *Communication Studies, 53*, 337–357.

Matusitz, J., & Breen, G. M. (2007). Telemedicine: Its effects on health communication. *Health Communication, 21*, 73–83.

Menachemi, N., Burke, D. E., & Ayers, D. J. (2004). Factors affecting the adoption of telemedicine—a multiple adopter perspective. *Journal of Medical Systems, 28*, 617–632.

Miller, G. A. (1956). The magical number seven, plus or minus two: Some limits on our capacity for processing information. *Psychological Review, 63*, 81–97.

Mosavel, M. (2005). The use of a telephone-based communication tool by low-income substance abusers. *Journal of Health Communication, 10*, 451–463.

Mosby (2009). *Mosby's medical dictionary* (8th ed.). St. Louis: Mosby/Elsevier.

Moyer, C. A., & Katz, S. J. (2007). Online patient-provider communication: How will it fit? *Electronic Journal of Communication, 17*(3/4). Retrieved September 1, 2010, from http://www.cios.org/EJCPUBLIC/017/3/01732.HTML.

National Cancer Institute (2009). *Evaluating health information on the Internet.* Retrieved December 12, 2009, from http://www.cancer.gov/cancertopics/factsheet/Information/Internet.

National Telecommunications and Information Administration (2000). *Falling through the Net: Toward digital inclusion.* Retrieved November 6, 2009, from http://search.ntia.doc.gov/pdf/fttn00.pdf.

Nemiro, J., Beyerlein, M. M., Bradley, L., & Beyerlein, S. (Eds.). (2008). *The handbook of high-performance virtual teams.* San Francisco: Jossey-Bass.

Oh, H., Rizo, C., Enkin, M., & Jadad, A. (2005). What is ehealth (3): A systematic review of published definitions. *Journal of Medical Internet Research, 7,* e1. Retrieved August 10, 2010, from http://www.jmir.org/2005/1/e1/#ref3.

Page, S. (2003). "Virtual" health care organizations and the challenges of improving quality. *Health Care Management Review, 28,* 79–92.

Perednia, D., & Allen, A. (1995). Telemedicine technology and clinical applications. *Journal of the American Medical Association, 273,* 483–488.

Prochaska, J. O., DiClemente, C. C., & Norcross, J. C. (1992). In search of how people change. *American Psychologist, 47,* 1102–1114.

Rains, S. A. (2008). Health at high speed: Broadband internet access, health communication, and the digital divide. *Communication Research, 35,* 283–297.

REM Health, Inc. (2009). Telemedicine case studies. Retrieved November 23, 2009, from http://www.remhealth.com.

Render, M. K. (2009, June 8), I learned that a PHR saves time, energy, and money. And it saved my life! Retrieved October 9, 2009, from http://www.myphr.com/Stories/SuccessStory.aspx?Id=345.

Revere, D., & Dunbar, P. J. (2001). Review of computer-generated outpatient health behavior interventions: Clinical encounters in absentia. *Journal of American Medical Informatics Association, 8,* 62–79.

Rimal, R. N., & Adkins, A. D. (2003). Using computers to narrowcast health messages: The role of audience segmentation, targeting, and tailoring in health promotion. In T. L. Thompson, A. M. Dorsey, K. I. Miller, & R. Parrott (Eds.), *Handbook of health communication* (pp. 497–513). Mahwah, NJ: Lawrence Erlbaum.

Rimer, B. K., & Kreuter, M. W. (2006). Advancing tailored health communication: A persuasion and message effects perspective. *Journal of Communication, 56,* S184–S201.

Rogers, E. M. (2001). *Diffusion of innovations* (5th ed.). New York: Free Press.

Simon, S. R., Kaushal, R., Cleary, P. D., Jenter, C. A., Volk, L. A., Poon, E. G., et al. (2007). Correlates of electronic health record adoption in office practices: A statewide survey. *Journal of The American Medical Informatics Association, 14,* 110–117.

St. Alexius Medical Center (2009). Examples: Telemedicine and videoconferencing services. Retrieved November 10, 2009, from http://www.st.alexius.org/customers/telemedicine/examples/.

Stewart, A. (Writer) (2009). *Farrah's Story.* F. Fawcett (Producer). National Broadcasting Company.

Suggs, L. S. (2006). A 10-year retrospective of research in new technologies for health communication. *Journal of Health Communication, 11,* 61–74.

Tabor, W. (2007). On the cutting edge of robotic surgery. *Nursing, 37,* 48–50.

Turner, J. W. (2003). Telemedicine: Expanding health care into virtual environments. In T. L. Thompson, A. M. Dorsey, K. I. Miller, & R. Parrott (Eds.), *Handbook of health communication* (pp. 515–535). Mahwah, NJ: Lawrence Erlbaum Associates.

U. S. Food and Drug Administration (2009). *HIV home test kits*. Retrieved December 11, 2009, from http://www.fda.gov/BiologicsBloodVaccines/SafetyAvailability/HIVHome TestKits/default.htm.

van Dijk, J. (2005). *The deepening divide: Inequality in the information society*. Thousand Oaks, CA: Sage.

Wantland, D. J., Portillo, C. J., Holzemer, W. L., Slaughter, R., & McGhee, E. M. (2004). The effectiveness of Web-based vs. non-Web-based interventions: A meta-analysis of behavioral change outcomes. *Journal of Medical Internet Research, 6,* e40.

Werner, P. (2004). Willingness to use telemedicine for psychiatric care. *Telemedicine Journal & e-Health, 10,* 286–293.

Werner, P., & Karnieli, E. (2003). A model of the willingness to use telemedicine for routine and specialized care. *Journal of Telemedicine and Telecare, 9,* 264–272.

Whitten, P., Steinfield, C., & Hellmich, S. (2001). Ehealth: Market potential and business strategies. *Journal of Computer-Mediated Communication, 6.*

Wilson, J., Coledan, S., Erwin, S., & Gourley, S. (2004). A better way to restart hearts. *Popular Mechanics, 181,* 17.

Wootton, R. (2001). Telemedicine. *British Medical Journal, 323,* 557–560.

Index

A

Active listening, 163
Active telemedicine, 374
Active voice, 174
Acts of engagement, social networks, 358
Actual support, 184
Advice giving, 166, 192–194
Advocacy, media, 349
  goal of, 352
Advocates, 326
Against Medical Advice document, 136
Agenda setting, 127
  research on, 340–342
Agenda-setting theory, 68, 338–339
Alcohol, misuse of, 12
Alternative media, 358
American health status, 7–14
  chronic diseases, 8
  death rates, 7–8
  health disparities, 9–14
  infectious diseases, 8
  risk factors for chronic diseases, 8
  unintentional injuries, 9
Announcement, public service, 360–363
Anonymity, 210
Apathy, 295
Arguments, decision, 68
Array of medical information available, 131
Arthritis, 13
Assessment, audience, 291
Asthma, 13
Attitudes, 223
Attributes of communication, 22–23
Audience, vicarious relationships, 315
Audience assessment, 291
Audience engagement, emotional, 317
Audience involvement, 291
Audience segmentation, 249–250, 386

B

Babrow, Austin, 84–85
Bad news, delivery of, 167
Barriers, perception of, 94, 222
Before I Die, 171
Behavioral capability, 231
Behavioral control, perception of, 224
Behavioral intention, 224, 396
Belonging, sense of, 206
Benevolence, 70
Bioethics, 48–54
Biomedical ethics, 42
Bioterrorism, 301
Blogging, 383
Boundaries

geographical, transcending, 381
temporal, transcending, 382
Breach of confidentiality, 64
  avoiding, 64

C

Campaigns. *See also* Health campaign practice
  attitudes, 223
  barriers, perception of, 222
  behavioral capability, 231
  behavioral control, perception of, 224
  behavioral intention, 224
  community building, 234
  community capacity, 235
  community organizing, 234
  community-organizing model, 234–238
  consciousness-raising, 227
  contemplation, 226
  conversation starters, 149–150
  counterconditioning, 227
  critical consciousness, 235
  cues to action, 222
  definition of theory, 220–221
  diversity, 177
  dramatic relief, 227
  ecological framework, 221–238
    health belief model, 221–223
    intrapersonal context of influence, 221
    stages of change, 225–230
    theory of planned behavior, 223–225
    theory of reasoned action, 223–225
    transtheoretical model, 225–230
  empowerment, 235
  environmental reevaluation, 227
  ethical analysis, 73–74
  health campaign theory, 238
  helping relationships, 227
  informing, 238
  interpersonal, 230–232
  intrapersonal context of influence, 221
  issue selection, 236
  large-scale, 275
    monitoring progress, 276–277
  mass communication context of influence, 233–238
  message channels, 265
  messaging model for, 252–267
  monitoring progress, 276–277
  motorcycle safety, 270–277
  multiple voices in, 304–305

observational learning, modeling, 230–231
organizational context of influence, 232–233
organizational development theory, 232–233
outcome expectations, 231
participation, 235
perceived benefits, 222
perceived severity, 222
perceived susceptibility, 222
practice, 243–278
pre-campaign survey, 259–260
precontemplation, 223
preparation, 226
process guides, 266–267
processes of change, 228
public communication, 233–238
public health perspective, 244–246
reciprocal determinism, 230
reinforcement management, 227
reinforcements, 231
research, 237
self-efficacy, 222, 231
self-liberation, 227
self-reevaluation, 227
small groups, 230–232
small-scale health, 275
  monitoring progress, 276–277
social cognitive theory, 230–232
social liberation, 228
stimulus control, 228
stress, 220
subjective social norms, 223
team contexts, 230–232
theories, 219–241, 275
working group, 253
working groups, 253
workplace wellness programs, 232
Campaigns practice, 243–278
Cancer, 13
Capability, behavioral, 231
Care provider communication, 157–159
  cultural influences, 160
  interpersonal influences, 159–160
  organizational influences, 157–159
  power dynamics, 160–161
Care provider patient power dynamics, 161
Careers, 28–35
  entertainment education, 326–330
  job market research, 31–35
  prospects, 28–31
Case-based ethics, 64–67
Casuistry/case-based ethics, 64–67
Categorical imperative, 57
Categories of adopters, 102
CDCynergy, 266–267

reinforcement management, 227
reinforcements, 231
research, 237
self-efficacy, 222, 231
self-liberation, 227
self-reevaluation, 227
small groups, team contexts, 230–232
social cognitive theory, 230–232
social liberation, 228
stimulus control, 228
stress, 220
subjective social norms, 223
team contexts of influence, 230–232
workplace wellness programs, 232
Health campaigns, 275
conversation starters, 149–150
diversity, 177
ethical analysis, 73–74
large-scale, 275
monitoring progress, 276–277
message channels, 265
messaging model for, 252–267
motorcycle safety, 270–277
multiple voices in, 304–305
practice, 243–278
pre-campaign survey, 259–260
process guides, 266–267
public health perspective, 244–246
small-scale health, 275
monitoring progress, 276–277
working group, 253
Health care communication scenario, 139
Health care provider defined, 156–161
Health care provider interaction, 155–180
active listening, 163
active voice, 174
advice giving, 166
bad news delivery, 167
care provider communication, 157
cultural influences, 160
interpersonal influences, 159–160
organizational influences, 157–159
power dynamics, 160–161
clarifying questions, 165
closed-ended questions, 165
communication, 157–161
cultural differences, acknowledging, 173
diversity, in health campaigns, 177
emotional contagion, 167
emotions, responding to, 170
empathetic concern, 167
fonts, 174
greater patient satisfaction, 162
Health Information Privacy Accountability Act, 159

Healthy People, 172
high-contrast colors, 175
Before I Die, 171
interpersonal influences, 159
knowledge, 170
malpractice, 162
manageable chunks of information, 174
mutuality, 161
open-ended questions, 165
organizational culture, 158
paternalism, 161
patient-centered care, 168
patient-centered communication, 162–177
benefits of, 162–163
health care provider skills, 163–171
health literacy, 171–177
skills training, 171
techniques for improving, 172–177
patient compliance, 162
patient power dynamics, intersection of, 161
perceptions of health status, 169
pretest messages, 176
question asking, 165
therapeutic interviewing, 164
Health care providers, 156
functional role of, 127
Health communication
defined, 14–28
milestones, 26–27
timeline, 25–28
Health Communication Division, International Communication Association, 26
Health disparities, 9–14
Health educators, 31
Health Information Privacy Accountability Act, 159
Health literacy, 132–133, 171–177, 342
Health status, Americans, 7–14
chronic diseases, 8
death rates, 7–8
health disparities, 9–14
infectious diseases, 8
unintentional injuries, 9
Healthy People, 172
Heart disease, 13
Helping relationships, 227
High-contrast colors, 175
HIPAA. *See* Health Information Privacy Accountability Act
Hippocratic oath, 46–47
classical version, 46
modern version, 47
HIV
prevention programs, 30
spread of, 62

Honesty, 70
Hum Log, 322
Hypertension, 13

I

ICA. *See* Health Communication Division, International Communication Association
Ideal speech situation, 58
Identification, 316
Illicit drug use, 12
Images, strong, 350
Imperative, categorical, 57
Improved health outcomes, 141
Improving patient-centered communication, 172–177
Inaccurate information, 209
Infectious diseases, 8
Influences, organizational, 129
Information, misunderstanding, 143
Information content, 290
Information overload, 393
Information processing theory, 393
Information quality, 393
Information seeking, 142
Information support, 186
Information verification, 147
Informational verifying, 147
Injuries, unintentional, 9
Injustice, framing health issue as, 350
Innovations, 99, 312–313
diffusion of, 398
Insurance plans, 130
Intention, behavioral, 224, 396
Interaction with patient, 119–153
Interactive, 356
Interface of profiles, source file, 386
Internal cues to action, 95
International Communication Association, 26
Internet, 355
Interpersonal influences, 125–126, 159
Intimidation, by health care providers, 142
Intrapersonal context of influence, 221
Involvement, audience, 291
Isolation, reduction in, 205
Issue selection, 236

J

Job market, 28–35
Joint Commission, 24

K

Knowledge, 170
Kosmoski, Carin, 275
Kreps, Greg, 237

WHO. *See* World Health Organization
Witte, Kim, 286–287
Working groups, 253–255
Workplace wellness programs, 232
World Health Organization, 15

Y

Young adults
    alcohol use, 12
    cigarette use, 12
    health status, 13
    illicit drug use, 12